The German Left and Aesthetic Politics

Historical Materialism Book Series

The Historical Materialism Book Series is a major publishing initiative of the radical left. The capitalist crisis of the twenty-first century has been met by a resurgence of interest in critical Marxist theory. At the same time, the publishing institutions committed to Marxism have contracted markedly since the high point of the 1970s. The Historical Materialism Book Series is dedicated to addressing this situation by making available important works of Marxist theory. The aim of the series is to publish important theoretical contributions as the basis for vigorous intellectual debate and exchange on the left.

The peer-reviewed series publishes original monographs, translated texts, and reprints of classics across the bounds of academic disciplinary agendas and across the divisions of the left. The series is particularly concerned to encourage the internationalization of Marxist debate and aims to translate significant studies from beyond the English-speaking world.

For a full list of titles in the Historical Materialism Book Series
available in paperback from Haymarket Books, visit:
https://www.haymarketbooks.org/series_collections/1-historical-materialism

The German Left and Aesthetic Politics

Cultural Politics between the Second and Third Internationals

Martin I. Gaughan

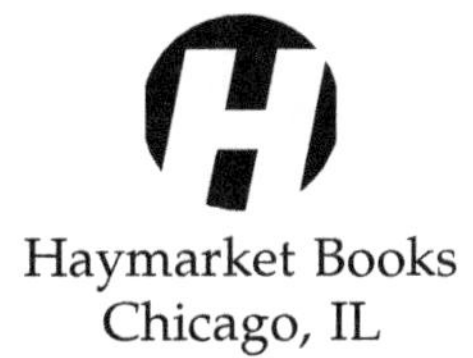

Haymarket Books
Chicago, IL

First published in 2021 by Brill Academic Publishers, The Netherlands
© 2021 Koninklijke Brill NV, Leiden, The Netherlands

Published in paperback in 2022 by
Haymarket Books
P.O. Box 180165
Chicago, IL 60618
773-583-7884
www.haymarketbooks.org

ISBN: 978-1-64259-783-7

Distributed to the trade in the US through Consortium Book Sales and
Distribution (www.cbsd.com) and internationally through Ingram
Publisher Services International (www.ingramcontent.com).

This book was published with the generous support of Lannan
Foundation and Wallace Action Fund.

Special discounts are available for bulk purchases by organizations and
institutions. Please call 773-583-7884 or email info@haymarketbooks.org
for more information.

Cover art and design by David Mabb. Cover art is a detail of *Die Kunst ist
tot*, paint and paper mounted on canvas (1996).

Printed in the United States.

10 9 8 7 6 5 4 3 2 1

Library of Congress Cataloging-in-Publication data is available.

Contents

Introduction

As the working class, in the process of its revolutionary reconstruction of the world, reconstructs its own nature, it produces its own literature – upon a level incomparably higher than the literature of the bourgeoisie.[1]

∴

The general trajectory of the approach taken in this text may be indicated by two quotations from the critical theorist Karl Wittfogel, the first to attempt to establish an elaborated Marxist aesthetic (see Chapter 5 below) and one from Marx. In the first, Wittfogel is describing the achievement of Franz Mehring, a member of the German Social Democratic Party (SPD) and founding member of the German Communist Party (KPD), designated by Lukács as the greatest German literary critic and theorist of the nineteenth century: 'but at the same time his work constitutes an original contribution to the deepening of our scientific insights into the class struggle as it has developed within the political and ideological husk of late feudal-bourgeois Germany'.[2] It is an aesthetic practice with a purpose, neither reductivist nor instrumentalist, giving rise to 'scientific insights' whilst allowing the cultural artefact the qualities proper to it. The second is from a conference of the Association of Proletarian-Revolutionary Writers (BPRS) on the eve of the Nazi take-over: 'Naturally overall the immediate prosecution of the economic-political struggle remains our central duty. Nevertheless the effective contribution of revolutionary cultural work, as experience shows, should not be undervalued'.[3] There is a passage in Marx which may provide a context for Wittfogel's statements. Marx is writing about engaging with 'real concrete terms': 'The totality as a conceptual entity seen by the intellect is a product of the thinking intellect which assimilates the world in the only way open to it, a way which differs from the artistic, religious and practically intelligent assimilation of the world'.[4]

---

1   Lifshitz 1973, p. 75. He is here summarising Marx's position as set out in his critique of Sue's *The Mysteries of Paris* in *The Holy Family*.

2   Brauneck 1973, p. 393.

3   Wittfogel, *Die Linkskurve*, 3, no. 1, p. 17.

4   Marx 1974, p. 141. This statement is rich in its implications for the deployment of a materialist

The present text traces how the programme summarily laid out above was pursued on the German left between the Second and Third Internationals, both in its theorising and its practices. It considers the arguments concerning proletarian culture and proletarian self-consciousness and how the developing political positions on the left articulated and contested the status of culture in the context of ongoing struggle. One major source of contention was the question concerning the art of the *Übergangzeit*, the art of the transitional period leading up to the seizure of power: was proletarian art possible before that moment or only after it?[5] What was the relation of the culture of the revolutionary era of the bourgeoisie (*das Erbe*) to that? The last chapter of Franz Mehring's renowned study of Lessing, *Die Lessing-Legende* (1893), carries the title 'Lessing und das Proletariat', his biography of Schiller *Ein Lebensbild für deutsche Arbeiter* (1905). Mehring's intention was to present this material as exemplary of radical potential of the proletariat in their own struggle (a position also shared by Lenin and Trotsky), not as a stage towards embourgeoisement of the working class.[6] But in a major revisionist, if also at times laudatory, essay in 1933, Lukács criticised Mehring's lack of commitment to proletarian art per se, thereby linking him with Trotsky's position.[7]

The issue of the art of the *Übergangzeit* and of proletarian revolutionary art became more acute after the failed November Revolution of 1918. The prewar hegemony of the SPD (Social Democratic Party) was challenged by the formation of the USPD (Independent Socialist Party), the KPD (Communist

---

    philosophy of language, the continuity of its operations across socially constructed discursive categories. Such a theory was developed in the 1920s by Vygotsky and Volosinov in the Soviet Union.

5   Morawski 1973, p. 75, notes that 'no recorded opinion of Marx on the need or likelihood of a proletarian art is extant, nor can his opinion be extrapolated from available texts with any certainty ...'.

6   What Lars T. Lih calls 'the merger formula' or 'the merger of socialism and the worker movement, common to both Kautsky and Lenin' (2008, Part I, 'Erfurtianism', pp. 44–61, a reference to the 1891 Erfurt Programme of the SPD) may cast light on the shared perception that the revolutionary proletariat might seek some common cause with the revolutionary bourgeoisie, but in the manner Rosa Luxemburg wrote of their active reception of Schiller, in whose work they 'deposited their ... own world view, ... picked through his intellectual work and fused it unconsciously into its own world of revolutionary thought and feeling' (see Chapter 1).

7   This essay, which will be considered further in Chapter 5, was a response to Stalin's questioning of the role of the German Second International party, particularly in literary criticism and theory. Lukács's assiduousness even discovered in a 1912 exchange of opinions on the possibility of proletarian literature in the pages of the SPD journal, *Die Neue Zeit*, organised by Mehring, 'the "original" German Trotskyism is encountered already in its present form' ('Hier ist der deutsche "urwüchsige" Trotzkiismus bereits in Reinkultur aufgetreten'). Mehring had not participated in the discussion but was reproached for his silence.

Party) and the KAPD (The Communist Workers' Party). The KPD continued with Mehring's cultural heritage for much of the 1920s, but the USPD and the KAPD pursued more radical programmes. The KAPD drew up its own (anti-) *das Erbe* programme of dissenting writers across the centuries, including Rabelais, Swift, Sterne, Jack London, the Irish 'navvy poet' and novelist Patrick Mac-Gill and playwright Franz Jung, a number of whose early plays were produced by Piscator in the Proletarisches Theater. Suspicious of democratic central-ism, inclined to political and cultural 'spontaneism', their objective was to energise proletarian revolutionary self-consciousness through culture, a pro-gramme that was influenced by the Dutch communists Pannekoek and Gorter. They claimed that the objective conditions for revolution were present but bourgeois culture in this industrially advanced Western society hampered the development of the subjective moment: the task of culture was to challenge, undermine, and displace that culture, replacing it with its own developing pro-duction.

Another concern of the text is to establish how these issues played out on the ground: what were the relationships between party politics, events (e.g. the 'German October' of 1923), the process of Stalinisation of the KPD, and cultural production? What kind of art was produced and by whom? Wieland Herzfelde proposed that artists from bourgeois backgrounds, particularly in the visual arts, would be needed for decades; by the end of the decade, arguments against 'fellow-travellers' would be pursued. Both he and the co-founder of the Pro-letarisches Theater, Hermann Schüller, warned against the bureaucratisation of culture. The fit between advanced theorising and proletarian revolutionary cultural production was problematic: the editorial board of the revolution-ary writers' journal, *Die Linkskurve*, had to suspend its course on dialectical materialism on the grounds of a lack of understanding – one former member described Lukács's contribution as a 'monologue'. This approach is meant to give body to the sometimes frictionless operation of theory, to meet the Marxist demand to work from the concrete, as emphasised, for instance, by Korsch and Sternberg in their engagements with Brecht (Chapter 6 below). In paying atten-tion to these moments in their particularity, the individual actors, the works produced, the texts written, one can better perceive the extraordinary intellec-tual and artistic energy expended and the level of achievement accomplished. To meet the trajectory proposed by Marx in the above quotation, this labour could not only be about a critique of bourgeois culture in decline, important though that is, as Mehring's detailed criticism of bourgeois critics in his *Lessing-Legende* made clear; it also had to produce theory and practice proposing a pro-letarian revolutionary conceptualisation of socio-cultural experience, enabling a corresponding practice by its addressees. Karl Wittfogel, for example, wrote plays for Piscator's Proletarisches Theatre, a theoretical essay on a new form of theatre, and introduced what was the first formal articulation of a Marxist aesthetic in the journal of the proletarian revolutionary writers, *Die Linkskurve*, in 1930. August Thalheimer, a founding member of the KPD and its leading theoretician, was an outspoken critic of the failures of the Soviet party and its role in the 'German October', penning a powerful rebuke in the form of a pamphlet, first published in 1931.[8] His insightful introductions to two volumes of Mehring's works, on literature and history of philosophy, in 1929, may very well have prompted Stalin's call for an analysis of the role of the pre-war SPD (see note six). Both Wittfogel and Lukács led a Third Period assault on him. Figures and incidents, such as these and others, provide the working fabric for engaging with this great departure for a cultural materialist praxis.

A proposal presented at the SPD conference in 1920, that culture be considered 'a third pillar of the movement' taking its place alongside the political and the economic, manifests the level of engagement.[9] It is the objective of this text to operate within that premise, specifically within the cultural tradition identified by Marx and Engels in their periodic engagements with the subject and elaborated by literary historians and theorists such as Mehring, Wittfogel, and Lukács, particularly their work on the revolutionary bourgeois heritage, 'das Erbe'. This, however, was not an uncontested contribution to the structuring of a Marxist theory of culture. Although the KPD embraced Mehring's 'das Erbe' programme in the immediate aftermath of the November Revolution of 1918, more 'spontaneist' committed activists and artists, particularly members of the USPD and the KAPD, espoused the immediate creation of a proletarian culture. These two strands would run in parallel during the early Weimar period, but with the gradual Stalinisation of the KPD from the middle of the Weimar decade, the spontaneist programme would wane and the heritage programme would be subject to revision, with an emphatic introduction of dialectical materialism as the necessary mode of investigation, stimulated principally by Lenin's reading of Hegel.

Another objective here is to align the cultural theorising and its practice with the shifting political landscape: both were interventionist but not func-

---

8   As Thalheimer worked, with Bukharin, on drafting Comintern programmes, its content must have been widely accessible.

9   A similar claim was articulated by the KPD-established 'Interessengemeinschaft für Arbeiterkultur' (Society for the Promotion of Working-Class Culture) founded in 1929: the Western European proletariat, under the direction of the Comintern, had fought on the political and economic front but 'the party has now seized the initiative to bring the struggle to the third, the culture front' ('Jetzt hat die Partei die Initiative ergriffen, um den Kampf auch an der dritten, an der Kulturfront aufzunehmen') (quoted in Lüdecke 1973, p. 46).

tionalist, hostile to an abstracted aesthetic as ascribed to the Kantian tradition, premised on socio-political disinterest. Pre-war Germany had been the most powerful industrial nation in Europe, with a large and well-organised working class. The SPD, its representative, survived Bismarck's anti-socialist laws. Germany's defeat in the First World War triggered the unsuccessful revolution of soldiers, sailors, and workers in November 1918, followed by intermittent and isolated insurrection and the failed 'German October' of 1923, a terminal point for armed resistance from the left. This setback was the occasion for a resetting of KPD politics, including its cultural programme. The danger of counter-revolution was also a constant presence – there had been the Kapp Putsch of March 1920 when the majority SPD-led government had to flee Berlin for Dresden, the attempted Munich 'beer hall' putsch of 1923, the murderous activities of the Freikorps and the rise of fascism. The Stalinisation of the KPD in the second half of the 1920s was to effect further changes, particularly in its cultural programme. Throughout the period, cultural theorising and its practice was enmeshed in and continuous with politics. Because of this intermeshing, the text is structured chronologically.

It is not concerned with the more general elaboration of a Marxist aesthetic practice (some Soviet ideas were contested, some adopted), but rather with how such a practice developed within the particular socio-historical conditions of Germany, a sufficiently rich context for its development. That is, it is temporally and spatially delimited with a positive purpose.[10] Lu Märten delineated the operations of this process in 1921:

> Artistic products originate and stimulate not only programmed energies, not only *intelligible ideas*, nor just only *non-conceptual representations*, but in their specificities, through their orientations and urgencies, clarify and confirm in an historical manner and achieve a considerable amount of knowledge, whilst simultaneously posing questions for the future.[11]

I am proposing that all the instances of practice and its theorising addressed within this text subscribed to the general principles perceived by Märten, the demands of a materialist aesthetic practice.

Chapter 1 is devoted to the extensive work of Franz Mehring. As he was not only the major literary historian, critic, and theorist of the Second Inter-

---

10   It should be borne in mind that important texts by Marx were not available until well into
      the 1920s and 1930s: for instance, *The Economic and Philosophic Manuscripts 1844* and *The
      German Ideology*.
11   *alternative* 1973, p. 101.

national in Germany, but also the subject of both positive acknowledgement and objective criticism by the Third International criteria of Wittfogel and Lukács in the early 1930s, his work is treated at some length in order to provide the specific context for such critical re-evaluation. Its material generally will be structured to anticipate Lukács's later criticism. Mehring was the first to deploy historical materialism at length as a theoretical instrument for investigating literary production, recognised by Engels in an exchange of letters in 1893. Rosa Luxemburg, who was a close friend, and Clara Zetkin, considered Mehring to be 'the true inheritor of Marx'. Lukács described him as 'the most significant German literary theorist of the 19th century' in 1932. His studies of Lessing, Schiller, and Heine were highly regarded. Wittfogel described his *Die Lessing-Legende* as 'a most imposing achievement', and praised his Schiller book 'whose socio-political content has never before achieved such clarity'. His work on contemporary Naturalism, characterised as the art of the declining bourgeoisie, received similar tribute: Lukács wrote of Mehring's 'incomparably higher standard in his presentation and criticism of the Naturalist movement in Germany'. This opening chapter therefore establishes a crucial benchmark against which later developments will be measured.

Chapter 2 introduces the immediate post-revolutionary developments. Mehring's cultural pre-eminence was promoted within the newly founded KPD, of which he was a founding member.[12] It was advanced by a student of his, Gertrud Alexander, the cultural editor of the Berlin paper, *Die Rote Fahne*. The contending parties for a claim to a Marxist cultural praxis were now the KPD, the USPD, and the KAPD. Alexander's programme was based on the exemplary role of the revolutionary bourgeoisie as set out in Mehring's writings. This position was not adhered to by all KPD members, particularly its cultural producers around the Berlin Dada group and the Proletarisches Theater. Here the bourgeois tradition was rejected in favour of an experimentally proletarian-oriented practice.[13] These efforts were subjected to vitriolic criticism by Alexander in the pages of *Die Rote Fahne* and other journals, most likely informed by Lenin's 1920 brochure *Left-wing Communism: An Infantile Disorder*. The KAPD programme would also be subject to such criticism, proposing as it did that the objective conditions for revolution were already to hand in Germany but were being held back by underdeveloped subjective factors: the problem of the German Revolution 'is the problem of the development of the self-consciousness of the German proletariat'. Franz Jung, co-founder of the KAPD, respected playwright

---

12   He died shortly after it was established in early January 1919.
13   This experimentation would later find a more considered voice in the work of Brecht at the end of the decade.

and novelist, attempted to realise this development of the 'subjective' factor, of the self-consciousness of the German proletariat, through his writings: intention and reception are set out. Beginning to emerge also was the question of the art of the *Übergangzeit*, the transitional period to the access to power of the proletariat.

Chapter 3 documents the first formal debate on the role of historical materialism within the field of culture, between Alexander, a heritage advocate, and Lu Märten, also a KPD member and freelance journalist who prioritised technical innovation over the ideological as the motivator for cultural production. An account of her pre-war development is presented through a number of essays and articles to provide some insight into how she came to propose such an apparently unorthodox approach. The debate was pursued in the pages of *Die Rote Fahne* and other KPD publications between 1920 and 1921, and has been described as the beginning of 'a fundamental discussion of the question of a materialist aesthetic which would continue through to the formation of the "Proletarian Revolutionary Writers Union" (BPRS) in 1928, at the end of the Weimar Republic'.[14] Central to the exchanges are the understanding of the roles of historical materialism and dialectical materialism in giving a comprehensive account of cultural production. Reference to Marx's texts is more pronounced than so far encountered, even if more limited than later in the decade. Alexander criticises Märten's position on the grounds of misrecognising the relationship between the forces shaping the economic and the technical response, of prioritising the latter over the former, contrary to Marx's thinking. Märten's counterargument, as in the passages over the Gothic cathedral, is that technical development enables the requirements of institutionalised ideologies, in this case the medieval Church, to be realised. For Märten, the technical needs to be developed within the cultural sphere in order to progress beyond the forms bequeathed by 'das Erbe', towards 'classless forms' and 'classless art', anticipating Brechtian concerns.

Chapter 4 traces the changes in the cultural programmes and policies after the failure of the 'German October' to take place. Expectations had been raised both in Germany and in the Soviet Union that the revolutionary seizure of power was possible in the Länder of Saxony and Thuringia, where the SPD and the KPD were sharing power. Inadequate preparation, confused advice from the Soviet party, lack of sufficient arms and the speedy intervention of the Reichswehr prevented the attempt. The result at the political level would be lingering tension between the two parties. Politics and culture came together

---

14   Fähnders and Rector 1973b, p. 14, n. 45.

in the figure of August Thalheimer, leading theorist of the KPD and a Comintern member. In 1928, he wrote a highly critical account of the Soviet role in the failure of the 'German October', accusing members of lacking understanding of the specifics of Western conditions: in 1929 and 1930, he wrote the introductions to collected editions of Mehring's writings on literature and philosophy. This became the occasion for a harsh Stalinist-inspired criticism by Wittfogel. The 'October' account will be presented here, together with the Mehring introductions and Wittfogel's critique in Chapter 5.

Culturally, an early outcome was Clara Zetkin's call for intellectuals to become politicised and organised in their support for the proletariat, in a move towards the creation of that 'Zweite Kultur', second culture, proposed by Lenin. 'Die Rote Gruppe' of communist artists, including Grosz and Heartfield, was formed in 1924, becoming in turn the model for the much larger 'Assoziation revolutionärer bildender Künstler Deutschland' (ARBKD: Association of Proletarian Revolutionary Artists) in 1928. The organisation of proletarian revolutionary writers followed in 1929. Another front was opened up by Wittfogel who began a series of articles in *Die Rote Fahne* in 1925, on proletarian art, which was essentially a critique of Trotsky's *Literature and Revolution*, an abbreviated version of which appeared in German translation in 1924 (favourably reviewed by Lu Märten). Trotsky's failure to support the possibility of a proletarian art in the transitional period before the seizure of power was negatively assessed and contrasted with Lenin's positive position on the subject. Lenin had just died, Trotsky was being marginalised, and Stalin was beginning to secure his power base, ushering in the Third Period.

Chapter 5 opens with the presentation of Wittfogel's critique of Thalheimer's introduction to the collected volumes of Mehring's writings, as mentioned above. After the failure of the 'German October', Thalheimer worked at the Marxist-Leninist Institute in Moscow and lectured on dialectical materialism. In 1928, he was reluctantly allowed to return to Germany where, with Brandler and others, he founded the Right Opposition within the KPD. His introductions are very positive even when he notes the absence of a theorised dialectical approach and the limited appearance of Hegel in Mehring's texts, omissions which generally characterised the Second International milieu. Nevertheless, Thalheimer identified the presence of a dialectical mode of thinking and the acknowledgement of Hegel, even if not pervasive, in Mehring's work. Wittfogel sees neither and accuses Thalheimer of ignoring all theoretical progress since the November Revolution, particularly the contribution of Lenin. Wittfogel's target is Thalheimer, not Mehring's achievement.

In 1930 and 1931, Wittfogel published a series of six articles in *Die Linkskurve*, the journal of the proletarian revolutionary writers, titled 'Zur Frage der marxistischen Ästhetik' (On the Question of a Marxist Aesthetic), recognised as the first published attempt to do so. Thalheimer and Mehring are again present but are then displaced by Lenin and Hegel. The objective of the series is to provide a guideline for members' practice. Slightly later, Lukács reviewed a number of contemporary novels, which provided the occasion for highly theorised criticism. In the case of the proletarian writer Willi Bredel, the guidelines are against the mistaken concepts of 'spontaneism' and 'Tendenzkunst' as subjective reaction to superficial appearance, in favour of partisanship, the objective understanding from a Leninist perspective: in the case of Ernst Ottwalt against formal experimentation at the expense of content, a criticism also directed towards Brecht, with whom Ottwalt had collaborated on the film *Kuhle Wampe*.

Roughly contemporary with the above – the dates cannot be established accurately – was the issuing of a letter from Stalin. The purported aim was to protect Leninism, which would be achieved by establishing the contributions of the non-Russian left, 'above all the German' left, including their 'limits and serious errors', specifically their work 'on the problem of the superstructure, especially in the field of literature'.[15] Wittfogel contributed a long article to the Soviet Encyclopedia in 1931, much on the line of the above – defensive of Mehring, accusatory of Thalheimer. Lukács responded later (1933) with an 85-page essay, 'Franz Mehring. 1846–1919'. What we get is a recognition of Mehring's considerable achievement and a generally objective Leninist appraisal of his merits and of his historically conditioned inability to deal with issues raised by the 1917 revolution. But there are also some poorly founded criticisms, which may be seen as conditioned by the Stalinist context.

The arc of the text is constructed by the figures of Mehring and Lukács, from the Second to the Third International and the transition to the Third Period, but not ignoring the many important actors in between. To terminate the main trajectory at Lukács's critique of Mehring seemed unsatisfactory, leaving important threads hanging. For this reason, some indication of the developing questioning of that trajectory was required, focusing on the critical dissident Marxisms of Sternberg, Korsch, and Brecht, setting down their challenging positions related to both political and aesthetic practice. This could be best accommodated in an Appendix (here Chapter 6). Some indication of the left's problematic engagement with visual culture, particularly in the period of the Second International, also needed to be addressed. This has been done in the Appendix, 'Towards a Materialist Art History', focusing on the work of the

---

15   It seems possible to see Stalin's letter as a rejoinder to Thalheimer's charge in his article
      on the debacle of the 'German October' of 1928.

art historian Wilhelm Hausenstein between 1909 and 1923. His work was widely published in the major socialist papers – *Vorwärts, Sozialistische Monatshefte, Die Neue Zeit* – and by major art publishers. The pre-emigration work of Max Raphael is also briefly considered.

Franz Mehring: Literary Practice as a Socialist Form

> It would be better if we sought ... also to connect literary criticism
> more closely with party work, to direct it through the party. Thus do
> the growing social democratic parties in Europe. This, too, we must
> also do.
>
> LENIN to GORKI, 1908[1]

This chapter considers the work of Franz Mehring, his major contribution to
the cultural programme of the German social democratic movement from the
1890s to the outbreak of the First World War. He was a founder member of the
German Communist Party (shortly before his death in 1919). During the 1920s
the party was subjected to increasing pressure by Stalinisation and the rise of
National Socialism, the former marginalising his influence, as will be set out,
the latter deleting it. His presence was re-established post-war in the former
German Democratic Republic.

The first two brief sections, 'A Portrait' and 'A Biographical Sketch', outline
some of that background. The former, as it were, situates him within the international socialist movement, the latter traces his indirect pathway to Marxism by way of liberal democratic politics to a pre-eminent position within the
movement. The section 'The Question of an Aesthetic Practice' precedes the
consideration of specific works by him in order to establish the complexity of
the issues which would be raised later. The first to address major literary works,
those of Lessing and Schiller, through historical-materialist analysis, his results
would later raise a question on the grounds of adequacy with respect to the dialectical dimension of his findings. The question focused on Mehring's stance
relative to Kant and Hegel: two of the questioners were Wittfogel and Lukács,
whose charges will be set out.[2] Mehring, as will be seen, rejected the idea of

---

1   Koch 1962, p. 591. 'Besser wäre es, wir versuchten ... auch die Literaturkritik mit der Parteiar-
beit, mit der Führung durch die Partei zu verbinden. So machen es die erwachsenen sozialdemokratischen Parteien in Europa. So müssen auch wir es machen'.

2   It should be borne in mind at this point that both Wittfogel and Lukács had access to texts

elaborating an aesthetic system per se, but did not reject the aesthetic dimension, achieving across his manifold writings a dialectical-materialist dimension, as defenders like Thalheimer and Koch would claim.[3] Engels's very positive reception of Mehring's *Die Lessing-Legende* raised the issue of form relative to content, a relationship he stated that he and Marx, because of the urgency of their tasks, neglected at times, a gentle reminder against possible sociological reductivism.[4] Highly regarded as a theorist, Mehring saw his more important role to be that of an interventionist and hence his reason for not elaborating an aesthetic theory. The works chosen for presentation here, those by Lessing and Schiller, proclaim his interventionist intentions: the final chapter of *Die Lessing-Legende* is titled 'Lessing und das Proletariat'; the title of the Schiller biography is *Schiller. Ein Lebensbild für deutsche Arbeiter*. His various writings on Naturalism generally contrast this late nineteenth-century bourgeois art as one of decline set against the work of Lessing and Schiller, but also one containing potential, the possibility of cultural history progressing by its bad side.

1 A Portrait

Mehring's only literary biographer, Hans Koch, writing in the late 1950s in the former German Democratic Republic, described him as 'a constellation of stars in the international workers' movement, whose light illuminated many

---

by Marx and Lenin not available to Mehring, amongst them the former's *Economic and Philosophic Manuscripts of 1844*, the latter's reading of Hegel's *Logic*.

3 Koch 1959, p. 69, notes: 'with regard to Marx's work – and this was true for most of the Second International cohort – it is the case, and particularly for the dialectical-materialist concepts of art, that most references by Marx and Engels were scattered': '… oft gar nicht zugänglichen Bemerkungen von Marx und Engels vorliegt'.

4 Morawski 1977, p. 18, writes that Marx and Engels 'wrote little on problems of form and this is explained only in part by Engels's letter of 1893 to Mehring, where he says he and Marx were bound to lay emphasis on content; … they gave primacy to content; theirs is a *Gehaltästhetik*'. He reinforces this point later on p. 37. Jost Hermand, a student of a student of Mehring's, Richard Hamann, at the SPD School in Berlin, has written more recently on that relationship: 'Relevant literature was for him always something which successfully achieved the synthesis of form and content. Accordingly he advocated neither an aesthetic formalism nor a (merely) correct ideological content, but demanded as an engaged avantgardist literary critic always both together: the linguistic formalism *and* the socio-political as shaping literature' ('Relevante Literatur war für ihn stets etwas, bei dem Form und Inhalt eine gelungene Synthese bilden. Er vertrat daher weder einen ästhetischen Formalismus noch einen ideologisch korrekten Inhaltismus, sondern verlangte als avantgardistisch eingestellter Literaturkritiker stets beides: die sprachlich-formale *und* die gesellschaftspolitische Qualifikation von Literatur' (Hermand 1996, pp. 17–31, 20)).

regions', but noted that 'his work has been as good as forgotten in recent years'.[5] Mehring's eclipse was specifically due to the eruption of major political and historical forces – the Stalinisation of the German Communist Party (KPD), the rise of National Socialism and the Second World War. We need to return to pre-World War One Germany to recover the lustre of Mehring's reputation. Another constellation may be imagined here, consisting of close associates and some of those in the wider socialist movement who were familiar with his writings, with the purpose of establishing his status both within German social democracy and the international community of social democrats. On the publication of his first major work, *Die Lessing-Legende* in 1893, a sympathetic investigation of the literary work of Lessing during the reign of Frederick the Great, considered to be the foundational document for an historical-materialist reading of an author's output, Engels wrote to him from London, 'it is by far the best presentation in existence of the genesis of the Prussian state. Indeed, I may well say, it is the only good presentation, correctly developing in most cases the interrelationships between all particulars'.[6] Two close associates, Rosa Luxemburg and Clara Zetkin, to whom he dedicated his biography of Marx, described Mehring as an 'inheritor of the Marxist spirit' and marked his seventieth birthday with tributes. Luxemburg wrote, '[T]hrough your books and articles you have forged for the proletariat unbreakable bonds not only with classical German philosophy, but also with classical literature, not only with Kant and Hegel, but also with Lessing, Schiller and Goethe'. Luxemburg further commended Mehring as 'the executor of the legacy' of Marx and Engels, mediated through 'the irreplaceable laws of the historical dialectic, clarified for the proletariat day in, day out'.[7] Clara Zetkin acknowledged Mehring's contribution in a long article she wrote in 1916 as editor of the socialist women's journal, *Die Gleichheit* (Equality), where she states: 'who comrade Mehring is and what he signifies for the theory and practice of international socialism is established for us in his works. ... They show him to be an exemplary executor and augmenter of that scientific

---

5   Koch 1959, p. 69.
6   Most of Mehring's work is not available in English translation but where it is I shall refer to it as the source. Here it is from Mehring 1975b, p. 59. This extensive theoretical essay was published as an Appendix to the *Lessing-Legende* and also met with Engels's approval. Unless otherwise indicated, all translations from the German are those of the author.
7   Mehring 1929, p. 10. 'Durch Ihre Bücher wie durch Ihre Artikel haben Sie das deutsche Proletariat nicht bloss mit der klassischen deutschen Philosophie, mit Kant und Hegel, sondern mit der klassischen Dichtung, mit Lessing, Schiller und Goethe ... so sind Sie der Vollstrecker dieses Vermächtnisses gewesen ... die ehernen Gesetz der geschichtlichen Dialektik, die Sie so meisterhaft dem Proletariat tagaus, tagein zu erklären'.

heritage which Karl Marx and Friedrich Engels left for us'.[8] Koch's later assessment reinforces the earlier evaluations: 'Working in their tradition Mehring brings to maturity what Marx and Engels began: literary science became at first hand an instrument of concrete political struggle for the workers' movement: it conclusively takes over as political tribune'.[9] Mehring's contemporary, the Russian Marxist theorist Plekhanov, in discussing Feuerbach's 'humanism', refers to him as follows: '[I] must admit that I do not know for certain how this question is regarded by Franz Mehring, whose knowledge of philosophy is the best, and probably unique among German Social Democrats'.[10] In the following passage from *Materialismus und Empiriokritizismus* (Materialism and Empirio-Criticism), Lenin wrote of Mehring's essay on the German scientist Ernst Haeckel that 'let one compare in conclusion Mehring's remark concerning Hekkel [sic], the remark of someone who not only wishes to be a Marxist but who also understands what that is'.

2   Biographical Sketch

Despite the central presence of Mehring's writing within the world of social democracy between 1891, when he became cultural editor of the most important socialist journal of the period, *Die Neue Zeit*, and the publication of his biography of Marx, *Karl Marx. Geschichte seines Lebens*, in 1918, little biographical material has been published on Mehring himself.[11] Mehring's path to social democracy and Marxism was markedly indirect and complex, by way of his journalism for a number of liberal and democratic, if to some extent left-leaning, papers. He was an unwavering supporter of the working class, hostile to the 'machine politics' of its representatives and, as political reporter, suspicious of Marx's familiarity with conditions on the ground in contemporary Germany, traces of which are still found in his very sympathetic 1918 biography. In light of

---

8   Zetkin 1957, pp. 706–17, 715. 'Wer Genosse Mehring ist und was er für die Theorie und Praxis des internationalen Sozialismus bedeutet, das sagen uns seine Werke. ... Sie erweisen ihn als ein vorbildlichen Verwalter und Mehrer des wissenschaftlichen Erbes, das Karl Marx und Friedrich Engels uns hinterlassen haben'.

9   Koch 1959, p. 62. '... Mehring bringt hier zur Reife, was Marx und Engels begannen: die Literaturwissenschaft wird zum direkten Instrument der konkreten politischen Kämpfe der Arbeiterbewegung; sie erobert die politische Tribüne'. The latter probably refers to Lenin's distinction between bureaucrat and tribune, where the latter is preferred.

10 Plekhanov 1941 [1908], p. 15.

11 Koch lists 44 pages of books, essays, and reviews on literature and history in his bibliography.

this journey it is necessary to consider what scant biographical material there is available, in this instance Clara Zetkin's essay, marking his seventieth birthday in 1916, and Thomas Höhle's biography of 1956, *Franz Mehring. Sein Weg zum Marxismus 1869–1891*.

Aware of certain hostilities within the SPD to Mehring's leading role in the recent past, Zetkin provides a sympathetic account of his career as briefly sketched out above: disillusioned with the puffed up claims of the liberals and democrats, Mehring chose the future, socialism. His enemies both inside and outside the party deliberately misconstrued this decision to discredit him in a personal manner. Zetkin calls to mind the 1903 SPD Conference at Dresden, 'with its disgraceful attacks [on him]', the questioning of his character and suspicion over his 'opportunistic' conversion to the cause of social democracy. The attacks resulted from exchanges over the principles and tactics of social democracy and were directed from the 'revisionist' wing of the party. Mehring was then political editor of the left-wing *Leipziger Volkszeitung* and, as Zetkin describes him, 'a clear-sighted and resolute leader of the left, whose knowledge, talent and experience tipped the scale in his favour'.[12] Höhle, whose biography of Mehring allows us to see that his entry into the SPD was neither opportunistic nor damascene but an evolution over a long period, also deals with the Dresden 1903 conference. When Mehring assumed editorship of the *Leipziger Volkszeitung* in 1901, he turned it into 'a Marxist, anti-revisionist paper of principle, whose importance soon spread beyond the confines of Dresden and the surrounding districts'. Due to his political activity and work as historian, literary historian, and editor, he had become 'one of the best known and most important personalities of the party', whose 'unconditional advocacy of Marxism made him the most hated opponent of the revisionists'. Hence his reception at the Dresden Party conference, where 'the right concentrated its fire on its sharpest, shrewdest and most strongly principled opponent'.[13]

---

12   Zetkin 1957, p. 711. 'Wir errinern an das schmachvolle systematische Kesseltreiben auf dem Parteitag zu Dresden. ... in der damaligen Auseinandersetzung um die Prinzipien und Taktik der Sozialdemokratie Franz Mehring, zumal als leitender Redakteur der *Leipziger Volkszeitung*, ein klarblickender, entschiedener Führer der Linken war und das grosse Gewicht seines Wissens, seiner Begabung und Erfahrung für ihren Erfolg in die Waagschale warf'.

13   Höhle 1956, p. 298. Detail from Höhle's biography indicates the turning points on Mehring's journey: the title of the dissertation on which the book is based, 'Franz Mehring. Vom bürgerlichen Demokraten zum proletarischen Revolutionär (1868–1891)' ('Franz Mehring: From Bourgeois Democrat to Proletarian Revolutionary') is a measure of the distance travelled. Mehring returned the fire in his *Meine Rechtfertigung* (*My Justification*), in which he challenged the false nature of the charges levelled against him and criticised the side-

Mehring was a working journalist all his life after leaving Berlin University, where he studied history and philosophy. He was awarded his doctorate on 'German Social Democracy: Its History and Theory' at Leipzig.[14] Two events which were to play a large part in his development occurred in 1869: he became acquainted with the writings of Ferdinand Lassalle, and he joined, whilst still a student, the editorial staff of *Die Zukunft* ('The Future'), the organ of radical bourgeois democracy in Prussia, founded by Johann Jacoby, edited by Guido Weiss, both of whom were to have considerable influence on him.[15] It is not necessary here to trace more fully their careers in the politics and journalism of Prussia at the time but to highlight those moments when their awareness of the writings and activities of Marx, Engels, and Liebknecht could have impacted on the student-journalist Mehring. Jacoby's politics were essentially those of a left-inclined reformer, informed by an understanding of more radical strains. He was a contributor to the *Deutsch-Französischen Jahrbücher* (German-French Almanacs) established by Marx in Paris, published in 1844. Although his attempt to found a radical democratic party had foundered and was further undermined by Liebknecht's and Bebel's formation of a social-democratic workers' party at Eisenach (known as 'die Eisenachers') in 1869, he nevertheless greeted its presence positively. A noted stylist, Weiss influenced Mehring's practice, as did his advocacy of the transmission of classical literature and the role of the aesthetic in social transformation. In 1875, he became Berlin political correspondent for the *Frankfurter Zeitung*, a paper with a less pronounced inclination towards the workers' movement than *Die Zukunft*, although sharing similar radical bourgeois democratic ideals.

Mehring polemicised in favour of the national socialism of Lassalle and against the international socialism of Marx and Engels. He characterised the quarrels on the left, 'in their decade-long dissensions on great and small', and 'representing the protracted and wearisome struggle which ends with the final victory of Marxian international communists against and over the tradition of Lassallean national socialists'.[16] As mentioned above, Mehring had been intro-

---

lining of Marxism within the SPD, the abandonment of theory, '[t]he undeserved contempt into which it has fallen amongst wide circles of the working class' ('die unverdiente Verachtung, der die Theories heute in weiten Kreisen der Arbeiterklasse anheimfallen ist …' (Mehring 1903, p. 36)).

14   Höhle 1956, p. 35. 'Die deutsche Sozialdemokratie. Ihre Geschichte und ihre Lehre'.

15   Höhle informs us that Marx and Engels were regular readers of the paper and often made use of it. This information is based on the *Marx-Engels Correspondence*, Vol. 3 (Berlin, 1950). 'Karl Marx und Friedrich Engels lasen damals ständing *Die Zukunft* und bedienten sich häufig des Blattes'. Höhle 1956, p. 45.

16   Höhle 1956, p. 128. 'So stellen sich diese inneren Zwiste eines Jahrzehnts … im grossen

duced to the writings of Lassalle by Jacoby and Guido Weiss. Although he was to modify his position on Lassalle, he was still protective of him in his last work, the biography of Marx, a position which would, for example, lead Lukács to question Mehring's understanding of dialectical materialism in his major 1933 evaluative essay on his achievement as a literary theorist (to be considered in Chapter 5).[17]

Accompanying his continuous attacks on Bismarckian politics, particularly the anti-socialist law, and monarchy – on the direct orders of Emperor William II, the Berlin newspaper Mehring edited, the *Volks Zeitung*, was temporarily closed down – was an emerging re-engagement with socialist politics. Höhle ascribes the first step to Mehring's writing on the Paris Commune, published in the prestigious *Preussische Jahrbücher* in 1879–80, a series 'which displayed a scientific character based on Mehring's research of a comprehensive range of sources, including Commune-friendly works such as Marx's General Council Address on behalf of the First International'.[18] Here 'the Commune socialists, members of the International Working Men's Association were surprisingly positively seen'.[19] In 1884, he published a series of articles on the origins of the German working-class movement, borrowing from Engels's *Der Bauern Krieg in Deutschland* (The Peasant War in Germany) where, as Höhle suggests, he 'came to sound and historical-materialist judgement, above all, in this context, on the important role of Thomas Münzer'.[20] For this series he had also researched

---

    und ganzen dar als der langwierige Kampf und der endliche Sieg des internationalen Kommunisten Marx gegen und über die Traditionen des nationalen Sozialisten Lassalle'. Höhle's quotation is from an early version of a history of social democracy which Mehring published in 1879.

17   By 1884, Mehring had begun to question aspects of Lassalle's politics, his ideas on 'social monarchy' ('sozialen Königtum') and his characterisation of the state as 'the primal source of all morality' ('seine Kennzeichnung des Staates als "des uralten Vestafeuers aller Gesittung"'). Höhle 1956, p. 185. Bismarck had contacted Lassalle on the role of the workers' movement. In correspondence between Bismarck and Lassalle only discovered in 1928 (and thus not available to Mehring), the latter suggested the monarchy become 'a social dictatorship', 'a social and revolutionary people's community'. This information is contained in the English translation of Mehring's biography of Marx, *Karl Marx: The Story of His Life* (Mehring 1936, p. 554).

18   Höhle 1956, p. 138. 'Die Arbeit über die Kommune trägt wissenschaftlichen Charakter und zeigt, dass Mehring ein umfangreiches Quellenmaterial verarbeitet hatte, darunter kommunefreundliche Arbeiten wie die Addressen des Generalrats der Internationalen Arbeiter-Assoziation ...'.

19   Höhle 1956, p. 139. '... dass die Sozialisten in der Kommune, die Mitglieder der Internationalen Arbeiter-Assoziation, überraschend positiv gesehen wurden'.

20   Höhle 1956, p. 187. '... kam er sicheren und historisch-materialistischen Urteilen, vor allem über die in diesem Zusammenhang wichtige Rolle Thomas Münzers'.

Marx's work on the *Rheinische Zeitung*, his understanding of detailed evidence that he had worked through the paper. In 1885, he wrote to Engels that he was intending to write a biography of Marx, inquiring about the possibility of having access to unpublished material. Engels did not respond but in a letter to Bebel we find a frank assessment of Mehring's relationship to and standing within the socialist leadership: Engels is writing of an article by Mehring in *Die Volks-Zeitung* against the anti-socialist law, '... it is certainly by Mehring, or at least I know no other in Berlin who writes so well. The fellow has so much talent and a clear head, but is a calculating rascal and by nature a betrayer'.[21] Prophetically, he continues: 'I hope that will be borne in mind, when he comes again to us, as he surely will, as soon as things change'.[22] Mehring's rapprochement with social-democratic politics continued to develop. He supported the mass strike of miners in 1889, his report on the Social Democratic Conference at Halle displays, according to Höhle, the first indication of his support (albeit indirectly) for the socialist organisation of society, an article 'Hohenzollern und die Reformation' announces his 'theoretical understanding of historical materialism'.[23] He published a wide-ranging attack on the capitalist-dominated bourgeois press, *Kapital und Presse*, enthusiastically received on the left, particularly by Liebknecht, now editor of *Vorwärts*, the SPD newspaper. In 1891, on Liebknecht's intervention, he joined the editorial staff of *Die Neue Zeit*, the leading socialist journal of the period, and took over editorship of the *Leipziger Volkszeitung*, which became a strong anti-revisionist organ.

Engels's reservations concerning Mehring were noted above, but when Mehring threatened to withdraw from politics as a result of a disagreement over the publication of a notice for one of his articles published elsewhere, Engels wrote anxiously to Bebel advising accommodation on the issue: 'furthermore it would be absurd should he be really thinking to turn his back on politics, it would be doing the authorities and the bourgeoisie a favour, his editorials in the "N[eue] Z[eit]" are in fact splendid and we await them with impatience. Such dash cannot be let rust or squandered on miserable belletristism'.[24] Mehring did not turn his back on politics and in 1895 Engels agreed

---

<ol>
<li value="21">Höhle 1956, p. 199. 'sind sicher von Mehring, wenigstens weiss ich keinen anderen in B(erlin), der so gut schreiben. Der Kerl hat viel Talent und einen offenen Kopf, ist aber ein berechnender Lump und von Natur Verräter'.</li>
<li value="22">Ibid. 'ich hoffe, man wird das im Gedächtnis, wenn er wieder zu uns kommt, was er sicher tut, sobald sich die Zeiten ändern'.</li>
<li value="23">Höhle 1956, p. 268. 'Die wichtigste Bemerkung in dieser Richtung stellte ein völlig unzweideutiges und rückhaltloses Bekenntnis zur materialistischen Geschichts-auffassung dar ...'.</li>
<li value="24">Koch 1959, pp. 321–2, 322. 'Es wäre übrigens Unsinn, wenn er wirklich an Rückzug aus</li>
</ol>

that Mehring should undertake to write the history of the German working-class movement.[25] Mehring was that type of bourgeois intellectual approved of by Engels, 'the one who really understands from the position of the proletariat what is most useful and welcome'.[26] At the end of her seventieth birthday greetings in 1916 to Mehring, Rosa Luxemburg refers to the herd-like betrayal and desertion by intellectuals of their burgher heritage in their return to 'the fleshpots' of the authorities: 'but let them', she continues, 'we have acquired the last and best of the German bourgeoisie, of that spirit, talent and character it had: Franz Mehring'.[27]

The above sketch has mapped out Mehring's career from an initially sympathetic position to socialist thinking (Johann Jacoby and Guido Weiss, their paper *Die Zukunft* and Lassalle's ideas), through hostility to the social-democratic party but not to the workers' movement, from disillusionment with the reformist programmes of the Democratic Party to gradual re-engagement with individual social democrats (Liebknecht, Bebel) and the works of Marx and Engels, to entry into the SPD, his anti-revisionist stance and, finally, his participation in the founding of the Spartakus Bund and the German Communist Party (KPD). Engels, Liebknecht, Zetkin, Luxemburg, and the other leading figures recognised what Mehring's extensive experience of German politics and literature had to offer the party and the workers' movement, even if revisionists, as exemplified by their behaviour at the Dresden party conference (described by Zetkin above), wished to use moments of his past against him.

3   The Question of an Aesthetic Practice

Mehring's work on culture will be considered within two broad categories: an appraisal of the class-based revolutionary nature of late eighteenth-century bourgeois culture, in particular the work of Lessing and Schiller, and a critique of contemporary bourgeois culture, particularly focused on Naturalist

---

der Politik denken sollte, er täte damit nur den Machthabern und den Bourgeois einen Gefallen, seine Leitartikel in der *N[euen] Z[eit]* sind in der Tat ganz famos, und wir lauern jedesmal mit Begierde darauf. Solch Schneid soll man nicht einrosten lassen oder an lausige Belletristen verschwenden ...'.

25   Höhle 1956, p. 296.
26   Engels's letter to Bernstein, quoted in Höhle 1956, p. 300. 'Haben sie aber diesen Standpunkt wirklich, dann sind sie höchst brauchbar und willkommen'.
27   Mehring 1929, p. 11. 'Geht nur. Wir haben der deutschen Bourgeoisie doch das Letzte und Beste weggenommen, was sie noch an Geist, Talent und Charakter hatte: Franz Mehring'.

drama. His declared purpose is to make both appraisal and critique accessible to the working-class movement as instruments in their emancipatory struggle: the 'self-freedom' (Selbstbefreieung) and 'self-education' (Selbsterziehung) of the proletariat.[28] Mehring's role was not that of a traditional academic, but rather that of an interventionist for whom the socio-political emancipation of the proletariat was the priority. August Thalheimer informs us that 'Mehring wrote literary history as a political fighter'.[29] Paul Frölich's description of him as surpassing 'everyone else in militancy of spirit and understanding of history' indicates succinctly the range of his activities and contribution.[30] Die Volksbühne serves as an example. Cecil W. Davies, in his *Theatre of the People: The Story of the Volksbühne*, informs us that it was founded 'by the party rank and file, not the party leadership', as the latter felt it might deflect energies from political activity.[31] Mehring himself reluctantly took over directorship of the club for those years, as a result of dissension at the SPD Conference in Erfurt in 1891, when some avantgardist writers and journalists left the party. He did, however, recognise its contribution as 'a serving member of the great struggle of the working class for emancipation'.[32] Mehring's 'multi-tasking' demands may be partially advanced to throw light on some areas of cultural work which he deliberately did not elaborate systematically and for which he would later be censured. These areas were aesthetics and philosophy and, more understandably given the pre-revolutionary era in which he lived, the absence of a concept of an art of transition – he states many times, as with the SPD line on the Volksbühne, that the proletariat must achieve socio-political emancipation before they can represent their transition.[33]

---

28   *Die Volksbühne*, 1892–93, Vol. 9, p. 3, quoted in Koch 1959, p. 100. This was not embourgeoisement.

29   Mehring 1929, p. 15. Thalheimer worked with Mehring and Luxemburg on setting up the journal *Die Internationale* in 1915, representing the views of the recently established Spartakus Bund in opposition to the SPD, eventually to become the KPD. He was recognised in the 1920s as a leading theoretician within the party.

30   Frölich 1983, p. 71. His wide-ranging publishing activities have been outlined already above.

31   Davies 1977, p. 38.

32   Ibid. Davies writes that 'a census of occupations of members made in the season 1893/4 shows strikingly that the association was predominantly working-class, with a particular appeal to skilled workmen' (Davies 1977, p. 45). Mehring states that this was the level at which he pitched his own writing: he edited *Die Volksbühne* journal, wrote essays and programme notes for the audience.

33   Mehring 1929, p. 31. In his introduction to the Mehring book, Thalheimer writes on the subject of the possibility of proletarian art that the argument 'appears to be richly scholastic and undialectic'.

In a brief introduction to a miscellaneous collection of essays on aesthetics, 'Ästhetische Streifzüge' (Aesthetic Excursions) (1899), Mehring states: 'To write a scientific aesthetic from the side of historical materialism would be as advantageous an undertaking as it is a complicated one. The following expositions do not intend to provide even a few stones to this large and spacious building: at most it wishes to clear the building site of some scrub'.[34] The clearing agent would be historical materialism. But Mehring himself raised the central question concerning the adequacy of historical materialism itself to accomplish that task: 'Can historical materialism, however, which is only a historical method, compensate the proletariat for philosophy, taken in its traditional meaning as a general and consistent Weltanschauung, into which flow all the currents of investigations in the natural and cultural sciences'.[35] Mehring's apparent neglect of philosophical systems also had a strategic purpose. What workers have wholly absorbed, he writes, is the 'Marxist idea', historical materialism, which 'can in fact fully satisfy their metaphysical needs, not through a new philosophy, but through a history of philosophy'.[36] The 'precise specific instrument' for writing such a history will take a long time to develop, so in the meantime 'we should guard against dragging philosophic speculation and trifles into the proletarian class struggle', whose 'metaphysical need in its deep urgency will better establish the correct way'.[37]

Mehring's oscillation between his use of the designations 'Methode' and 'Weltanschauung' was to raise questions concerning the ideological status of his critique, even amongst those who recognised the extraordinary importance of his contribution, as Koch so clearly states: 'thanks to Franz Mehring Marx-

---

34   Koch 1961, p. 141. 'The aesthetic', Mehring wrote in a review of proletarian poetry in 1908, 'is not a fully autonomous region, the boundaries cannot be drawn between feeling, understanding and projection'. Koch 1961, p. 489. 'Die Ästhetik ist nicht ein völlig abgeschlossenes Gebiet für sich: mit dem Zirkel lassen sie sich Grenzen nicht ziehen, wo sich Empfindung, Erkenntnis und Wille scheiden'. It is notable that understanding, the cognitive, and projection, phantasy, are major elements in Mehring's sense of the aesthetic.

35   Mehring 1931, p. 271.

36   Mehring 1931, p. 272. Karl Korsch describes the mind-set of orthodox Second International Marxists as 'reassuring each other that their Marxism by its very nature had nothing to do with philosophy ... and thought they were saying something important *in favour* of it'. It had become 'scientific socialism'. Korsch 2012, p. 33.

37   Mehring 1931, p. 273. Korsch provides a persuasive account of Mehring's position here, writing 'how sound Mehring's political instinct was when he rejected philosophy altogether in the face of philosophical fantasies *like these* ... Kantian, Dietzgenian and Machism'. Korsch 2012, p. 34, n. 7.

ist literary research begins to be established as a specialist Marxist science'.[38] If Mehring does not formally set out a theoretical dialectical position as such, we must therefore look to his practice to see how he deploys 'Methode' and whether there may be pathways to 'Weltanschauung', as a sometime admiring, sometime adversarial critic, Georg Lukács, seems to concede, even if he reproves him for 'methodological dualism' or 'eclecticism': 'Mehring's praxis is often so much better than his theory ... that his correct critique stands in contrast to his incorrect theory'.[39] Indeed, Lukács may provide us with a category for Mehring's practice, that of 'instinctive dialectics': he is writing on revolutionary bourgeois writers of the eighteenth century, that their method was based on naive materialism and 'instinctive dialectics'.[40] Mehring was not ignorant of the crucial role the dialectic had, as the following statement clearly demonstrates: 'The dialectical mode of thinking will certainly be learned and whoever understands the laws of dialectical thinking will penetrate the dialectical mediations of reality very differently from one who has for so long knocked their head against the hard facts, until in a more or less thorough manner they arrive at the proper interrelationship'.[41]

In much of his writing, the boundaries between 'Methode' and 'Weltanschauung' are permeable. He writes of historical materialism that 'it is not an infallible dogma, but a scientific method ... [I]t is much more the proletarian class struggle grasped in thought: it is from events themselves, rising up from historical development and responds to them'.[42] This does not sound like the mechanical imposition of an inflexible method, more an openness to the dynamics of change – he uses a similar phrasing to acknowledge Hegel's philo-

---

38   Koch 1959, p. 64. '... dass dank Franz Mehring sich die marxistische Literaturforschung als marxistische Spezialwissenschaft zu konstituieren beginnt'.

39   Lukács 1954, pp. 369–70. '... in dieser Frage die Praxis von Mehring sehr oft viel, viel besser als diese Theorie. ... liegt die Lage auch so, dass Mehring seine richtige Kritik im Gegensatz zu seiner unrichtigen Theorie schreibt'.

40   Lukács 1980, p. 24, n. 6. This appeared originally in *Die Linkskurve* in 1932 in his article 'Reportage or Portrayal'. Given Engels's praise for Mehring's Appendix on historical materialism (see below on the *Lessing-Legende* passages), the category of naive materialism does not apply.

41   Mehring 1931, p. 11. This was in response to an exchange of articles on the dialectic between Kautsky and Bernstein, published under the title 'Nachlese' in *Die Neue Zeit*, 1899, quoted by Thalheimer.

42   Koch 1959, p. 46. 'Er ist kein unfehlbares Dogma, sondern eine wissenschaftliche Methode ... er ist vielmehr der proletarische Klassenkampf in Gedanken erfasst: er ist aus den Dingen selbst, aus der historischen Entwicklung emporgewachsen und wandelt sich mit ihnen; ...'. As we shall see from Chapter 6, Karl Korsch agrees with Mehring on this conceptualisation, supported with a reference to Marx.

sophical superiority over Kant, 'his philosophy was for him his time seized in thought' ('seine Zeit in Gedanken erfasst').[43] The working of the dialectic may also be subliminally present in his mode of articulation. Here, in an article commemorating Marx's anniversary, 'Karl Marx und das Gleichnis', a German term which may be read as the figurative in general or as image or trope, he is responding to charges by 'young university people' that Marx's figurative language betrays 'by no means an acute thinker' ('keineswegs ein scharfsinniger'), rather 'a spiritual man' ('geistreicher Mann'), constrained by 'unclear mysticism' ('unklarer Mystik'), who sought to make 'historical materialism understandable in a totally vague way with patched together images' ('selbst den historischen Materialismus nur in ganz unbestimmter mit Bildern zusammengeflickter Weise ...').[44] Mehring very succinctly canvasses the opinions of Lessing and Goethe on the productive role of the figurative, glances at Hegel and then addresses Marx's doctorate and first chapter of *Das Kapital*, 'the summit of his literary achievement' ('den Gipfel seiner schriftstellerischen Leistung'). 'For Marx', he writes, 'the figurative is never decorative, never merely a rhetorical flourish. But it is not so much, as it is also with Lessing, a lever only for easier understanding, an obligation, not only to have an effect on the intellect but also on the imagination; it is an originating simultaneous manifestation of equivalences, the realised ideal of complete presentation of which Lessing said that concept and image belong together ... The figurative, as Marx uses it, is the sensuous mother of thought from which it receives its living breath'.[45]

In a passage from *Kapital und Presse* Mehring more directly addressed the deployment of the dialectic where he criticises Nietzsche from a Hegelian perspective, on the socio-historical nature of morality, of 'good' and 'evil' as in *Jenseits von Gut und Böse* (Beyond Good and Evil). Nietzsche, Mehring writes, considers these as polar opposites, undialectically, whilst for Hegel they are dialectically related. The context for the passage is the French Revolution and morality, the former characterised by Hegel as progressive, derided by Nietzsche 'as farce to excess' ('überflüssige Posse'). 'That "evil"', Mehring writes, 'in which Hegel perceived the emerging force of historical development has,

---

43   Mehring 1931, pp. 79–80.
44   *Die Neue Zeit*, 1908, Vol. 3, pp. 851–4, 851.
45   *Die Neue Zeit*, 1908, Vol. 3, p. 853. 'Bei Marx ist das Gleichnis niemals Zierat, niemals ein blosser Schmuck der Rede. Aber es ist auch nicht einmal nur wie bei Lessing ein Hebel des besseren und leichteren Verständnisses, ein Bemühen, nicht nur auf den Verstand, sondern auf die Phantasie zu wirken, sondern es ist ein ursprüngliches Zusammenschauen der gleichen Dinge, das verwirklichste Ideal jener vollkommenen Darstellung, von der Lessing sagte, dass Begriff und Bild zusammengehören ... Das Gleichnis, wie es Marx handhabt, ist die sinnliche Mutter des Gedankens, der von ihr den lebendigen Odem empfängt'.

according to his dialectical method, with its conservative and revolutionary sides, another sense', that 'every new advance appears as an outrage against the hallowed, the customary, the passing'. In a clear account of Hegel's method he writes that 'its revolutionary character conceives historical development as an uninterrupted process of development and decline, which despite apparent contingencies and occasional reversals accomplishes progressive development'. The intent of Nietzsche's discourse on good and evil is characterised by Mehring as the attempt to discover the developmental stage of contemporary capitalism's class morality and to 'burst apart the ties to earlier class moralities – notions of petit-bourgeois honour and bourgeois respectability – that still apply'. Nietzsche is 'not the social philosopher of the aristocratic, rather that of capitalism' ('... nicht ... der "Sozialphilosoph der Aristokratie", sondern der Sozialphilosoph des Kapitalismus').[46]

But the dialectic was also more overtly present. This text is concerned only with Mehring's work on literature. Schleifstein reminds us of Mehring's histories of the SPD and the working-class movement, that 'it bears witness that he employed the dialectical method and *masterfully* demonstrated how to employ it across many areas ... that he clearly understood the significance of the dialectic for the historian'.[47]

There are many instances throughout his work where the dialectic is in play, even if instinctively. The absence of an overt dialectic rigorously applied was seen as a disabling position: Lukács, for instance, claimed that it prevented Mehring from making his anti-neo-Kantian stance more effective than it was. Schleifstein wrote that although Mehring greatly admired Goethe, he failed to fully understand the nature of his 'spontaneous philosophical mater-

---

46   Mehring 1891, pp. 121–7. '... jenes "Böse", in welchem Hegel die Triebkraft der geschichtlichen Entwicklung erblickte, hat nach seiner dialektischen Methode mit ihrer konservativen und revolutionären Seite noch einen zweiten Sinn ... dass jeder neue Fortschritt auftritt als ein Frevel gegen den Heiliges, als Rebellion gegen die alten absterbenden aber durch die Gewohnheit geheiligten Zustände. ... aber ihr revolutionärer Charakter fasste die geschichtliche Entwicklung als einen ununterbrochenen Prozess des Werdens und Vergehens auf, in welchem sich trotz aller scheinbaren Zufälligkeiten und zeitweiliger Rückschläge doch eine fortschreitende Entwicklung ... vollzieht. ... ist der Versuch, die Klassenmoral des Kapitalismus auf der heutigen Stufe seiner Entwicklung zu entdecken und die Bande zu zersprengen, welche die Klassenmoralen seiner früheren Entwicklungsstufen, die kleinbürgerliche Ehrbarkeit und die grossbürgerliche Respektabilität, ihm noch anlegen ...'.

47   Schleifstein 1959, p. 109. '... seine historischen Arbeiten zeugen davon, dass er die dialektische Methode anzuwenden und die Dialektik der geschichtlichen Entwicklung auf weiten Gebieten *meisterhaft* darzulegen weiss. [...] dass er zwar die Bedeutung der Dialektik für den Historiker anerkannte ...'.

ialism' ('spontaner philosophischer Materialismus'), even if 'contradictory and pantheistically clothed', that he did not 'comprehend its ideological roots' ('nur wurde er sich ihrer *weltanschaulichen* Wurzel nicht bewusst').[48] But both Schleifstein and Lukács commend Mehring's 1908–09 review essay on the publication of Goethe's letters to Charlotte von Stein: the former 'as a remarkable revision of his earlier representation of Goethe' ('zu einer sehr bemerkenswerten Korrektur seines Goethes-Bildes'), the latter that Mehring's 'outstanding analysis' ('ausgezeichnete Analyse') identified correctly and in a 'Marxist manner' ('sehr richtig und marxistisch nachweist') that Goethe's flight from Weimar was not that of a love tragedy but 'the failure of the burgher Enlightener Goethe to implement his programme there' ('sondern die Folge des Scheiterns der Pläne des bürgerlichen Aufklärers Goethe gewesen ist ...').[49]

The question of Mehring's use of the dialectic was inevitably related to the source of his aesthetic thinking, Kant or Hegel. Consequently, I am concluding this passage with a glance at Thalheimer's introductions to Mehring's collected works on literature and philosophy and with brief reference to Mehring's essays on each of them. I begin with a passage titled 'Zur historisch-materialistischen Ästhetik'. 'Mehring', Thalheimer writes, 'did not construct an aesthetic theory on the basis of historical materialism but provided cues to its structure'.[50] Just as Marx had engaged critically with classical English political economy, so too had Mehring with classical German literature and philosophy. He had 'correctly considered Kant as "the founder of the scientific aesthetic" ... recognised Kant's groundbreaking contribution ... in demonstrating that art was a proper and natural human faculty'.[51] But to what extent did this recognition make Mehring a Kantian *avant la lettre*? Nowhere does Mehring deploy the concepts of 'taste' or 'beauty', nor display any interest in the concept of 'disinterest'. He rehearses briefly some arguments around taste and beauty, presumably because they were part of the Kantian-Schillerian discursive world. He wrote: 'a suprasensuous idea can have no historical development and therefore all aesthetic judgement is historically conditioned'.[52] Counter-intuitively, Lukács charges him with Kantian disinterest yet notes that 'his revolutionary instinct armed him' ('sein revolutionärer Instinkt wehrt er sich'), that he prevails, as in his criticism of the neo-Kantians and other situations, where deficiencies

---

48   Schleifstein 1959, pp. 143–4.
49   Schleifstein 1959, p. 144; Lukács 1954, p. 376.
50   Mehring 1929, p. 21.
51   Ibid.
52   Koch 1961, p. 165. 'Eine übersinnliche Idee kann keine historische Entwicklung haben, und doch ist alles ästhetische Urteil historisch bedingt'.

in the dialectic might have hindered him. Mehring's operative practice dispensed with Kant's categories including the primacy of form as one finds in his comments on Hauptmann's 'Florian Geyer': 'Disregard for conventional dramatic forms is a great step forward when, as a result, a new content can be seized ...'.[53] There are many passages throughout his writings where he fundamentally disagrees with Kant's theories. In his 1904 essay 'Immanuel Kant', we find numerous criticisms, mostly primed as responses to contemporary neo-Kantian claims to re-establish socialism on an ethical rather than a Marxian-materialist foundation. Against Kant's moral precept of Man as an end, not as a means, Mehring wrote: 'To present the dissolution of the feudal form of production exclusively as the emancipation of the worker, rather than simultaneously its transformation to capitalist exploitation was a general illusion of the bourgeois Enlightenment ...'.[54] 'With the whole Kantian *Weltanschauung*', he writes, 'nothing binds us but the historical recognition of indebtedness to the groundbreaking men of the bourgeois Enlightenment'.[55] The purpose of his essay is to establish the limits of Kant's theory of knowledge: although based on practice, it ignores most of social interaction. Hence the senselessness of the street cry 'Back to Kant' with which currently the proletarian emancipatory struggle is so pestered. Kant's complete lack of a sense of history was unique even amongst the proponents of Enlightenment. In his essay 'Kant und Marx', also of 1904, responding to the commemoration of Kant's centenary and again directed against the neo-Kantians, Mehring writes that 'Kant has no significance for the present and its problems'.[56]

Mehring criticises former mentors Jacoby and F.A. Lange for their adherence to a Kantian morality on which to base socialism, in the case of the latter the complete unawareness of historical materialism, with the former

---

53   Koch 1961, p. 309. 'Die Missachtung der überkommenen dramatischen Formen ist ein grosser Fortschritt, wenn durch sie ein neuer Inhalt des Dramas erobert kann ...'. Lukács provides a less intrinsic account of Mehring's self-declared position on form: 'His sound revolutionary spirit in any case propels him against all form experiment, to protest strongly against all "literary revolutions" of form': 'Sein gesunder revolutionärer Instinkt treibt ihn in jedem Fall dazu, gegen alle Formenexperimente gegen alle "Literaturrevolutionen" von der Form aus heftig zu protestieren'. Lukács 1954, p. 369. Obviously Lukács recognises that Mehring does not share the Kant/Schiller position that it was the role of form to 'annihilate' content.

54   Mehring 1931, p. 230. 'Die Auflösung der feudalen Produktionsweise ausschliesslich darzustellen als Emanzipation des Arbeiters, statt zugleich als Verwandlung der feudalen in die kapitalistische Ausbeutungsweise, war eine allgemeine Illusion der bürgerlichen Aufklärung ...'.

55   Mehring 1931, pp. 58–9.

56   Mehring 1931, p. 76.

selecting Kant over the 'Hegelian dialectic'.[57] In contrast to Kant, Hegel is not 'a timeless thinker', rather 'his philosophy was for him his time seized in thought'.[58] In developing his absolute idea from Fichte's subjective way of thinking, 'Hegel's historical dialectic inhabited innumerable provinces of the spirit which he enriched through the principle of development of the historical which Kant's philosophy was totally incapable of doing'. Mehring, in his essay 'Philosophieren und Philosophie', writes of the demise of Hegelianism: 'Thus the Hegelian philosophy did not perish in the Young Hegelians, but rather they perished from it'.[59] Marx and Engels survived Hegelianism by rejecting the 'Spirit-motivating idea', retaining only the dialectical method. He quotes Engels: 'What remain usable from all previously existing philosophy are the precepts of thought and its laws – formal logic and the dialectic. Everything else unfolds in the positive science of nature and history'.[60]

The purpose of Thalheimer's introductions is to produce a reading of Mehring which gives to his historical materialism a dialectical dimension. In addressing the absence of an elaborate engagement with Hegel's aesthetics in Mehring's work, he writes of the former's work that '[h]is class-based characterisation of Cervantes's Don Quixote, the knightly epic, of Ariosto, of Dutch painting can with only slight modifications be incorporated into an historical-materialist art history or aesthetic'.[61] To counter what would be considered to be reductionist dangers in an historical-materialist account of art, Thalheimer selects passages from Hegel, whose perceptions are also embedded in Mehring's writings, critical of the perception of art as the imitation of nature ('die Nachahmung der Natur'), of tendentious art ('Wird aber der Zweck der Belehrung so sehr als Zweck behandelt'), where the message is prosaically presented and not through the indirect and implicit means of art ('nicht nur indirekt in der konkreten Kunstgestalt implicite enthalten sein soll'), where

---

57   Mehring 1931, p. 157. This is from his essay 'Johann Jacoby und die wissenschaftlichen Sozialisten' (scientific socialists).

58   Mehring 1931, p. 76.

59   Mehring 1931, p. 268. 'So ist die Hegelische Philosophie nicht an den Junghegelianern umgekommen, sondern umgekehrt diese an der Hegelschen Philosophie'.

60   Ibid. 'Was von der ganzen bisherigen Philosophie noch selbständig bestehen bleibt, ist die Lehre vom Denken und seinen Gesetzen – die formelle Logik und die Dialektik. Alles andere geht auf in die positive Wissenschaft von Natur und Geschichte'. Schleifstein suggests that Mehring misreads Engels's claim that the 'overturning' of Hegel was the end of philosophy as such, when in fact Engels's intention as such was to announce a philosophical thinking established on a real foundation.

61   Mehring 1929, p. 26.

the artwork is broken ('und das Kunstwerk ein in ihm selbst Gebrochenes') 'in which form and content no longer seem to grow together' ('in welchem Form und Inhalt nicht mehr als ineinander verwachsen erscheinen').[62] His final quotation concerns Hegel's 'Kunstideal': 'to draw out reality from the spread of the particular and the accidental in such a way that the core of this sublated externality appears as a living individuality'.[63] An historical-materialist aesthetic cannot avoid Hegel, he writes, although neither can it stop with him. Yet when we read Thalheimer's account of Mehring's achievement in his Schiller biography, it may be read as an example of that historical/dialectical crossover he defends. Only part of this may be presented here:

> He investigates Schiller's literary sources, the influences of the 'Sturm und Drang'. He characterises the particularity of Schiller's lyrical gift, his philosophical position and the influence of Kant, of antiquity etc. and he brings all of this into relationship with the changing class relationships in the Germany of his era, the state as it existed, the developing stages of bourgeois class consciousness, with economic development. He transformed the general formulation of historical materialism into such a clear and rich representation. The economic skeleton has been clothed in muscles, nerves and skin. Multiple series of mediations establish the relationship between the economic base and the ideological superstructure, the development of the poet, the construction of his individual works, its material content and form.[64]

Thalheimer resolves this 'anxiety' around Mehring's status between historical and dialectical materialism on the level of practice. In Germany he is equalled only by Rosa Luxemburg. 'The dialectical materialist', Thalheimer writes, 'is to be as little sought in the work of Mehring as in that of Marx, Engels, Rosa Luxemburg or Lenin, except where they expressly address questions of dialectical materialism or philosophy of history: it is much more in Mehring's overall the-

---

62   Mehring 1929, pp. 26–7.

63   Ibid. 'die Wirklichkeit zurückgenommen aus der Breite der Einzelheiten und Zufälligkeiten, insofern das Innere in dieser der Allgmeinheit entgegengehabenen Äusserlichkeit selbst als lebendige Individualität erscheint'.

64   Mehring 1929, p. 19. As we shall see below, Rosa Luxemburg's review of the Schiller biography was equally positive. In his response to Mehring's *Die Lessing-Legende*, Engels would praise him for 'correctly developing in most places the interrelationships between all particulars'. The Engels-Mehring correspondence will be dealt with in the *Lessing-Legende* section.

oretical and practical work that the dialectical thinker is disclosed and from which one can learn of the operation of the dialectic'.[65]

Koch, his literary biographer, also finds much that is dialectical in Mehring's thinking, if not systematically articulated. In a section in chapter five titled 'Über die ästhetische Bedeutung der revolutionären subjectivität' (On the aesthetic significance of revolutionary subjectivity), Koch writes that Mehring considered that 'progressive, revolutionary ideological positions were a determining moment in the promotion of artistic talent [...] and were the most important guarantee of aesthetic worth and effectiveness'. Drawing on Marx's theses on ideology, Mehring recognised that the precept 'for *all* ideological form, including art and literature, is to be dialectical and revolutionary, to accomplish the dialectical and revolutionary development of reality'.[66]

These last comments from Koch are based on his readings of two collections of shorter articles and essays by Mehring: his 'Ästhetische Streifzüge' (Aesthetic Excursions) of 1898–99, and his 'Literarhistorische Streifzüge' (Literary Historical Excursions) of 1899–1900. Not having to engage with the wider canon of *Die Lessing-Legende* or even less so with his Schiller biography, Mehring's concern with form, content, and language, with social class and contradiction within the bourgeois order, is more immediately perceptible. It is possible to speculate that the renown of the two major studies led commentators (including Wittfogel and Lukács) to neglect the range of his work, and to discover, as Thalheimer and Koch claim, the significant presence of dialectical thinking. This should be borne in mind when considering Mehring's contribution to a materialist aesthetic.

---

65   Mehring 1931, p. 7. 'vielmehr ist es bei Mehring seine gesamte theoretische und praktische Arbeit, in der sich der materialistische Dialektiker offenbart und an der man materialistische Dialektik lernen kann'.

66   Koch 1959, pp. 275–6. '... dass er progressive, revolutionäre ideologische Positionen als ein bestimmendes Moment bei der Ausbildung und Förderung potentzieller künstlerischer Veranlagung ansah und in der Verkörperung solcher progressiver ideologischer Positionen in literarischen Werk das gewichtigste Unterpfand ästhetischen Wertes ästhetischer Wirksamkeit erblickte ... das es erste Gebot, für *jede* Form der Ideologie – auch für Kunst und Literatur, ist dialektisch und revolutionär zu sein ...'.

4   *Die Lessing-Legende*

> Mehring is thereby a self-conscious successor of Lessing and has achieved
> in the course of his activity something very significant in the destruction
> of glorifying and defaming legends.[67]
>
> LUKÁCS

4.1   *Introduction*

The text of *Die Lessing-Legende* was first published in the pages of the SDP
journal *Die Neue Zeit* across 21 issues during the years 1891–92. In his brief preface to the ensuing book, published in 1893, with its subtitle 'Eine Rettung' ('A
Recovery'), containing the Appendix 'Über den historischen Materialismus',
Mehring succinctly sets out the two crucial advantages afforded by the latter
mode. The additional material enabled a more ample and detailed account
of the 'Frederikan state' (Frederick the Great) to be produced: 'that the more
clearly this state emerged as the historical product of class conflict between
East-Elben princes and the major estate holders [Junkers], the sharper our
classical literature emerged as the emancipatory struggle of the German bourgeoisie'.[68] The Appendix arose out of responses and questions from the readership of *Die Neue Zeit* but it also allowed him, as he wrote, 'to acknowledge his
indebtedness to the writings of Marx and Engels more clearly than had been
possible in the text of his study'.[69] When the second edition was published in
1906, the initial subtitle 'Eine Rettung' was dropped in favour of a more forthright declaration, 'Zur Geschichte und Kritik des preussischen Despotismus
und der klassischen Literatur', clearly indicating the direction of his objective.[70]

The two subtitles establish the dynamic of his study: there are two legends
here, that of the 'Frederikan state' and that of Lessing's relationship to it,

---

67   Lukács 1954, p. 387. 'Mehring ist dabei ein bewusster Nachfolger Lessings und hat während
      seiner Tätigkeit in der Zerstörung von verherrlichenden und verleumenden Legenden
      sehr Bedeutendes geleistet'.

68   Mehring 1975, p. 3. '... die ausführlichere Schilderung des friderizianischen Staats dienen.
      Denn je klarer sich dieser Staat als das geschichtliche Erzeugnis eines Klassenkampfes
      zwischen estelbischen Fürsten- und Junkertum herausstellt, um so schärfer tritt unsere
      klassische Literatur als der Emanzipationskampf des deutschen Bürgertums hervor'.

69   Mehring 1975, p. 4. '... auf die rückhaltlose Anwendung der materialistischen Forschung-
      methode, die Marx und Engels in so einleuchtender, so klarer, so unwiderleglicher und
      deshalb so epochenmachender Weise entwickelt haben'.

70   Koch 1959, p. 399. The Appendix was also dropped and Mehring in his Preface to the
      second edition, republished in the 1975 edition being used here, draws the reader's atten-
      tion to work he has published since, including his editing of the literary heritage of Marx,
      Engels, and Lassalle in 1902.

both fashioned by bourgeois historians, amongst whom are the literary historians.[71] Mehring's objective is to deconstruct both legends, effecting the recovery (die Rettung) of Lessing, 'who belongs not to the contemporary bourgeoisie but to the class who possess his revolutionary commitment, the proletariat'.[72] Mehring's objective here – to make available to the proletariat the literary heritage of the emerging bourgeoisie of the late eighteenth century, including Lessing, Schiller, and Goethe – clearly parallels Engels's claim that the proletariat were the true inheritors of classical German philosophy, made accessible to them by the writing of Marx and his own. In my initial treatment of Mehring's texts, I will be operating within the positive assessments of his contribution to the cultural horizons of the working-class movement, as set out in the opening 'A Portrait' section, including the voices of Engels, Luxemburg, Zetkin, and Lenin, where the emphasis was on his role as historical materialist, that is, as his work was initially received and understood.

4.2 Contemporary Reception

Engels may be considered as Mehring's 'first reader'. He praises the text itself and its Appendix on historical materialism in letters to Bebel, Kautsky, and Mehring himself. To Bebel, Engels writes from London in March 1892:

> I have also just read Mehring's *Lessing-Legende* in the *Neue Zeit* and enjoyed it very much. The work is excellent. I would change and nuance much in a different way but in general he has hit the nail on the head. It is a joy when one sees how the materialist concept of history, after twenty years of being held back by the extravagant endeavours of young party members is finally beginning, being deployed as it should properly be: a guide to the study of history.[73]

---

71   Mehring comments on claims in bourgeois criticism, 'we shouldn't forget that we are less concerned with Lessing than with the Lessing legends ...'. 'Doch wir dürfen nicht vergessen, dass wir es weniger mit Lessing als mit der Lessing-Legende zu tun haben ...'. Koch 1975, p. 269.

72   Koch 1975, p. 364. '... Arbeit gehört nicht der Bourgeoisie, sondern dem Proletariat'. The title of the last chapter is 'Lessing and the Proletariat'.

73   Koch 1959, pp. 322–3, 322. 'Die Arbeit ist wirklich ausgezeichnet ... im ganzen und grossen hat er den Nagel mitten auf den Kopf getroffen. Es ist doch eine Freude, wenn man sieht, wie die materialistische Geschichtsauffassung, nachdem sie – in der Regel – seit 20 Jahren in den Arbeiten der jungen Parteileute als grossmäulige Phrase hat heranhalten müssen, endlich anfängt, als das benutz zu werden, was sie eigentlich war: ein Leitfaden beim Studium der Geschichte'.

Mehring had surpassed the contributions of Kautsky and Bernstein in his concentration on Prussia and the decisive strength of his writing.[74] Engels judges the text 'as the most thoroughgoing siege of the citadel of the Prussian legend: one says Lessing but one means Old Fritz. Such destruction is absolutely necessary before Prussia can be absorbed into Germany'.[75]

In a brief letter to Mehring in April 1893, Engels responds positively to his work on combing through the confusions of Prussian history and of 'having established the correct interrelations', culminating in a work 'which is by far the best on this period of German history'.[76] Engels responds at greater length to its Appendix on historical materialism in July 1893. 'I begin with the end', he writes, 'with the Appendix on historical materialism, in which you have excellently summarised the principal issues and convincingly so for the impartial reader', and reiterates his comment on 'correct interrelations'.[77] Mehring's credentials as an historical materialist receive validation in Engels's letters. But in the paragraph following on from this later validation, Engels introduces the problematic issue of the interrelationship of content and form and places it in a context of neglect, of which both Marx and he are also guilty, of 'consistently not foregrounding it enough', that is to say, 'we have all laid in the first instance, and *were bound to lay*, the main emphasis on the derivation of political, juridical and other ideological notions, and of actions arising from these notions, from basic economic facts. In doing so we neglected the formal side – the ways and means by which these notions come about – for the sake of the content'.[78] After a number of paragraphs on the historical effectivity of the ideological, in which Engels criticises their opponents of 'the undialectical conception of cause and effect as rigidly opposite poles, the total disregarding of interaction', he approves of Mehring's assertion against his opponents that because materi-

---

74   His contemporaries acknowledged the quality and effectiveness of his language, as did his post-war East German commentators on his exceptional style: these qualities were not lost on his opponents – the major social theorist, Werner Sombart, criticised the historical-materialist analysis in *Die Lessing-Legende* but noted 'incidentally the stimulating German' ('beiläufig reizendes Deutsch').

75   Koch 1959, p. 323. 'Es ist die beste regelrechte Belagerung der Zitadelle der preussischen Legende, die ich kenne; den Lessing sagt man, den alten Fritz meint man. Und die Zerstörung der preussischen Legende ist absolut nötig, ehe Preussen in Deutschland verschwinden kann'.

76   Koch 1959, p. 326. '... dass Sie sich durch diesen preussischen Geschichtswust durch geackert und die richtigen Zusammenhänge nachgewiesen haben ... dass Ihre Arbeit weitem das Beste ist, was über diese Periode der deutschen Geschichte existiert'.

77   There is an English translation of this letter in Mehring's *On Historical Materialism* (Mehring 1975, pp. 57–60, 57).

78   Ibid.

alism denies 'an independent historical development to the various ideological spheres which play a part in history, we also deny them any *effect upon history*'. Having been guilty of the neglect of form himself he does not wish to reproach Mehring, rather to draw his attention to it for future consideration.[79] Mehring is confirmed as an historical materialist but a question has been raised about the dialectical dimension of his thinking, if by indirection.

Engels's judgement that 'one says Lessing but one means old Fritz' cannot be left there: Mehring has both in his sights. His objective is to dismantle the bourgeois-sustained myth of 'old Fritz' and that of a Lessing incorporated into that overall myth, and to establish the Lessing who was in opposition to princely Absolutism and the Enlightenment practised in Berlin, the cultural producer of texts which generated representations of his struggle to establish a stage for a potential bourgeois culture. The issue of form and content arises in what seem to be two traditionally distinct registers, that of materialism and its conceptualisations and, more narrowly, that of culture, which since Kant had privileged the realisation of form over content. It would become the task of the dialectical materialist to dissolve the seemingly distinct registers and to establish the mediations through which intelligible interrelationships could be founded. For a number of reasons, including political activism, Mehring was not that fully instantiated dialectician, as set out in the previous section, nor was this deficiency noted by those who realised the considerable contribution to the cultural life of the working class he had achieved.

In his 1906 introduction to the *Lessing-Legende*, Mehring sketches in the context for his own interventionist text. After the economic crisis of the 1870s there had been a modest upswing in bourgeois confidence, also reflected in the field of culture. Naturalist dramatists, experimentally inventive, were more inclined towards the mystical and symbolic and distanced themselves from the proletarian struggle for freedom. Similarly with bourgeois critics and aestheticians, who had achieved modest work in the aesthetic-philological area: 'But their understanding disappears [...] where the literary comes into contact with the economic and political, with the overall historical development'.[80] He responds

---

79   Ibid. Koch suggests *contra* Lukács that Engels's reference was to the Appendix rather than the text itself. Engels n.d. [1888], p. 29, provides a foundational moment for this interrelationship in 1888, shortly before the exchange of letters with Mehring. He is writing on Hegel and Feuerbach's 'disposal' of his work: 'It had to be "sublated" in its own sense, that is, in the sense that while its form had to be annihilated through criticism, the new content which had been won through it had to be saved'. The letter is quoted by Mehring in his Appendix and as the latter is available in English it is the source being used here.

80   Mehring 1975, p. 8. 'Aber ihr Verständnis schwindet ... wo sich die literarische mit der ökonomischen und politischen, mit der allgemeinen historischen Entwicklung berührt'.

to some critics of his work: to Famulus Sauer, who accused him of neglecting 'the impelling power of religious ideas', although Mehring devotes much space to Lessing's detailed critique of Lutheranism and the shaping of his ideas. An Austrian professor accused him of fashioning Lessing as 'a social-democratic revolutionary and materialist'. Surprisingly, his text received a guarded commendation in the prestigious *Historische Zeitschrift* which, under its editor Sybel, promoted strongly the 'friderizianische Legende'. Dismissive of 'sozialdemokratische Wissenschaft' Sybel nevertheless advises that 'it would be wrong to simply ignore such books, and that from an unbiased assessment of a so fundamentally different perception of the state and the forces of historical life to draw no lesser benefit than in its way the National Economy has done'.[81] Given that Mehring was most clearly committed to deconstructing the 'enemy camp', this reinforces Engels's assessment above. Mehring claims that since 1892, the year of the serialised publication of the *Lessing-Legende*, the dissolution of the 'Frederikan Legende' has satisfactorily progressed and the 'patriotic rubbish' of Sybel, Treitschke, and related historians has been fully dropped. Confirming, by implication, Engels's reservation on the form/content interrelationship in the 1893 letter cited above, Mehring declares that his Appendix 'On Historical Materialism' will not be reprinted, as his understanding has deepened as a result of editing the Marx-Engels-Lassalle literary archive, published in four volumes in 1902.

A more thoroughgoing engagement with textual matters arose in the exchange between Paul Ernst and Mehring in the pages of *Die Neue Zeit*. Ernst's 'Mehrings "Lessing-Legende" und die materialistische Geschichtsauffassung' was published in two issues of the journal in 1892–93, with Mehring's response, upon which the exchange is considered here, appearing in 1893–94.[82] Ernst asserts, Mehring writes, 'that I infer directly from the economic whilst at the same time avoiding its translation into the psychological, that accordingly I am compelled to a rationalist construction and to arrive at propositions that do not accord with the real, and are therefore of hardly less worth – Paul Ernst really means: hardly more worth than – the elaboration of a wholly ideolo-

---

81   Mehring 1975, pp. 10, 11. '... dass es falsch wäre, dergleichen Bücher einfach zu ignorieren, und dass die historische Wissenschaft aus der unbefangenen Würdigung einer so grundsätzlich verschiedenen Anschauung vom Staate und von den Mächten des geschichtlichen Lebens keine geringeren Vorteil ziehen wird, als es in ihrer Weise die Nationalökonomie getan hat'.

82   Ernst was a writer also involved with the theatre club Die Volksbühne. He joined the SPD at the end of the 1880s, broke away with others on the issue of cultural politics at the 1893 Conference.

gical historian'.[83] Ernst wants to know how, in addition to contemporary economic conditions, individual endowment, social milieu and social position, spiritual influences and other matters impacted on Lessing. As Mehring has dealt with such issues in detail, he wonders whether Ernst has really read the book. The range of material is beyond the scope of the present exercise to rehearse, so the discussion will be curtailed. Mehring chooses a number of social types and literary related tropes deployed by Ernst to produce his own critique. Ernst proposes the role of the pastor's son, which Lessing was, as a constant factor in German culture. But Mehring counters with the artisanal background of Winckelmann, Herder, Kant, Fichte, Goethe, and Schiller. Lessing the 'Bohemian' is dispatched by reference to Mehring's detailed textual account of the writer's early years and the interests he pursued at university, in the theatre and as a correspondent for a Berlin newspaper. He questions the usefulness of Ernst's tropes of literary fashion and tradition through his own wide-ranging knowledge of the contemporary theatre of Lessing's time, down to the translations of English work available at book fairs – Lessing's first play 'Miss Sara Sampson' was based on the example of Samuel Richardson's *Clarissa*. Ernst reads Lessing through the eyes of the nineteenth-century bourgeois, not through the experience of the eighteenth-century burgher, Mehring asserts – the opening chapter of the book is, as set out above, a critique of the nineteenth-century bourgeois reception of Lessing. Against the charge of an over-rationalistic construction at the expense of the psychological, Mehring counters by stating that rather than over-emphasising the economic, he has probably under-emphasised it, that 'a scientific history of our classical literature would not be possible if the eighteenth century was not freed from the ideological confusion of its myths and fairy tales, and set on its economic base'.[84] Lagging behind the social and economic development of the English and French bourgeoisie, some advances were nevertheless made in Germany which allowed them, despite all the economic and political backwardness, 'to achieve, at least culturally, parity with their western contemporaries'. This cultural achievement is certainly 'the most striking demonstration of the struggle

---

83   Mehring 1975, pp. 369–85, 369–70. '… dass ich aus der ökonomischen Bewegung direkt, mit Umgehung ihrer Übersetzung in Psychologie schlösse, dass ich dadurch zu rationalistischer Konstruktion gezwungen würde und zu Behauptungen gelangte, die der Wirklichkeit nicht entsprächen und daher kaum einiger wert seien wie – Paul Ernst meint wohl kann mehr wert als – die Elaborate eines ganz ideologischen Historikers'.

84   Mehring 1975, p. 383. '… eine wissenschaftliche Geschichte unserer klassischen Literatur werde erst möglich sein, wenn das achtzehnte Jahrhundert aus dem ideologischen Fabel- und Märchenwust gelöst und auf seine ökonomischen Füsse gestellt sein werde'.

for freedom of the German bourgeoisie'.[85] Who could deny, he concludes, that historical materialism continues to examine not only its own premises, but also its findings relative to its context.

Mehring's next critical and very revealing defence of his work was directed against Jean Jaurès, founder-leader of the French socialist party and author of the comprehensive, three-volume history of the French Revolution, in one of whose chapters Mehring's methodology in the *Lessing-Legende* received severe criticism. Jaurès rejected the historical materialism of Marx and therefore Mehring's account of the eighteenth-century German bourgeoisie, together with his deconstruction of the myth of Frederick the Great. As this is an absorbing but wide-ranging response by Mehring, attention will be focused on the more narrowly cultural dimension relating to his construction of the text of the *Lessing-Legende*. It appeared under the title 'Pour le roi de Prusse', echoing Marx's title, and was published in *Die Neue Zeit* in January 1903. Amongst Mehring's criticisms were Jaurès's failure to engage with the work of any German economist of standing and his dependence on quotations 'taken from official historical writing which were used to construct a house of cards'. One of these was a much used quotation from the young Goethe on the 'renowned situation' ('die berühmte Stelle'), the 'Golden Age' which existed in the time of Frederick the Great. Here Goethe, in Mehring's paraphrasing, celebrates the 'Borussian Despot' (Frederick the Great) as 'without doubt the animating genius of our classical poetry and sees in Lessing the principal witness for this perception'.[86] 'Later', Mehring writes, 'Goethe deplored Lessing's treatment', quoting him: 'that this extraordinary man should have had to live in such wretched times that provided him with no better material on which to work for his plays, that in his "Minna von Barnhelm" in the absence of anything better, he had to interest himself in the affairs of Saxony and Prussia'.[87] Mehring

---

85   Mehring 1975, p. 384. 'Fortschritte, die ihr erlaubten, bei aller ökonomischen Rückständigkeit wenigstens geistig auf gleicher Höhe mit den westlichen Kulturvölkern zu bleiben. ... Der schlagendeste Beweis des bürgerlichen Emanzipationskampfes wird freilich immer unsere klassische Literatur bleiben ...'. Lukács 1971, p. 17, concurs with Mehring's assessment of the high achievement of German bourgeois literary culture.

86   Mehring 1975, p. 393. '... worin Goethe den borussischen Despoten allerdings als den belebenden Genius unserer klassischen Poesie feiert und in Lessing einen Hauptzeugen für diese Ansicht sieht'.

87   Mehring 1975, pp. 412, 3. '... in dem er an Lessing beklagte, "das dieser ausserordentliche Mensch in einer so erbärmlichen Zeit leben musste, die ihn keine besseren Stoffe gab, als er in seinen Stücken verarbeiten musste, dass er in seiner 'Minna von Barnhelm' an den Händeln der Sachsen und Preussen teilnehmen musste, weil er nichts Besseres fand"'. These affairs generally were the military and financial demands of Prussia on Saxony, as detailed by Mehring.

explains how he proceeded with this quotation, much used by later nineteenth-century critics to support the claim for the culturally progressive role of the Hohenzollerns. It is, in essence, a brief discourse on method. 'I initially explore', he writes, 'this quotation from its subjective side, that is, how its originator Goethe had come, from the social milieu in which he lived, to such a perception, and then from its objective side, that is, whether the Frederikan system, that I thoroughly depicted relative to its diplomacy, pursuit of war, administration, justice, church and educational politics, could be a force for promoting culture or hindering it'.[88] His conclusion is in the negative. Jaurès, Mehring notes, was quite satisfied to see the quotation of the 18-year-old Goethe but to ignore the older Goethe's re-assessment, and criticise Mehring's historical materialism on the basis of his own often decontextualised use of quotations.

By drawing on the above sources, a number of general issues on Mehring's *Lessing-Legende* have been brought to attention. The exchange of letters with Engels has established his standing as an historical materialist, but although he has pursued particulars in their finest detail, the interrelationship of form and content may be a future concern. Mehring rejects Ernst's accusation that he is reductivist, that he ignores the subjective moment, affirms his understanding that ideology is not an autonomous sphere but has historical effectivity, and charges Ernst with thinking metaphysically and not dialectically. In his response to Jaurès, on the question of Goethe's famous quotation 'die berühmte Stelle', which seems to underpin the notion of a Frederikan 'Golden Age', we have a succinct statement of his working method, working initially from the 'subjective side', Goethe in his social milieu, before moving on to the 'objective side', the Frederikan System. When Mehring wrote the *Lessing-Legende* he had not had access to the Marx-Engels-Lassalle literary archive, which he would edit in 1902. As the editor of an abridged English translation of the text wrote: 'The most important problem which Mehring had to solve as the originator of historical-materialist criticism was the problem of developing a Marxist aesthetics'.[89] Later in the Introduction, he characterises it as

---

88   Mehring 1975 p. 393. 'Ich untersuche dies Zitat zunächst nach seiner subjektiven Seite, nämlich wie sein Urheber Goethe aus dem sozialen Milieu heraus, worin er lebte, zu dieser Ansicht gekommen sei, und dann nach seiner objektiven Seite, nämlich ob das frideriz-ianische System, das ich eingehend nach seiner Diplomatie, Kriegführung, Verwaltung, Rechtsprechung, Kirchen- und Schulpolitik usw. schilderte, eine kulturfördernde oder kulturhemmende Macht gewesen sei'.

89   An abridged version of the text was published by A.S. Grogan in the USA in 1938. Extracts of this are available at http://www.marxists.org, from which the above quotation is taken (p. 5).

'a pioneer achievement in dialectical-materialist literary criticism'.[90] It is now time to consider what Frederikan myths Mehring was deconstructing and what accounts he gave of specific works, particularly Lessing's dramatic works. As Mehring's achievement in the fields of political, economic, and military history had been recognised by Engels and, as noted above, by Sybel, editor of the prestigious bourgeois academic journal *Historische Zeitschrift*, no further comment is required on those.[91]

In his fifth chapter, 'König Friedrich und Lessing', Mehring quotes four statements by Frederick on his intentions for his rule: 'the Prince as first servant of the State', his role as 'King of the poor', 'no restriction on press freedom', and finally, 'freedom of worship'. Mehring examines these claims, the last two of which were decidedly social and would impact seriously on cultural production – Lessing's work was conditioned in various ways by them, for example, theology and the politics of religion which were to inform some of his work; he also inveighed against the hypocrisy of press freedom, designed to allow those he characterised as the 'shallow' Enlighteners around the court to publish what they liked about religion but nothing else.[92] Mehring establishes that these four seemingly modest and liberal proposals are essentially cynical gambits in state aggrandisement. He summarises Frederick's intentions from a text he wrote as crown Prince, his 'Antimachiavell'; here, whilst modestly conceding that 'the Prince is no more than his least subaltern', he nevertheless arrogates to himself the role of 'first judge, first finance minister and first minister for society', roles through which he exercised his Despotic Absolutism. He became, as Mehring points up ironically, 'King of the poor' through the impoverishment resulting from the levies and taxes he exacted on individuals and communities in pursuit of his war aims, particularly the Seven Years' War. Mehring undermines the 'beautiful legend of Frederikan "Socialism"' ('die schöne Legende des friderizianischen "Sozialismus"') and shows that his 'social reform' led in fact to 'the proletarianisation of the peasantry' ('auf die Proletarisierung der

---

90   Grogan, http://www.marxists.org (p. 10). He had earlier noted Lukács's criticism of Mehring in his 1934 *Partisan Review* essay.

91   Although not being dealt with here, Mehring's comprehensive history of the SPD *Geschichte der Deutschen Sozialdemokratie* addresses not only the history of the working-class movement but cultural politics as well.

92   Mehring 1975, p. 297. Here Lessing is writing to one of his Berlin acquaintances: the 'shallow' Enlightener, Nicolai: 'but let someone in Berlin come forward who wishes to speak up for the rights of the repressed, where it so often now happens in France and Denmark, against the extortion and despotism and you will soon realise which country today is the most enslaved in Europe'.

bäuerlichen Bevölkerung hinaus').[93] His exactions on the city of Leipzig – a city with which Lessing had close ties, including that of attending its university – were particularly destructive from a cultural point of view. Leipzig, Mehring writes, was the primary centre for trade in Germany and had achieved an almost republican independence. Accordingly, it was here that its importance 'for the re-awakening of bourgeois self-consciousness comes to light'. Already the site of the book fair, it also became 'an intellectual and economic power'.[94] It was in Leipzig that 'as we may say today: the whole bourgeois world then achieved its highest development'.[95] Lessing and Klopstock built on the contributions of their predecessors. The *Lessing-Legende* finds its context in the complex post-Reformation settlements with regard to the Hohenzollern rule in Prussia and that of the Wettiners in Saxony.[96] Frederick's religious tolerance was strategic: he supported Catholicism because he needed access to southern German recruits, and the Jesuits because they were strict disciplinarians. Lessing took a principled stance against the repressive character of orthodox Lutheranism and in his 'Lemnius Letters' he shows how Luther had committed calumny against the minor poet Lemnius and driven him into exile.[97] He cam-

---

93   Not only Frederick's 'social reform' is in the frame here: Wilhelm II, now rid of Bismarck, introduced strengthened legislation for the protection of workers and called an international conference on the issue. Mehring was highly suspicious of the motives: 'bureaucrats and diplomats, major holders of capital and employers produce no social reform, even when blessed with the salving oil of the Prince-Bishop's eloquence ...'. This quotation is from the lead article in the *Volks-Zeitung*, 4 March 1890, prior to the *Lessing-Legende*. Hölle 1956, p. 256. 'Bürokraten und Diplomaten, Grosskapitalisten und Unternehmer machen keine Sozialreform, auch wenn ein Fürstbischof das salbungsvolle Öl seiner Beredsamkeit dazugibt ...'.

94   Mehring 1975, p. 216. 'so tritt die Bedeutung Leipzigs für das Wiedererwachen des bürgerlichen Selbstbewusstsein erst in dass rechte Licht ... Schon als Sitz des deutschen Buchhandels war Leipzig zugleich eine intellektuelle und ökonomische Macht'.

95   Mehring 1975, p. 217. '... wie wir heute sagen möchten: die ganze bürgerliche Welt auf dem höchsten Punkt ihrer damaligen Entwicklung'.

96   Mehring 1975, p. 206. As with Frederick's 'social reforms' and the contemporary reflection in Wilhelm II's calling for an international conference on greater worker protection (see above), Mehring also makes a parallel reference here: that of the bourgeois moment in Leipzig with that of the contemporary bourgeoisie, including those appropriating Lessing for the Hohenzollern myth: 'and since then the German bourgeoisie have sought refuge under the cover of Prussian bayonets'.

97   Mehring 1975, p. 346. 'Nathan der Weise' ('Nathan the Wise'), his final play from 'my pulpit', the theatre, manifests his humanist stance with regard to religion. The Hegelian David Strauss, in his *Life of Jesus*, describes a short piece by Lessing, 'New Hypotheses on the Evangelists' as 'containing the fruitful seeds of all later research on the subject'. '... die fruchtbaren Keime aller späteren Forschungen über den Gegenstand enthalte' (Strauss 1835–36, p. 102).

paigned against orthodoxy 'only as a weapon of social repression, an obstacle to scientific progress, as an ideological accomplice of princely despotism. For Lessing Enlightenment was nothing other than the self-understanding of the bourgeoisie concerning their vital interests'.[98]

4.3   *The Bourgeois Myth*

Part One of the text, 'Kritische Geschichte der Lessing-Legende' ('Critical History of the Lessing-Legend'), introduces us to the bourgeois construction of the writer's contribution to German culture – the first chapter is titled 'Lessing und die Bourgeoisie'. 'Among the great thinkers and writers of the German bourgeoisie', Mehring writes in his opening sentence, 'none had in the course of life more difficult fortune nor after death, to all appearances, a more fortunate fate than Lessing'.[99] Mehring's ironic 'to all appearances' announces his intention to rescue Lessing (the subtitle of the first edition was 'Eine Rettung', a rescue) from the 'Golden Age' myth of the Hohenzollern King of Prussia, Frederick the Great, propagated within the Hohenzollern Empire established in 1871. Lessing's constant qualities, 'hatred of the exploiters, love for the exploited, indomitable rejection of the great, his readiness to fight injustice', ensure that his character 'stands in sharpest contrast to that of today's bourgeoisie'.[100] Mehring ascribes an emerging 'Lessing-Kultus' – he was celebrated at the Jubilee Exhibition of 1886 and in 1890 a Lessing monument was unveiled in Berlin, to an historical need of the bourgeoisie. After Prussia's military success in 1866 'it was of concern to the bourgeoisie', he writes, 'that they reconcile their actuality with their idealised past, to construct from the period of our classical formation an Age of Frederick the Great'. As two of the most outstanding cultural Prussians of Frederick's age, Herder and Winckelmann, had fled Prussia because of its backwardness, the role fell to the Saxon Lessing, who had spent some time as a literary critic in Berlin. Mehring sketches briefly a history of Lessing's representations: pre-1848 revolution 'a revolutionary genius' (Gervinus in the 1830s),

---

98   Mehring 1975 p. 325. '... aber er bekämpfte sie als Organ der sozialen Unterdrückung, als Kappzaum der wissenschaftlichen Forschung, als ideologische Begleiterscheinung des fürstlichen Despotismus. Für Lessing war die Aufklärung nichts als die Selbstverständigung der bürgerlichen Klassen über ihre Lebensinteressen'.

99   Mehring 1975, p. 29. 'Unter den grossen Denkern und Dichtern des deutschen Bürgertums hat keiner im Leben tatsächlich ein schwereres, nach seinem Tode anscheinend ein glücklicheres Los gezogen als Lessing'.

100   Mehring 1975, pp. 30, 31. '... der Hass gegen alle Unterdrücker und die Liebe zu allen Unterdrückten, die unüberwindliche Abneigung gegen die Grossen der Welt, die stete Kampfbereitschaft gegen das Unrecht ... dass Lessings Charakter im schroffsten Gegensatze steht zu dem Charakter der deutschen Bourgeoisie von heute'.

not 'a revolutionary' but 'a religious reformer' according to the great conservative historian Treitschke in the 1860s, not 'a reformer' but 'a Liberal', is the judgement of Erich Schmidt, the leading bourgeois literary historian, in the 1890s. Speculating on the near future Mehring would not be surprised to see him characterised 'not as a "reformer" but rather as a free-marketer (ein Nichts-als-Freihändler)', a projection based on an 1870s biography of Lessing by Stahr, in which Lessing's political position is described as an 'irrefutable rejection of Communism'. From the foregoing one can see the difficult task Mehring had undertaken to rescue a Lessing for the proletariat, the title of the last chapter of his book. Mehring's text is concerned with reading the bourgeois myth in the context of the Frederikan myth.

Mehring recognises that the intertwining myths are not without origin, as in the young Goethe's cultural 'Golden Age' ('die berühmte Stelle') of Frederick and Lassalle's essays on Lessing, but he distinguishes between mid- and late nineteenth-century authors on Lessing, being more tolerant of the former.[101] He grants that Danzel's biography of Lessing understands the political dimension of Frederick's Seven Years' War, 'calling it by its correct designation as a dynastic brawl over a province', but criticises his historical method because of his Hegelianism, from which 'he sought on metaphysical-speculative grounds to understand Lessing's life and work as a moment in the spiritual history of Germany'.[102] The negative presence of Hegelianism, in his writing on the State, is found in Stahr's biography and Lassalle's essays, which were a response to Stahr's biography. Stahr too was originally a Young Hegelian, an enthusiastic contributor to the Halle Almanac and was, as with Ruge, hostile to socialism; this hatred he also ascribed absurdly to Lessing's open spirit.[103] Mehring quotes from Marx's critique of Hegel's *Philosophy of Right* in the 1848 *Deutsch-Französischen Jahrbücher*, that not the State but civil society ('bürgerliche Gesellschaft') held the key to an understanding of historical development. 'Following the works of Marx and Engels', Mehring writes of the work of Stahr and Lassalle, 'it is very easy to uncover the basic flaw in that conception of

---

101   Mehring 1975, pp. 33–4. '... dass kein Geringerer als Goethe ihren ersten Keim gepflanzt hat, dass revolutionäre Köpfe wie Lassalle ihrem Einfluss bis zu einem gewissen Grade unterlegen sind'.

102   Mehring 1975, p. 52. '... und dieser 'historischen' Methode Danzels vorzuziehen, der ursprünglich Hegelianer war und auf metaphysisch-spekulativem Wege dass Leben und Wirken Lessings als einen Teil der deutschen Geistesgeschichte zu verstehen suchte'.

103   Mehring 1975, p. 65. '... und gleich Ruge den Sozialismus hasste und diesen abgeschmackten Hass auch in Lessings freie Seele hineindichtete ...'.

history. It stems from the idealisation of the State indebted to Hegel's speculation, the State as the regulative archetype of human development'.[104] From this conception of history Stahr can conceive of King Frederick as standing forth as a 'fellow-struggler and a fellow-worker among his eminent contemporaries'; Lassalle sees the King and Lessing as the German 'revolutionaries' of the eighteenth century.[105] Mehring was more tolerant of Lassalle's position; he had a deeper historical understanding but 'his conception sprang from a Hegelian source ... This ideological understanding has been superseded by the writing of Marx. Today it is so easy to clear up individual errors in Lassalle, but thirty years ago it was difficult to equal his intellectual standing'.[106] As will become apparent from these later passages, Mehring's critique of Hegel's historical conception of the State is focused on the manner in which it has bolstered bourgeois ideological representations of the Prussian state and the incorporation of Lessing's life and work within those representations. He called on Marx above to support his stance here and Engels commended this text for undermining the foundations of the Prussian state.

As Mehring takes two positions on Hegel in his final chapter, the 'statist' Hegel can be seen in the first as an observation on an applied, functionalised Hegel, Hegel captured by the Prussian state ('gar preussische Staatsreligion'). The Ministry of Education warned candidates against 'the other shallow philosophical systems' ('von sonstigen "seichten Philosophemen"') promoting and, as Mehring ironically observes, using this principle to pursue dissidents and return them to the reasonable, the reality of the Prussian state, including its prisons and fortresses. Mehring may not use the term 'dialectical' in the following passage but he recognises its functioning:

> But what Hegel said of the French Revolution also applies to his philosophy: it stood things on their head. This state of affairs had to be inverted

---

104 Mehring 1975, p. 60. 'Nach den Arbeiten von Marx und Engels ist es leicht, den Grundfehler in dieser Geschichtsauffassung zu entdecken. Er liegt in der idealistischen auf Hegel zurückführenden Auffassung des Staats als der massgebenden Urform der menschlichen Entwicklung'.

105 Mehring 1975, p. 61. '... Dass, wie Stahr sagt, der König Friedrich als "Mitstreiter und Mitarbeiter seines grossen Zeitgenossen" dastehe oder dass der König und Lessing wie Lassalle meint, die deutschen "Revolutionäre" des achtzehnten Jahrhunderts gewesen seien'.

106 Mehring 1975, p. 81. '... aus seiner ideologisch-hegelianischen Geschichtsauffassung entspringt ... durch die Arbeiten von Marx, lange überholt worden ... Es ist heute ebenso leicht einzelne Irrtümer Lassalles klarzustellen, wie es vor dreissig Jahren schwer war, auf der geistigen Höhe Lassalles zu stehen'.

in order to disclose the revolutionary rational core in its husk of the reactionary real. From the Prussian state philosophy revolutionary socialism was born.[107]

In a statement which is central to his undertaking, Mehring draws a parallel between Marx and Lessing: 'Marx concluded classical philosophy with the optimistic struggle for the working class, as Lessing had initiated it after the hopeless struggle for the bourgeois class'.[108] Mehring's reference here to Lessing concerns the latter's anti-theological writings, where it was 'in the interests of the bourgeoisie to endeavour to free secular science from the chains of theology'.[109] 'Notwithstanding', Lessing writes, 'I do not have absolute confidence that sometime a flatterer is sure to come, one who will designate this current era of German literature, that of Frederick the Great, as admirable'.[110] For Mehring, Scherer and Schmidt were the anticipated flatterers. Scherer's type of literary history 'ignores the economic and political history of the period and conveniently declines into aesthetic-philological hot air. ... Each apparent better insight is nothing other than a courtly idiom to smuggle in King Frederick as the great spiritual pioneer of our classical literature'.[111] Both Scherer and Schmidt depict Lessing as an ambitious bourgeois of contemporary stripe, seeking to bring himself to the attention of Frederick, 'guest of Frederick', where he met Voltaire. There is no record to substantiate the claims: Lessing admired

---

107   Mehring 1975, pp. 361–2. 'Aber was Hegel von der Französischen Revolution sagte, dass galt auch von seiner Philosophie: Sie stellte die Dinge auf den Kopf. Sie musste umgestülpt werden, um ihren revolutionär – vernünftigen Kern in ihrer reaktionär – wirklichen Hülle zu offenbaren. Aus des preussichen Staatsphilosophie entpuppte sich der revolutionären Sozialismus'.
108   Ibid. 'Marx schloss die klassische Philosophie mit dem hoffnungsfrohen Kampfe für die arbeitende Klasse, wie Lessing sie eingeleitet hatte nach dem hoffnungslosen Kampfe für die bürgerliche Klasse'.
109   Mehring 1975, p. 207. 'Es war im Interesse der bürgerlichen Klassen, wenn Sie weltliche Wissenschaft aus den Fesseln der Theologie zu erlösen trachten'.
110   Mehring 1975, p. 186. 'Gleichwohl will ich nicht darauf schwören, dass nicht einmal ein Schmeichler kommen sollte, welcher die gegenwärtige Epoche der deutschen Literatur die Epoche Friedrichs des Grossen zu nennen für gut findet'.
111   Ibid. 'Wenn man Literatugeschichte eines Zeitalters erzählen will, ohne die ökonomische und politische Geschichte desselben Zeitalters zu kennen, so verfällt man günstigenfalls in eine ästhetisch-philologische Kannegieserei. ... Denn jener scheinbare Anflug von besserer Einsicht ist bei ihm nichts als eine höfische Redewendung, um den König Friedrich als die geistig bahnbrechende Grösse in unsere klassischen Literatur einzuschmuggeln'.

Voltaire's middle-class dramas but was highly critical of his court drama. Lessing's ambition was not that as implied by Scherer and Schmidt. Commenting on Frederick's custom of surrounding himself with 'a host of refined spirits' ('... eine Menge schöne Geister'), he wrote: 'I will never feel able to play such an abject role, even if royal decorations were in the offing. A king may rule over me forever, he may be more powerful but better he cannot seem to be. He cannot bestow so large a pension on me that I would consider it recompense for the commission of unworthy acts'.[112] The case of Frederick's sponsoring of German literature is dismissed by Mehring, initially in a quotation of an apocryphal statement claimed to be by Frederick to the French writer Mirabeau, to the effect that he left German writing alone so that it could better develop by itself, but further on the more solid evidence of Frederick's pamphlet on German literature fittingly written in French, 'De la literature allemande', published in the year of Lessing's death, is referenced. For Mehring this makes clear the 'insuperable gulf between German culture and Prussian despotism'; Frederick was not acquainted with the development of the German bourgeoisie. 'But it is also undeniable', Mehring writes, 'that in giving way to a fit of despotic megalomania, he intended to pour scorn on German literature'.[113] Mehring contrasts the hostility of earlier bourgeois writers – Herder, Klopstock, and Schiller – to the pamphlet with its reception by literary historians like Scherer and Schmidt, and concludes that its content exposes the 'humbug of the Lessing-Legende!'

5   The Plays: 'Minna von Barnhelm' and 'Emilia Galotti'

Lessing's major dramatic text, the play 'Minna von Barnhelm', will be briefly considered to examine how it represents the issues raised by Mehring in his questioning of the Frederikan 'Legend' constructed by nineteenth-century bourgeois literary historians on the basis of their highly ideologically inflected

---

112   Koch 1962, p. 430. 'Nimmermehr werde ich mich fähig fühlen, eine so niedrige Rolle zu spielen; und wenn auch Ordensbänder zu gewinnen stünden. Ein König mag immerhin über mich herrschen; er sei mächtiger, aber besser dünke er sich nicht. Er kann mir keine so starken Gnadengelder geben, dass ich sie für wert halten sollte, Niederträchtigkeiten drum zu begehen'.

113   Mehring 1975, p. 355. '... die unüberschreitbare Grenzscheide zwischen deutschen Geistesleben und preussischen Despotismus. ... Aber unbestreitbar ist auch, dass er einem Kitzel despotischen Grössenwahns nachgab, dass er der deutschen Literatur einem blutigen Schimpf zuzufügen beabsichtigte'. Although his minister Hertzberg pointed out the most serious errors, Frederick refused to alter 'these trifles'.

representations of the Prussian state.[114] An initial surprise for the spectator of 'Minna von Barnhelm', this fundamental bourgeois text, is that its hero, Tellheim, is an army officer in Frederick's army: 'What could be more German', Mehring rhetorically asks, 'than that the classic comedy of our bourgeois life should be about military life?'[115] Mehring addresses the apparent paradox by suggesting that during that era, including the Seven Years' War, the officer class was one of the limited spaces available for possible ethical behaviour: the miserable conditions prevailing in Germany 'compelled him to engage with army life when he wished to depict the serious conflicts of honourable characters, and he knew how to extract, notwithstanding this kind of life, the social side and to assume here also the struggle against social repression'.[116] He quotes Goethe to establish his perception, that 'this outstanding man had to live in such miserable times, which provided no better material, that his "Minna von Barnhelm", for lack of anything better, had to work on Saxon-Prussian affairs', and from Schiller's 'Wallenstein' to the effect that 'in time of war individuality and excellence could develop'. The play is based on Lessing's own experience of military life and on a real event. In Leipzig, Lessing came into contact with the poet Kleist, then a major in the Prussian army, and through him Lieutenant Tauentzien, whose secretary he became, a period Mehring described as probably the happiest of his life, even if it was spent in a military camp during the Seven Years' War and not in bourgeois surroundings. This experience would inform the qualities of Tellheim, the captain-hero of 'Minna'.[117] The event arose from Frederick's despotic treatment of his army, where he was continually engaged in his own war of attrition against factions, including the Junkers: 'The less the King was able to undermine the economic foundations of the

---

114 The author of the recent standard biography of Lessing, Hugh B. Nisbet, wrote in a review of nineteenth-century essays on 'Minna von Barnhelm': 'It is also significant that, like nearly all of the play's commentators before Franz Mehring's *Die Lessing-Legende* of 1893, the contributors to the present volume show little or no awareness of the play's politically subversive elements and veiled criticisms of the Prussian regime which Mehring and more recent scholars have since brought to light'. Nisbet 2012, pp. 189–91, p. 190.

115 Mehring 1975, p. 280. 'Denn was kann deutscher sein, als dass die klassische Komödie unseres bürgerlichen Lebens ein – Soldatenstück ist?'

116 Ibid. 'Zwang ihn die Erbärmlichkeit der deutschen Zustände, ins soldatische Leben zu greifen, wenn er ernste konflikte ehrenhafter Charaktere schildern wollte, so wusste er diesem Leben trotzdem die soziale Seite abzugewinnen und auch hier den Kampf gegen soziale Unterdrückung aufzunehmen'.

117 Mehring 1975, p. 265. Mehring makes a crucial historical point here, where he writes that 'militarism as a self-sufficient opponent of bourgeois culture had not yet developed, which held good as long as the army was the private property and war the private industry of the Princes'.

Prussian army, and the higher he had to elevate the noble officer-caste and the more carefully he had to indulge it, the more he tormented and harassed the individual officer'.[118] The real event probably involved a Major Dyherrn, who was tasked with 'extracting from the exhausted city of Leipzig every last farthing of the most monstrous levies'. He felt compelled to make serious objections, which were unavailing, awaiting the peace to place himself at the king's mercy.[119] Frederick's response, peace being declared, was to dismiss all the middle-class officers. He also reneged on his policy to repay war damages. It was in this context that Lessing wrote 'Minna'.

Tellheim contains 'a good deal of Lessing himself', but also an idealised 'Frederikan officer' based not only on Kleist and Dyherrn but on many others.[120] 'One has only to read the three dozen cabinet orders from Frederick to Dyherrn on the levies on Leipzig', Mehring writes, 'to understand the figure of Tellheim'.[121] Lessing, Mehring proposes, found more class and moral purpose in this officer class than amongst his contemporary bourgeoisie, a class which Lessing, according to Mehring, felt to possess 'a less materialist but more bourgeois spirit, which in the face of princely despotism held steadfastly to its sense of justice'.[122] It is continuous with this spirit that Tellheim 'thinks and acts' ('denkt und handelt'). For him 'the great are superfluous': 'service for the great is dangerous and does not repay the effort, constraint and humiliation which it costs'.[123] He does 'little by inclination for them, not much more from duty but all in terms of his own honour'.[124] Tellheim believes that every honour-

---

118   Mehring 1975, p. 280. 'Je weniger der König an den ökonomischen Grundlagen des preussischen Heeres rütteln konnte, je höher er die adlige Offizierskaste stellen und je sorgfältiger er sie schonen musste, um so mehr peinigte und quälte er die einzelnen Offiziere'.

119   Mehring 1975, pp. 281–2. 'er legte der schon bis auf den letzen Groschen ausgepumpten Stadt Leipzig so ungeheurliche Kontributionen auf, dass der mit ihrer Eintreibung beauftragte Major und Flügeladjutant v. Dyherrn ...'.

120   Mehring 1975, pp. 283. 'In Tellheim ist der friderizianishe Offizier, ist selbst ein Kleist sehr idealisiert; ... ein gutes Stück Lessing steckt mit darin'.

121   Mehring 1975, p. 282. 'Aber man braucht nur die drei Dutzend Kabinettsordres Friedrichs an Dyherrn wegen der Leipziger Kontribution zu lesen, um das Bild Tellheims vor sich zu sehen'.

122   Ibid. '... sondern jenen gar nicht militärischen, sondern sehr bürgerlichen Geist, der auch dem fürstlichen Despotismus in die Zähne hinein unbeugsam an seinem Rechtsbewusstsein festhält'. Mehring remarks that the balance in the 1890s has altered: militarism is now a powerful cult, the bourgeoisie relatively no more advanced.

123   Mehring 1975, p. 283 'Ihm sind "die Grossen sehr entbehrlich"; "die Dienste der Grossen sind gefährlich und lohnen der Mühe, des Zwanges, der Erniederung nicht, die sie kosten"'.

124   Ibid. '... er tut "für die Grossen aus Neigung wenig, aus Pflicht nicht viel mehr, sondern alles der eigenen Ehre wegen"'.

able man should spend some time in this profession 'to make himself familiar with danger, to learn courage and resolve'.[125] To become a soldier for the sake of being a soldier is just wandering about as 'a butcher's boy' ('Fleischerknecht').

Unlike Mehring, contemporary bourgeois critics had not, amongst other historical omissions, read the correspondence between Frederick and Dyherrn (three dozen cabinet orders) on levies on the city of Leipzig. They sought the origin of the play in literary sources, in Shakespeare, in Spanish cloak-and-dagger plays; 'even in Plautus'. Further, what Mehring designates the 'Byzantinismus' of contemporary bourgeois literary history falsely facilitated the reception of 'Minna' 'as a homage to the Prussian militarist state of King Frederick'.[126] 'The plot of "Minna" is nothing other', Mehring writes, 'than a biting satire on the regime of Frederick'.[127] Like Dyherrn, the play's Tellheim has been charged with enforcing the most severe levies on estates, but being unable to pay he advances his own money. Frederick has promised to 'rectify debts', a commitment Tellheim had expected to be discharged. Instead he was dismissed from the army and subjected to a harsh trial on grounds of bribery. Frederick's brother supported him, the money was refunded and Tellheim re-admitted to the army. Despite the reprieve this was a daringly negative representation of the Frederikan regime. Lessing's contemporaries understood the play better than his own contemporaries, Mehring informs us. Nicolai, Lessing's Berlin Enlightenment friend, complained as a Prussian subject about 'the many thrusts against the Prussian government', but when it was staged there 'it was performed ten times to great applause'.[128] Goethe wrote that 'Minna' was 'the most genuine product of that war' and 'the first theatre production significantly and specifically grappling with the content of contemporary life and for that reason has had incalculable consequence'.[129] The poet Anna Luisa Karschin,

---

125   Ibid. '… dass es für jeden tüchtigen Mann gut sei, sich in diesem Stande eine Zeitlang zu versuchen, um sich mit allem, was gefahr heist, vertraut zu machen und Kalte und Entschlossenheit zu lernen'.

126   Mehring 1975, p. 416. '… womit dem modischen Byzantinismus erleichet wird, Lessings Lustspiel als eine Huldigung an den preussischen Militärstaat oder den König Friedrich zurechtzufälschen'.

127   Ibid. 'Die Fabel der "Minna" ist nämlich nichts anderes als eine schneidende Satire auf das friderizianische Regiment'.

128   Mehring 1975, pp. 284–5. 'Nicolai beklagte als "preussischer Untertan" die "vielen Stiche gegen die preussische Regierung" … die "Minna" in Berlin auf die Bühne prachte, wurde sie zehnmal hintereinander unter lautem Jubel gespielt'.

129   Mehring 1975, p. 412. '"… Minna von Barnhelm" als die wahrste Ausgeburt jenes Krieges ehrenvoll erwähnen zu müssen, als die erste aus dem bedeutenden Leben gegriffene Theaterproduktion von spezifisch temporären Inhalt, die deswegen auch eine nie zu berechnende Wirkung gehabt habe'.

Lessing's contemporary, described by Mehring as possessing a sharp critical edge, wrote to fellow poet Gleim: 'Prior to Lessing no other German writer has succeeded in infusing both well-born and the people, the learned and the uninitiated with a kind of enthusiasm and so thoroughly pleased them'.[130]

If 'Minna von Barnhelm' is 'perhaps the finest German comedy', 'Emilia Galotti' may be considered 'the revolutionary bourgeoisie's most important tragedy' Lukács wrote in 1922.[131] Lessing based his play on an episode from Livy's *History of Rome*, on the abuse of power by the patrician Council of Ten against plebeians. A young woman of noble birth, Virginia, refused the demands of a member of the Council, placed her virtue above her life and sought solution in death by the hand of her own father. The episode led to an uprising in which the Council lost power. Mehring briefly summarises the narrative: the tearful request of the daughter to her father to take her life because she fears her own blood against the advances of the despot, who had ordered the assassination of her lover on the steps of the marriage altar. The father is executed for the murder of his daughter. The play was met with derision and censure: Goethe offered as plot solution that Emilia was secretly in love with the prince. Mehring rejects that: Emilia does not love the prince – it is the dramatist's intention that she should not ('... soll ihn nach des Dichters Absicht nicht lieben ...'), otherwise the father, Odoardo, would merely have wielded the knife to secure his daughter's 'anatomical purity' ('anatomische Unschuld') and deprive the tyrant of his prey.

The action undertaken was the only one possible against despotic power. The outcome is severely demanding on the spectator: 'the monstrous evokes neither fear nor pity' ('das ist jenes Grässliche, das weder Furcht noch Mitleid erregen ...').[132] Nor even if traced back in history, as Lessing had convincingly set out in the context of Aristotle, could it have a tragic effect.[133] Rather,

---

130   Mehring 1975, p. 416. 'Vor Lessing hat's noch keinen deutschen Dichter gelungen, dass er den Edlen und dem Volke, den Gelehrten und Laien zugleich eine Art von Begeisterung eingeflösst und so durchgängig gefallen hätte'. For Mehring, who had been involved in the workers' theatre club, the play, apart from being the first classical drama, also brought a modern theatre public into being.

131   Lukács 1971, p. 17. 'It was the first bourgeois tragedy of high literary quality produced by eighteenth-century literature, and not only German literature but that of Britain or France ...' (Lukács 1971, p. 16). In this essay, first published in *Die Rote Fahne*, Lukács supports Mehring's reading of the play against that of Goethe.

132   Koch 1975, p. 305.

133   The reference here is to Lessing's major writing on theatre, *Hamburgische Dramaturgie*. He had been invited to Hamburg to participate in the founding of a National Theatre as its dramaturg, an enterprise which failed.

Mehring claims, 'the young Lessing recognized above all the most shocking and violent connection between social oppression and the violation of young women in the eighteenth century' ('die empörendeste und erschütterndste Begleiterscheinung der sozialen Unterdrückung, die Vergewaltigung der jungfräulichen Ehre ...'), just as it had always been and is so today, as long as social oppression continues. Lessing confirmed his sharp social insight that the tragic moment is evidently more significant in its world-historical generality than is the individual case which through the accidental brings about political upheaval. Lessing wishes to write a 'middle-class Virginia' ('Eine bürgerliche Virginia ...'): the Livy episode is tragic enough and capable of shocking the soul 'even if no political revolution follows' ('... wenn auch gleich kein Umsturz des ganzen Staatsverfassung darauf folgt'). Anti-Dühring, who claimed that Lessing had reduced the affect, Mehring maintains that Lessing deepened the fate of Virginia. He cites an event which took place in Lessing's own Saxony shortly before he wrote the play: a noble family had arranged a marriage celebration since their daughter had been selected by the ruling despot as his mistress. In such circumstances, Mehring continues, 'a middle-class Virginia with a really tragic outcome was impossible' ('eine bürgerliche Virginia schreiben wollte, musste denn nun freilich wohl um einen tragisch versöhnenden Ausgang verlegen sein'): on German soil 'neither an Emilia or Odoardo was possible'. Lessing would not have been 'champion of the middle classes' ('... der Vorkämpfer der bürgelichen Klassen sein müsse') if he had been 'more scornful of than angered by such outrage' ('... um ihre Schmach nicht viel mehr zürnen als spotten zu sollen'). To secure the psychological suppositions of the play he transplanted the action from 'the boring wretched philistine world of his homeland' to Italy, the origin of the tale. Petty despotism ruled all over, maybe more 'refined' in Italy, there was no atonement for its grotesquely terrible misdeeds. The fate of an Emilia 'is grounded in the economic structure of the society in which Lessing's characters lived, boundaries beyond which the dramatist could not go' ('Über diese Schranke konnte der Dichter nicht hinaus').[134] Renowned contemporaries recognised the social content of the tragedy. Herder suggested that the play carry the motto 'Discite moniti' – 'be warned, take heed', addressed to despotism. Despite his difference with Goethe over the plot line, Mehring quotes him: 'he saw in it the "decisive step" to morally inspired opposition against tyrannical despotism ...' 'full of a deep view of a world that on the whole gave rise to a monstrous culture' ('... eine ungeheure Kultur').

---

134   Koch 1975. All quotations from pp. 304–6.

'In "Emilia Galotti"', Mehring wrote slightly later, 'middle-class conscious-ness undoubtedly reached its pinnacle ... In the fate of this play was reflec-ted the fate of the contemporary middle class'.[135] It found its last and most powerful echo 'in the young Schiller's revolutionary plays'. But the greater mass of the philistine middle class, amongst whom were the Berlin Enlighteners around Frederick's court, remained cold and silent. 'Emilia Galotti' became more uncomfortable for a middle class displaying weakness in its comprom-ises with absolutism. Mehring concludes: 'The middle class for whom "Emilia Galotti" was written had never understood the "monstrous culture" and allowed themselves to become "barbarian". But the play remains new for every strug-gling revolutionary class as though it had just come from the dramatist's stu-dy'.[136]

5.1   *Schiller for German Workers*

In her review of Mehring's study of Schiller, Rosa Luxemburg emphasised its currency: 'Mehring's study appears at exactly the right time as a most welcome gift for the German working class, providing an image of the great poet free from the distortions of biased bourgeois reception on the one hand and on the other from biased party reception'.[137] As with his mission of 'a recovery' (eine Rettung) with regard to Lessing, Mehring is on a similar but more complex mission here, as indicated by the Luxemburg quotation, not just from the bour-geoisie but also from the party, particularly in light of the hostility occasionally manifested by Marx and Engels towards Schiller's aesthetic-philosophic posi-tion. A particular instance of this is found in the exchange of letters between Marx and Engels with Lassalle in 1859 on their responses to the text of his play 'Franz von Sickingen', which he had sent them. Generally positive they both raised the same issue – more Shakespeare, less Schiller. Engels wrote:

---

135   Mehring 1929, p. 58. 'In "Emilia Galotti" gipfelte gewissermassen das bürgerliche Klassen-bewusstsein ... In dem Schicksal dieses Stücks spiegelt sich das Schicksal des damaligen Bürgertums'. This essay first appeared in 1894–95 in *Die Volksbühne*, the journal of the theatre, where Mehring notes 'Lessings dramatisches Meisterwerk' is being performed.

136   Mehring 1929, p. 59. 'Die "ungeheure Kultur" der "Emilia Galotti" haben die bürgerlichen Klassen, für die sie gedichtet war, nie verstanden und darüber mögen sie zu "Barbaren" geworden sein. Jeder revolutionär-aufstrebenden Klasse aber wird das Stück immer so "neu" erscheinen, als käme es frisch aus der Gedankenwerkstatt des Dichters'. Mehring was quoting Goethe on 'the monstrous culture' and 'barbarism'.

137   *Die Neue Zeit* 1904–05, pp. 163–5. Online at Friedrich Ebert Stiftung, Bonn. 'Die Studie Mehrings erscheint gerade zur rechten Zeit wie eine hochwillkommene Gabe an die deutsche Arbeiterschaft, um ihr ein von bürgerlicher-tendenziöser und anderseits auch von parteitendenziöser Verzerrung freies Bild des grossen Dichters zu liefern'.

'In accordance with my view of the drama, which consists in not allowing the ideal to oust the real, or Schiller to oust Shakespeare'. Marx recommended to '"Shakespearise" more, whereas your principal failing is, to my mind, Schillering'.[138] Both objected on the grounds that dialogic exchange between characters in their socio-historical situations was displaced in favour of the 'ventriloquised' exchange of ideas, as they perceived it in Schiller's later work.

Aware of this legacy and as a kind of preparatory text to the Schiller biography, Mehring wrote the essay 'Schiller und die grossen Sozialisten' (Schiller and the great socialists), also in 1905, addressing the status of Schiller on the left. The Schiller commemoration that year 'inevitably raises the question of the influence that Schiller had on Marx, Engels and Lassalle' ('auch die Frage nach dem Einfluss auf, den Schiller auf Marx, Engels und Lassalle gehabt hat'): with Marx and Engels there is only occasional mention but Lassalle speaks more often of him and with open sympathy. The 'story goes' that Marx and Engels did not choose to engage much because Schiller was philosophically idealist, a vague characterisation, the product of his bourgeois commentators ('... den nicht sowohl Schiller selbst, als Schillers bürgerliche Ausleger aufgebracht haben'). On the other hand, Marx and Engels had spoken with the highest admiration 'for Fichte and Hegel, the most notable of Idealists, whose students they acknowledged themselves to be' ('... Von Fichte und Hegel ... haben Marx und Engels mit grösster Hochachtung gesprochen und sich gern als ihre Schüler bekannt'). 'Under differing circumstances', Mehring states, 'Idealism can signify antithetical views' ('Idealismus und Idealismus können je nachdem ganz verschiedene und unter Umständen ganz entgegengesetzte Anschauungen bedeuten').[139] Schiller's aesthetic-philosophical idealism ('ästhetisch-philosophischer Idealismus') was captured by the bourgeoisie in a wholly misunderstood and distorted form in its flight from the German 'misery' ('... in ganz missverstandener und verzerrter Form, das Ideal des deutschen Philisters werden musste'), whilst Hegel's Idealism found in Marx and Engels its 'creative transformers' ('... bis sie in Marx und Engels die schöpferischen Umbildner'). Mehring sees in the capture of Schiller's Idealism by the bourgeoisie the origin of the hostility of Marx and Engels to his philosophical position and quotes them to this point: 'Marx once said that Schiller's flight into the ideal is only the exchange of the general misery into rapture, and Engels on another occasion that philistine disparagement of philosophical materialism

---

138   Online at http://www.marxists.org. Mehring edited *Aus dem literarischen Nachlass von Karl Marx, Friedrich Engels und Ferdinand Lassalle* in 1902.

139   *Die Neue Zeit* 1904/05, pp. 153–6, 153. Online at Friedrich Ebert Stiftung, Bonn.

by the petit-bourgeoisie fed on crumbs from Schiller's poetry'.[140] It is at this point in the 1840s and 1850s that the issue of Idealism becomes more acute: 'in their most powerful years of development Marx and Engels had to fight the bogey the petit-bourgeoisie had constructed from Schiller's Idealism, and their anger was so much the greater in light of that class-fraction's patching together of a hotch-potch of the misunderstood Idealism of Schiller with the misunderstood Idealism of Fichte and Hegel'.[141] A particular figure on whom their anger was focused was Karl Grün, a one-time colleague of Marx at Berlin University, a Young Hegelian and a proponent of German or 'True Socialism'.[142] In the *Manifesto of the Communist Party* they devote a section to 'True Socialism', a scathing critique of the role of this movement: 'it directly represented a reactionary interest, the interest of the German Philistines. In Germany the petty bourgeois class, a relic of the sixteenth century, and since then constantly cropping up again under various forms, is the real social basis of the existing state of things'. Threatened with 'the industrial and political supremacy of the bourgeoisie ... and the rise of a revolutionary proletariat ... "True Socialism" appeared to kill these two birds with one stone. It spread like an epidemic'.[143]

But Mehring feels that with regard to Schiller himself Marx and Engels, given the burden of their own struggles, may understandably have been too peremptory in their dealing ('nun freilich Schiller selbst bei Marx and Engels zu kurz gekommen'), had not taken the trouble to differentiate between Idealism as Schiller understood it during his epoch and his later petty-bourgeois interpreters ('sie haben sich nie die Mühe genommen, zu unterscheiden ...'). Lassalle was no less a student of Fichte and Hegel and also criticised the petty-

---

140   *Die Neue Zeit* 1904/05, pp. 153–6, 154. Online at Friedrich Ebert Stiftung, Bonn. '... weshalb Marx einmal sagt, Schillers Flucht ins Ideal sei nur die Vertauschung der gemeinen Misere mit der überschwenglichen Begeisterung, oder Engels ein andermal die Verketzerung des philosophischen Materialismus so erklärt, dass der Philister davon nur so wiel verstehe, als er an einigen Bildungsbrocken aus Schillers Gedichten aufgeschnappt habe'.

141   Ibid. '... mit dem Popanz zu kämpfen, den die deutsche Spiesbürgerei aus dem Idealismus Schillers gemacht hatte, und ihr Unwille darüber war um so grosser, ... den missverstandenen Idealismus Schillers mit dem missverstandenen Idealismus Fichte und Hegels in ein unglaubliches Sammelsurium zusammenkoppelten'.

142   Grün was, for a period, a central figure on the left. He participated in the 1848 revolution. Charged with 'intellectual responsibility' for a related insurrection in Berlin, he was imprisoned.

143   Marx and Engels 1977, p. 8. In a footnote added by Engels in 1890, he wrote: 'The chief representative and classical type of this tendency is Herr Karl Grün' (Marx and Engels 1977, p. 86). Mehring includes a short section on 'True Socialism' in his biography of Marx, in which he states: 'Marx and Engels attacked Karl Grün more violently than any other of its representatives' (Mehring 1936, p. 113).

bourgeois distortion of this Idealism, but he distinguished between Schiller and his interpreters ('... er unterscheidet zwischen Schiller und dessen bürgerlichen Interpreten'). He wrote a pamphlet criticising Grün and Julian Schmidt and defending Schiller's achievement ('... durchaus treffende Charakteristik des Schillerischen Idealismus').[144] Unavoidably Marx and Engels had to oppose this tendency ('True Socialism') if they were to achieve their great purpose: 'even if Schiller were not accorded his rights this is easier to bear than that a spiritual infection of the masses by the belletristic twaddle in the manner of Karl Grün should result'.[145] This formidable history confronted Mehring when he set out to reclaim Schiller for the German workers. Mehring's strategy to contest this downgrading of Schiller is twofold: to contextualise him historically and to establish his distance from Kant, thereby proposing that his Idealism was not that of the 'True Socialism' of the nineteenth century. As biographer he is here guided by 'the conception of history of the modern proletariat as has been classically grounded by Marx and Engels' ('... so gibt uns die Geschichtsauffassung des modernen Proletariats, wie sie von Marx und Engels in klassischer Weise begründet worden ist ...').

Schiller grew up under the absolutist court of Württemberg at a time when, as Mehring writes, 'the feudal world undermined by the capitalist mode for centuries, collapsed irreparably: the bourgeois era dawned, the new sun paradoxically rose in the west and shone on the Germans from afar'.[146] Shocked by the violence of the French Revolution, Schiller, 'the strongest representative of German "Sturm und Drang" buried his head when the bourgeois revolution confronted him in reality' ('Der kühnste Vertreter des deutschen Sturm und Drang verhüllte entsetzt sein Haupt, als ihm die bürgerliche Revolution leibhaftig entgegentrat'), leaving him 'incapable of grasping the bourgeois revolution' ('Unfähig, die bürgerliche Revolution zu begreifen ...').[147] He consequently 'lent Kantian philosophy a specific orientation, constructing from Kant's realm of nature a state based on nature, which he understood the feudalist-absolutist

---

144   *Die Neue Zeit* 1904/05, pp. 153–6, 155. Online at Friedrich Ebert Stiftung.

145   *Die Neue Zeit* 1904/05, pp. 153–6, 156. '... ist Schiller selbst dabei nicht zu seinem Rechte gekommen, so war das – ungleich leichter zu ertragen, al seine geistige Verseuchung der Massen mit belletristischen Salbadereien im Stile der Karl Grün ...'.

146   Mehring 1929, pp. 139–40. 'Die feudale Welt, vom kapitalistischen Maulwurf seit Jahrhunderdten untergraben, brach rettungslos zusammen: das bürgerliche Zeitalter dämmerte herauf. Aber umgekehrt wie in der Natur ging diese Sonne im Westen auf und den Deutschen leuchtete sie erst von fern'.

147   Mehring 1929, p. 213. Ironically, he had been elected an honorary citizen of the French Republic in 1792: when it arrived three years later, its signatories, including Danton, had been executed.

state of his era to be, but fashioning from Kant's realm of human free will "a building of true political freedom", and, as Kant had erected the realm of art as the binding agent between the two, so Schiller wished to progress from the absolutist state to that founded on bourgeois reason by way of aesthetic culture'.[148] For Schiller, the most complete work of art was the construction of political freedom. 'Nonetheless Schiller relentlessly drew out the consequences of the bourgeois state of reason' ('Schiller zieht auch hier rücksichtlos die Konsequenzen des bürgerlichen Vernunftrechts'). Living in a Germany 'that knew almost nothing of large industry and hardly anything of manufacture' ('das noch nichts von der grossen Industrie und kaum etwas von der Manufaktur wusste'), he was sufficiently aware to condemn existing practices: 'Endlessly tied to a single fragment of the whole man himself becomes a fragment: endlessly with only the monotonous clamour of the wheel he rotates in his ears he never develops the harmony of being, and instead of shaping man in nature man becomes an impress of his work, of his science'.[149]

In his essay 'Goethe and Schiller', Mehring comments that Goethe pays no attention to social issues and quotes a long passage from Engels, who contrasts the different responses of the two poets to the German 'misère': 'Goethe took flight on his Italian travels, but Schiller by no means "took flight" into the Kantian Ideal, rather in grasping it passionately he committed himself more actively to German society than Goethe'.[150] Mehring seems to imply that too hasty a judgement may have been visited upon Schiller, as noted earlier. 'Instead of bemoaning this state of affairs in a reactionary manner', Mehring continues, Schiller responds positively: 'To develop the manifold abilities of humans requires no other medium but that they be set in opposition to one another. This antagonism of forces is the great instrument of culture' ('Dieser Antagonismus der Kräfte ist das grosse Instrument der Kultur'). In his play 'The Robbers',

---

148   Ibid. '... nun der Kantischen Philosophie die eigentümliche Wendung, dass er aus Kants Reiche der Natur den Naturstaat machte, worunter er den feudalistisch-absolutischen Staat seiner Zeit verstand, aus Kants Reiche der menschlichen Willensfreiheit aber "den Bau einer wahrhaft politischen Freiheit", und wie Kant das Reich der Kunst als verbindendes Glied zwischen dem Reiche der Natur und dem Reiche der Freiheit errichtet hatte, so wollte Schiller aus dem Naturstaat über die Brücke der ästhetischen Kultur in den bürgerlichen Vernunftstaat'.

149   Mehring 1929. p. 215, 'Ewig nur an ein einzelnes kleines Bruchstück des Ganzen gefesselt, bildet sich der Mensch selbst nur als Bruchstück aus: ewig nur das eintönige Geräusch des Rades, das er umtreibt, in Ohre, entwickelt er nie die Harmonie seines Wesens, und anstatt die Menscheit in seiner Natur auszuprägen, wird er bloss zum Abdruck seines Geschäfts, seiner Wissenschaft'.

150   Koch 1961, p. 151. Wittfogel too would be critical of Goethe's inattention to contemporary social conditions.

Schiller 'opposed the dominant social order with the sharp weapons of materialism' ('... bekämpfte Schiller ... die herrschende Gesellschaftsordnung mit den schneidenden Waffen des Materialismus').[151]

Describing some of Schiller's love lyrics as being of interest 'more for their philosophical content now' ('... um ihres philosophischen Gehalts wegen'), Mehring writes, 'It can be claimed, not without reason, that the poet manifests himself in them as "Kantian" without a trace of Kant' ('... dass der Dichter in ihnen sich schon als Kantianer offenbare ohne noch eine Ahnung von Kant zu haben'). To the extent that Schiller also drew his aesthetic ideas from the general context of the Enlightenment, he went beyond Kant ('... ging er ... über Kant hinaus'). 'He sought', Mehring continues, 'the possibility for aesthetic judgement not any longer in "the transcendental sphere" but in the historic conditions of human beings'.[152] He shared the prejudice of fellow Enlighteners that the Enlightenment was not bound by its era, but possessing a passionate temperament he rejected 'the lifeless abstractions of Kant's aesthetic theory'.[153] Mehring's final judgement is not that Schiller is a materialist, even if he is more engaged with the social and political than his Kantian mentor, Körner, or Goethe: 'Though Schiller was a major philosophical thinker as a poet his philosophical poems only offer pleasure': for 'the aesthetic redemption did not supersede philosophical dualism but only further postulates it'.[154] His early plays in particular, however, supplied 'the first and greatest weaponry' for the emancipatory struggle of the proletariat.

In the introduction to the second edition of his biography of Schiller, *Schiller. Ein Lebensbild für deutsche Arbeiter*, published on the 150th anniversary of the writer's birth, Mehring greets 'the proletarian youth movement, which at present has made further advance and with newly acquired strength strives for lofty objectives'.[155] But Schiller is not unproblematically a model for the workers, nor was he for the bourgeoisie so often led astray by his idealism. As with

---

151   Koch 1961, p. 153.

152   Koch 1961, pp. 150–60, p. 156. 'Er suchte die Möglichkeit ästhetischer Urteile nicht mehr in dem "übersinnlichen Substrat", sondern praktisch in der historischen Bedingtheit der Menschen'.

153   Ibid. '... was in Kants ästhetischer Theorie leblose Abstraktion war'.

154   Mehring 1929, pp. 229–30. 'Aber wie Schiller nur als Dichter ein grosser Philosoph war, so bieten seine philosophischen Gedichte nur einen ästhetischen Genuss. ... Die ästhetische Erlösung hebt den Dualismuus nicht auf, sondern setz ihn auch immer nur erst voraus'.

155   The edition being used here is reprinted in Mehring 1929, pp. 117–267, 117. '... sie würde gern ... die proletarische Jugendbewegung begrüssen, die gegenwärtig einen neuen Anlauf genommen hat und mit frisch gesammelter Kraft hohen Zielen zustrebt'. The first edition had been published in 1905, on the centenary of Schiller's death, and had sold out.

Lessing, Schiller encountered the misery of late eighteenth-century German conditions but instead 'took flight into the domain of art'.[156] Mehring writes that 'the bourgeois class consciousness of his time was not very marked in Schiller and in this he cannot be compared with Lessing'.[157] For today's proletariat, 'who strain and must strain every nerve of their power to destroy the inhuman reality they experience in order to seize an existence worthy of human beings, such a flight is defeatist'.[158] Notwithstanding that 'our classical literature and philosophy wandered through the clouds it has preserved the spirit ... provided for the emancipatory struggle of the proletariat their first and greatest armourers'.[159] Mehring will base his assessment of Schiller's works on their capacity for contributing to the emancipatory struggle of the proletariat, distinguishing between the earlier 'republican'- and 'bourgeois tragedies' ('republikanisches'- und 'burgerliches Trauerspiel'), and the later more speculative and philosophical modes. 'The antithesis between life and the ideal is reconciled through proletarian class struggle', Mehring writes, 'not through art as Schiller endeavoured to do'.[160] Nevertheless, the practice of historical materialism can produce a significant relationship between Schiller's work and the proletariat, with its objective of 'presenting what has marked most clearly the lives and events of a period in order to re-present them in all their humanity. Should one consider Schiller from the standpoint of that Idealism which he acknowledged, he would appear, as so often is the case, as a shadowy phantom who had little to offer to a powerfully motivated and future-oriented class'.[161]

------

156   Assessment of Schiller's activity was not rigidly set. As we saw above Engels contrasted him positively against Goethe: Mehring here seems to oscillate in promoting Marx's more negative critique, 'that Schiller's flight into the realm of the Ideal only exchanged the general *misère* for the rapturous ...' ('Schillers Flucht in das Reich Ideals vertauschte nur die gemeine *misère* mit der überschwenglichen ...'). Mehring 1929, p. 266.

157   Mehring 1929, p. 118. As Mehring had pointed out in response to Paul Ernst (above), Schiller was from an artisanal background, Lessing the son of a pastor. 'Auch prägte sich nicht in ihm das bürgerliche Klassenbewusstsein seines Zeit am schärfsten aus, darin konnte er sich nicht mit Lessing messen'.

158   Ibid. '... wo die Arbeiterklasse jeden Nerv ihrer Kraft anspannt und anspannen muss, um eine entmenschte Wirklichkeit zu zerstören und sich ein menschenwürdiges Dasein zu erobern ...'.

159   Ibid. 'Aber eben dadurch, dass sie auf Wolken wandelte, hat sie den Geist gerettet, der dem proletarishen Emanzipationskampfe seine ersten und grössten Waffenschmiede erzog'.

160   Mehring 1929, p. 119. 'In dem proletarischen Klassenkampf ist der Gegensatz zwischen Ideal und Leben versöhnt, den Schiller nur durch die Kunst versöhnen konnte'. There is an echo here of Marx's critique of Hegel where contradictions are resolved at the level of ideas only.

161   Mehring 1929, p. 121. '... da diese historische Methode vielmehr überhaupt erst ermöglicht, die menschlichen Gestalten, in denen sich das Leben und Weben einer historischen Peri-

Mehring's literary biographer, Koch, writes of his practice that 'it was informed by the awareness of the dialectical deployment of the progressive dreams and ideals of the past'.[162]

Despite many structural weaknesses – Schiller himself felt it flagged in the middle – Mehring describes 'The Robbers' as quintessentially a 'Sturm und Drang' work, 'it was symbolic for the German "Sturm und Drang"'.[163] A brief contextual outline will suffice to establish the socio-political background. The princely absolutist state of Württemberg was described by Schiller's contemporary, the writer Schubart, as a 'Sklavenplantage' ('slave plantation'): in common with other such states it engaged in 'people trafficking' ('Menchenshacher'), the selling-off of the sons of peasants and labourers to serve as mercenaries abroad, many used by Britain in the American War of Independence.[164] Schiller too was not his own man but in service as a military orderly, the property of the prince. In January 1782 he travelled to Mannheim to see the premier of 'The Robbers' without permission: upon his return he was imprisoned for 14 days. Against this absolutist background, the play gains its significance.[165]

It is set in the court of Count Moor, with his two sons Karl and Franz being the chief protagonists. Exiled through intrigue from the court, instigated by Franz, the idealist Karl takes to the woods where he joins a band of robbers and becomes their leader. In a text marked by highly emotional language and passages of extreme violence, Franz and Karl represent the machinations of court repression and active resistance to that: 'In Franz Moor only the revolutionary hesitation of the writer is brought to life, but in Karl Moor his revolutionary

---

ode am klarsten ausgeprägt hat, in all ihrer Menschlichkeit wieder aufleben zu lassen. Betrachtet man Schiller vom Standpunkt jenes "Idealismus" zu dem er sich selbst bekannt hat, so erscheint er – und wie oft ist sein Bild so bezeichnet worden! – als ein Schatten und Schemen für den eine lebenskräftige und zukunftsfrohe Klasse nichts übrig haben kann ...'.

162 Koch 1959, p. 136. 'Mehrings Konzeption wird von dem Wissen um die dialektische Aufhebung der fortschrittlichen Träume und Ideale der Vergangenheit bestimmnt'.

163 Mehring 1929, p. 145. '... er war symbolisch für den deutschen Sturm und Drang'.

164 Mehring, in his *Lessing-Legende* text, informs us that an English Adjutant, William Faucit, signed a contract with the Prince of Brunswick's government for 4,300 men (p. 312). He also refers to the Earl of Richmond's condemnation of it in the House of Lords in 1776 as 'a scandalous commerce in hired men (Mietsknechte)', as though like 'animals driven to slaughter' (p. 314). With the exception of Saxony, waging war was the economy of the German absolutist princes, Mehring asserts.

165 It may be noted that George Grosz borrowed Schiller's title to depict the 'robber barons' of post-war capitalism in Weimar Germany in a series of pen and ink drawings.

enthusiasm flares and radiates'.[166] 'Without a deep interest in a materialist world view', Mehring writes, 'Franz's monologues could not have been written, but the shocking vision of the miscreant, as seen in so many scenes and throughout the drama, was indebted to Schiller's biblical influences, perceptions and images'. The monologues succeed 'more by the power of the poet's genius than by his design'.[167] Rejecting the admonitions of a priest he justifies his actions in his criticism of authority: 'This ruby I drew from the finger of a minister whom I stretched at the feet of his prince during the chase. He had risen through flattery from the humble populace to become his favourite, the fall of his neighbour was his step to advancement, the tears of orphans raised him up. This diamond I took from a treasury official who sold offices of trust and honour to the highest bidder ...'.[168] He justifies his activities outside the law: 'the law has not yet shaped a great man but freedom incubates the colossal and the extremes', Karl proclaims.[169] Mehring paraphrases Karl's most republican statement: 'Set me at the head of an army of fellows like myself and out of Germany shall spring a republic compared to which Rome and Sparta will be as nunneries'. Fired by his incendiary language his 'spirit thirsts for action, his breath for freedom – murderers, robbers – with this word the law was trampled underfoot by me'.[170] 'Unlike the heroes of contemporary dramatists', Mehring writes, Karl 'strode through the German present as invincible, punishing the villainy of the ruling class ... never had the lion of the "Sturm und Drang" raised its forepaw so menacingly against German tyrants'.[171] 'Die Räuber' was staged in the work-

---

166 Mehring 1929, p. 143. 'Immer ist in Franz Moor nur der revolutionäre Zweifel des Dichters lebendig geworden, in Karl Moor aber flammt und leuchtet seine revolutionäre Begeisterung'.

167 Ibid. 'Ohne ein tiefes Interesse für die materialistische Weltanschauung konnten die Monologe des Franz nicht geschrieben werden, aber wie erschütternde Vision des Bösewichts, so zeigt noch manche andere Szene, und im Grunde das ganze Drama, dass Schiller noch tief in biblischen Anschauungen und Vorstellungen lebte'. Mehring adds that Schiller rejected Kant's position on the natural inclination to evil [Böse] and sourced its origins in the socio-historic.

168 Mehring 1929, p. 144. 'Diesen Rubin zog ich einem Minister von Finger, den ich auf der Jagd zu den Füssen seines Fürsten niederwarf. Er hat sich aus dem Pöbelstaub zu seinem ersten Günstling emporgeschmeichelt, der Fall seines Nachbars war seiner Hoheit Schemel – Tränen der Waisen huben ihn auf. Diesen zog ich einem Finanzrat ab, der Ehrenstellen und Ämter an die Meistbietenden verkaufte ...'.

169 Mehring 1929, p. 143. 'Das Gesetz hat noch keinen grossen Mann gebildet, aber die Freiheit brütet Kolosse und Extremitäten aus'.

170 Mehring 1929, p. 144. 'Mein Geist dürstet nach Taten, mein Atem nach Freiheit – Mörder, Räuber! – mit diesem Wort war das Gesetz unter meine Füsse gerollt'.

171 Ibid. '... mitten durch die deutsche Gegenwart ging er mit den Schritten eines Niebesiegten und strafte die feige Schurkerei der herrschenden Klassen. ... aber noch nie hatte der

ers' theatre club, Die Volksbühne, with which Mehring was closely involved: '"The Robbers" has proven itself to be an imperishable theatre piece to this day', which despite its setting and language, 'still thrills with its powerful hyperboles and passion'.[172] These qualities had a profound effect on its first night audience in Mannheim as an eye-witness reported: 'The theatre was like a mad house, rolling eyes, clenched fists, stamping feet, hoarse cries in the auditorium … it was like a general disintegration into chaos from whose mist a new creation broke forth'.[173] Its more widespread effect was hindered by theatre censorship.

For Mehring 'Kabale und Liebe' ('Intrigue and Love') signals the transition from the 'republikanisches Trauerspiel' to the 'bürgerliche Trauerspiel'.[174] 'Schiller', Mehring writes, 'raised the bourgeois drama to a revolutionary height neither previously nor subsequently reached, not even by Lessing's "Emilia Galloti"'.[175] In the play, courtly despotism and the petty bourgeois (Schiller's artisanal background), 'the contemporary driving forces in German life are brought out into open conflict, a social opposition nowhere more clearly manifested than in Württemberg, Schiller's home state'.[176] Mehring rejects the accusation of 'fawning critics' that Schiller caricatured the nobility in their depravity in contrast to the upright morality of the petit bourgeois, 'what he reflects dramatically was simply the horrible truth'.[177] For the purpose of this text the plot is

---

     Löwe des Sturmes und Dranges seine Pranke so drohend gegen die deutschen Tyrannen erhoben'.

172   Mehring 1929, pp. 144–5. '… haben sich die Räuber als ein unverwüstliches Theaterstück erwiesen, bis auf den heutigen Tag … deren gewaltige Hyperbeln doch immer von heisser Leidenschaft beben'. This review appeared in *Die Volksbühne*, 1909.

173   Mehring 1929, p. 150. 'Das Theater glich einen Irrenhaus … rollende Augen, geballte Fäuste, stampfende Füsse, heissere Schreie im Zuschauerraum! … Es war eine allgemeine Auflösung wie im Chaos, aus dessen Nebeln eine neue Schöpfung hervorbricht'.

174   'Republikanische' is a term Schiller himself used. Writing to a friend about the play between 'Die Räuber' and 'Kabale und Liebe', 'Fiesko', he notes, 'Republican freedom is here in this region a sound without a meaning, an empty name'. 'Republikanische Freiheit ist hierzulande ein Schall ohne Bedeutung, ein leerer Name'. But he also adds that it was played 14 times on demand in Berlin (quoted in Mehring 1929, p. 169).

175   Mehring 1929, p. 164. 'Schiller hob das bürgerliche Drama auf eine revolutionäre Höhe, die es vordem nicht und nachher nicht erreicht hat, weder in Lessing's "Emilia" …'. Engels described it in a letter to Minna Kautsky, 1885: 'the main merit of Schiller's "Love and Intrigue" is that it is the first German political tendentious drama [Tendenzdrama]'. Reprinted in Baxandall 1977, p. 114.

176   Ibid. '… die damaligen treibenden Kräfte des deutschen Lebens, in offenem Kampfe so klar gegenüber … Nirgends in Deutschland standen sich Despotismus und Kleinbürgertum, wie in Württemberg'.

177   Mehring 1929, p. 165. '… aber was er dramatisch widerspiegelt, ist einmal grauenhafte Wahrheit gewesen'.

too complex to summarise. The play was well received in Mannheim, as Schiller reported to a friend, had moderate success elsewhere, but a respected Berlin critic, Mehring informs us, washed his hands of this 'Schillerian filth'.

From Mehring's perspective these two early plays of republican and bourgeois tragedy constitute the core of Schiller's contribution to the radical cause based as they were on his experience of this immediate context. Influenced by his Kantian friend Körner, who was, as Mehring writes, 'devoid of any sense of history', his plays became more speculative.[178] Through the writing of 'Don Carlos' Schiller clearly 'evolves from the wild revolutionary Robber Moor to becoming the statesman-like Liberal Marquis Posa', drawing, as Mehring suggests, 'on the ideas of other named friends on the subject of Freemasonry and the Order of the Illuminati'.[179] Although Schiller may claim that 'All Posa's principles and salient feelings revolve around republican virtue', Mehring describes the ideas as those of an 'empty Enlightenment'.[180] Unlike Lessing, Mehring asserts, 'Schiller was incapable of conceiving of the bourgeois revolution' and instead sought to found true political freedom on Kantian ideas.[181] But, in a passage reminiscent of Marx and Engels on Balzac and the historians, Mehring evaluates Schiller's historical trilogy 'Wallenstein' very positively: 'What Schiller used to call his "idealised art", the "major task of idealising" is here brought to artistic perfection': he has 'idealised Wallenstein and Wallenstein's world but even in doing that he has grasped its historical essence in a sharper and deeper measure than his contemporary historians' and 'in a profound sense related the present to the past'.[182] Mehring describes the relationship between his dramatic text and history writing: 'As dramatist Schiller was a great historian, whilst his historical writing was only the byproduct of the marble from which he chiselled

---

178 Mehring 1929, p. 297. 'Als echter Kantianer hat Körner keinen historischen Sinn'.

179 Mehring 1929, p. 188. '... wonach sich Schiller vom Räuber Moor bis zum Marquis Posa aus einem wüsten Revoluzzer zu einem staatsmännischen Liberalen abgeklärt habe'. The Illuminati were a secret Enlightenment grouping formed in Bavaria, close to Württemberg, in the third quarter of the eighteenth century, opposed to absolutist rule and religion.

180 Mehring 1929, p. 189. 'Alle Grundsätze und Lieblingsgefühle des Marquis drehen sich um republikanische Tugend ... für eine überaus leere Aufklärung'. Mehring is probably borrowing the characterisation from Lessing, who used 'soft Enlightenment' for the Berlin variety around Frederick's court.

181 Mehring 1929, p. 213. 'Unfähig die bürgerliche Revolution zu begreifen, gab Schiller nun der Kantischen Philosophie die eigentümliche Wendung ...'.

182 Mehring 1929, p. 243. 'Was Schiller seine "Idealisierkunst" die "Riesenarbeit des Idealisierens" zu nennen pflegte, hier zeigte es sich in künstlerischer Vollendung .... Er hat Wallenstein und Wallensteins Welt idealisiert, aber eben dadurch ihr historisches Wesen schärfer und tiefer erfasst, als die damaligen Historiker .... Und voll tiefen Sinnes verknüpfte er die Gegenwart mit der Vergangenheit ...'.

the forms of his historical dreams'.[183] This is reflected in Mehring's praise for 'Wallenstein' whilst he is critical of errors in Schiller's history writing on the Thirty Years' War, in which Wallenstein was a major figure.

Aware of hostility on sections of the left to Schiller's 'aesthetisch-philosophischer Idealismus', Mehring nevertheless argues for the relevance of the dramatist to the contemporary working-class movement. He acknowledges the difference between Hegel's 'historisch-philosophischer-Idealismus' and Schiller's aesthetic philosophy, how Hegel's 'historische Dialektik' was 'capable of grasping in thought innumerable regions of the spirit'. He recognises Hegel's 'fundamental and striking criticism of Schiller's Idealism'. Nevertheless, Mehring proposes that 'not only the bourgeoisie have a claim on him, but equally the proletariat. The working class was still part of the bourgeois class when Schiller worked and fought'.[184] The author of 'Die Räuber', 'Kabale und Liebe', 'Wallenstein' and 'William Tell', 'with his voice against tyrants, will always find echo in the hearts of the working class'.[185]

That Schiller was a more problematic writer for the left to deal with than Lessing is documented by Gisela Jonas in a 1988 publication, the *Schiller-Debatte 1905*, where she writes that Kautsky specifically requested that Rosa Luxemburg would be the reviewer of Mehring's text, a review to which I now turn.[186] Luxemburg's ideologically nuanced review reads like a complement to the Mehring text, it is highly supportive of its major trajectory, and occasionally registers difference of emphasis – Mehring doubted Schiller's capacity to represent the bourgeois revolution, specifically here the Great French Revolution, whilst Luxemburg suggests that with historical distance he could have succeeded, as he did with his 'Wallenstein'.[187] Her forthrightness alerts us

---

183   Mehring 1929, p. 200. '... nur die Abfälle der Marmors sind aus dem er die Gestalten seiner historischen Dramen meisselte'.

184   Mehring 1929, p. 266. 'Nicht nur die Bourgeoisie hat einen Anspruch an ihn, sondern ebenso das Proletariat. Die Arbeiterklasse war noch ein Teil der bürgerlichen Klasse, als Schiller arbeitete und kämpfte'. Thalheimer in his Introduction to this collection makes a related claim when he writes that during the early stages of the bourgeois revolution, its art for a time was companionable to the struggles of the proletariat and remained so for a time afterwards: 'Typical examples of German literature of this orientation are Heine and Herwegh, the most typical Freiligrath' (p. 29). Mehring had written at length on all three and their relationships to Marx.

185   Ibid. 'Immer wird sein Ruf gegen die Tyrannen durch ihre Reihen schallen ...'.

186   The full title of Jonas's study is *Schiller-Debatte 1905. Dokumente zu Literaturtheorie und Literaturkritik der revolutionären Sozialdemokratie* (East Berlin: Akademie Verlag, 1988).

187   The review was published in *Die Neue Zeit*, Vol. 25, 1904–05. An English translation by Esther Leslie was published in *Rosa Luxemburg: Selected Political and Literary Writings* (Luxemburg 2009, pp. 16–19). This is the version being used here. In the general literature

to the problematic reception of Schiller within the SPD: 'Mehring's study has appeared at just the right moment. It comes as a welcome gift to the German working class, delivering an image of the great poet free of the distortions prevalent in both the biased bourgeois version and the biased Party version'.[188] Ideological dissension within the Party is directly addressed: 'However precisely those circles who, at any other moment, are bravely prepared to participate in all possible revisions of the "sore points" of Marx's doctrine, do not exhibit the tiniest desire to revise the customary uncritical judgements of Schiller'.[189] Schiller's work has now 'become part of the intellectual family scrapbook of the enlightened, combative proletariat in particular' and has played 'its part in the work of the emancipation of the working class'.[190] Her comments on the mode of reception stress the dialectical nature of that process, not a passive reception of Schiller's work as such, one that is dependent on 'what the revolutionary working class deposited in Schiller's poems based on its own world view, its striving and its feelings ... but rather picked through his intellectual work and fused it unconsciously into its own world of revolutionary thought and feeling'.[191] This dialectical engagement is further emphasised: 'Schiller must also be confronted objectively and scientifically by the working class as a major manifestation of bourgeois culture instead of subjectively merging with him or, more accurately, dissolving him into their own world view'. Dissatisfied with reductivist historically materialist readings of Schiller as 'a *revolutionary* poet *par excellence*', she invokes the concept of 'revolutionary', 'as deepened and ennobled by Marxist doctrine, by dialectical historical materialism ...', a concept which is not satisfied with the mere external manifestation of protest but attends to 'its inner tendency, its social content'.[192] Corresponding to this superficial reading of 'revolutionary' is 'a type of materialist reading' in which 'the deep inner structure of Schiller's whole world view and life-work' is 'not explained by the existing historical and social misery of his time' but

---

one finds the statement that Mehring had reawakened Luxemburg's strong empathy with Schiller's work. Her review is also very complimentary towards the manner of Mehring's achievement: not a biography in the usual sense of chronology, but a real portrait with painterly refinements of line and tone which provides 'pure aesthetic pleasure from start to finish'.

188   Luxemburg 2009, p. 17. 'Dichter' is translated here as poet but Mehring also uses it for dramatist, as also with Lessing. As mentioned above, Mehring refers to the hostile reception of Schiller's work by Marx and Engels.

189   Luxemburg 2009, p. 18.

190   Luxemburg 2009, p. 17.

191   Ibid.

192   Luxemburg 2009, p. 18.

that his 'alleged revolutionary collapse' is explained by the direct personal pressure exerted by the courts of Stuttgart and Weimar. For Luxemburg, 'the creator of *Wallenstein* finds vindication in the cool-headed "orthodox" materialist Mehring'.[193] 'Schiller', she writes, 'found his materials in the struggles of history, not because and in as much as they were *revolutionary* but rather because they embodied tragic conflict at its highest potency and effect'.[194] Mehring's contribution was that he understood this: 'Mehring solved this whole problem in two sentences, by saying: "As poet he needed historical material" and "as dramatist Schiller was also a great historian"'.[195] Mehring's text will 'render the most important service to the reading public, which matters especially now with party literature'.[196] This is no doubt a reference to Lenin's thinking on the role of party literature in struggle.

6 The Critique of Naturalism

> Mehring's presentation and critique of the Naturalist movement in Germany is of an incomparably higher level.[197]
>
> LUKÁCS

In his 1898 essay 'Naturalismus und proletarischer Klassenkampf', Mehring provides a brief socio-historical background for the emergence of Naturalism. With the economic crash of the 1870s 'the spiritual strength of the bourgeoisie seemed to be extinguished' and bourgeois literature seemed to have experienced its 'death knell'. But such a powerful social formation 'never expires just like that'. Capitalism, as expected by the revolutionary proletariat in the 1870s, and much later, did not collapse dramatically. The 1880s saw bourgeois society revive economically and spiritually: a wide range of scientific literature was published, an array of economic publications undertook a relatively sharp and deep analysis of modern society, and literary Naturalism developed. 'An irresistibly expiring culture', Mehring writes, 'gathered all its strength to sustain its existence, the maximum it could muster', but it was not sufficient to

---

193   Luxemburg 2009, p. 19.
194   Ibid.
195   Ibid.
196   Ibid.
197   Lukács 1954, p. 385. 'Auf einem unvergleichlich höheren Niveau steht Mehrings Darstellung und Kritik der naturalistischen Bewegung in Deutschland'. The comparative relates to Mehring's relative neglect of non-German Naturalism.

'ward off its demise'.[198] From this context one can account for 'the strengths as well as the weaknesses' ('... kann man wie den Stärken, so auch die Schwächen ...') of contemporary Naturalism. In an incredibly constrained context Naturalism lacked the conceptual range to negotiate the historical: 'it must helplessly confront every historical problem' which explains why 'it clung to the slavish copying of appearance'.[199] Nevertheless, there had been a perception, shared by Mehring, that Naturalist artists and writers might have come to 'an artistic understanding' ('zum künstlerischen Verständnis') of the contemporary working-class movement but as his various essays and reviews across the period indicate, this was only infrequently achieved.

Mehring was not only a critic of Naturalist texts, he was also heavily involved as an investigative journalist in the politics of a dominant Berlin clique of writers and theatre people, their control of what was staged and their involvement with the capitalist press. His subject was corrupt practices. The beginning of the campaign was a letter by an actress to him as editor of the Berlin *Volks-Zeitung*, claiming not only unfair dismissal but also boycotting by the powerful Berliner Ring: for Mehring she was a 'social type', a 'Proletarierin'. Mehring's campaign experience is recounted in two brochures, *Der Fall Lindau* (*The Case of Lindau*) 1890, and *Kapital und Presse* (1891), the latter of which is a searing criticism of late nineteenth-century bourgeois society and its cultural politics. Lindau was the focus of Mehring's criticism: sensationalist Naturalist playwright, including representations of the sexual lives of the Lumpenproletariat; a journalist characterised by Mehring as Bismarck's 'serf' ('Leibjournalist'), who advocated the continuation of the anti-socialist laws even after the Chancellor's departure; spurned by the actress against whom he instituted the boycott across Berlin theatres. For Mehring the corruption of the cultural system could not be more blatant.[200] The focus here, however, will be on Mehring's comments on Naturalism, not the more general scene.

The first paragraph of Mehring's essay 'Der heutige Naturalismus' (Contemporary Naturalism) indicates the nature of the issues at stake. There he uses

---

198   Koch 1961, p. 223. 'Eine unaufhaltsam absterbende Gesellschaft sammelte ihre ganze Kraft, um sich am Leben zu erhalten, und es war gewisss die stärkste Kraft, die sie überhaupt noch aufzubieten, hatte ...'.

199   Ibid. 'Man versteht dann, weshalb er sich an die sklavische Nachahmung der Natur klammert, denn es muss ratlos vor jedem gesellschaftlichen Problem stehen'.

200   In the opening paragraph to Chapter 9 of *Kapital und Presse* titled 'Zur Philosophie und Poesie des Kapitalismus', Mehring writes 'that the inscription on the banner under which the Lindau-Ring flourishes is Nietzsche's *Beyond Good and Evil*, Nietzsche, the "Sozial-Philosoph des Kapitalismus"'.

the terms 'Widerschein' (reflection) and 'Wiedergabe' (reproduction). In the brief first paragraph he states that there is no formal characteristic which encompasses the concept of Naturalism but that one must in each individual case establish 'what position it tends to take in the contemporary class struggles' ('... welche Stellung die naturalistische Richtung in den Klassenkämpfen ihrer Zeit einnimmt'). This is the standard ('der Massstab') through which we interrogate it, so that 'we do not misrecognise that it is, in fact, the reflection that the increasingly powerful blazing workers' movement casts upon art'.[201] In its 'avantgardist' struggle Naturalism denounces the essence ('das Wesen') of all art through the demand that the significance of an artwork be judged solely on its truth to nature ('... nach seiner Naturwahrheit zu beurteilen ...'), that the value of art be conceived as 'the so-called' literal reproduction of nature, that every individual addition from the artist's fantasy, every artistic sensibility and composition should be discarded. Mehring is drawing a distinction between the terms 'Widerschein' and 'Wiedergabe': reflection, augmented by the dynamic concept of refraction, is the fundamental ground for the Marxist theory of knowledge, the dialectical engagement with the immediate; reproduction is the unmediated response to the given, the former addressing essence (Wesen), the totality, the latter, appearance (Wirklichkeit), the particular.

Mehring is not uniformly negative in his critique of Naturalism: read through the lens of historical materialism 'it could be a storm-signal for world history' ('Er kann ein Sturmsignal der Weltgeschichte sein ...').[202] 'Does it announce a new era of art and literature as some proclaim', he asks, 'or does it signify the inevitable decline of both, as others say. Without further questioning no answer may be made'.[203] He is concerned by a consensus at the SPD Gotha Conference of 1896 that 'modern art exists in a period of decline and can therefore only represent decline': Naturalism is 'an artistic rebellion: it is the art that begins to track capitalism ... concerning itself with the waste of capitalist society'.[204] 'The period of decline in which we live', he writes, 'is also a period of rebirth. However honestly and truly modern art may depict the ruins, it will remain false in that it overlooks the new life rising from the ruins'. But to progress

201 Koch 1961, p. 131. '... so lässt sich nicht verkennen, dass er [Naturalismus] des Widerschein ist, den die immer mächtiger auflodernde Arbeiterbewegung in die Kunst wirft'.
202 Koch 1961, p. 130. Originally published as 'Etwas über Naturalismus' ('A Note on Naturalism') in *Die Neue Zeit*, 1892.
203 Koch 1961, p. 127. This was published in *Die Volksbühne*, 1892–93.
204 Koch 1961, pp. 131–2. Originally published as 'Der heutige Naturalismus' ('Contemporary Naturalism') in *Die Volksbühne*, 1892–93.

from spontaneous disgust to 'clearer understanding of a new art and Weltan-schauung is a farther journey, and as yet the artistic movements which strive after a more truthful art have taken only unsteady and uncertain steps'.[205]

Mehring's assessment of Naturalism pursues a dual approach: as a critique of bourgeois culture in decline, unable to provide representation pointing towards the future, and scrutinising it for the outside possibility that it might marginally, in its formal innovation, accommodate the new content of the world of the forward-looking proletariat.[206] In the context of immediately preceding art Naturalism had the potential to be progressive ('... einen gewissen Fortschritt bedeutete'): '... it has the courage and love of truth to depict the passing as it is, but its fate – today still uncertain – depends on whether it will find the higher courage and higher love of truth to also depict the emerging, as it must be and will daily become'.[207] But there is also the possibility that it could become 'dominated by a hopeless and despairing pessimism, which by its nature is a reactionary current ...'.[208] In his report on the SPD Gotha annual conference in 1896, in which contemporary literature was on the programme for discussion for the first time, he warns against the total rejection of modern art by assuming that 'the working class was divorced from it' ('... was die arbeitende Klasse von der modernen Kunst trennt ...'), 'to fail to recognise that within bourgeois society it is certainly progressive' ('... gar zu verkennen, dass sie innerhalb der bürgerlichen Gesellschaft allerdings ein Fortschritt ist').[209] 'The bourgeois Naturalists are socialistically inclined', he writes, 'as the feudalising Romantics were inclined towards the bourgeoisie': but 'they have only

---

205   Ibid.

206   This potential for formal invention he most clearly articulates in comments on the work of the French Impressionists: 'The Impressionists are in the realm of the artistic arena a type of bourgeois socialism, they strike with biting criticism the excesses of capitalist society ...'. 'Where French Impressionism', he wrote, 'has broken through the capitalist mode of thinking it is able to seize the beginnings of a new world in essence, it has a revolutionary affect, it becomes a new form of artistic representation to which no earlier compares in its particular dimension of power' ('... wirkt er revolutionär, wird er wie neue Form künstlerische Darstellung die schon jetzt, keiner früheren an eigentümlicher Grösser und Kraft nachsteht ...'). *Die Neue Zeit*, 1890–91, pp. 649–53, 653. Online at Friedrich Ebert Stiftung, Bonn.

207   Koch 1961, p. 131. 'Sie hat den Mut die wahrheitsliebe, das Vergehende zu schildern, wie es ist, aber ihr – heute noch ungewisses – Schicksal hängt davon ab, ob sie den höheren Mut und die höhere Wahrheitsliebe finden wird, auch das Entstehende zu schildern, wie es werden muss und täglich schon wird'.

208   Ibid. 'Sie wird noch allzu sehr beherrscht von eine hoffnungs- und trostlosen Pessimismus, der seiner Natur nach eine reaktionäre Strömung ist ...'.

209   Koch 1961, pp. 134–40, 139.

completed half the journey and should they stop there the outcome would be the inevitable decline of art and literature'.[210] So far 'they have only seen the old decaying but not the newly developing world; they have found the lumpenproletariat in brothels and bars but they do not know where the class conscious proletariat works and fights'.[211] Caught between rejection of the 'grosskapitalistische Gesellschaft' and ignorance of the organised working-class movement, positive representations of a class-conscious proletariat were not to be expected. The mediating index for both Naturalism and the working class, often referred to in these writings, is the classical heritage (das Erbe) of Lessing and Schiller, marking the reasons for the level of decline of bourgeois culture and the potential for the revolutionary proletariat. 'The spiritual requirements of a monopoly capitalist society for which our contemporary writers write are entirely different', he states, 'than for the spiritual requirements of the burgher society for which Lessing, Goethe and Schiller wrote'. What is crucially different 'are the restrictions imposed by the monopoly capitalist mode of production' ('Es sind die Bedingungen der grosskapitalistischen Produktionsweise ...').[212]

In a passage which would lay him open to the charge of rejecting the possibility of an art of the transition, he writes that 'it is most unlikely that a new era of art will emerge during the period of the struggle, but it is certain that the victory of the proletariat will usher in a new epoch ...'.[213] Mehring does not absolutely exclude it as his review of a work by a young proletarian makes evident. The Volksbühne, of which Mehring had become Chairman, had a programme of promoting the work of promising young playwrights' production denied staging by commercial theatre. One such was the dramatist Paul Bader, whose play 'Andere Zeiten' ('Other Times') was put on there in 1892 and was very positively reviewed by Mehring. It enacts wide-ranging confrontations from contemporary struggles: 'for the first time the proletariat are brought to the stage, not the lumpenproletariat from the brothels and the local drink-

---

210 Koch 1961, pp. 224, 133. 'Die bürgerlichen Naturalisten sind sozialistisch gesinnt, wie die feudalen Romantiker bürgerlichen gesinnt waren ...'. 'Aber er hat soweit nur erst den halben Weg zurückgelegt, und wenn er dabei stehenbliebe, so würde er allerdings den unaufhaltsamen Verfall von Kunst und Literatur einleiten ...'.

211 Mehring 1961, p. 447. A similar charge would be laid against Expressionist work by Jost Hermand in the 1960s. Hermand was a student of Richard Hamann's who, in turn, was a student of Mehring's.

212 Koch 1961, pp. 227–9, 228. Mehring does not detail these restrictions in his reviews or articles but, as his history of the workers' movement indicates, he understood their greater social role.

213 Koch 1961, p. 226. Lukács would detect evidence of pre-Trotsky German 'Trotskiism' in Mehring's attitude.

ing dives, as in much "Naturalistic" writing – rather the real proletariat, not one consumed by hopeless pessimism or stupefied in wasteful pleasure, but despite everything working and struggling in joyful optimism, stirred by the great potentialities of humanity'. Bader sees 'not only the declining world but also the coming one' ('... nicht bloss die versinkende, sondern auch die aufsteigende Welt ...'). It is not obvious if the play was meant to be tendentious or whether it has become so despite the intention of the dramatist: its newspaper editor is neither caricature nor monster, 'nor is he a mere photographic copy of random individualism but a real individual as formed by capitalist development, almost more its victim than its support' ('... er ist auch keine brutale Photographie eines zufälligen Individuums, sondern ein lebendiger Mensch, wie in die kapitalistische Entwicklung schafft, und fast noch mehr Opfer als Träger des Kapitalismus'). Similarly with the proletarian family: 'Whoever sees these splendid creations recognises at first glance that they are from the life, that they breathe the sorrow and joy of the modern proletariat. In the simple, moving image of Frau Oppelmann resounds the iniquitous fragmented life of a woman, but the males are full of boisterous humour and regard the future clear-sightedly ... forging with a strong fist the structure of a more fortunate world'.[214] Although Mehring points to deficiencies in the play, its achievements are a standard against which Naturalist drama is evaluated. With the exception of Hauptmann's 'Die Weber', Naturalist dramas rarely produce such significant representations.

Hauptmann was one of those playwrights Mehring described as 'socialistically inclined', as is manifest from the two plays considered here, 'Vor Sonnenaufgang' (Before Sunrise) and 'Die Weber' (The Weavers), the former summarily dealt with here as it registered the failures overcome in the latter.[215] Hauptmann described 'Vor Sonnenaufgang' as a 'social drama' ('soziales Drama'), which instantly created the impression that he had introduced to the stage 'a social image of the world, the struggle between capitalism and socialism' ('... er habe sofort ein soziales Weltbild, den Kampf zwischen Kapitalismus und Sozialismus auf die Bühne geführt'). The scene is set in a mining area, where the discovery of more coal seams leads to the purchase of more land and the enriching of some locals. But Hauptmann does not think to 'confront in dramatic terms miners and their exploiters' ('... die Bergleute und ihre Ausbeuter

---

214   Koch 1961, pp. 471–5, 473, 475. 'In der rühendschlichten Gestalt der Frau Oppelmann klingt die tiefe Wehmut eines schnöde zerbrochenen Frauenlebens wider, aber die Männer sind voll grimmer Humors, und mit hellem Blick schauen sie in die Zukunft ... sie hämmern mit kräftiger Faust den Bau einer glücklichen Welt'.

215   Mehring wrote more than 20 essays on and reviews of Hauptmann's work.

dramatisch gegenüberstellen ...'); this fortuitous enrichment of some is, like the lottery, a product of capitalism but it 'lies outside the capitalist mode of production and from which spring class conflicts'.[216] His newly enriched drunken peasants are no more 'Kapitalisten' than his heroes are 'Sozialisten'. 'Against the millions of workers who are directly tossed into the abyss by the capitalist mode of production', Mehring comments, 'not a hundred peasants achieve wealth in the manner Hauptmann has depicted it'.[217] Three years after the earlier failure he understood how to create from 'the spring of a genuine socialism' 'The Weavers' ('... aus dem Born eines echten Sozialismus zu schöpfen verstanden hat ...'). Indeed Hauptmann's failure to identify class representatives means his play could be seen not as 'socialist' but 'anti-socialist'. But the Silesian Weavers' uprising was something other.

The uprising was an historic event; the play had an objective 'preparatory' text by Wilhelm Wolff, to whom Marx dedicated the first volume of *Capital*, 'brave, true, noble champion of the proletariat', a text first published in 1845 and republished by Mehring in *Die Volksbühne* journal in 1893, the year of the staging of the play. Police censorship followed by court proceedings meant the play could only get a theatre club performance, therefore a middle-class audience. More personally Hauptmann came from a Silesian weaver's background, dedicated the play to his grandfather whose family stories formed 'the nucleus' of his play. As Mehring wrote, 'here he was offered material that had only to be arranged and was in fact only arranged, to create the framework for a play' – in his major review Mehring checks Wolff's text against Hauptmann's.[218] With this background the play could not, therefore, 'be a crude copy of some accidental actuality' ('... doch keine brutale Kopie einer zufälligen Wirklichkeit').

Mehring's intertextual reading of the texts is in the interest of pointing up the socialist dimension of the dramatic text: 'this brief comparison should suffice to establish the extent to which Wolff's text forms the skeletal structure of Hauptmann's play'. 'We say this', he continues, 'not to discredit Hauptmann's play, but that this comparison should put an end to the loose and rambling talk about the "filtering out of all references to politics and socialism"'.[219] Mehring's

---

216   Koch 1961, p. 190. '... aber sie liegen abseits der kapitalistischen Produktionsweise und den aus ihr entspringenden Klassenkämpfen ...'.

217   Ibid. 'Gegenüber den millionen von Bauern, die von der kapitalistischen Produktionsweise unmittlebar in den Abgrund geschleudert werden gibt es nicht hundert Bauern, die von ihr in der von Hauptmann geschilderten Weise mittlebar zu Reichtum gekommen sind'.

218   Koch 1961, p. 192. 'Hier bot sich ihm ein Stoff, der nur eingeteilt zu werden brauchte und auch wirklich nur eingestellt worden ist um den Rahmen eines Dramas zu schaffen ...'.

219   Koch 1961, p. 283. 'Wir sagen das nicht zu Hauptmanns Unehre, ... aber jener einfache

focus is a review by an influential left-leaning Naturalist, Julius Hart: '"The Weavers" breathed "revolutionary spirit" and "social-democratic anger", but what roused the storm of approval was not "the revolutionary language of the party politician but the overall greatness of mankind's"'.[220] 'I fear', he writes, 'that our readers have more than enough of this bombast' and points them to the playwright's source, 'the text of a genuine social democrat' ('... nach dem Text eines unverfälschten Sozialdemokraten'), Wolff. Mehring notes that the 'unvarnished bourgeoisie' ('ungeschminkte Bourgeoisie') recognise the play for what it is when they say '"The Weavers" is a socialist Tendenz piece, that's it!' ('die Weber sind ein sozialistisches Tendenzstück und damit basta!'). Modernist critics like to throw socialist expressions around but guard against offending capitalism, but 'we must not allow an important play to be withdrawn to "pure regions of art"' ('... wollen wir uns eine bedeutende Dichtung doch lieber nicht in "reinere Regionen" entrücken lassen').[221]

In his essay 'Entweder-Oder' (Either-Or) 1893, Mehring summarises extracts from the Police President's Office, which exercised the authority of censorship. He had set out his reasons, based on 'well-founded apprehension' ('... wohlbegründete Befürchtung ...'). Theatre-goers would hear, under the guise of theatre, the daily rallying cries of social democracy on the suppression of the proletariat and their coming victory, their inclination towards violent rejection of the current order would be strengthened, it would permit partisan passions to break out. Mehring rejects all of these grounds and points to their absence in Hauptmann's 'harshly depicted events', in which the indifference of blatantly exploitative employers and of state functionaries determine the lives of the weavers. Mehring questions how the police president could categorise this 'literary representation of indisputable facts' as 'tendentious', a punishable charge. Hauptmann was not tendentious, 'colouring facts to his own ends but the writer of "The Weavers" had with the most scrupulous truth adhered to the actual unrolling of events'.

'It is difficult to accept', Mehring writes, 'that a so enlightened administration as the Berlin Police President's office wishes to exceed the behaviour of the petty princes of the eighteenth century', who did not prevent public performances of Lessing's 'Emilia Galotti' or Schiller's 'Kabale und Liebe',

---

Sachverhalt sollte das schwatzschweifige Gerede von der "Abklärung alles Politischen und Sozialistischen" u.s.w. wirklich unmôglich machen'.

220 Koch 1961, p. 277 '... die "Weber" atmeten "revolutionären Geist" "sozialdemokratischen Ingrimm" ... aber was zu stürmischen Beifall hinreisse, sei nicht die "revolutionäre Rede eines Parteipolitkers, sondern nur die allegemeine grosse Menschlichkeit"'.

221 Koch 1965, p. 283.

even though these truly represented injustices of absolute rule. Hauptmann's advocate for permission to stage the play argued that the revolutionary dimension was only apparently so, that the author did not 'stand on the side of the uprising' and allowed the restoration of order through the intervention of the troops, that the uprising was purely the result of hunger and had nothing to do with today's social movement, that today's social protection for workers had made such a situation redundant, that three quarters of a potential audience would be of 'higher standing'. Summarising, he claimed that given the above the work would be considered only as 'a true to life literary work' ('... nur um eine lebenswahres dichterisch Werk handle'), so no prohibition on performing was justified. Mehring resists 'dismembering this nonsense from the advocate' ('Es sei ferne von uns, alle diese advokatarischen Mätzchen im einzelnen zu zergliedern'). The advocate's argument was rejected and Hauptmann took his appeal to a higher court. This ruled in Hauptmann's favour, 'but one should not have to think to protect the right of literature and art against the police cudgel'.[222] ('Man darf sich nicht etwas einbilden ... oder auch nur das gute Recht der Literatur und Kunst gegen den Polizeiknüppel wahrte'). Nor did permission to perform in the luxury of the Deutsches Theater threaten the peace.

The above speaks to the politics of the play, but what of its aesthetic values? No other Naturalist drama can compare with 'The Weavers' ('... kann sich nur entfernt mit den "Webern" messen'). It contrasts sharply 'with that clever scribbling that counterfeits some arbitrary banal and gross actuality with photographic accuracy', he continues.[223] It overflows with 'the most genuine sense of life' ('quellen über von echtesten Lebens') but only because 'it has been worked through assiduously with the finest artistic awareness' ('über nur weil sie mit dem angestrengten Fleisse eines feines Kunstverstandes gearbeitet sind'.) This 'careful balancing and nuancing' ('Abtönung und Abwägung') were necessary 'to give the colourful mosaic of genre scenes dramatic tension' ('... um einem bunten Mosaik genrehafter Szenen dramatische Spannung zu geben'). What serious consideration was devoted to shaping the striking and fully masterly successful forms from which 'the appropriate masses must emerge, if they are to be really activated in dramatic movement' ('... aus denen die handelnden Massen bestehen mussten, wenn sie wirklich in dramatische Bewegung gesetzt werden sollen').

---

222   Koch 1961, p. 294.

223   Ibid. 'Sie stehen in schärfsten Gegensatze zu jener "genialen" Kleckserei, die irgendein beliebiges Stück banaler und brutaler Wirklichkeit mit photographischer Treue abkonterfeit ...'.

For Mehring, a 'mass-theatre' seemed to be on the agenda: 'Together with the dramatic hero the virtuosic performance would also disappear', an insight pointing towards Piscator and Brecht.[224] Hauptmann's play might only be 'a summer's swallow' for which we should be grateful. By the end of the decade rigorous examination confirmed how Naturalism's promise had faded. Mehring now turned to the workers' own theatre club, Die Volksbühne, the familiar-ising with the classics (Lessing, Goethe, and Schiller) and the encouragement of homegrown talent, like Bader above.

Although Mehring may have rejected the elaboration of an aesthetic *per se* there is no doubt that his writing on culture is suffused with a refined political aesthetic, sensitive to the concerns of artistic forming. The sense of his engage-ment with the artefact is one of highly mediated investigative practice, meeting not only the requirements of historical materialism but also of the dialectical, as persuasively proposed by his contemporaries and later researchers as refer-enced above.

---

224   Brecht, writing in post-World War Two Germany, can recognise the qualities Mehring points up: 'Even Hauptmann's *The Weavers*, which is full of beautiful things, is a play with a message, in my opinion'. Brecht 2019, p. 273.

Political Spontaneism and Cultural Practice

In this sense Lenin characterised spontaneism as the nucleus of consciousness.[1]

∴

1 Political Spontaneism and Cultural Practice

The development of an historical-materialist aesthetic in the pre-revolutionary period was the product of the SPD's engagement with the Marxist heritage. But the post-revolutionary period, November 1918, would immediately and fundamentally change the cultural landscape, involve new players, asking different questions and making different demands. The 'Erbe' position was still central, but now also the programme of the KPD. The USPD and the KAPD elaborated a cultural programme which privileged the 'subjective moment' in the revolutionary process, the cultivation of a proletarian class consciousness through culture, indispensable preparation to seize the opportunity when the 'objective conditions' materialised. Bogdanov's writings on Proletkult became available in translation, an event which raised the issue of an art for the transitional period to the dictatorship of the proletariat. Mehring's 'Erbe' theory was increasingly questioned within the KPD itself, particularly from the second half of the decade.[2]

In anticipating the major political and cultural conflicts which will arise, it will be very informative at this juncture to introduce Lenin's brochure *'Left-Wing' Communism: An Infantile Disorder*, in order to obtain a succinct theoretical characterisation of what was happening in immediate post-revolutionary Germany. Whilst it directly addressed the political situation it may with advantage be considered as indirectly throwing some light also on the cultural polit-

---

1 Assmann 1978, p. 620. 'In diesem Sinne bezeichnete Lenin die Spontaneität als "Keimform" der Bewusstheit'.

2 The exchanges between two KPD members, Lu Märten and Gertrud Alexander, cultural critic of the KPD paper, *Die Rote Fahne*, provide an important focus for understanding what was at issue, and will be examined in Chapter 3.

ics. The relevant passage comes towards the end of the Conclusion, where he is commenting on 'right' and 'left doctrinairism': 'the former', he writes, 'persisted in recognising only old forms and became totally bankrupt, for it did not perceive the new content', whilst 'left doctrinairism persists in the unconditional repudiation of certain old forms and fails to see that the new content is breaking its way through all and sundry forms, that it is our duty as Communists to master all forms, to learn how to supplement with the maximum rapidity one form by another, to substitute one for another, and to adapt our tactics to every change that is called forth by something other than by our class or by our efforts'.[3] In 1920, Lenin, in his 'On Proletarian Culture' (in German translation, 'Über proletarische Kultur'), also clearly reinforced his 'Left-Wing Communism' stance: 'Marxism has acquired its world-historical significance as the ideology of the revolutionary proletariat by not having rejected the most valuable achievements of the bourgeois era but, to the contrary, has appropriated and worked on what in the more than 2,000-year development of human thought and human culture was valuable'.[4]

There are three parties here in 'Left-Wing' Communism, the right and left doctrinairists and the Communist, who is called upon to activate this energised dialectic, 'to master all forms [...] to substitute one for another, and to adapt our tactics to every change that is called forth'. This is an intelligible demand in the political arena, the one laid on members of the avantgarde party. There is much in the language and concepts used here that could also be found in an avantgardist cultural programme, but whilst direct translation between party programme and cultural programme is not feasible, there is enough that is suggestive of potential crossover between these different discursive practices, if only to deploy one to criticise the other. The question of the art of the transitional period to the dictatorship of the proletariat is a point at which the relationship between the above politics and cultural practice might provide some insight. Broadly speaking there were two positions. Lenin and the KPD proposed the leading role of the party and the support of the cultural heritage in its revolutionary moments, a position which when viewed from the KAPD stance was 'right doctrinairist', that is, 'they persisted in recognising only old forms'. The KAPD proposed political spontaneism and emphasised the 'subject-

---

3 Lenin 1934, p. 82.
4 Fähnders and Rector 1974b, pp. 125–6, 'Der Marxismus hat seine weltgeschichtliche Bedeutung als Ideologie des revolutionären Proletariats dadurch erlangt, dass er die wertvollsten Errungenschaften des bürgerlichen Zeitalters keineswegs ablehnte, sondern sich umgekehrt alles, was in der mehr als zweitausendjährigen Entwicklung des menschlichen Denkens und der menschlichen Kultur wertvoll war, aneignete und verarbeitete'.

ive moment' in the revolutionary process as against the 'objective moment', the development of the self-consciousness of the proletariat by way of an art which rejected the constraints of the cultural heritage in favour of an experimentally open production which would be designed to shape that consciousness. Subscribing to Marx but not to Leninism they would be 'left doctrinairists' in both politics and culture, although on the latter it might be argued that they were 'trying to master all forms, to learn to substitute one for another', unlike supporters of the heritage. The 'left doctrinairists' seized the initiative in the immediate post-revolutionary period in both cultural theory and practice and though their politics may have been as Lenin characterised them, their production would nevertheless have a lasting impact on left Weimar culture. Wieland Herzfelde attempted to address this complex and conflictual position in his 1922 brochure 'Gesellschaft, Künstler und Kommunismus', existential in his own case: as a KPD member he supported its political programme but favoured the KAPD cultural programme. This work will be examined below.

The situation in Germany was very different from that in Russia, where the party representing the proletariat was in power. Consequently that tension between the political programme of the party and cultural politics could be negotiated at state level, as seen in the exchanges between the Commissariat of Enlightenment and the claims of Proletkult to remain autonomous, where Lenin's intervention played a crucial role in ensuring the latter's incorporation within the Commissariat.[5] In Germany, no such centralised constraint was possible and as a result the elaboration of a spontaneist theory and related practice held sway amongst groupings on the left, particularly the KAPD. Designated as 'Linkskommunisten' they developed from within the Marxism of pre-war SPD and became formalised as the KAPD after their expulsion from the KPD in 1920. They played a very active role in the immediate post-revolution phase, both politically and culturally. That the revolution was not planned but resulted from spontaneous uprisings, initially with sailors in Kiel refusing orders and determining their own decisions, supported the argument for spontaneism more broadly, an ideological position which had much currency at the time. Its core instance was the issue of the mass strike and its articulations in the writings of Lenin and Luxemburg, on the relationship between democratic centralism (the party) and spontaneism (bottom-up). The argument would determine the organisation of the left in the post-revolutionary phase: the KPD following the Lenin line, the KAPD the Luxemburg line, but in the form modified by the Dutch socialist theorists Pannekoek and Gorter, whose role has been described

---

5   The leading account of this process is Fitzpatrick 1970, where the three-way struggles between
    Lenin, Lunacharsky, and Proletkult's founder, Bogdanov, are detailed.

as follows: 'before and during the war had influenced the self-understanding process of the German revolutionary left and after the November revolution were amongst the leading mentors of left-communism'.[6]

Just as this ideological difference determined political practice, so too did it affect cultural practice.[7] The central focus for the KAPD was the current relationship between the objective and subjective components of the revolutionary moment: where the objective component was present, as the KAPD believed was the case in Germany, but had not been made full use of, 'elements of a subjective nature must have been present which provided obstacles to an accelerated execution of revolution', thus elevating the role of the subjective component.[8] Writing in 1920 Pannekoek raised further the role of the subjective component: 'the roots of capitalist power lie much deeper. They lie in the dominance of bourgeois culture over all the people, including the proletariat. Across the centuries the cultural life of the bourgeoisie has saturated all of society, established organisations and categories that penetrate the masses through thousands of tributaries and dominate them'.[9] 'Everything comes down to this', the KAPD programme states, 'to assist the proletariat realise their own consciousness, a process that only requires stimulated activity to make use of the power it already possesses'; the problem of the German revolution is consequently 'the development of the self-consciousness of the German proletariat'.[10] That the pervasiveness of bourgeois culture as a barrier to proletarian self-consciousness was not only the concern of Pannekoek and the KAPD is borne out strikingly in the following statement by Lenin: 'it would

---

6   Fähnders and Rector 1974a, p. 52. '... für die Spontaneitätstheorie der holländischen Anton Pannekoek und Herman Gorter ... vor und während des Krieges auch in den Selbstverständigungsprozess der deutschen revolutionären Linken eingriffen und nach der Novemberrevolution zu den führenden theoretische Mentoren des deutschen Linkskommunismus gehörten'.

7   The KAPD founding document declared that it was 'not a party in the traditional sense', 'not a leader party', its task was to sustain the proletariat in 'freeing itself from such leadership'. An abbreviated version is published in Fowkes 2014, pp. 343–6.

8   Fähnders and Rector 1974a, p. 63. '... müssen Gründe *subjektiver* Natur vorhanden sein, die dem beschleunigten Fortgang der Revolution als hemmende Faktoren im Wege stehen'. The quotation is from the KAPD founding programme.

9   Ibid. 'Die Wurzeln der Kapitalmacht liegen viel tiefer. Sie liegen in der Herrschaft der bürgerlichen Kultur über das ganze Volk, auch über das Proletariat'.

10   Fähnders and Rector 1974a, p. 64. 'Komme alles darauf an, dem Proletariat zu dem Bewusstsein zu verhelfen, dass es nur eines energischen Zugreifens bedarf um von der Macht die es eigentlich besitzt, wirksamen Gebrauch zu machen. Das Problem der deutschen Revolution ist das Problem der Selbstbewusstseinsentwicklung des deutschen Proletariats'.

be more difficult to promote revolution in western European lands because the high standard of culture there operates against the revolutionary proletariat and the working class finds itself in cultural slavery'.[11]

Artists sympathetic to the cultural programme of the KAPD took up this challenge of rejecting the bourgeois heritage and of contributing to the enhancement of the subjective moment in its relationship to self-consciousness. A number of paradigmatic instances of their praxis will be examined in detail below in their specificities: the 'Kunstlump' (Art Scoundrel) debate, the Erste Dada Messe (the First Dada Fair), the Proletarisches Theater and Franz Jung's play 'Die Kanaker', all of 1920, where the opposing critical voices of the KPD and KAPD will be clearly heard.

2 The 'Kunstlump' Debate

The first instance of controversy concerning the 'Erbe', known as the 'Kunstlump' ('Art Scoundrel') debate was raised in the pages of two KPD publications, the journal *Der Gegner* ('The Adversary'), supportive of KPD politics but opposed to its cultural politics, and *Die Rote Fahne*, official organ of the KPD.[12] As with most cultural politics on the left during the post-revolution decade,

---

11   Fähnders and Rector 1974a, p. 9. '... schwieriger sei die Revolution zu beginnen, weil dort der hohe Stand der Kultur gegen das revolutionäre Proletariat auswirkt und die Arbeiterklasse sich in Kultursklaverei befindet'. The statement is from the report on his address to the fourth Conference of Trades Unions and Factory Committees in Moscow, June 1918. There is a passage in Herzfelde's 'Gesellschaft, Künstler und Kommunismus' which bears on Lenin's perception. Herzfelde is reflecting on the insignificant number of visual artists who critically engaged with the system and writes: 'If in Germany this were more so than elsewhere, the cause lies in the fact that industrial development and capitalist organisation here is more intensive, more consistent, more all-encompassing than in other European countries ... possessing only the most limited possibility and propensity for social engagement or social and political development'. '... so liegt das daran, das die industrielle Entwicklung und die kapitalistische Organisation in Deutschland intensiver, lückenloser und allumfassender gewesen ist als wohl in irgendeinem anderen europäischen Lande ... die die geringste Fähigkeit und Neigung zu sozialer Eingliederung und politischer oder ökonomischer Entfaltung besassen'. Fähnders and Rector 1974a, p. 140.

12   *Der Gegner* was not an official KPD publication but was published by the Malik Verlag, run by poet and Berlin Dadaist Wieland Herzfelde, John Heartfield's brother. It was, however, recognised as the KPD publishing house for culture. The Malik circle included fellow Dadaists Grosz, Heartfield, Piscator, founder of the Proletarisches Theater, Franz Jung, experimental novelist and dramatist, and others, including Märten, who published in it. It should be emphasised that all but Lu Märten had experienced the war, which is reflected in their writings and visual work.

its origin was in a complex political series of events, in this case the counter-revolutionary Kapp Putsch of March 1920, which attempted to seize power from the socialist government. In Dresden fighting took place in the vicinity of the Zwinger Art Gallery between armed workers and the reactionary Freikorps troops supporting Kapp, as a result of which a Rubens painting was slightly damaged. Oskar Kokoschka, leading Expressionist and Professor at the Academy of Fine Arts, wrote a letter to a local paper requesting the combatants to remove themselves to the nearby heath where human culture would not be endangered, thus protecting for future generations 'their holiest treasures'.[13]

Predisposed as Dadaists to be hostile to the idealist aesthetic values of Expressionism with its emphasis on inwardness and individualism, Grosz and Heartfield wrote 'Der Kunstlump' with Kokoschka as 'The Art Scoundrel'. The article attacks the bourgeoisie in general and its cultural values in particular. Its vehemence is, no doubt, conditioned by its moment, not only the 'Kapptagen' ('days of Kapp Putsch'), but also the reversal in Hungary, where the Soviet republic led by Bela Kun was violently overthrown by Horthy ('siehe jetzt auch Horthy-Ungarn'). In this article and many others we are made aware of the formidable task confronting that left constituency intent on producing a counter-culture. The battle line is drawn up in the opening sentence: the bourgeoisie 'has constantly armed itself with "culture", amongst other things, against a rebelling proletariat' ('gegen das aufbäumende Proletariat stets unter anderen auch mit "Kultur" gepanzert'). The bourgeois cultural interior in all its luxury and indulgence is sketched here verbally as it is in Grosz's numerous visual depictions, the relationship between exploitation and cultural possessions – Rubens, Rembrandt, Kokoschka himself are mentioned, clearly established. The text is then punctuated with questions directed towards workers and their exploited conditions. What is art's relevance to the worker given his impoverished milieu? What relevance to him in the context of the betrayal of his revolution by Ebert and the SPD; if an art which seeks to buoy him up with false promises, why bother with the work of artists who feel no obligation to protest against the exploiters? Art is a decoy 'to sabotage your class consciousness, your will to power' ('sabotiert man Euer Klassenbewusstsein, Euren Willen zur Macht'). Kokoschka's letter is quoted in full, introduced by a reminder to the worker: 'you who have constantly produced the surplus value ("der Mehrwert") on which such culture depends hear what such an artist thinks'. The concepts of art and artist are 'a bourgeois invention' ('eine Erfindung des Bürgers') and art's role in the state can only be on 'the side of the ruling class' ('auf Seiten der

---

13   Fähnders and Rector 1974b, pp. 47–54.

Herrschenden'). The designation 'art' is the 'abolition of human equality' ('eine Annulierung der menschlichen Gleichwertigkeit'). The artist does not stand higher than the society which gives him recognition. And a statement which reflects on the collage/montage technique practised by the Dadaists, the artist does not produce from within his self the content of his works, but 'processes (like a sausage machine its meat) the world picture of his public' ('sondern verarbeitet [wie ein Wurstkessel Fleisch] das Weltbild seines Publikums').[14] They call on all to take a stance against the 'masochistic awe of historic values, against culture and art!'[15]

This polemic raises at least three related issues. Firstly, there are the problems of producing a revolutionary counter-culture under the pressures both of the continuing bourgeois order and its cultural institutions but also of militarised counter-revolutionary action – here the Kapp Putsch. Secondly, there is the question of the role of 'das Erbe', here scathingly dismissed in the figures of Rubens and Rembrandt, in the context of the socio-economic conditions of the working class. Thirdly, there is the indication of the mode of cultural production and critique, here that of the collage/montage cutting and pasting practice associated with the writers of the article as members of Berlin Dada, of putting through the mangle the public images of the day, a non-elitist practice which they encouraged workers to take on.

Gertrud Alexander, advocate of 'das Erbe', responded to the article in *Die Rote Fahne*, directly addressing the writers: 'Herrn John Heartfield und George Grosz': *'Der Gegner* believes it has done the working class a service by supporting pure vandalism'.[16] 'To the contrary: such a polemic neither advances nor revolutionises the workers'. She agrees with them on their criticism of Kokoschka and his skewed values and is critical of recent bourgeois culture as no longer socially sustaining, with its flight from reality ('Wirklichkeitsflucht'). The revolutionising of art cannot be erected on such grounds but the worker 'would either be a vandal or a fool to wish to begin this revolutionising by destroying the whole of the heritage'. Apart from the art value the artefacts also possess historical value. The worker himself, 'the new humanity' ('die neue Menschheit') will decide what of value to retain from the past, what best facilitates knowledge, historical understanding and the critique of humankind. 'What if not this', she asks, 'have communists and Marxists made available, to direct the event on its necessary pathway, to recognise the necessity of revolu-

---

14 Fähnders and Rector 1974b, pp. 47, 52, 53.
15 Fähnders and Rector 1974b, p. 54.
16 Reprinted in full in Fähnders and Rector 1974b, pp. 55–7, 55.

tionary advance'?[17] The past is not empty ballast to be thrown overboard, the proletariat cannot destroy the ground on which it stands and upon which it must build. She asks Heartfield and Grosz if they realise that what they want destroyed has been purchased at the expense of workers' labour – should not their descendants have the benefit of it? 'Indeed', she concludes, 'you render society a disservice in openly demanding vandalism'. The editor of *Der Gegner*, Julian Gumpertz, replied, supporting the Grosz/Heartfield broadside against bourgeois culture, accusing Alexander of misrepresenting their position by characterising it as 'vandalism' and in the interest of defending 'the eternal values of art' ('und die "Ewigkeitswerte" der Kunst vor diesem Angriff in Schutz nehmen'). He is unmasking 'your rebuke of vandalism' ('... Ihren Vorwurf des Vandalismus') and the defence of art's eternal values for what it is: ideological links of bourgeois society which must not be abolished. Alexander has criticised the lack of historical analysis in the article but provides none herself. He concludes by stating that 'ideological freedom from the bourgeois order can be achieved only by the working class itself, neither through him nor Alexander'.[18]

Alexander responded immediately and in a manner which altered the somewhat generalised nature of the debate in the opening two articles and set the agenda for a more grounded historical analysis of the cultural heritage: her charge against the argument mounted by Grosz and Heartfield and defended by Gumpertz is essentially that of spontaneism and non-mediation. The issue is deeper than the designation 'vandalism', that it represents 'a totally anarchistic view of art and culture ... an anarchism revealing itself as a primitive remedy to overcome capitalism' ('... dass es sich um eine vollständig anarchistische Anschauung gegenüber Kunst und Kultur handelt ... ein Ausweg primitivster Art, den Kapitalismus zu überwinden'). She draws a parallel with the English artisans of the nineteenth century who wrecked machines, and adds: 'the proletariat has long since become immune to such hopeless radicalism' ('Von diesem aussichtslosen Radikalismus ist der Proletariat längst geheiligt'). So little can capitalism and imperialism be fought and destroyed through the destruction of the means of production, so little will the destruction of the cultural heritage save the proletariat from the despised influences of bourgeois

---

17   Fähnders and Rector 1974b, p. 57. '... was gerade die Kommunisten und Marxisten befähigte, das Geschehen in seine notwendige Bahn zu lenken, die Notwendigkeit des revolutionären Weiterschreitens zu erkennen'.

18   Fähnders and Rector 1974b, pp. 57–60, 59. Originally printed in *Die Rote Fahne*, June 1920, as 'Kunst, Vandalismus und Proletariat. Eine Antwort an GGL', Alexander sometimes signed herself 'GGL'. Gumpertz edited Karl Liebknecht's writing and speeches, was the KPD representative on the Proletarisches Theater board, later became a member of the Frankfurt School for Social Research.

culture. Just as the proletariat must take over the existing means of production, so in a similar fashion must the heritage of the collective culture ('das Erbe der Gesamtkultur'), whether it pleases them or not. It must be of concern to ensure that the heritage is unharmed. Alexander is in this passage adhering closely to Lenin's position on left-radicalism ('Linksradikalismus'): 'Left doctrinairism persists in the unconditional repudiation of certain old forms and fails to see that the new content is breaking its way through all and sundry forms, that it is our duty as Communists to master all forms'.[19] She accuses the '*Gegner*' writers of having an insurrectionist understanding, a pitchfork ('Heugabelsinne') sense of revolution, that an article is revolutionary when bound together with grossly abusive language. She reminds Gumpertz that she had unmasked the revolutionary pretensions of Expressionism when he had defended them.[20] She clarifies her use of 'eternal' ('das Ewige') as not connoting 'timeless' ('das Zeitlose') but rather a surviving document from the era 'in which it was created and to which it is bound, potentially revolutionary in content, informative of its class interest'. The task is not to destroy the culture but to supersede (aufheben) bourgeois society. She questions Gumpertz's dismissal of individualism as a cover for egoism, believing that communism will produce the conditions for true individualism.

A short coda to this debate in the pages of *Die Rote Fahne* is provided by August Thalheimer, a founder member of the KPD and its leading theoretician until the mid-1920s. Titled 'Proletariat and Art. Political Observations' (*Proletariat und Kunst. Politische Bemerkungen*), Thalheimer writes that the bourgeoisie have sufficiently vandalised their own culture without any need of assistance; the task of the proletariat is to transform (umgestalten) it for its own purpose, a pre-echo of Piscator's and Brecht's 'umfunktionieren'?[21]

The 'Kunstlump' debate is the first major post-revolution theoretical debate on the role of the cultural heritage under the conditions of revolutionary and counter-revolutionary struggle. Cultural and political spontaneism are intertwined in the work and writing of Grosz, Heartfield and Gumpertz. The first three align themselves with the political programme of the KPD but espouse a cultural politics more in line with the KAPD cultural programme, a tension

---

19   Lenin 1920, p. 82.

20   Nothing more will be said of Expressionism here but to draw attention to Ernst Bloch's defence of its ambivalent politics in the Moscow-based journal *Das Wort* in 1937–38. Amongst many contributors was Lukács.

21   Thalheimer was a younger colleague of Mehring's and would write important introductions to two volumes of his collected writings on literature and philosophy at the end of the 1920s (see Chapter 5 below).

which would continue to trouble the left throughout the Weimar period.[22] Alexander's critique is based on the cultural tenets of Mehring's 'Erbe' theory and Lenin's politics. It was noted above that her response to Gumpertz was more focused than her initial criticism and it is tempting to believe that she may have read Lenin's critique *'Left-wing' Communism: An Infantile Disorder* in between her two articles. Her second article was spread across the issues of 23 and 24 June. Lenin's brief text was available in German translation from 20 June. This then is the nucleus of the KPD aesthetic programme, as yet more directed towards cultural reception than cultural practice. The cultural practice side of the debate would come to the fore when the Berlin Dadaists, particularly Grosz, Heartfield and Erwin Piscator, presented their work to the public in support of the revolutionary movement as members of the KPD. Work of such a radical departure would inevitably raise questions about the relevance of the 'Erbe' theory, especially in the transitional period where, for example, Proletkult was an alternative. From her position Alexander would mount hostile attacks on the major Dada exhibition in June 1920, Erste Internationale Dada-Messe, and on the opening night of Piscator's Proletarisches Theater: Lu Märten, a fellow KPD member, would take a more understanding position on the innovations proposed in both.

3   Erste Dada-Messe (The First Dada Fair): 'Die Kunst ist tot. Es lebe
        die neue Maschinenkunst Tatlins'[23]

Wieland Herzfelde wrote a brief introduction to the exhibition, prefacing it with quotations from two nineteenth-century French painters, Wiertz and Delacroix, on the challenge posed to painting by photography, more as a general statement for context. However, the Dadaist does not want 'either to compete with the camera or to infuse it with soul' ('mit dem Photographenapparat zu konkurrieren oder ihm gar eine Seele einzuhauchen') but to use its archive as a source. The image 'Leben und Treiben in Universal-City 12 Uhr 5 mittags'

---

22   Grosz for instance would continue to admire Max Hölz, branded by the KPD as an incendiary, as is evident from his autobiography *Ein kleines Ja und ein grosses Nein. Sein Leben von ihm selbst erzählt.*

23   'Art is dead. Long live the new machine art of Tatlin'. Grosz and Heartfield held a poster containing this statement in front of one of their mechanomorphic assemblages. Tatlin had constructed a large model of the building of a tower celebrating the Third International, rivalling the 'bourgeois' Eiffel Tower. This material has been dealt with in detail in my *German Art 1907–1937: Modernism and Modernisation* (Gaughan 2007, Ch. 2).

('Life and Times in Universal City 12:05 midday') by his brother, John Heart-field, manifests this practice as described by Herzfelde, 'depicted through filmic means' ('... schildert mit den Mitteln des Filmes'). By this cultural practice, Roland März writes, 'the Dadaist contributes to the unravelling of a world obviously in dissolution – revolutionary and counter-revolutionary (Kapp Putsch) Germany'.[24]

Viewing the exhibition through the lens of 'das Erbe', Alexander ironically sees elements of a new aesthetic but fails, to a degree unsurprisingly, to recognise them: 'on first sight this exhibition looks like an advertising hotch-potch for a cinema'. Too serious and pretentious, it lacks the spirit of the joke. She reads the artefacts as objects from the bourgeois world, stuck together mosaic-like with extracts from papers, tram tickets, postcards, pressed into 'images' and signed, the whole redolent of bourgeois decadence. What she describes as 'Militäreffekten', including the uniformed dummy of an army officer (by Heart-field and Schlichter) suspended from the ceiling, cap fixed on a pig's head, should be consigned to 'an anti-militarist panopticon where no one would raise an objection'. To present this collection of 'perversities' as a cultural or artistic achievement is not only not a joke but insolence. The besmirched copies of Leonardo and Botticelli reignite the vandalism charge of her 'Kunstlump' responses. 'How derisively trivial', she continues, compared with the powerful struggle of the proletariat to overthrow bourgeois society, a struggle which will succeed without the campaign against art and culture mounted by this 'bourgeois literary clique' ('... den eine bürgerliche Literatenclique unternimmt'). Nor should they consider themselves communists. 'But what', she wonders, 'has all of this to do with the proletariat? Without damage to their proletarian spirit, class consciousness and readiness for struggle they can seek beauty in the better days of the bourgeois, a period which produced human beings no less revolutionary probably than the worker-revolutionaries of today'. She cautions the workers against such cultural practices, responding to the Dadaists' address to them: a banner proclaimed: 'Dada kämpft auf Seiten des revolutionären Proletariats' ('Dada fights on the side of the revolutionary proletariat'), whilst a catalogue entry claimed 'Der dadaistische Mensch ist der radikale Gegner des Ausbeutung' ('The Dadaist is the radical adversary of exploitation'). She concludes: 'The workers are warned' ('Die Arbeiter sind gewarnt').[25]

---

24   März 1981, p. 42. Herzfelde is less 'Kunstlump' critical of the heritage, accepting its 'histori-cal-scientific' ('wissenschaftlich-historisch') role, but not its relevance for contemporary practice.

25   Fähnders and Rector 1974b, pp. 101–2.

One of the posters at the Dada-Messe advises its visitors 'Nehmen Sie DADA Ernst, es lohnt sich' (Take Dada seriously, it repays you), which is what the next two reviews do, those by Adolf Behne and Lu Märten. Behne was writing for the USPD paper *Freiheit* and Märten was in transit between the USPD and the KPD and whose review would be published in its paper, *Die Rote Fahne*.[26] The USPD cultural programme inclined more towards that of the KAPD, which prioritised the 'subjective' moment of revolutionary readiness over that of the 'objective' conditions, about which more will be said below. It was not bound by the heritage and was open to innovation. One of the leading proponents of this theoretical position was the highly regarded Dadaist, Franz Jung. For Behne, 'Dada shows the world of 1920', the human being is a machine, culture is in tatters, the military is dominant. Dada manifests the state of the spirit through its assemblages, which contain 'an uncanny discord' ('unheimliche Spannung') and which is doubtless a powerful enrichment for our painting. More percipiently he links Dada practice to film: 'here are present an abundance of important suggestions – eventually for film, whose future in general I imagine to be dadaistic' ('... eine Fülle wichtiger Anregungen – nicht zuletzt für den Film, dessen Zukunft ich mir überhaupt sehr dadaistisch vorstelle'). Dada is an important event: 'it understands and supersedes through understanding' ('Er erkennt – und hebt durch Erkennen auf').[27]

Märten's response to the Dada-Messe work is more nuanced than Alexander's, more consonant with Behne's on materials, and can be seen as a comment on the former's narrowly focused heritage-influenced account. Alexander invoked the one-dimensional trope of the joke (Ulk) and criticised the *Berlin Morning Post* for mentioning Rabelais in the context. Märten, on the other hand, does invoke that world and the historically more resonant trope of satire. The bourgeoisie cannot tolerate satire as to recognise it would require their

---

26 Behne and Märten shared certain cultural involvements which would dispose them towards a more open-ended experimental mode. Both had been involved with the Werkbund ethos, art and design as informing a more aesthetically aware industrial product; Behne, an architect, was a member, and both came to reject its programme. In his critique of the Werkbund and its inflexibility on the totally designed interior, he proposed the playfulness and fantasy potential of kitsch. The Dada Messe material was not alien to his thinking, as it was for Alexander, who described the exhibited work 'als blöden Kitsch' ('imbecilic kitsch'). 'It is incomprehensible', she writes, 'how A. Behne, critic for *Freiheit*, could be so well disposed towards such revolutionary nonsense'.

27 März 1981, pp. 44–5. Eisenstein confirmed Behne's insight in a 1923 essay on his development of his practice of the 'Montage of Attractions' as being completely 'analogous to the montage sections of the pictures of George Grosz or elements of the photo-illustrations by Rodchenko'.

own supersession ('sich selbst aufheben würde'). They now find their satire in the pages of the humorous magazines (*Witzblatt*), 'What Dada attempts satirically with distinctive means' ('mit bestimmten Mitteln satyrisch versucht'), she writes, 'may be beyond its reach', that the 'satiric dialectic of capitalism' ('die satyrische Dialektik des Kapitalismus') is inoperative when, as today 'the substance of capital itself is thoroughly satiric' ('... der materielle Körper des Kapitalismus in allen Dingen an sich selbst Satyre ist'), renders obsolete traditional forms and conceptions of art. Claiming that the simple reproduction of conditions is sufficient in itself she refers to 'the recently published *Die Kloake* (*The Cesspool*) where through the compilation of material *grotesque* effect is achieved in representing the contemporary history of war and counter-revolution'.[28] The bourgeoisie are still willing to see their snouts reflected in art: should Dada wish to deconstruct 'capitalist satire' then they must abandon the ambition for art and, problematically, the 'bridge to capitalism' ('die Brücke zum Kapitalismus') with it.[29] Dada, earnestly revolutionary as it appears, must become the enemy of the bourgeois order, not a mirror of its spectacle. Its practice will have to concern itself with the technical world first developed by capitalism ('... mit Techniken ... die der Kapitalismus ... erst entwickelt hat'), to the extent that we can hope that 'we are at a beginning of an art, in line with an original instance ... one probably technically impoverished but one showing an honest artistic countenance'.[30] Märten's writing here intuits an important concept, whose role will only be recognised much later, that of anti-art, a concept which would address that moment of bridge breaking and reconstructing which she believed Dada must accomplish.[31]

---

28   *Revolution und Realismus* 1978, pp. 85–6. '... und ich weise auf das eben in München erschienene Buch *Die Kloake*, wo nur noch Anordnung des Stoffes nach *grotesker* Wirkung hin geschiet: der Stoff selbst aber der Auschnitt: Weltkrieg – grosse Zeit und Konterrevolution – von Zeit und Geschichte, von Geist und Wirken dieser Gesellschaft selbst im Original geliefert ist. Und dies ist allerdings blutige Satyre genug'.

29   Grosz's many images of 'snouted' bourgeoisie were, however, unlikely to please them. Her friendship with two Berlin Dadaists, Hannah Hoch and Raoul Hausmann, must have informed much of her thinking on Dada. Hausmann's interest in the mechanical and the optical: his hostility to capitalism, his espousal of montage as revolutionary not only in content but also form, the technical as a source for the refocusing of social consciousness.

30   *Revolution und Realismus* 1978, p. 86. '... soweit wir auf einen künstlerischen Anfang hier, dem ursprünglichen Wesen der Künste nach ... ein vielleicht technisch hilfloses – aber künstlerich ehrliches Gesicht zeigen wird'.

31   Berlin Dadaist Hans Richter introduces the designation of the concept in his 1971 book *Dada, Art and Anti-Art*. Adorno in his *Aesthetic Theory* (1986, pp. 42–3) articulates dialectically its critical function: 'Just as all art is secularised transcendence, so all art participates in the dialectic of enlightenment. Art has faced the challenge of this dialectic by develop-

As her Dada article is to a great degree a new departure in her work, it is necessary to provide a context for this. Between 1917 and 1919 she was employed by the Russian Telegraph Agency (ROSTA) in Berlin, where she met some Russian employees who transmitted knowledge of cultural developments taking place in Russia. Two articles, both of 1919, indicate if not a completely newfound interest, then at least a newly informed engagement with them: they were 'Proletkult' and 'Maschine und Diktatur'. The former is an exhortatory address to the readers of the USPD paper *Freiheit*, in the rhetorical manner of much post-revolution writing on art as an agent of social transformation. General in detail there is no specific reference to the Proletkult programme, although some of Bogdanov's writings, including *Die Kunst und das Proletariat*, were available in German translation that year. It does contain the explicit rejection of 'the bourgeois heritage in total' ('... doch nicht den Kult des Bürgertums erben ... wir alles überwinden, was von da kommt').[32] In her Naumann/Werkbund-influenced phase she wrote of the 'dictatorship of the machine' with its dehumanising capitalist division of labour as the enemy of art but now in Russia a productive alliance between workers' interests and artists leads to a 'social dictatorship' ('... sozialen Dikatur').[33] Under 'communist production', with artists participating as engineers, a 'rationality of the medium' (*Vernunft des Mittels*), commensurate with the artistic skills of earlier art becomes possible. The question of 'how do we overcome capitalism?' has been answered: the question now is 'how do we overcome the existing broader effects' of the system? On the question of art – 'an art of the machine'. 'The materialist insight and answer', she concludes, 'can only be: Overcome the machine through the machine' ('Überwindung der Maschine durch die Maschine').[34] There is a third text which provides a more informative context for the perceptions advanced above, referencing historical and dialectical materialism, the arts in Russia and other related material. This is *Historisch-Materialistisches über Wesen und Veränderung der Künste* (Historical Materialism on the Substance and Transformation of the Arts). This brochure is a more substantial work than her previous articles. The original text is dated 'Summer 1920', contemporary with her Dada review. As it forms the starting point for a series of exchanges between Alexander and Märten, its consideration is postponed until Chapter 3.

---

ing the concept of anti-art. From now on, no art will be conceived without the moment of anti-art. This means no less than that art has to go beyond its own concept in order to remain faithful to itself'.

32   May 1982, pp. 43–5, 45.
33   This phase will be set out in detail in Chapter 3.
34   This article is summarised in Kambas 1988, p. 127.

4 Das Proletarische Theater

The same forces – the critics Alexander and Märten, the Dadaists, now including Erwin Piscator, co-founder of the Proletarisches Theater, came into conflict later in the year. The occasion was the opening of the theatre and, in the case of Alexander, its first night programme in October 1920. The central issue is again that of heritage and innovation, but Piscator introduces a new dimension, that of deploying heritage in a radically 'umfunktioniert' (ideologically restructured) manner. Whereas Behne saw the future potential of Dada in filmic structure its practice could also be employed in theatre as a type of 'applied' Dada, Dada 'in the round' as it were. Piscator's experimental theatre would later have a profound effect on the theory and practice of leftist cultural production.[35]

As with many of the theories and practices of culture during this immediate post-revolutionary period, and not just in Germany, the urgency of political events must be borne in mind – these exchanges are not mere hypothetical speculation: Grosz and Heartfield wrote their 'Kunstlump' philippic in the context of the counter-revolutionary Kapp Putsch and the workers' armed opposition to it: Alexander's negative critique of the opening night was undoubtedly influenced by the continuing White Terror forces – the programme for the opening was framed with the slogan 'Gegen den weissen Schrecken – für Sowjetrussland' ('Against the White Terror – for Soviet Russia'), and one of the plays staged was 'Vor dem Tore' ('At the Gate'), to which Piscator refers in the programme, '... of a camp where your comrades are imprisoned in Horthy's Hungary'.[36]

Unlike the Dada-Messe the Proletarisches Theater had a more institutional dimension as its full title proclaimed: Das 'Proletarsche Theater, Bühne der Revolutionären Arbeiter Gross Berlins' ('The theatre of the revolutionary workers of Greater-Berlin'). A call for the founding of such a theatre was published in their council paper *Räte-Zeitung*. Factory organisations were invited to contribute, as were the factory councils; also represented were the USPD, KAPD, and the KPD, who, as Piscator noted, 'the KPD, or at least its spokesmen, were

---

35 Piscator 1980. Piscator studied theatre history and acting in Munich. He experienced trench warfare. He joined the KPD on the day that Grosz, Heartfield, and Herzfelde did, and, as John Willett wrote, 'was turned into a Dadaist by Herzfelde'.

36 Piscator 1980, p. 44. The play was written by a Hungarian communist for the Proletarian Theatre in Budapest at the time of the Hungarian Soviet. Admiral Horthy suppressed the Hungarian Council Republic and was to remain dictator of Hungary into the 1930s.

so cool to us from the beginning ...'.[37] Politically united in their objective of overthrowing the bourgeois order, they differed markedly on cultural grounds, as their programme and their protagonists would make manifest, particularly between the KPD and the KAPD. The outlines of such programmes were set out in the opening night special issue of *Der Gegner*, edited by Herzfelde, whose fellow board member Gumpertz was delegated as KPD representative to the theatre committee.

There are at least three crucial points raised by Piscator relative to a developing materialist aesthetic. He recognises the contribution of Dada but announces its supersession: 'Dada laughed! And thus the whole buffoonery was consummated. Dada, although recognising where eradicating art led, was not the solution'. He proposes a progressive strategy with regard to the heritage. It will not always be necessary to prioritise the political tendency of the author, for as long as the public and the theatre want revolutionary culture, 'it will be possible to make almost any bourgeois play, be it that it expresses the decline of the bourgeoisie or that the capitalist principle is clearly recognisable in it, serve to strengthen thought for the class struggle or to deepen insights into historical necessities'.[38] Just as world history can be deployed in the furthering of politicising class consciousness, 'so also can the greater part of world literature serve the same purpose'.[39] Then there are the questions of form and style. 'Form is everything', he writes, 'but form alone can never be revolutionary. Content makes it that ...', later suggesting that the author 'must learn from political leaders'. Style, too, may be discovered there, as he proposes in an earlier passage: the style must be 'completely concrete (rather like the style of a manifesto written by Lenin ..., which by its simple, composed fluency, its unambiguous clarity, produces a great emotional effect')'.[40]

---

37   Piscator 1980, p. 51.

38   Piscator's adaptation of Schiller's *Die Räuber* in 1929 is a pertinent instance of this project in light of Mehring's and Luxemburg's pre-war evaluation of the playwright's relevance for the proletariat; see above and Piscator 1963, Ch. 12.

39   The other co-founder, Herman Schüller, spells out the range of sources for proletarian theatre ('die proletarische Schauspielkunst'): 'it will have to learn from Impressionism and Expressionism, from all the "isms", from Sudermann, from Goethe and Dada'. 'Proletkult-Proletarisches Theater', Fähnders and Rector 1974b, pp. 198–203, 201. Impressionism was sometimes used for Naturalism, Sudermann was a major Naturalist playwright, in whom Mehring had detected socialist sympathies.

40   Fähnders and Rector 1974b, pp. 194–7, 196, 194. Ironically, Lenin brought his 'unambiguous clarity' to bear on some of the activities of the KAPD and 'left-wing' communism, which was considered above.

The opening paragraph of Schüller's contribution to the programme introduces probably the most contentious issue confronting the development of a materialist aesthetic practice. He briefly introduced what Proletkult was and differentiated it from the Commissariat of Enlightenment, whose function was to execute 'the cultural politics of the Soviet state' ('die Durchführung der staatlich – sowjetischen Kulturpolitik'). 'The work', he continued, 'can be opportunistic and dangerous for the proletariat if it is not executed from the point of view of Proletkult', chief amongst which is 'the awakening of the cultural consciousness of the proletariat' and the promotion of their artistic work. The aim of the revolution for Proletkult is 'not the dictatorship, rather the elimination of the dictatorship' ('... das Ziel der Revolution ist nicht die Diktatur, das Ziel die Beseitigung der Diktatur überhaupt'), not democratic centralism.[41] 'Culture', Schüller wrote, 'is the logical completion of the social revolution, which is dependent on the development of self-consciousness of the proletariat'. Within this cultural-political ambience, the 'subjective revolutionary moment' pressed hard upon the 'objective revolutionary moment' for precedence at the interface of KAPD and KPD programmes, marking a fault line of high tension, to be discussed further below. Schüller acknowledges the dialectical mediations between the economic, political, and cultural but emphasises that on these grounds alone it is not possible to raise the 'strength of spirit of the revolution' (... die Atemkraft der Revolution). Drawing upon the work of Bogdanov he writes, 'The most important means here is the organisation of feelings and ideas through art which is in accordance with revolutionary class struggle' ('Das wichtigste Mittel hierzu ist die Organisation der Gefühle und der Vorstellungen durch die Kunst ...'). He had earlier referred to the psychological dimension of collective consciousness: the proletarian theatre can achieve the organisation of feeling and ideas 'through its formal means, oratorical, recitative, imagistic, musical, cinematographic, theatrical', whereby the evening becomes a celebration 'transformed into the living embodiment of communist

---

41   A passage in the 'Räte-Zeitung', calling for the establishing of a proletarian theatre (see above) also draws attention to these issues. As the economic conditions for the victory of the socialist revolution are being daily fulfilled, 'the major revolutionary requirement is clarification, strengthening and deepening of revolutionary consciousness. Revolutionary art is the means for this revolutionary consciousness: it organises, as Rosa Luxemburg taught and as Proletkult shows, our feeling, it mobilises heads and hearts for proletarian class struggle' ('Sie organisiert, wie uns Rosa Luxemburg lehrt und es der russische Proletkult zeigt ...'). Fähnders and Rector 1974a, pp. 203–5, 204. Luxemburg opposed Lenin on democratic centralism, Proletkult claimed autonomy, positions which represented those of the KAPD.

thought' ('einer lebendigen Verkörperung des kommunistischen Gedankens gestaltet werden').[42]

Alexander's critique of the first night performance confirmed Piscator's remark on the 'coolness' of the KPD spokesmen towards their enterprise. There was a need for a proletarian theatre but this wasn't it: 'Proletarian Theatre! The entrance swarmed with bourgeois literati related to Dada, with their pretension to erase bourgeois art'. The programme, which she seems to have bought from Herzfelde's wife, convinced her that what was being presented was propaganda: why call it theatre and not propaganda? 'The designation theatre commits to art, to artistic achievement'. Art should be a 'hallowed undertaking' ('ein zu heilige Sache'), its name not sacrificed to bungling propaganda. And is not communism also to be so hallowed that it should not be subject to such coloured poster-style treatment and bad caricature?[43] 'Is it not grotesque', Alexander continues, 'that now when daily events cry out for action, where all await, Russia awaits, Hungary awaits, the proletariat of the entire world awaits, that the German proletariat decides at this moment to open in

42   Fähnders and Rector 1974b, pp. 198–203, 198, 199, 200, 202. Schüller was the strongest advocate of Proletkult in Germany at this time, where it had a low profile. Psychoanalysis had a particular resonance in the KAPD, especially in the writing of the Dadaist Franz Jung, whose work will be considered below: briefly, the psychoanalyst Otto Gross, an associate of Berlin Dadaists, had, in opposition to his teacher, Freud, elaborated a socially informed psychoanalysis.

43   The programme in *Der Gegner* anticipated such a response: they were presenting this despite its shortfalls, its almost simplification of the problems, anaemic dialogue. But it was not about art and virtuosity, but rather the will to life, the awakening of the communist world view should seize the stage. Märten's perceptions for the 'impoverished' beginnings for the new art in her Dada review are echoed here. A much later positive judgement on the contribution of these artists towards a proletarian art is to be found in an essay by the former East German art historian Ursula Horn, in her 'Einflüsse des Anarchismus auf die Anfänge proletarisch-revolutionärer Kunst' ('The Influences of Anarchism on the Beginnings of Proletarian-Revolutionary Art'): 'The developmental path of Felixmüller, Grosz, Heartfield and others indicate that from an anarcho-radical desire to overthrow ... the way to the scientific world view of the party of the working class was possible. The revolutionary works of Dix ... Grosz, Heartfield belong in the art which fulfilled, through the deployment of avantgardist artistic mediums and methods, specific demands in class struggle' ('... dass von einem anarcho-radikalistischen Umsturzverlangen ... der Weg zur wissenschaftlichen Weltanschauung der Partei der Arbeiterklasse möglich war ... und anderen gehören zu einer Kunst, der es darum ging unter Ausnutzung avantgardistischer künstlerischer Mittel und Methoden spezifische Aufgaben im Klassenkampf zu erfüllen'), Horn 1977, pp. 29–43, 40–1. Lu Märten's work was being reassessed by a colleague, Rainhard May, at the same time. He delivered a paper on her 1920s work to the same forum in 1979. His assessment of her contribution will be set out in Chapter 6.

Berlin a theatre they call "proletarian" and put Bolshevism on the stage'![44] She devotes short passages to each of the three one-act plays and finds that 'the spark ignited by the art work is absent'.[45] Alexander broadens her critique to that of the relationship between intellectuals, workers, Proletkult and proletarian art. Do intellectuals mislead workers with talk of Proletkult and worker art (Arbeiterkunst), when workers 'are not yet ready for independent judgement' ('... noch nicht reif zu selbständigen Urteil') and impose their ideas on them? The programme 'Comrade Schüller' has set out could have value but 'unfortunately it is for the most part condemned to remain theory' ('... nur leider verurteilt zum grössten Teil Theorie zu bleiben ...'). There is almost no proletarian art and art is not something to be produced by decree, propaganda or encouragement. In what is a very traditional conceptualisation, she states that the production of art requires the creative personality, 'an innate gift', not instruction. What the worker needs today is 'a strong art which sets the spirit free'. Such art can be of bourgeois origin but it must be art. Rather than the representation of the immiseration on view here – she imagines the spectators crawling back home dispirited – something that outsoars it, which feels powerful and combative must replace it. 'Do what only you can do', she writes, 'elect a poet from your ranks but he must be a poet! Such a poet is Max Barthel', 'select him as your banner'.[46] 'Should you produce a dramatist', she continues, 'then a proletarian theatre could be established; in the meantime you could look to Schiller' ('The Robbers', 'Love and Intrigue') until one emerges. She reverses to a degree Piscator's statement on the determining relationship of content to form: 'Form makes content into art – without form content remains mere actuality' as that evening's presentation was. 'I must insist', she concludes, 'I am not talk-

---

44   'Russlands Tag' dealt with the Allied intervention in Russia. A passive German worker is 'informed' by Russian and Hungarian workers of the intervention and the 'White Terror', the armed operations of world capitalism. The German worker and spectators join their comrades, breaking down international barriers. The programme note underlined the urgency, quoting Luxemburg: 'Entweder Sozialismus oder Untergang in der Barberei' ('either socialism or the descent into barbarism'). The text of the play was published in *Der Gegner* in 1920–21, no. 4. It is available in the 1979 reprint of the journal by Das Arsenal Verlag, pp. 94–103.

45   One of the plays, 'Der Krüppel', appears under the name of 'Julius Haidvogel', a pseudonym for Karl Wittfogel, who would later ignite a crucial debate from the mid-1920s on a revision of Mehring's contribution, a critique of Trotsky, culminating in a series of articles in *Die Linkskurve* in 1930 on the issue of a Marxist aesthetic, to which Lu Märten would respond.

46   Alexander would later write very positively on his work in 'Literaturbesprechung' ('Literature Review') in 1921. Fähnders and Rector 1974a, pp. 96–100, 98–9. She also mentions Erwin Hoernle approvingly, who would later become a critic and theorist of worker photography.

ing about artistic pleasure but about experience ("Erlebnis"), as exemplified in Greek tragedy'.[47]

Two articles by Märten from 1921, on the need for a revolutionary press, particularly its feuilleton or cultural section and for a proletarian theatre, address these issues but in a more indirect manner.[48] For Märten the feuilleton is, like the proletarian theatre, the potential site of proletarian presence and participation. Presently, like mainstream theatre, it is the arena of bourgeois culture. In order to incorporate it fully into cultural struggle, a Brechtian-type 'umfunktionieren' is called for: 'the specialised and technically virtuosic journalism and feuilleton style developed by the bourgeois press, and to which all cultural workers who are engaged in it succumb, more or less unconsciously – cannot undertake the new cultural tasks demanded, so consequently it must be revolutionised': 'Only those committed to the left can do so. Increasingly there is the necessity to make available material hitherto found only in books and journals, not just on politics and economics' but also 'on the general context of cultural issues' ('... an den gesamten Komplex geistiger Dinge'.) The constant struggles of working-class life prevent in general the possibility of accessing these resources: the revolutionised feuilleton will allow the worker to realise that these cultural goods 'are very close to him and reside within him, and that the historical roots of all cultural manifestations are not to be thought of as separated from his own class struggle'.[49] Polemics and discussions on particular questions on the arts belong there, 'all that in historical and economic interrelationships remain to be analysed' ('... alles das, in dem

---

47   Gumpertz responded briefly, on Herzfelde's behalf also, accusing *Die Rote Fahne* critic of 'judging such experimental attempts with bourgeois criteria' ('... mit den maßstäben der bürgerlichen Kunstkritik heranzutreten ...'). Fähnders and Rector 1974a, pp. 211–12, 212. Alexander's understanding of the role of form here is at odds with Marx's theorising on the relationship, the shaping role of content vis-á-vis form: Piscator is in agreement with Marx.

48   'Die revolutionäre Presse und das Feuilleton' was published in *Der Gegner*, in an issue which also contained Herzfelde's 'Gesellschaft, Künstler und Kommunismus' and extracts from Franz Jung's play 'Wie lange noch, du Hure, bürgerliche Gerechtigkeit?' ('How much longer, bourgeois justice, you whore?'), written whilst he was imprisoned for his political activities. Both Herzfelde's and Jung's work will be considered later. This particular issue of *Der Gegner* can be read as a manifesto supporting the KAPD cultural politics, avantgardist/experimental in formal terms but politically engaged, in opposition to the KPD 'Erbe' (cultural heritage) programme. 'Über proletarisches Theaterbedürfnis und proletarisches Theater' was published in *Die Arbeit*.

49   May 1982, p. 102. '... dass diese Dinge ganz nahe bei ihm und in ihm liegen und dass die historischen Wurzeln jeder geistigen Erscheinung nicht zu denken und zu trennen sind von seinem eigenen Klassenkampf'.

tiefere wirtschaftliche und historische Zusammenhänge noch zu analysieren bleiben'). The starting point for such a programme, for instance, would be 'what is considered as revolutionary art or not' ('... was etwa als revolutionäre Kunst anzusehen ist oder nicht ...'), an assessment which can only be established on the basis of historical-materialist analysis and not merely a confirmation of pre-judgement. Nor must it be reductivist, that what is involved is 'simple analogy with economic phenomena to arrive at understanding' ('... um einfache Analo-gie der wirtschaftlichen Erscheinungen handelt um zur Klärung zu kommen'). As Marx has established the scientific understanding of the economic is a cent-ral but preparatory orientation and pathway to the cultural complex, 'it does not account for the specifics of the work, but rather initially points towards it' ('... aber sie erübrigt die eigentliche Arbeit darüber nicht, sondern weist auf diese erst hin').

As with Piscator's theatre, the role of the writer would be to engage the reader actively, stripping away the 'conceptual clothing of bourgeois terms'. Until now some articles on what was 'good or bad' in art were provided for the worker, before which 'he *must* remain uninformed and which he must accept uncritically, *because he was not provided with the tool of the critic – only with the criticism*' ('... *das er kritiklos hinnehmen muss, weil ihm nicht das Werkzeug der Kritik geliefert wird sondern nur die Kritik*').[50] On the basis of these demands – revolutionising the relationship of writer to reader (collabor-ators) and for analysis supported by 'deeper' investigation of the relationship of the economic and the historical to the cultural – Märten raises a number of important issues; for instance, the supposition that the cultural products of high capitalism (Hochkapitalismus) are inescapably decayed and reprehens-ible, whilst at the same time those of early capitalism (Frühkapitalismus) are judged considerately – and deserve to be saved, at least for cultural memory: such an approach possesses 'negligible revolutionary knowledge value' ('... hat ebenso wenig revolutionäre Erkenntniswert'). Controversially, and in what can be read as an anti-Erbe position, she claims that historically considered, the art of early capitalism betrays the same elements as those found in high capital-

---

50   In the brief introduction to her 1920 brochure *Historisches-Materialistisches über Wesen und Veränderung der Künste* (Eine pragmatische Einleitung), Märten indicates clearly that this passive reception has to be radically altered. Her purpose in the brochure is 'to mark the entry points in order to stimulate the collaborative thinking of the readers ... in a cer-tain direction. ... As an orientation for collaborative work every listener and questioner is here a co-worker' ('... Als Orientierung für Mitdenken und Mitarbeit, den jeder Hörende, Fragende ist hier Mitarbeiter'). As this publication was to initiate the important exchanges between Märten and Alexander on the question of historical materialism and the arts, it will be considered separately below, in Chapter 3.

ism. Unless analysis which clarifies difference takes place, she continues, 'an unexplained synthesis results; opinion, not knowledge'.[51] Cultural aspirations on the left must also be subject to rigorous analysis, for instance 'the vague promise expressed for a renewal and flowering of all the arts under socialism remains an empty phrase so long as its probability is not more clearly indicated'.[52] Similarly with the claim that only in a communist society 'will the arts be renewed and become fruitful again': such an overwhelming thesis cannot be used as a measure of judgement for the manifold appearances of cultural artefacts, 'it must be the result of analysis, not its point of departure' ('... sie ist Ergebnis, nicht Ausgangspunkt der Analyse').[53] The core of her theory is the dialectical interrelationships between the irreducibility of the specificity of the cultural artefact and its historical-materialist environment, as contained in the penultimate paragraph of her article. There she writes: 'Artistic products originate and stimulate not only programmed energies, not only *intelligible ideas*, nor just only *non-conceptual representations*, but in their specificities, through their orientations and urgencies, clarify and confirm in an historical manner

---

51   This passage reflects a larger historical enterprise Märten was engaging in, which would be published in book form in 1924. Its shorter 1920 version as a brochure was referred to in the previous footnote. Briefly, she seeks to give an account of the origin and development of the arts based on Marx's theory of labour: 'art arose from labour and primitive life form' ('Dass Kunst aus Arbeit und primitiven Leben entstand') is how she succinctly presents it in her article on the revolutionary press. The reference to the art of earlier and later capitalism may owe something to her knowledge of her friend Hausenstein's materialist accounts of late medieval, Renaissance and Baroque visual art (see the Appendix below).

52   This criticism is probably directed at some of the ecstatic Expressionist manifestos and declarations published immediately after the November revolution, in particular by 'Die Novembergruppe', 'Der Arbeitsrat für Kunst', 'Rat geistiger Arbeiter' and others, where the presence of 'Rat' (council) attempts to indicate solidarity with workers, soldiers and sailors. They were the subject of Dada critique.

53   This last passage reflects an approach she articulated in an article from 1920, 'Revolutionäre Dichtung in Deutschland', published in the journal *Die Erde*. Establishing the decline of bourgeois culture is only part of the issue: it remains 'to investigate in which direction the dissolution and emancipation from the form and content of the transition is proceeding and to which solutions and new developments it is pointing – which new human artistic ideas (today it is proletarian) are already there in preparation' ('... zu untersuchen in welcher Richtung die Auflösung und die Emanzipation von Form und Inhalt der Überlieferung vor sich geht und zu welchen Lösungen oder Neubildungen sie hinweisen – welche darin neuen menschlichen, (d.h. heute proletarischen) Kunstvorstellungen darin schon enthalten oder vorgebildet sind'). This was a special edition of the journal *alternative* devoted to 'Lu Märtens Kunsttheorie zwischen, marxschen Arbeitsbegriff und sozialdemokratischer Technikgläubigkeit', containing a selection of her writing and articles on them (*alternative* 1973, p. 101).

and achieve a considerable amount of knowledge, whilst simultaneously posing questions for the future'.[54]

In her article on the need for a proletarian theatre, Märten does not address the Piscator theatre as did the Alexander review, but places the necessity within an historical outline of theatre. Two major positions concerning the development of a materialist aesthetic, consistent with her ideas in the Dada and revolutionary press articles, are reinforced here. In her Dada review she speculated on the art of the future, that it might be a 'technically impoverished' art, at least to begin with. She supported Piscator's deployment of the strategy of recycling contemporary material from newspapers ('... politische Propaganda in Rede und Schrift'), and agreed with the decision not to employ the distractive technical advances of bourgeois theatre ('... nicht die technische Mittel des bürgerlichen theatrakalischen Herkommens zu übernehmen'). Even within such apparent limitations, workers would experience something more than could be obtained purely through political propaganda, she speculates that 'theatre could once again become genuine theatre, genuine play, the pure freedom of play' – she has in mind its pre-bourgeois history. More radical is her questioning of the continuing existence of any particular artistic genre *per se*, here the theatre, a questioning which was crucial for the argument on the culture of the transitional, post-revolutionary period in its progress towards the dictatorship of the proletariat. 'Until now', she writes, 'we have always thought and debated ... that the old contents and forms of art must change. In my opinion the first revolutionary question is not that, but rather to what extent that which exists, the presence of a specific art – here the theatre – is really and self-evidently necessary for a future culture'.[55]

Her position here is less clearly articulated than that of the founders of the Proletarisches Theater, Piscator and Schüller, who saw the 'umfunktionieren' of any drama from the past as available for their purposes, but nonetheless she is in agreement with that seemingly technically impoverished undertaking in its 1920–21 moment. At this point then clearly opposed positions on the practice and theory of art are becoming marked – between the Mehring-derived doc-

---

54 May 1982, p. 104. 'Die künstlerischen Produkte erregen und entstammen eben nicht nur programmatischen Energien, nicht nur *verstandesgemässen* und eben so *nicht nur begrifflosen* Vorstellungen. Sie in ihren Gattungen nach der einen oder andern Neigung und Notwendigkeit historisch erklären und festellen, heisst schon ein gut Stück auch für diese Erkenntnis – und sie ist immer auch eine Frage der Zukunft zugleich – leisten.'

55 Kambas 1988, p. 143. 'Meines Erachtens aber ist die erste revolutionäre Frage nicht das, sondern, inwiefern ein Vorhandensein, das Dasein einer bestimmten Kunst – hier das Theater – überhaupt für eine künftige Kultur notwendig und selbstverständlich ist'.

trine of the role of the heritage, now also the orthodoxy of the KPD, and the 'avantgardist' formal tendencies of the KAPD programme. The novels and plays of Franz Jung, the third figure in that *Gegner* issue would further exacerbate that division.

5   Franz Jung: Activist and Artist

Jung was an extraordinary rather than an exemplary figure in leftist cultural politics at the time and for that reason it is enlightening to briefly outline a biographical sketch in order to be aware of what engaging in cultural work might entail. He studied economics, law, and art, wrote his dissertation on the effects of taxation on the match industry (later, in temporary exile in post-revolutionary Russia, he would be instrumental in setting up a match factory). Working in Munich he came into contact with the art world, including the psychoanalyst Otto Gross, described as one of Freud's most brilliant students. Moving to Berlin he became acquainted with Franz Pfemfert, editor of the prestigious political and cultural journal *Die Aktion*, then supportive of Expressionism but which would after the war become a major agent of KAPD cultural politics.[56] Jung supported himself by writing for the stock market pages of a major Berlin economics publisher. He volunteered for military service, deserted and was incarcerated. Released on the advice of Otto Gross, he established the journal *Die Freie Strasse* (*The Open Road*) in 1916, which espoused the social psychoanalysis of Gross, placing property and patriarchy as the core components of individual psychic malfunctioning, a position which had led to his split with Freud. He edited *Die Neue Jugend*, which would become the first Dada journal in Germany, became co-editor of Club Dada, through which he met all the members of the Berlin Dada grouping. George Grosz described him and his effect as follows: 'The aesthetic dimension was retained but increasingly put under pressure by a type of anarcho-nihilistic politics whose principal proponent was Franz Jung ... a Rimbaud-type figure, audacious, an adventurous nature which held back from nothing. He allied himself with us, and as the powerful personality he was, he immediately influenced the whole Dada movement'.[57]

---

56   In a cultural sense, he may fit a pattern in that his progress towards a radical left position
        was via war-time Expressionism. The relative German interest in Proletkult was informed
        by this Expressionism. The co-founder of the Proletarisches Theater, Hermann Schüller,
        was an example of this trajectory.

57   Grosz 1974 [1955], p. 129. '... und als der Gewaltmensch, der er war, beeinflusste er sofort
        die ganze Dadabewegung'.

As a Spartacist he participated in the November Revolution, was imprisoned but escaped. He joined the KPD but was expelled in 1919, whereupon he became a founder-member of the KAPD. With two others he captured a fishing trawler and sailed to Russia to plead the KAPD's cause for membership of the Communist International but discussions with Lenin, Bukharin, and Radek failed to convince them. Upon his return to Germany, he was found guilty of 'piracy on the high seas' and was imprisoned. Whilst there he wrote a number of novels and two plays later to be staged by Piscator at the Proletarisches Theater. On release he participated in the 'March Days' armed insurrection in central Germany (described by Chris Harman as the 'March madness' – see Chapter 4), escaped to Holland, from where he was deported to Russia in temporary exile. From the foregoing it is obvious that here is a complex assemblage of political activity and cultural engagement: the following paragraphs will delineate how these components interacted and how they related to the KAPD's programme.

Jung published a polemical article, 'Proletarische Erzählungskunst' (Proletarian Narrative Art) in the paper *Proletarier* in 1920, which begins with a very clear statement about the present condition of literary production in Germany. 'Proletkult', he wrote, 'had nothing to do with proletarian art; at best it was one of the means by which proletarian art might be developed'.[58] Art is the product of class, class ideology and struggle. Bourgeois ideology speaks only for the individual, not the universal. Influenced by Otto Gross's social psychoanalysis and a concept of 'Vitalism' from his artistic contacts in Munich, Jung characterises bourgeois society as being no longer creative, of being devoid of the originary strength of the community, of lacking the 'vitalism' to shape life, the 'Lebendigen im Leben'. Proletkult thinking is included within this perception – in Germany Proletkult is confused with proletarian art, a sign that Proletkult is still a bourgeois affair: 'of course there is no proletarian art in Germany but possibly it is at a very early stage'.[59] Now bourgeois feuilletonists suddenly discover proletarian works past and present: even the feuilletons of *Die Rote Fahne* (KPD), *Freiheit* (USPD), the literary critics of the *Junge Garde* are no different. Parties supportive of the proletariat must declare what they perceive its essence to be and what its role in the renewal and humanisation of society is to be. The question of proletarian art, not incidental as many believe, must not become a parade ground for literati who have nothing to do with the proletariat. The community thinking of an oppressed class in its struggle against its oppressor whilst simultaneously establishing its own structures finds little space in world

---

58   Fähnders and Rector 1974b, pp. 125–8.
59   Berlin Dadaists were sceptical of Proletkult: Raoul Hausmann satirised it in 'Puffke propagiert Proletkult', Puffke being the self-satisfied philistine.

literature, in Germany almost none. Strangely, however, it is stronger in Western Europe and in Anglo-American literature.[60] For Jung the difference between East and West is understandable: the problem of proletarian art is dependent on the level of development of the self-consciousness of the proletariat ('abhängig ist von dem Grad der Selbstbewusstseinsentwicklung des Proletariats'). For him it is further indication that the centre of gravity of revolutionary strategy had increasingly shifted westward, having to adapt to the already fully developed self-consciousness of Western proletarians from the moment when the security and experience of proletarian ideas had become the inevitable condition for the preservation of the political power seized. Art was the source of incitement for the development of this self-consciousness. KAPD cultural strategists had drawn up a counter-heritage tradition of writers and artists, including Rabelais, Swift, Georg Büchner, Zola, Anatole France, the contemporary Irish writer Patrick McGill, Upton Sinclair, and Jack London. Jung discusses some of these and singles out Jack London on two grounds: the absence of artistic quality in the accepted sense and the presence of the 'rhythmic collectivity' of events throughout ('... enthalten durchaus den Rhythmuskollektiven Geschehens'), a quality Jung espoused and strove for in his own writing. H.G. Wells's works he praised for their fantasies within which proletarian art was to be found.

An anonymous sympathetic article on Jung's own writing appeared in *Die Rote Fahne* in 1922, under the title 'Was soll der Proletarier lesen. Franz Jung?' (What Should the Proletarian Read?)[61] 'Working-class men and women read the popular novels of the day, why so – not having anything in common with their class enemy? Certainly one cannot always be reading books on politics but "there must be a type of novel possible which engages with the real and serious in life", those aspects with which we struggle daily, confused, but of which we say "despite everything it must be otherwise"'. 'This revolutionary struggle', the writer continues, 'in which we engage daily on two fronts, with others and with ourselves' ('... den wir heute täglich gleichsam gegen zwei Fronten, mit den anderen und mit uns selbst führen ...'). Nor do we want sermons on street struggles from political novels. It must be possible to pursue answers to the

---

60   His remarks on the 'new Russia' repeat those on Germany: it also 'offers no proletarian art' ('Das neue Russland bietet noch keine proletarische Kunst'). 'It sticks obstinately to proclaiming art *for* the proletariat' ('Es versteift sich auf eine Riesenpropaganda der Kunst *für* das Proletariat'). This echoes Schüller's reservations above that Proletkult might become 'democratic centralism' in the cultural arena and reflects the general suspicion of Leninism in the KAPD.

61   Brauneck 1973, pp. 162–5.

questions that precisely address our struggle for the revolution, 'the question the Russian Tolstoy expressed so unambiguously but never answered: What is to be done?' Such novels do exist but are mostly ignored, are even ignored by many of the workers' press. Franz Jung ruthlessly poses that question and answers it ('So rücksichtslos stellt die Frage Franz Jung und er gibt auch eine Antwort darauf'). The writer lists Jung's works, all published by Herzfelde at the Malik Verlag. It is not a matter of 'good' or 'bad novels': whatever Jung writes is fundamentally different from bourgeois writing. There are no agitational or accusatory books: 'one could call them experiments for a revolutionary life' ('man könnte sie Versuche zum revolutionären Leben nennen'). Bourgeois writers have developed, as a diversionary tactic, a structure of literary technique and articulation, employed for the most refined ideological instrument of domination along set narrative lines. To the contrary, 'Franz Jung addresses from the start those whose lives the social revolution benefits, proletarian life and no other' ('... deren Leben der sozialen Revolution gilt, deshalb handelt es sich bei ihm um das proletarische Leben, um sonst nichts'). There are no heroes, the address is to the present, not some distant future. Jung speaks of 'proletarians' as they act together in a revolutionary manner, class in all its dimensions is represented. Here lies 'our present duty' ('unsere gegenwärtige Aufgabe ...'). Jung's answer to the question 'What is to be done?' is compressed into a few sentences at the end of *Arbeitsfriede*, a novel set in the housing estate of that name: 'We, believers in community ... intend power to be the wider unfolding of the human, the deeper understanding of that which lives. One day all will see justice and truth. Who will decide – not you, but later life, the community'. The writer is here picking up on a particular dimension of Jung's perception of a communal rhythm (Gemeinschaftsrhythmus) which owed something to Otto Gross's social psychoanalysis.

Die Rote Fahne also reviewed the first production of Jung's 'Die Kanaker' at the Proletarisches Theater in April 1921.[62] The reviewer describes it as a 'piece between theatre and reality', an extract from our life today, images typical of the way in which the fate of the proletariat proceeds. The performance begins with what might be seen as an early instance of a Verfremdungseffekt (distancing effect): the curtain rises to disclose a couple 'standing and kissing', they are 'startled and embarrassed' before the public and run off. 'The distance between

---

62   Brauneck 1973, pp. 117–21. The title comes from the name of a mythic cannibalistic tribe whose leaders devoured its own members lest they should challenge authority. For Jung this represented the fundamental thinking of the bourgeoisie in its class struggle with the proletariat ('Dies ist der Grundgedanke des bürgerlichen Klassenkampfes gegen das Proletariat').

stage and reality is removed', the reviewer continues. The spectator feels that a 'forbidden view' into real life has occurred, that 'she has witnessed not a piece of theatre but rather a moment in real life'. Such a feeling is generated at many points throughout; 'here', the reviewer continues, 'lies the specific quality of this art ... the fusion of art and propaganda, not through the lecture, nor through the obtrusive precision of the propagandist's purpose, but simply that the spectator is drawn into its play, that everything played on the stage matters to her' ('... die Verschmelzung von Kunst und Propaganda, nicht durch Lehrhaftigkeit und nicht durch aufdringliche Deutlichkeit der propagandischen Absicht ...'). There is spontaneous audience participation at certain moments, responses to happenings on the stage, for example, recognition of a police attack on workers. The reviewer identified two related core concepts in Jung's intentions, the potential social productivity of Proletarian life ('das Lebendigen im Leben') and 'Gemeinschaftsrhythmus' (communal rhythm), or as Jung also expressed it in his passage on Jack London above, 'the rhythmic collectivity of events' ('... den Rhythmus kollektiven Geschehens'). He recognises the work as 'a powerful attempt to discover the new form for the content of proletarian art' ('... ein gewaltiger Versuch, zu dem Inhalt einer proletarishen Kunst die neue Form zu finden'). Just as the proletariat gropes its way forward 'in clouded consciousness' towards freedom, so too is Jung's work an attempt 'to give expression to the new which is initially unclear and fragmentary' ('... worin das Neue sich erst unklar und fragmentarisch ausdrückt') and, in a reprise of Lu Märten's assessment of the Dadaist cultural contribution above, he continues, 'it is in its unfinished manner more important and serious than all the high cultural products of the bourgeoisie'.

In its notice the KAPD provided a succinct summary of the plot. The play opens with two industrialists, one German, one Japanese, discussing the deal of selling-off the machinery for export to the latter, thereby sabotaging production and throwing the workers to their fate – the German is possibly Stinnes, who made an enormous fortune through dealings made possible by inflation in buying and selling industrial enterprises.[63] Provoked by the factory manager a quarrel erupts, the factory is occupied by the police, a lockout is imposed. Unanimous resistance, followed by anxiety, brawling, mistrust, torpor amongst the workers. The following scene switches to a bourgeois interior, the site of collaboration between police and management. The workers now rebel, occupy the factory and start it up again, celebrating by singing 'The Red Flag'. More

---

63   Stinnes was negatively represented in the visual work of Grosz, Scholz, and Schlichter
      amongst others at this time.

class-conscious workers expect a bourgeois counter-attack, which comes in the form of the 'White Terror'. The leader is shot, the occupation defeated, the curtain falls.[64]

The plot development between Acts One and Two is suspended to allow discussion on the events so far by two philosophers, Lenin (played by Piscator) and H.G. Wells. The discussion centres on revolution and class war, priming the audience to think beyond the particulars they have seen, to recognise the struggle and the cunning nature of bourgeois hegemony, the distressing stupor of the workers who are not able to see through its disguises, who see individualised instances of capitalist domination, who mistrustfully quarrel amongst themselves and fail to comprehend the totality. Neither Lenin nor Wells is quite the historical figures they were – Wells despite being praised in Jung's 'Proletarische Erzählungskunst' above is here presented as a social Darwinian. The outcome of class conflict will be a fusion of bourgeois and proletarian elites, 'a new society of men of steel – something totally new, a totally other social level', in which antagonism will be overcome. Lenin, who articulates Jung's position to an extent, rejects this social-Darwinist elite theory as the ideological justification of a bourgeois intellectual, a cynical betrayal of the masses. He acknowledges the presence of 'cannibalistic' impulses, even within the working class but it was not inherent, rather the outcome of class conflict: 'Proletarian class struggle is the opposite of cannibalism. With us those in need will not be eaten. That is capitalism, and the civil war between capital and work will be fought through the medium of capitalist ideology'. The workers must strengthen collective consciousness in this difficult present. '[O]nly the power of consciousness will steel us'.

After the final curtain falls on present defeat, male and female representatives of the working class discuss the uncoordinated actions of the workers in light of the exchanges between Lenin and Wells. The man defends spontaneous response, the discharge of pent-up anger; the woman characterises this as 'cannibalism' amongst the workers, as merely the satisfaction of a feeling of hatred in the interest of a minority, leaving the majority more vulnerable to defeat. 'Hatred deprives us of our best weapons', she claims and demands that the man attend to Lenin's assessment, not to engage in senseless actions but

---

64   Fähnders and Rector 1974b, p. 244. A reminiscence of a performance by Jung's wife Cläre
       underlines the play's actuality: 'from my own experience I can confirm the impression
       of the immediate contemporaneity: in the play there is a scene set in the backroom of
       a workers' pub whilst from the street outside the theatre the sound of police gunfire'
       ('Die Arbeiter beraten hier weitere Pläne ihres Vorgehens, während man Schüsse der Pol-
       izeitruppen hört'). Ibid.

in strengthening proletarian collectivity, the most important weapon in their struggle, and also a prerequisite for individual freedom. Their goal must be the potentially simultaneous development of individuality and real community, through which strength is achieved; in this way they would knock the sharpest weapons of the new 'war class' from their hands. Because the 'collective rhythm' ('Gemeinschaftsrhythmus') of the proletariat is not yet fully developed, they continue to suffer defeat. Within this articulation the present defeat is now being seen as a way-station to the full realisation of class self-consciousness.

6   Herzfelde's 'Gesellschaft, Künstler und Kommunismus' (1922)

As poet and participant in the Erste Dada-Messe (see above), editor of *Der Gegner*, the organ of the KAPD's aesthetic ideas, publisher of the Malik Verlag, which published Franz Jung's work amongst others (including Lukács's *History and Class Consciousness*, written in 1922 and published in 1923), and supporter of Piscator's Proletarisches Theater, Herzfelde played a crucial role in the experimental works attempting to establish cultural practices consonant with perceived proletarian potential.[65] These works were seen as enhancing the cultivation of proletarian self-consciousness, the subjective stage crucial to the realisation of the dictatorship of the proletariat, activities informed by a politically engaged cultural avantgardism parallel with the vanguard role of the party, albeit not always an easy relationship. His brochure is a sober account of the enormous difficulties confronting such a programme and is quite blunt in his presentation of them. The long essay is divided into four sections: The relationship between society and artist; The path of the artist to Communism; The duties of the communist artist in bourgeois society; and The artist in the Communist State. The focus in the following will be almost entirely on the last.

A major problem is the differing temporalities of socio-political change and cultural change. 'Whilst for almost a century', he writes, 'the practice of socialism was to hand ... artists were left to their own limited perceptions ... almost without theoretical or experiential knowledge'.[66] The primary cultural ques-

---

65   There are passages in Lukács's 'Introduction' to the 1971 reprint of the book which give a sense of the turmoil, theoretical and otherwise, of the period, if in a different register: it 'was born in the midst of the crises of its transitional period' ... 'the often mistaken tendencies of the age gives the book a certain claim to be regarded as representative. A momentous, world-historical change was struggling to find a theoretical expression' (Lukács 1971, pp. xvi, xxv).

66   Fähnders and Rector 1974b, p. 159. 'Während man politisch, ökonomisch eine fast hundert

tion is the art of the transitional period, to that time when the power attained by the proletariat facilitates proletarian art and culture. But in the meantime? This transitional period (*Übergangzeit*) may last years, decades even ('Jahre', 'Jahrzehnte'), and will require a great number of artists who worked for the bourgeoisie to now commit themselves to serving the interests of communism, a requirement common to both Germany and the Soviet Union, centred on the role of Proletkult. Herzfelde is forthright in his criticism of the lack of knowledge and interest exhibited by members of the KPD in contemporary cultural practices, particularly the visual.[67] The visual artist is not proletarian and would have to reconstruct his whole world view, indeed must to an extent relearn to think. Herzfelde suggests two stages in this process. The first is relatively quickly traversed: when he recognises his role within the party, his duties in combatting exploitation in solidarity with his comrades. But a mediated understanding is demanded, 'an intense awareness of structure and function of the diverse social elements, with true comprehensive insight into the real conditions arising from the forces of production, all to be understood from the position of communism'.[68] The second is more problematic and concerns his vocational activity (Berufstätigkeit). Until the seizure of power the party has neither museums nor stages, the proletariat provides no patronage; consequently, the artist feels left hanging ('er fühlte sich plötzlich in der Luft hängen'). The revolutionary parties in Germany have made no attempt to understand the circumstances of communist artists, nor from their Marxist training to resolve the artists' dilemma: 'Indeed', he comments, 'for revolutionary Marxists they have more often in their criticism manifested a shameful lack of understanding concerning the various "isms" and other experiments and whose convenient assertion is that all this, because it is muddled, immature, unintelligible, must be a product of bourgeois

---

    Jahre alte Praxis wie Theorie des Sozialismus zur Verfügung hat ... die Künstler sind sich selbst überlassen und ihnen individual begrenzten Anschauungen ... und ausserdem hat man hier theoretisch und erfahrungsgemäss fast kein Rüstzeug'.

67   He recounts the following instance: when a propagandist of the KPD was questioned as to why the party press did not regularly carry reasonably large images in prominent positions (as was the case in French and American papers on workers' campaigns), he replied: 'there was no room, also the party organ was not a comic paper'. There are two issues here: the activity of the Dadaists, who recognised the explosive quality of appropriated images and shredded papers for their purposes; the literary bias of the party's cultural programme. Not until the later 1920s would a more informed engagement begin to emerge, which included 'comic' papers.

68   Fähnders and Rector 1974b, p. 152. '... nur dann fruchtbar sein kann, wenn sie sich paart mit intensiver Kenntnis der Struktur und der Funktionen all der verschiedenartigen gesellschaftlichen Zellen mit wahrhaft universeller Einsiciht in die realen produktionen Kraft, diese bis in alle Einzelheiten im Sinne der kommunisten Entwicklung zu beinflussen'.

decadence' – clearly a response to Alexander's critique of the Dadaists and Piscator's Proletarisches Theater in *Die Rote Fahne*, as detailed above.[69] Herzfelde returns to this issue in a later passage, where he repeats how inappropriate the attitudes of 'our politicians' are to the immature experiments of young artists to overcome their bourgeois ways of working and thinking. The tone is now sharper: 'But this tendency is not only unjustified but extremely harmful for the whole movement today and for the further development of proletarian culture'.[70] 'It is here', he claims, 'a question of a type of academic intellectualism which almost takes on in the Marxist parties a rampantly unhealthy appearance'.[71] He is not defending any type of 'intuited' or 'mystical' cultural politics but attacking what he sees as the damage done by 'propagandistic logic' and 'objective psychology' through 'our schooled theoreticians from Kautsky to Thalheimer'.[72]

The question of literary form, he contends, has been slowly resolved over the past decades but this is still a problem for the visual arts. The real question here is 'to what extent the art of the present contains deposits and shoots, fertile soil for the art of a proletarian communist society': to explore this question is not the duty of the communist artist (such activity would interfere with his creativity), rather that of the cultural researcher.[73] 'As yet', he writes, 'Proletkult', the embryo of the coming classless culture, 'has no programme'. In the meantime, all the communist artist can do is 'to put his abilities wholly and unreservedly

---

69   Fähnders and Rector 1974b, p. 143. '... sie haben sich jedoch des öfteren mit einer für revolutionäre Marxisten beschämenden Verständnislosigkeit in ihren Kritiken über die verschiedensten "ismen" ... ergangen'.

70   Fähnders and Rector 1974b, p. 155. '... sie ist äusserst schädlich für die ganze heutige Bewegung und in den Weiterungen auch für die Entwicklung einer proletarischen Kultur'.

71   Ibid. 'Es handelt sich hier um eine Art akademischen Intellektualismus, eine in den Marxistischen Parteien geradezu krankhaft wuchernde Erscheinung'. It should be noted that Herzfelde uses the plural – 'Marxist parties' – throughout: his political allegiance to the KPD, a cultural inclination towards the KAPD.

72   Ibid. 'Gerade die Verletzung aller propagandistischen Logik und sachlichen Psychologie durch unsere "geschulten Theoretiker" von Kautsky bis Thalheimer wird angegriffen'. Kautsky was editor of *Die Neue Zeit*. Thalheimer was a leading theoretician of the KPD and in 1929 editor of two volumes of Mehring's work, which will be dealt with in Chapter 4.

73   Fähnders and Rector 1974a, p. 151. '... Die Frage zu untersuchen ist jedoch nicht Aufgabe der kommunistischen Künstlers (das Grübeln müsste seine Phantasie zersetzen), sondern die des Kulturforschers'. The KPD did set up a committee on culture, which included, amongst others, Gertrud Alexander and Karl A. Wittfogel, who would play a leading role during the 1920s, but communist artists also set up their own groups, including 'Die Rote Gruppe' in 1924, and ASSO ('Assoziation revolutionärer bildender Künstler Deutschlands', or ARBKD) in 1927.

at the disposal of the revolutionary present. Then and only then does he serve the future'.[74]

To this point a number of issues have been raised: art and artist of the *Übergangzeit* (the transitional period) vis-à-vis the bourgeois cultural traditions, the KPD's limited understanding of visual art in particular, constrained by a cultural ideology unduly influenced by 'schooled Marxists', and a certain reservation about 'Proletkult', shared with Franz Jung, who claimed that 'Proletkult' (a centralised organisation) and proletarian culture were not the same thing. Herzfelde does advocate that artists organise within the party and seems to suggest, possibly, to 'educate' the party functionaries, that a research programme be set up. Despite these last two proposals, he mentions that art practice should be a matter of negotiation: 'first, communist interests, then the artistic; on artistic questions not compulsion but example, not dictatorship but democracy'.[75] Against the danger of 'bureaucratisation' it would be foolish 'to leave everything to party proceedings': artists 'must seize the initiative, down to the most precise details'. Many precedents need to be examined – the role of art in other revolutions, 'which mass-psychological affects did they engender' ('welche massenpsychologischen Gesetze machten ihre Wirkung aus'). Reflecting on the role of artists in the Soviet Union, he writes: 'The communist artist must assume the responsibility that Communism becomes the principle of a living consciousness rather than that of a matter of statecraft and means of existence'.[76]

7   Art and/or Politics 1919–22

The trajectory sketched out above, from the 'Kunstlump' debate to Herzfelde's brochure, charts the immediate post-revolutionary response to the perceived

---

74   Fähnders and Rector 1974b, p. 152. '... als seine Kräfte ganz und rückhaltlos in den Dienst der revolutionären Gegenwart zu stellen. Dann und nur dann dient er wahrhaft der Zukunft'.

75   Fähnders and Rector 1974b, p. 158. 'Erst die kommunistischen Interessen, dann die künstlerischen Fragen aber nicht Zwang ... sondern Beispiel, nicht Dikatur, sondern Demokratie'. The model here would appear to be the KAPD.

76   Fähnders and Rector 1974b, p. 160. 'Der kommunistiche Künstler wird die Verantwortung auf sich nehmen, dass der Kommunismus vom Staats- und Existenzprinzips des lebendigen Bewusstseins wird'. The 'lebendigen Bewusstsein' is one of Jung's phrases. Herzfelde, writing on young Soviet artists, describes their activity as 'the cultivation of the social rhythm' ('... zur Belebung des sozialen Rhythmus'), another concept in Jung's theorising, emphasising the importance of the 'subjective moment'.

requirements for a culture answering to the needs of the proletariat. Inevitably, as Herzfelde wrote, the artists would have to come from the ranks of the bourgeoisie, whilst the revolutionary parties (KPD and KAPD in particular) would have to engage with what those artists sympathetic to their politics were proposing as cultural representations of the way forward for the proletariat. Herzfelde was critical of the cultural conservatism of the latter. All the artists mentioned above were members of the revolutionary parties, their production both politically and formally 'avantgarde', in that they sought, as in Märten's term 'conduit', new formal pathways for a new content. Contemporary critique, even in the parties' papers, was limited, as may be seen from the sources quoted above. However, as also suggested above, Lenin's critique of 'Left-wing Communism' as an 'infantile disorder' does indirectly allow a more mediated consideration of the relationship between the politics and the culture than, for instance, Alexander's non-mediated response to the Dadaists and to the Proletarisches Theater. Lenin rejected spontaneism as a political practice, conceding only that 'the spontaneous element exhibits nothing else but a germ of consciousness' ('Keimform der Bewusstheit'). The task then for the artist would be to give a dialectical dimension to this spontaneism, to find a representational form to embody it if the artist's work were not to be judged a failure in terms of its ideological aspiration.

In the light of hindsight, Fähnders and Rector apply this criterion of judgement to Jung's work. They are commenting on a couple of novels he wrote in 1921, 'in which he represents the present class struggles not from the perspective of a historically-blind dogmatist of spontaneism but from the basis of his own practical experiences, both as a leading member of the KAPD and in the spontaneous resistance of the workers themselves'. In these works based on concrete experience, the novels achieve a higher level of the problematisation, central to the immediate post-revolutionary period, of 'the discrepancy between spontaneism and consciousness in the workers' movement'. Nevertheless, according to Fähnders and Rector, Jung fails to recognise this discrepancy as 'a dialectical, tensional interrelationship', and sees it rather in terms of 'static antinomy', of 'self' and 'other', 'of feeling and reason, of natural instinct and synthetic politics': Jung 'displaces the correctly diagnosed dilemma at the political-organisational level to an anthropological-psychological level, thus removing its political effect'.[77] This sophisticated critique of Fähnders and

---

77 Fähnders and Rector 1974a, p. 209. '... nicht aus der Optik eines geschichts-blinden Dogmatikers der Spontaneität schildert, sondern auf Grund eigener praktischer Erfahrungen, sowohl in der Führungsgruppe der KAPD als auch in den spontanen Kämpfen der Arbeiter selbst ...', '... der Diskrepanz zwischen Spontaneität und Bewusstheit in der Arbeiterbe-

Rector is informed by half a century of greater availability of Marx's texts and consequent theorising.

Jung, on the other hand, is that type of artist described sympathetically by Herzfelde, as one moving over from a generalised bourgeois camp. Indeed the antinomies described by Fähnders and Rector may be re-codified in terms of Jung's pre-war 'revolutionary' thinking, where the ideas of Otto Gross's social psychoanalysis were propagated by Jung in the journal he edited, *Die Freie Strasse*, and the attendant politics of a utopian Expressionism and early Dadaism. There is an interesting passage in Seth Taylor's *Left-Wing Nietzscheans: The Politics of German Expressionism 1910–1920* which throws light on this politics, where he is commenting on two articles by Gross, the second of which was published in the *Räte Zeitung*, the paper of the Berlin Council of workers, soldiers, and sailors. The articles propose 'an educational system that would prepare the way for a real revolution ... by first bringing about the requisite inner revolution'. Gross paid tribute to Lunacharsky's 'technical schooling', but 'revolutionary education must include teaching the basic tenets of modern psychology from which the workers will gain their own emancipation through self-knowledge'.[78] Gross and Pannekoek (see above) rather than Hegel and Lenin were the models present to Jung, the need to supplement the knowledge gained through practice with another level of self-knowledge, that through culture – both Lenin and Pannekoek stressed the penetrative power of bourgeois culture, a potential bulwark to revolutionary success. The multi-levelled analysis of Fähnders and Rector is by no means tending towards a reduction but there seems to be an insistence on the cural text conforming to the demands of political theory, a demand which the former cannot fully achieve. Non-mediation rather than mediation was the major characteristic of some of the art of the period, as Alexander noted of Dadaism in her advocacy of the heritage argument. But here a space must be kept open for consideration of the immensity of the task – new forms for a new content, a content scientific in its materialist aspirations and rigour, unimaginable in contemporary bourgeois culture.

----

wegung ...'. 'Jung begreift diesen Widerspruch nicht als ein dialektisches Spannungverhältnis ... sondern als statische Antinomie von "Eigenem" und "Fremden", "von Gefühl und Ratio" ... Er verschiebt dadurch das richtig diagnosierte Dilemma von der politisch-organisatorischen auf eine anthropologisch-psychologische Ebene und entzieht es dem eingreiffenden politischen Handeln'.

78   Taylor 1990, pp. 114–15.

CHAPTER 3

Märten and the Development of a Theoretical Position: From Reformism to the November Revolution

As we have seen in Chapter 2, the role of 'das Erbe' became more contentious after the November Revolution of 1918, with the fragmentation of the left into different parties and fractions. Gertrud Alexander, cultural editor of *Die Rote Fahne*, vigorously promoted Mehring's programme.[1] A figure who exemplifies many of the issues at stake in the politically charged and rapidly changing circumstances was Lu Märten: she had been a member of the SPD but critical of their focus on 'great art' ('Grosse Kunst'), she moved through the left USPD and their greater sympathy with artistic experiment, to the KPD, where she advocated a practical aesthetic based on experimental art forms and founded on the principles of historical materialism, rejecting 'das Erbe' and its forms as a conduit for working-class consciousness. Some of Märten's work has already been encountered above in Chapter 2, her positive critique of Dada, of proletarian theatre, the espousal of the role of the machine in art and the need to challenge the existing cultural pages of the press, including those in left-wing papers. The theoretical exchanges concerning culture between the cultural editor of *Die Rote Fahne* Alexander and Märten have been described by more recent commentators in the following manner: 'The controversies which she [Märten] had with Gertrud Alexander from 1919 to 1921 over questions of content and method extend beyond issues of Mehring's [classical heritage] position and left-wing communism: with them [Alexander and Märten] begin a fundamental discussion on the question of a materialist aesthetic which would continue through to the formation of the Proletarian Revolutionary Writers League (BPRS) in 1928 at the end of the Weimar Republic'.[2]

---

1   She had two essays on Gothic architecture published in *Die Neue Zeit*, a subject germane to her defence of the 'Erbe' position. She may also have attended the SPD School in Berlin where Mehring taught.

2   Fähnders and Rector 1974a, p. 129. 'Die Kontroversen, die sie von 1919 bis 1921 mit Gertrud Alexander über verschiedene inhaltliche und methodische Fragen führte, standen jedoch ausserhalb der Auseinandersetzung zwischen Mehring-Nachfolge und Linkskommunisten und wiesen auch über das Problem des Erbes hinaus; mit ihnen beginnt eine grundsätzliche Diskussion über Fragen der materialistischen Ästhetik, die bis in den Bund proletarisch schriftsteller am Ende der Weimarer Republik reicht'. Another commentator, Richard

The stages of Märten's development are markedly different from those of Mehring and indeed Alexander. Mehring's biographical trajectory was that of someone entirely engaged in the public space of major journals, party conferences, organisation, author of publicly appraised works. Alexander was educated at the University of Jena and the Royal Academy of Arts in Berlin, where she later taught drawing, whilst Märten's formal education, on the other hand, was seriously disrupted by economic circumstances and illness. Through her efforts and interests she found her way into sympathetic Berlin circles whose activities would prove crucial to her development as critic and theorist. Her only biographer to date, Chryssoula Kambas, has characterised this development as follows in commenting on her earliest art-theoretical ideas: 'They lay in the energised fields of journalism, creative writing, the processes in the most recent developments in painting and handicraft, as demonstrated in the great exhibitions, amongst them the Secession; in issues raised by the radical bourgeois wing of the women's movement: they also lay in tensions between the Nationalsozial Verein (National Social Association) and the SPD and its cultural aspirations'.[3]

There are a number of areas here not encountered in Mehring's cultural theory of 'das Erbe': her creative writing – an early novel and a play, encouraged by members of a Berlin bohème she knew, including major figures like the Hart brothers and Else Lasker Schüler; there are also visits to artists' studios and major exhibitions, a visual dimension totally lacking in Mehring's work, experience which leads to essays on major painters; finally, there is the reference to the National Social Association, which promoted a contemporary industrial culture including both handicraft and machine work, in contrast to the SPD concentration on 'great art' ('Grosse Kunst').[4]

H. Schütz, writes of 'Lu Märten's contribution to the discussion of the theory of form which lasted almost twenty years, from the "old" Social Democratic Party to the "Stalinisation" of the KPD' (*alternative* 1973, p. 71).

3   Kambas 1988, pp. 95–6. The German 'Werkstatt' translates as 'workshop', 'place of work', including the artist's studio. Kambas's title is astute, signifying the continuum of the concept of work across different practices as Märten understood it. Her biography is based on material provided by Märten in the 1950s to her nephew, now in the family collection, and on correspondence contained in the International Institute of Social History in Amsterdam and Die Akademie der Künste in Berlin. I am greatly indebted to Kambas's text for the biographical details and the sourcing of Märten's publications.

4   Friedrich Naumann, a Protestant pastor, was the leading figure in the Association. He had familiarised himself with the writings of Lassalle, Marx, and Bebel and believed that the workers were not supportive of Marxist revolutionary ideology, that the cartelisation of industry was producing new relationships between capitalists and workers, many boardroom meetings now sounded more like socialist gatherings. A founder-member of the Deutscher

There are two distinct strands to Märten's thinking during the pre-war period, one social, the other cultural, with handicraft (Handwerk) in terms of design providing a shared role at times.[5] The social strand was concerned with the women's movement (*Frauenbewegung*), increasingly with proletarian women, and domestic work (*Hauswirtschaft*), the home and the proletarian environment. She is here influenced by the reformist thinking of John Ruskin and, more immediately, Friedrich Naumann's ideas.[6] Two of her earliest published articles reflect both the exigencies of her own experience in a less well-off area of Berlin and her interest in the general reformist movements of the period. The first, 'The Centralisation of Housework', supports the communalisation of living in buildings to be furnished with the most developed domestic equipment.[7] In the second, 'To the Women of the Proletariat', she suggests that proletarian women can open up another front against capitalism through their own co-operatives.[8]

Although a member of the SPD since 1898 her espousal of the reformist approach was at odds with the party's official line. An article in their journal

---

Werkbund in 1907, he proposed that better designed products and factory environments would wean workers from the Marxism of the SPD. Frederic J. Schwartz's *The Werkbund: Design Theory and Mass Culture Before the First World War* is indispensable for an understanding of the political and cultural issues raised by the reformist movement in design, providing the background for Märten's engagement (Schwartz 1996).

5   The most theoretically inclined Marxist art historian at the end of the 1920s, Max Raphael, would write the following: 'A problem of particular interest to Marxists is that of the industrial arts, i.e., the creation of objects that serve to gratify our most ordinary needs, such as food, drink, clothes, lodging etc.', and asks: 'Does the creative artistic faculty begin with such objects?' Unfortunately he does not pursue the subject any further. Both Märten and Raphael taught courses at MASCH (the Marxist school in Berlin) at the end of the 1920s, when the topic could have been discussed. There is a copy of Raphael's 'Zur Kunsttheorie des dialektischen Materialismus', published in *Philosophische Hefte*, 1932, in Märten's archive in the International Institute for Social History in Amsterdam. The above quotation is taken from the English translation of the essay by Inge Marcuse, contained in Raphael's *Proudhon, Marx, Picasso: Essays in Marxist Aesthetics* (1981, p. 88). Raphael's work will be considered at length in the Appendix.

6   She reviewed the third volume of Ruskin's work in 1902 in Naumann's journal *Die Zeit*. The journal promoted the English Arts and Crafts, but also an art education movement for workers in France, 'Art for All' ('Art pour tous').

7   May 1982, pp. 14–18. 'Die Zentralisation der Hauswirtschaft' was published in *Genossenschaftpionier*, a co-operative journal, in 1903. Amongst other contributions published on the subject were reports on domestic work exhibitions in *Arbeiterinnen-Zeitung* (*Working-Women's Paper*) 1906, *Frauen-Zukunft* (*Women's Future*) 1910.

8   May 1982, pp. 18–21. 'An die Frauen des Proletariats' was published in the SPD paper *Vorwärts* in 1904. She also published in the most prestigious left-feminist journal of the period, Clara Zetkin's *Die Gleichheit* (*Equality*).

Die Neue Zeit proposed William Morris rather than Ruskin or Naumann as their model, quoting him: 'Resolve the economic and you solve all the other questions. It is the magic wand for everything else, the expressive means for the spiritual and sensuous'.[9] In another article from the same period she begins to address an issue which she will explore in a more historical-materialist sense later: 'The Artistic Factors in Work Past and Present'.[10] Here she is directly concerned with the experience of the worker in large factories under the capitalist division of labour. She quotes Ruskin on the ideal relationship: 'a work of the head, the heart and the hand', the work embodying the personality of the worker. This history, she writes, was not, however, without its contradictions: it gave on to new abilities which also gave rise to social distinctions, tensions, and conflicts. It may be hoped, she continues, that present production and working methods will bring constructive factors into being, psychological, even artistic. The contemporary factory worker, male or female (Arbeiter oder Arbeiterin), is a more social being, recognising their own interests in those of the wider working class in general and its growing consciousness of its own strength. At present much of their time is consumed in political struggle and campaigns but through these will arise greater demand for more complex subject formation. A new moment will emerge, through the working process and not by way of formal teaching, as workers recognise their products as elements in a greater social whole – 'what worker', she asks, 'would not greet with pride the Eiffel Tower and the contents of industrial exhibitions as products of their labour, evoking the joy in creativity just as the Handwerker did?' Thus artistic and philosophical thought, the aesthetic sense, enters the working community. In this manner the statement that 'not only do the people need art but that art also needs the people' is confirmed. Under the present conditions this is not the case, but possibilities should be identified and developed.

This is still very much a reformist programme, now more Naumann than Ruskin. Amongst her circle at this time was Theodor Heuss, co-founder with Naumann of the Deutscher Werkbund in 1907, whose ideas are clearly reflected here. There is muted criticism of one aspect of the SPD educational programme (Bildungsprogramm) and the transmission of 'great art'. Although not emphasised there is a pointer towards the future, her contentious insistence that form arises through engagement with the material and the working pro-

---

9   Hermann Wendel, quoted in Kambas 1988, p. 104. Joan Campbell gives a very good account of the SPD hostility to the politics of reform in her *Joy in Work, German Work: The National Debate 1800–1945* (Campbell 1989).

10   Märten 1903, pp. 800–4. This was Naumann's journal, organ of the Nationalsozial Verein.

cess and should not be considered as a passive conduit for content. An essay on proletarian housing in Berlin further develops this strand of her thinking. Two statements encapsulate what will become the core of her practical aesthetic: 'From purely material, functional forms will develop the expressive means for the spiritual and the sensuous', and, some sentences later, through the search for solutions to architectural demands 'emerges the abundance of resources and the cultivation of form'.[11] In an unpublished essay from 1913, Märten calls on the SPD to modify its educational programme for culture and address 'the first cultural educational requirement' engagement with the objects of everyday use, 'the aesthetic objects and forms offered today by industry'. She distances herself from the Naumann position: this pseudo-culture is the product of the 'dictatorship of capitalism', to be understood not in terms of social harmony but rather of class difference. Handwerk production is not the way forward, 'we must educate ourselves in imagining the possible new capacity in machine production'.[12]

As yet what we have in the above articles written between 1903 and 1913 is an assemblage of ideas addressing social concerns related to work and worker, the machine and the role of design, the reformist objective of aestheticising the working environment (the new factory architecture) and its products – the work of Peter Behrens for AEG being a paradigm for such ambition.[13] To the extent that Naumann's National Social Association and the Deutscher Werkbund were significant reformist institutions with the specific aim of combatting the Marxism of the SPD, Märten's involvement with them and their programmes gives some purchase to these early writings. The opening sentence of Märten's 'The Artistic Factors in Work Past and Present' indicate what she was trying to negotiate between these very different positions, bearing in mind that she was an SPD member. 'At a time', she writes, 'when the worker is to a

---

11   Kambas 1988, p. 32. 'Aus reinen materiellen Zweckformen wurden Ausdrucksmittel seel-
      ischer und sinnlicher Notwendigkeiten. ... und suchen nach den Mitteln, die die Aufgabe
      lösen sollen, wächst der Reichtum der Mittel und entsteht die Kultur der Form'. Kambas
      convincingly suggests that Märten must have become aware of the work of the nineteenth-
      century architect and theorist Gottfried Semper at this time, his emphasis on material and
      function in the determination of form.

12   'Ästhetik und Arbeiterschaft. Das Arbeitersein und seine Gestaltung', in Lu Märten Ar-
      chive, International Institute of Social History, Amsterdam, Portfolio 1 (hereafter IISG).

13   A major modernising architect, Behrens was the 'ideal' Werkbund representative. Emp-
      loyed by AEG, the General Electric Company in Berlin, he was responsible for all its design
      requirements, from advertising, through product design and its major factories, one of
      which still stands.

large degree conscious of the significance and worth of his class as a political and economic force, to the contrary he is designated a "wage-slave" ("Lohnsklave"), his work as "wage-slavery" ("Lohnsklaverei")'. Such a designation may have acknowledged the contribution to the struggle but it does not address the changing nature of the work process under the conditions of the large factory and changing technology. Reference to the recent work of Joan Campbell, in her chapter 'Work and Revolution', suggests some of the positions in play within the SPD at this time. 'When the German Social Democrats turned to Marx in the last decade of the nineteenth century', she writes, 'they virtually ignored the strain in Marxism which sought to change work itself into a free creative activity, "life's prime want"'. In their fight 'for tolerable conditions of employment and basic civil rights', she continues, 'their Marxism had little room for the notion of joy in work'. She notes the presence in the literature of the ambivalence within Marxism on whether to humanise labour or to abolish it, but that 'Engels's prompting helped to ensure that not joy in work but more free time *after* work became the prime objective of German Marxists'.[14] Märten would remain at odds with the SPD cultural programme throughout her membership: that she should secede from the reformist Naumann circle marks a step in her development towards an historical-materialist aesthetic.

Märten's articles on culture introduce a subject not found to any extent in the SPD's 'Erbe' programme: the visual. There are articles on the German women artists Käthe Kollwitz and Paula Becker Modersohn [sic] and, more generally, on women in the Fine Arts, more specifically, on women represented in the second jury free exhibition in Munich, 1911. There are also essays on the major modernist figures, Eduard Manet and Vincent Van Gogh. There is a study of the socio-economic situation of artists, *Die wirtschaftliche Lage der Künstler*. There are also articles on art, class, and socialism, on the artists and socialism and 'Tendenz Kunst', programme-led or content-led art. These pre-war writings, together with the socially oriented articles addressed above, still tentative, are stages on the way to the more pointed theoretical positions she would deploy in the post-November Revolution culture arguments.

Märten's sensitivities to the visual were formed through her contact with practicing artists in her 'bohemian' Berlin circle, visiting their Werkstätte – there are images of two sculpted heads of her in Kambas's book from the early period, one of 1911 by the man she would later marry, Repsold. Two art historians, Wilhelm Hausenstein and Martin Wackernagel, were also part of that

---

14   Campbell 1989, p. 25.

circle: both supported her theoretical approach.[15] Indicative of the problems Märten would encounter were the rejections she received from the SPD *Die Neue Zeit*, both from Karl Kautsky as editor and Mehring. She submitted 'Kunst, Klasse und Sozialismus' in 1906: Kautsky thanked her for sending the article and apologised for rejecting it, 'because in its present form it is too difficult to understand and for the majority of our readers, I fear, more bewildering than enlightening'.[16] In 1910 she submitted an article on Van Gogh to *Die Neue Zeit* but this time it was rejected by Mehring.[17] She suggested a review of Hausenstein's book on contemporary art in 1914 but Kautsky's response was the same; '*Die Neue Zeit* is above all for a reading public of workers. Hausenstein repeatedly uses a language little understood by workers, a situation further reinforced by a reviewer. Because this art-jargon is infectious, as, for example, philosophical jargon is'.[18] In her Van Gogh article, she struggles to provide a quasi-Simmelian account of how the tempo of the modern might be represented: 'we must', she wrote, 'find the immediate expression, the immediate form for our experience, in speech, in fine arts (as in the technique of pure communication: the telegraph)'. Impressionism, no mere style as such, has found signs for experience. Although one may have an understanding of Kautsky's unwillingness to publish Märten's article in *Die Neue Zeit*, there is a discernible concern with trying to establish a theoretical position, more clearly articulated in 'Von der Mietskaserne'

---

15   Hausenstein would later become a major art historian, see the Appendix below. He joined the SPD in 1907. Of significance relative to Märten, he published a sociology of art, *Soziologie der Kunst. Bild und Gemeinschaft*, in 1912 and a history of contemporary art, *Die bildende Kunst der Gegenwart*, in 1914. Wackernagel graduated under Heinrch Wölfflin, the most influential art historian of the period. He spent time in Rome working for the Royal Prussian Historical Institute. Again, relative to Märten, who, 'with friends, spent time in Rome with him', he was specifically interested in the artists' studio and the organisation of artistic life, patrons, and the art market. Wackernagel stayed in contact with Märten until his death in 1961. Another important contact in this field was Felix Hartlaub, art historian and theorist, Director of the Mannheim Art Gallery, advocate for Expressionism and contemporary art.

16   Lu Märten Archive, IISG, Amsterdam, Portfolio 34. Mehring had promised it to Hausenstein; it appeared in the journal in 1911.

17   Lu Märten Archive, IISG, Amsterdam, Portfolio 34. Similar reservations concerning literature were articulated by Bebel and Liebknecht at the 1896 Congress. Mehring, in his articles on Naturalism, did see some positive possibilities in Impressionism in a general sense (its formal innovations might be of use), but he did not concern himself with any particular artist.

18   Lu Märten Archive, IISG, Amsterdam, Portfolio 34. Philistine as this response may appear to be, it does contain in essence the problem of constructing a cultural programme for a class rapidly establishing its presence on the historical stage.

roughly a year later, as quoted above: 'From purely material, functional forms will develop the expressive means for the spiritual and sensuous'. For Märten colour is primarily material, technical, not an expressive medium per se. The Van Gogh article is a stage in the development of her major contentious argument on the priority of the technical in the origin of the work. It is opposed to the SPD position of prioritising the ideological as the source of the work, a programme determining its formal presentation, a position Märten expressly rejected, a critical position she more explicitly maintained against 'das Erbe' in the post-revolutionary phase.[19] Her response to an article in the SPD newspaper *Vorwärts* in 1910 on the issue of a proletarian 'Tendenz' art prior to the future state, i.e. an art of transition, reinforced her view on the form-content issue: the formal aesthetic developments of modern art could not be calibrated to a decisive turning point in the revolution.[20]

Märten's pre-war development stands in marked contrast to the aesthetic programme of the SPD, founded on the solid base of 'das Erbe', represented by Mehring's considerable output; Märten's practice is very much that of the bricoleur sourcing her materials across a range of sites, heterogeneity rather than the uniformity of the 'Erbe' doctrine. Unlike that, with its conscious grounding in the writings of Marx and Engels, there is negligible reference here either to Marx or historical materialism as a world view. Her intellectual milieu was more disparate but she shared, as an SPD member, core or related values with social-democratic ideals: the provision of adequate housing and living conditions for the Berlin working class, informed in her case by ideas emanating from the reformist Deutscher Werkbund circle. This experience of debates on Handwerk, the machine and materials led her to think about work, the worker, and creativity within the confines of the capitalist division of labour. It concentrated her attention on the prioritising of material and its forming potential relative to the production of meaning, extended into the arena of the fine arts, thus challenging and inverting the SPD position on the priority of the ideological in this relationship. Such a trajectory would allow her to align her ideas with those of Bogdanov on Proletkult in the immediate post-November Revolution period in Berlin, when she met some Russians associated with cultural programmes there. Particularly relevant to Bogdanov's emphasis on physical labour and materials, that 'almost all "fortuitous" and unnoticeable discoveries

---

19   It should be pointed out that Mehring's articulation of the artistic qualities present in 'das Erbe' was much more sophisticated and nuanced than a fetishised class or ideological reductivism.

20   Kambas 1988, p. 84, summarising Märten's response, which was published in *Die Neue Zeit*, 1912.

have been made through a selection of materials and not through "spiritual" labour'.[21] She also rejected the prescribing of the art of the transitional period on the grounds that the formal innovations inherent in the experimentations of contemporary art could not be determined in advance. Set against the *gravitas* of Mehring's achievement, Märten's pre-war theorising seems highly speculative, yet its implications as developed in the early post-revolution period would represent a wider questioning of the 'Erbe', now being firmly established as the aesthetic doctrine of the KPD.

1 The Historical Materialism Debate 1920–21

In the practice-initiated debates set out in Chapter 2 – the orthodox KPD critic responding negatively to the heterodox KAPD-inclined cultural production – a generalised materialist commitment was taken for granted, if disputed. Historical materialism as a programme found no elaborated articulation. This was to change in the early years of the 1920s. The first post-Mehring treatment of the theory may be Lukács's address at the inauguration of the Institute of Research into History in Budapest in 1919, and subsequently printed in the Berlin journal in the same year, titled 'The Changing Function of Historical Materialism'.[22] Unlike in the above debates, Mehring is mentioned twice. The greatest successes of historical materialism, Lukács claimed, are in the 'analysis of social formations, of law and of related phenomena, e.g., strategy', and continues: 'For this reason studies such as those of Mehring's – one thinks here of the *Lessing Legend* – are profound and subtle when they are dealing with Napoleon's or Frederick the Great's organisation of the army and the state. But they become much less definitive and exhaustive when he turns to the literary, scientific and religious institutions of the same epoch'. Despite these 'scientific errors', Mehring is commended for having awakened 'the class consciousness of the proletariat': 'as the instruments of the class struggle his books have brought [the] author immortal renown'. Märten's brochure *Historich-Materialistisches über Wesen und Veränderung der Künste (Eine pragmatische Einleitung)*: (Historical Materialism on the Substance and Transformation of the Arts. A Pragmatic Introduction) and subsequent writings are not indebted to either Mehring or Lukács theoretically and her starting point is not the consideration of 'great art', her objection to the SPD pre-war programme and its

---

21   Taylor 1991, p. 81.
22   It was subsequently reprinted in *History and Class Consciousness* published by Herzfelde's Malik Verlag in 1923. The edition being used here is the 1971 Merlin Press reprint.

espousal of 'das Erbe' (the heritage).[23] The Mehring (and Lukács) position was represented by Gertrud Alexander in her critique of Märten's theorising.

Before considering the exchanges in detail, a couple of points relative to the brochure need to be made. Although not published until 1921, the signing-off date printed on the original is 'Summer 1920', that is roughly contemporary with her review of the Dada exhibition (see Chapter 2 above) in which her thinking is more overtly radical, as is also the case with her 1921 articles on the revolutionary press and the proletarian theatre. Märten's brochure, however, contains references from her earlier allegiances, here from Ruskin, where she is writing on architecture: 'every member of such a production is constructed and emerges from the objectivity of a material function: the achievement of head, heart and hand', a phrase she quoted in her earlier review of his work, but somewhat at odds with the three more radical publications referred to above. Handwerk (artisanal and craftwork) is still the prioritised site which sustains the continuum between work and art.[24] She is pursuing two courses simultaneously: in the brochure she is tracing the historical relations between work and art, in which material, not ideology, plays the leading role, whilst in her articles she still proposes the leading role of material but now free from the Handwerk connection, recognising the role that the technical (if now sometimes impoverished, as with the proletarian theatre) has to contribute to what she will later describe as a 'practical aesthetic', one intervening in the issues of the day from a proletarian point of view.

The brief introduction to the original brochure describes it as 'an extract from a work which on external technical grounds is not yet ready for publication', a reference to a commission for a book from the Soviet Commissariat for Popular Education.[25] This probably accounts for an uneven quality in the brochure, the result of material being compacted, a mode of assertion rather than development in a number of passages.[26] 'The text is grounded', she wrote,

---

23   The brochure was published as no. 15 in the Internationale Jugendbibliothek series, under the aegis of the Exekutivkomitee der Kommunistischen Jugendinternationale, by the Verlag Jung Garde, Berlin. It is 63 pages long. It is reprinted, without the brief introduction, in May 1982, pp. 46–94. Page references are to this edition.

24   The German term 'Handwerk' will be used as it covers the artisanal/craft range.

25   Kambas 1988, pp. 176–8, details the fortunes of that commission, which was terminated when Soviet funds were frozen in Germany. It was published in book form (vastly extended) in 1924 but was again hit by financial problems when its communist publisher became bankrupt, as a result of which its distribution was seriously disrupted.

26   Abbreviated passages on eighteenth-century German culture for instance, including Lessing, could have been taken from Mehring but lacking his grounding. Interesting ideas on the epic rather than the novel as the appropriate form for proletarian theatre is sketched

'in the collective will of the proletariat for power and knowledge', providing 'an orientation for shared thinking and work, because every listener, every questioner, is here a co-worker'.

The first page of Märten's text acknowledges the work of Marx, his clarification of the historical origins of class war and his exposure of the economic roots underlying social change, with a new emphasis for her. These processes affected not only man's species-being, but also 'his consciousness, thinking modes and life processes'. But how do such things operate in the specifically spiritual ('geistige') arena?[27] Much sharp criticism of capitalism and bourgeois culture is available but nothing 'by any means informed by the historical materialist method' ('... nicht durchaus vom Wesen der historischen und materialistischen Methode abhängig blieb ...'), nothing about 'the development and transformation of all those things gathered together under the designation "art"'. Because the arts represent classes and the ideological contents of epochs, their understanding will be more complex than the harsh and unambiguous facts of everyday economic life. There can be no scientific objection ('... eine Berechtigung haben kann so jedenfalls keine wissenschaftiche ...') to mediating economic and cultural forms and contents; 'an analytical tool is required and that tool is historical materialism'.[28] This is the scientific principle of the revolutionary communist intent, which will deconstruct the anarchic theories and practices of culture under late capitalism. Having set out the scientific dimensions of historical materialism as the key to understanding cultural production, Märten then moves on to another core interest of her argument, the relations between Handwerk, art, and the machine. 'If, for example', she writes, 'it is confirmed by historical materialism that the arts in general, more or less materially dependent on the economic and the technical, have lost their foundations with the decline of Handwerk, there therefore arises to be considered the pressing and by no means easily resolved question of how these will fare in a communist society where machine production will be retained'.[29]

---

out only – a contemporary work, Becher's 'Arbeiter, Bauern, Soldaten' is commended as a 'dramatisch-episch-musikalisches Werk', the music to be provided by the young Kurt Weill. Claimed relations between music, work, and the technical are briefly set down. Concentration here will be mainly on the basic theoretical position rather than detailing the many examples given.

27   'Cultural' would be the acceptable translation, rather than 'spiritual' or 'intellectual'.

28   May 1982, p. 48. 'Es hiesse die Brauchbarkeit eines Werkzeuges, wie der historische Materialismus es darstellt ...'.

29   May 1982, p. 50. '... wie in der kommunistischen Gesellschaft, die ja doch die Maschinenproduktion beibehalten wird, zu denken ist'.

The issue then emerges 'if the whole question of the rebirth of art, especially that of the plastic and design areas, will also become one of the re-establishing of Handwerk as the working mode' ('... als arbeitstechnische Grundlage ...') 'of the artist'.[30] As the machine will remain a crucially important factor in production, Märten advocates that acquired Handwerk artisanal skills be applied to the machine, establishing a 'dictatorship over the machine' ('... eine Diktatur über die Maschine') rather than a dictatorship of the machine.[31] The deeper question is 'what demands will devolve upon the arts in accordance with their material assumptions and their historical conditions'?[32] She quotes Lunacharsky on the technical and spiritual ('geistigen') in Russia and his reference to Marx. 'What can he mean', she writes, 'other than on these issues more fundamental historical and materialist work must be carried out. The reference to Marx can only mean that we treat the material as he himself did. No new method needs to be established, it only requires the dialectical application of our method to the genesis and operation of the spiritual categories'.[33] Without such analysis, no certainty in this area can be achieved – she notes the lack also in revolutionary critical reviews ('... revolutionären kritische Rezensionen'). Even where difficulties arise in addressing the cultural field with workers, 'the Marxist method with its dismantling and reconstructing dialectic' ('... die Marxsche Methode mit Hilfe ihrer zerlegenden und wieder verbindenden Dialektik ...') 'is the best means for achieving the purpose set'.

The emphasis on the materialist dimension is not mechanistic but denotes a kind of 'metabolic' exchange: 'the exchange emanating from the technical – of capitalism or another system – undergoes a physical-psychic expressive energy'.[34] From the external debates of the technical and mechanical, for exam-

---

30 These ideas were also much the provenance of a liberal or non-Marxist left in the immediate post-war period. The 'Arbeitsrat für Kunst' ('Council for Art') was one example; one of its leading members, Adolf Behne, advocated such a policy in his *Die Wiederkehr der Kunst* (*The Return of Art*). Another member, Walter Gropius, implemented it in the early Bauhaus, but would significantly extend it with 'A New Unity: Art and Technology' in 1923.

31 She had published an article on the subject, 'Maschine und Diktatur', in *Das Neue Reich* in 1919.

32 May 1982, p. 50. '... welche *Aufgabe*[*n*] den Künsten, entsprechend ihren materiellen Voraussetzungen und ihren historisch weiterweisenden Bedingungen – zufallen werden'.

33 Ibid. 'Die Berufung auf Marx kann immer nur heissen, den Stoff so behandeln, wie ihn Marx behandelt hat. Nicht eine neue Methode braucht für derartige Arbeit erfunden werden, sondern nur die dialektische Anwendung unsrer Methode für Werden und Wirken der geistigen Kategorien'.

34 May 1982, p. 54. 'Die Wechselwirkung, die aus der technischen Mechanik – die des Kapitalismus oder einer anderen – mit dieser physisch – psychischen Ausdrucksenergie im Menschen erfährt'.

ple, 'the transformative effect of the technical on the spiritual, so-called purely spiritual production, is substantial'.[35] As an example she gives the 'art of the compositor' ('Schriftsetzerkunst') and its effect on the press and other areas: to introduce these is to remember that also 'the anti-bourgeois spiritual workers, the revolutionary and the communist – the outcomes and tendency of which they oppose – cannot remain free from its influence and constant formal constraint' ('... nicht von ihrer Einwirkung und ihrem stehenden formalen Zwang frei sein kann ...'). In the transitional period, such cultural workers will be indebted to these influences: consideration of the organisational in terms of cultural production in the coming society, on the restoration of quality suitable to sense and intellect 'notwithstanding the retention of machines and modern technology – will have to resort to these processes and forms' ('trotz Beibehaltung der Maschinen und moderner Technik – auf Wege und Formen zu denken haben wird'). Märten also references Marx's comments on the relation of technological discoveries (the microscope and other instruments) to a greater understanding of nature and in turn philosophy.[36]

Central to her claims in the brochure for an understanding of the genesis of culture are the following: that work is the basis on which art arises; that Handwerk is the foundation for art; that the material and the technical take precedence over the ideological in the realisation of the artefact, that form takes precedence over content, in the sense that the shaping potential of the technical and material establishes limiting conditions within which the ideological can be formally realised and represented. These positions she states clearly in a number of passages. 'Historical data', she writes, 'establish that the arts originally emerged related to work and human craft – and further, that in the earliest possibilities for human expression the seeds of artistic capacities are already contained, realised through the means to hand'. 'The whole history of the arts since the Middle Ages', she continues, 'indicates that the foundations of work were decisive for the possibilities of the arts, not the ideological', and adds that individual achievement can be ascribed to the tools available for use. She pursues this line of argument in remarks on the Gothic cathedral 'whose supreme artistic character is only to be conceived of as arising from spiritual sources'. But such thinking, she adds, 'confuses not only the substance of individual art genres, ignores their conditions but also forgets the primary material

---

35   Ibid. '... ist z.B. die Wandlung der Technik auf die geistige, sogenannt reingeistige Produktion sehr wesentlich ...'.

36   May 1982, p. 61. 'Marx hat schon diejenigen erwähnt, die mit der Wirtschaft und ihrer Technik unmittelbar zusammenhängen wie die Naturwissenschaft vom Mikroscop und andere; die Philosophie wiederum von den Resultaten der Naturwissenschaften'.

foundations from which the Gothic rose and which alone can bestow on every spirituality wishing to express itself a convincing corporeal presence'.

The mode of capitalist production has undermined the role of Handwerk. When capitalist technology removed the substance of work from the worker ('... die Arbeit des Arbeiters vom Inhalt befreite'), it also removed the artistic possibility whose sovereignty lay hidden in that working process, it simultaneously removed the work of the artist from the medium of work ('... so befreite sie auf der andern Seite die Arbeit des Künstlers vom Mittel der Arbeit'), destroyed the interrelations connecting the most inward substance with collective being ('... riss sie aus Zusammenhängen, die ihr innersten Wesen mit dem Kollektivwesen und Bewusstsein aller verband').[37] As a result, artistic practices sought new foundations, particularly in the traditional plastic arts – painting, sculpture, design, including architecture, 'through ideologies which it set as objectives for itself' ('... durch Ideologien die sich auf sie selbst als Selbstzweck beziehen'), through abstract precepts derived from other disciplines, by borrowing from philosophy and associated subjects. Today we have moved beyond the derision and disparagement of extreme modern art with its dissolution of the objective social world in favour of 'inwardness' ('... die blosse malerisch erschöpfte Gegenständlichkeit der Dinge aufzulösen in Gestalten der Innerlichkeit ...'), and Märten refers to the work of the German Expressionist painter Franz Marc as exemplary of this: 'The world envisaged through the dreams of animals' is the clearest example of this. But for the historical materialist, these developments within culture and in work procedures are understandable. Historical-materialist research, she remarked earlier, in dialectical mode, 'nevertheless cannot ignore the negative manifestation'.[38] Bourgeois cultural anarchy manifests itself more clearly in the plastic arts than anywhere else 'as the lack of an artistic consciousness which can recognise and grasp the new dialectical formation'. Current art discourses fail totally here and 'the few attempts to bring artistic or spiritual processes to dialectical and historical clarification' unfortunately remain unknown or not understood.[39]

In summary, given the early date and context of this publication (1920–21), the Kapp Putsch, splits on the left, and sporadic armed conflict, there is little

---

37   May 1982, p. 87. She is probably influenced by reports of productivist art in Russia, the artist-engineer, where a high level of Handwerk is maintained, she claims. She does not elaborate on this in the brochure but will do so in the 1924 book.

38   May 1982, p. 81. 'Eine historische-materialistische Untersuchung jedoch kann auch an der negativen Erscheinung nicht vorbeigehen'. History, as it were, advancing by its bad side.

39   May 1982, p. 85. '... die wenigen Versuche, künstlerische oder geistige Prozesse im Zusammenhang mit wirtschaftlichen dialektisch und historisch zur Klärung zu bringen, blieben leider unbekannt oder unverstanden'.

that could have been more projective about the brochure. The emphasis on the continuing role of Handwerk, present in her pre-war work, is probably here bolstered by what she may have been hearing through her Russian contacts in Berlin, of the prospect of the artist-engineer there and the possibility of the dictatorship over the machine.[40] Her historical-materialist theorising, based on the precedence of the material and the technical over the ideological, was challenging to the bourgeois conceptualisation of art and the supporters of the classical heritage on the left, as will be seen in Gertrud Alexander's response and the following exchanges.

Alexander initially responded to Märten's brochure in *Die Internationale* under the title 'Historischer Materialismus und Kunstkritik'.[41] More schooled in Marxist theory – a student of Mehring's – and art history, Alexander rejects fundamentally Märten's major premises: that the material and technical take precedence over the ideological; that art and Handwerk have always been identical; that the creative process for artists and Handwerker are similar. The criticism is based on her perception of the absence of the play of the dialectic in Märten's deployment of the historical-materialist method. Despite the sophistication of her presentation of the grounds for rejection, she also left herself open to counter-objections which Märten deployed in her own response.

To counter putative bourgeois objections to the use of historical materialism in the context of art, that art must be experienced not explained, Alexander uses traditional terms for engaging with art – respect for its formal qualities, the genius of its creator, its effects on our soul, its timelessness – but adds that all must be considered in their relations to the social, that the psychic be contextualised within the requirements of historical materialism ('Die Frage nach dem psychischen Erleben wird also ausgelöst werden innerhalb der historisch-materialistischen Betrachtung'). But the questions Märten asks are different ones, Alexander continues: at this point in time, how historical materialism relates to art criticism; if new propositions for the arts could be recognised on the bases of historical-materialist research on the origins of artistic decline; and how best to communicate to the worker knowledge, thinking, and understanding ('Wissen, Denken und Verstehen') of the arts and spiritual things, whether through the criticism of everyday bourgeois art and literary production in the daily press of the left or through the results of research, as her brochure attempts to do. For Alexander, the choice of medium is not important; what matters is the mode of questioning: the outcome depends

---

40   In her exchanges with Wittfogel at the beginning of the 1930s to be addressed below, she will be critical of the suppression of 'laboratory art' under Stalinisation.
41   May 1982, pp. 156–66. This reprint is the copy being used here.

'on exact deployment of the historical-materialist method *dialectically* and not mechanically from without' ('... es kommt nur darauf an, eben jene historisch-materialistische Methode *dialektisch* und nicht mechanisch und äusserlich anzuwenden'). It should not have escaped 'so sharp a thinker as Lu Märten' that 'the execution of a bourgeois artwork can also be grasped by historical materialism and discussed, and must be in the daily press a process of great interest for the proletariat'. She criticises Märten for her exclusion of artists, for example Wilde, Shakespeare, and others, as historical materialism dialectically used can identify the revolutionary nature of their work and make it available for the daily struggle of workers, an echo of Mehring's work on Lessing and Schiller for the proletariat.[42] Alexander recognises the effort Märten has made to provide for the worker 'the longed-for knowledge for the understanding of the spiritual, social, and individual development and substance of human beings through the historical-materialist method, but it lacks overall the spiritual bonds and the authoress does not succeed in penetrating to the recognition of the dialectic of phenomena' ('... es gelingt der Verfasserin nicht, bis zur Erkenntnis der Dialektik der Erscheinungen durchdringen'). Märten, she writes, fundamentally thinks that these can be grasped in their externality ('... dies tritt aber äusserlich in Erscheinungen ...'): she lacks the 'intuitive perception of interrelations, their interactions and integrating articulation' ('Es fehlt ihr das intuitive Erschauen von Zusammenhängen und ihr klarer Zusammenfassen und abgerundetes Aussprechen').

Alexander then addresses Märten's claims for Handwerk and the perceived threat of the machine ('... die Maschine den Ruin der Kunst bedeutet ...'). The mastery of the technical is an element but not in general *fundamental* ('... aber nicht in dem Masse *wesentlich* ...'), a world separates the artist from the Handwerker. Alexander's account of the artist's role is conventional: intuition, the will to form (a concept borrowed from contemporary art history discourse, originating in the work of Alois Riegl), finding the lasting and supraindividual ('... überzeitlichen und überindividuellen ...') in the here and now. Where these qualities are powerfully present, the technical is happily superseded. 'I remember what Marx once said', she continued, 'every epoch discovers its required forms of expression and means' ('... jede Zeit schafft sich die ihr notwendigen

---

42   Concomitant with this criticism is her questioning of Märten's invocation of the 'Geist des Volkes' in the context of her espousal of Handwerk as the origins of art, 'a vague and problematic concept for proletarians, who too often encounter it as oppositional, nationalistic sounding' ('... unbestimmter Begriff für Proletarier ... und im nationalen Sinne entgegenklingt ...'); the recent Kapp Putsch and the murderous activities of the Freikorps were only too present.

Ausdrucksformen und – mitteln'). As Märten increasingly stresses the technical towards the end of her text, 'she departs from the proper substance of historical materialism in that she regards the technical in the first instance as the economic foundation of the arts'. Marx is again invoked here – this is 'a narrowing of the wide horizon Marx had opened up for us, in which he recognised under "economic foundations" the total complex of the socialisation of human beings, their general conditions of existence in their transformation, and their associated practical organisation of work, through which the organisation, the conscious formation and unconscious coming into being of their spiritual orientation and creativity was achieved' ('… sah die Organisation, das bewusste Bilden und unbewusste Werden ihrer geistigen Orientierung und ihres geistigen Schaffens').

Alexander's next major area of disagreement is with Märten's assertion that the material and technical takes precedence over the ideological: the site she chooses is the Gothic cathedral, an ensemble resonant with powerful artistic and ideological energies, and upon which she possessed some expertise, having published two essays in *Die Neue Zeit* prior to the war.[43] Here again she uses conventional art-historical discourse: 'art in contrast to Handwerk involves an incarnation and such is the Gothic cathedral: the Gothic cathedral is essentially the artistic expression of spiritual powers'. The imaginative and material are so complex in their co-presence that little can be established from external perception. To prioritise the material, as Lu Märten does, is 'to mechanise and reduce the scope of historical materialism. Incarnated in the Gothic cathedral art was still present to the consciousness of the populace, a common property' ('… noch im Bewusstein des Volkskörper, Gemeingut …'). Architecture and the art of masonry were sufficiently well established to solve a problem of form such as that of the Gothic. But it was first resolved when it presented itself, on economic and ideological grounds (in the Marxist sense), as arising from the spiritual-religious needs (which are the reflection of particular economic relations of domination and dependency). The mere presence of the 'folk collective' ('Kollektivität des Volkes') invoked by Märten does not accomplish that.[44]

---

43   Alexander is obviously aware of the ideas of major contemporary art-historical discourse, particularly that of Riegl and Heinrich Wölfflin. But to read the exchanges between Märten and herself against that high bourgeois theorising is to understand how radically different this way of thinking is. For a brief but conceptually concentrated passage on the ideas of Riegl and Wölfflin, see Frederic J. Schwartz's essay 'Walter Benjamin' (Schwartz 2006).

44   Alexander also provides brief historical-materialist analyses, similarly grounded, for Renaissance Italy and the France of Louis XIV.

In the present era, the collective spirit cannot arise from the manual activity of the people but from the complex of socio-economic relations. As Alexander sees the role of the machine only in the sphere of design, she does not consider it a hindrance to accomplished artistic work ('… kein Hinderungsgrund für die Entstehung vollendeter Kunstwerke im Umfange der handwerklichen Sphäre zu sein'). Commenting on the recent high class design work being produced across Germany (the objective of the Deutscher Werkbund), she notes that in most cases Handwerker do not complete the work from start to finish, but execute the designs of artists, unlike practice in the Middle Ages. Nevertheless, the play of invention and fantasy need not be excluded: 'This should also be possible today by machine and despite it' ('Dies wäre aber auch heute mit der Maschine, trotz der Maschine möglich'), echoing Märten's 'dictatorship over the machine' in the sphere of art.

Alexander, in concluding, concedes that Märten has raised an important issue. When considering the problem of a proletarian art as an art for the future, Lu Märten may well be right if she means that 'new art is first conceivable through a more serious engagement with society's work process, through a realisation of a material mass culture'. But she does not agree that Handwerk can give rise to artistic creation. For Alexander, the way forward to a more complete penetration of the everyday is by the production of more significant artefacts, with the education of the spirit and development of a new ethos, through a material culture of the masses by communal bonding in communism: a shared purpose for work and living is the prerequisite for a new unfolding of the arts. In a conciliatory closing statement, she writes that 'in the final analysis this is also the meaning of Lu Märten's writing', but stresses the precaution against the narrowing and limiting of the historical-materialist horizon through the ascription of a phenomenon to one source, instead of the dialectic of the spiritual and the material.

When she published a shorter review the same year in *Die Rote Fahne*, 'Kunst und historischer Materialismus', Alexander's tone is sharper.[45] She began by drawing the readers' attention to precedents for Märten's study, including Franz Mehring, Clara Zetkin, Eduard Fuchs, and Heinrich Cunow ('when he was still a Marxist') and others in the pre-war *Die Neue Zeit*, the SPD journal. The issues addressed there were the relations between ideology and production, including art. Lu Märten believes she has something new to say relative to her predecessors in the emphasis on the influence of the development of the technical element on the arts (Kunsttechnik), the dependence of the success or fail-

---

45   May 1982, pp. 166–9.

ure of the arts on this element. In response, she quotes the above-mentioned Cunow's critique of Werner Sombart's essay 'Technology and Culture': Märten, she claims, holds a similar, totally mechanistic 'technological causality' as a 'Marxist derived concept of history, falling into the error, as many Marxists and anti-Marxists did, of thinking that the economy and technology were identical'. From this position Märten sets the issue out incorrectly and ignores the dialectical grasp of the process ('geht sie an der dialektischen Erfassung des Geschehens vorbei ...').[46] 'Marx', she writes, 'emphasised that the development of the technical, of the Handwerk process, is *not identical* with the mode of production, but that the deployment of the technical first develops from the mode of production. Machine and Handwerk are not decisive for the development of the mode of production but to the contrary, similarly with art'.[47] For Marx, 'the arena of Handwerk activities does not generally take its place in the historical-materialist connections between the economic and the ideological, with which analysis he had assigned the technical to its appropriate place'.[48] Alexander again quotes Marx to support her position – 'Every age discovers for itself its necessary forms of expression and means' – and accuses Märten of inverting the meaning of the phrase: it is important to consider the role of the technical in art but not in this manner.[49]

---

46 The Cunow-Sombart reference will be returned to below relative to Märten's theorising of the technical in music. Both Cunow and Sombart were important figures on the left but only a brief indication of their roles may be outlined here. Engels named Sombart as the only German professor who understood *Das Kapital*. A colleague of Max Weber's, he joined the Verein für Sozialpolitik (Association for Social Politics), an association of German economists who recognised the role of their discipline in resolving social problems. In 1902 he published his major work, *Der moderne Kapitalismus*. Cunow was politically educated through the SPD, studying Marx and Hegel. He became an editor at *Die Neue Zeit* and later at *Vorwärts*, both SPD. He taught at the party school alongside Mehring, Hilferding, and Luxemburg. Whilst colleagues defected to the USPD, he became a postwar SPD parliamentary representative. In 1921, contemporary with the Alexander-Märten exchanges, he published his major work, *Die Marxsche Geschichts-, Gesellschafts- und Staatstheorie* (*The Marxist Theory of History, Society and State*).

47 May 1982, p. 167. 'Gerade Marx hat betont, dass die Entwicklung der Technik, des Handwerksmässigen *nicht identisch* ist mit der Produktionsweise, sondern dass die Anwendung der Technik sich erst aus der Produktionsweise ergibt. Maschine und Handwerk sind also nicht *ursächlich bestimmend* für die Entwicklung der Produktionsweise, sondern umgekehrt ...'.

48 May 1982, p. 168. '... nicht in die Sphäre der Erkenntnis historisch-materialistischer Beziehungen zwischen dem Ökonomischen und Ideologischen, nachdem er der Technik einmal den ihr gebührenden Platz in der Produktion angewiesen hatte'.

49 Ibid. '... aber man darf dabei nicht diesen Satz umkehren, wie es Lu Märten tut ...'. Alex-

Alexander now considers the example of music as it appears in Märten's text, where the latter examined the relation between the development of musical instruments and the sound world of music. Märten claimed that newly invented technical means (musical instruments) enabled the more advanced development of music in the seventeenth century: a few sentences earlier she had correctly recognised that because of the 'knout of Absolutism' ('... unter der Peitsche des Absolutismus') with its censorship of word and image, 'music was the only form of expression available in the seventeenth and eighteenth centuries through which everything that could be made understandable and knowable was possible' ('die Musik bleibt, da durch sie allein alles das verständlich und bewusst gemacht werden kann ...'). But Märten fails to recognise that 'inner compulsion' ('innere Nötigung') was also determining, the 'will to form of a collective body' ('... hier der Gestaltungswille eines Kollektivkörpers'), that the invention of instruments and of music were dialectically related. Alexander compares Märten's approach with that of Sombart, thoroughly bourgeois, quoting the latter from his essay 'Technik und Kultur' in *Die Neue Zeit*: 'when you therefore compare the sound world of Wagner and [Richard] Strauss with that of Beethoven, you clearly grasp that the essential difference is a technical one. These are other instruments producing different sounds'. Alexander adds that Sombart says nothing about the true motive of this sound.

Irritated by what she perceives as 'the comrade's ... schoolmasterish criticism of her "so-called brochure"', Märten has space only 'to consider the essentials of her article': those who do not understand them 'may boast a thousand-fold with their dialectic or invoke all the sanctities of historical materialism but remain only cloaked ideologues'.[50] Historical materialism was an instrument for radical investigation, not 'intuitive recognition'; it was an ideological ideal, but one of deductive, exact reasoning based on data ('sondern die der deduktiven exakten Tatsachenbeweisführung'). Fear of vulgarisation ('Verflachung') of the historical-materialist method is the ideologue's fear that his beloved phenomenon, 'soul or art', would be erased once it appeared naked ('... die von ihm geliebte Erscheinung – "Seele" oder "Kunst" – würde vernichtet, wenn sie in ihrem Grundmaterial einmal nackt zum Vorschein kommt'). What counts

---

ander may be referring to Märten's referencing above, to Marx on the mediations of technological innovations e.g. the microscope on progress in the natural sciences and, in turn, on philosophy.

50   May 1982, pp. 95–8. Märten's reply was published in *Die Rote Fahne* at the end of May 1921. Alexander was its cultural editor.

is not the method per se but the ability to use it ('sondern allein die Fähigkeit dessen, diese das Handwerkzeug, zu benutzen'). Those who come up with such explanations as 'religious requirements', 'victorious church', 'spirit of revolution', have no right to judge the results of historical-materialist investigation. If we wish to use a concept such as 'economic-ideological' everywhere in order to spare ourselves toil and work ('... um uns Mühe und Arbeit zu sparen ...'), one can only think that we do not need the historical-materialist method for that. Returning Alexander's class censure of her theorising ('bourgeois' and 'petit-bourgeois'; 'kleinbürgerlich'), Märten writes that 'such intuitions are to be found even in good bourgeois art history'. She then ascribes to Alexander the claim that Handwerk never had anything to do with art, a claim which shows that there is no understanding of the basis of scientific investigation. Work stands at the beginning of all historical phenomena, the determining substance of all ideologies – but above all it remains the material research factor for all the so-called plastic arts. Märten suggests that Alexander apparently does not know 'the great chapter on Handwerk in *Capital*' ('Offenbar kennt sie die grosse *Kapitel* über das Handwerk im *Kapital* nicht'), an imperative for the historical materialist. Nor does she seem to know the brilliant sentence in Marx that 'the machine had *separated work from its content*' ('... dass die Maschine die Arbeit von ihrem Inhalt befreit habe'): its sense points to a spiritual-personal loss, and consequently also an artistic one. As Marx could not accomplish everything, there was an obligation on the part of his successors to follow his example, to grasp a situation as he did and not to conjure up old gods. Turning directly to Alexander, Märten queries what these statements mean: 'Gothic as the flowering of art signifies the victorious church', or 'Architecture was long prepared ... to solve the problems of the Gothic cathedral'. This calls itself the depth of historical-materialist analysis. One can appreciate the Gothic cathedral visually and aesthetically, but this is not the scientific method, which considers the structural dimensions. To explain this 'spirit', that is, the material and structural, is the task of the historical materialist. Handwerk and Technik underlie the soaring achievement of the building and 'the ideology of the Church *used* this symbol but it did not invent or determine it' ('... und die Ideologie der Kirche benutzte dieses Symbol, aber sie erfand es nicht und bedingte es nicht'). Märten then refers to some building types of Asian religions, which also display for the materialist the standing of work and the technical. This is the basis of an epoch into which all spiritual expression is tied. That is historical materialism. Elaborating on this point, Märten writes that only with that, by pursuing the numerous pathways which such a relation evokes within *general* social relations, can one situate in clear historical and material significance the 'spirit of a thing', 'the essence of the artist', as all the beautiful ideological phrases characterise them.[51] Although this summarising statement is not couched in Alexander's more structured understanding of the dialectic, it assembles elements which have the potential to perform that function.

Alexander replied to this a couple of days later in *Die Rote Fahne*, under the title 'Noch einmal Kunst und historisch-materialistische Methode' ('Art and Historical Materialism Once More').[52] She begins by pointing out that Märten has used inaccurate citations ('... nicht gerade genaue Zitate ...') on a number of occasions; for example, concerning the ideological supremacy of the Gothic, 'leaving the problem of form, so to say, hovering in the air' ('das Formproblem lag sozusagen fertig in der Luft'). Alexander was more nuanced than that in her initial *Internationale* review: she does ascribe the phenomenon of the Gothic cathedral to belief, but also writes that the formal architectural problem was of the opening up of the wall, the penetration of its screen, competencies that were already in train. The refutation gives her the opportunity 'to make precise my basic position'. Her first point concerns Märten's 'vulgar Marxist' confusion of production with the technical, which is 'not only shallow: it is false' ('... ist nicht nur flach: er ist falsch'). 'Work does not only stand at the beginning of all historical phenomena', she writes, 'it is the condition of *all* human exist-ence and accordingly *all* relations of production that humans enter into amid the course of history ... the constant in all human development. The trans-formable and the transformative is [sic] the social form of human work ...'.[53] Her second point addresses the charge against ideology: 'to recognise the sig-nificance of ideology for history is not to be an ideologue. The discovery of dialectical mediation between relations of production as base and ideology as superstructure does not expunge the ideological from the historical process'. Nor are ideological fantasies (e.g. religion) excluded; instead they are treated as firm historical data. She returns to the Gothic in her third point and, con-tra Märten, describes it as a 'sociological problem' ('... soziologisches Problem') and refers Märten to her own articles on the Gothic in *Die Neue Zeit*, the second of which was titled 'Über die sozialen Grundlagen der Gotik' ('On the Social

---

51   May 1982, p. 97. '... die ein solches Verhältnis in den *gesamten* sozialen Verhältnissen hervorruft – kann man den "Geist einer Sache", das "Wesen des Künstlers", und wie die schönen ideologischen Formeln alle heissen, in die klare geschichtliche und materielle Bedeutung stellen'.

52   May 1982, pp. 169–71.

53   May 1982, p. 170. 'Die Arbeit steht nicht nur am Anfang aller geschlichtlichen Erschein-ungen, sie ist die Bedingung *aller* menschlichen Existenz und damit die Grundlage *aller* Produktionsverhältnisse, die die Menschen im Laufe ihrer Geschichte eingehen. Sie ist das Beharrliche in aller geschichtlichen Entwicklung. Das Veränderliche und das Verändernde ist die gesellschaftliche Form des menschlichen Arbeit ...'.

Basis of the Gothic'). Fourthly, she also corrects a misquotation, that Handwerk and art never had any connection, concluding that 'I have concerned myself with indicating dialectical relations: that is the basic purpose of my criticism' ('Das ist der Grundgedanke meiner Kritik'). This was the final statement in the exchange between Märten and Alexander on the subject of historical materialism in art.

This may have been the end of this particular exchange, but it was not the end of the argument. Alexander departed the German scene to take up a post in the Women's Bureau in Moscow in 1923, but by the end of the 1920s, Wittfogel would carry the argument and dialectical materialism forward, as will be set out in Chapters 4 and 5. In the early 1930s, Märten would confront him in the pages of *Die Linkskurve* on the structuring of a Marxist aesthetic.

The 'German October' and Reconfiguration

In every national culture there are – be they also undeveloped – elements of a democratic and socialist culture, because in every nation there is a working and exploited mass, whose living conditions inevitably produce a democratic and socialist ideology ...[1]

LENIN

∴

This chapter addresses political-cultural developments subsequent to the series of events which culminated in what is known as the 'German October', a defining event for both the political and cultural programmes. The opening section provides a summary of the politics surrounding the event. The following sections explore two interrelated and inter-penetrating strands: that of the practice of culture, the production of artefacts, and the theorising of that practice. Practice, of course, entails its own theorising, as for example in the work of Grosz and Heartfield, where there is strong ideological affiliation without the necessity of rigorous articulation, although both also powerfully represented their positions through texts. The other strand is a more rigorously structured theoretical elaboration sourced in the demands of dialectical materialism, represented during this period by the writing of Karl A. Wittfogel in a series of articles he published in *Die Rote Fahne* in 1925, criticising Trotsky's theory of proletarian art before their access to power. The practice is informed by general class principles of Marxism, as is the theoretical side albeit more focused, as in the instance of Wittfogel. Despite a seeming parallelism, they can be grasped as complementary in their objectives – the critique of the existing bourgeois cultural value system which bolsters that class's dominant socio-political role. The passage on practice involves the question of the role of intellectuals relative to the party, particularly in relation to the elaboration of the 'second culture', a concept originating with Lenin. The formation of artists' groups such

---

1   Kuhirt 1979, p. 119, quoting Lenin from the German translation of Lenin's work, *Kritisiche Bemerkungen zur nationalen Frage.*

as 'Die Rote Gruppe', 1924, and the 'Assoziation revolutionärer bildender Künstler Deutschlands' (ARBKD), 1928, institutionalised this role. The chapter closes with Thalheimer's introductions to two volumes of Mehring's collected works, on literature and the history of philosophy. Wittfogel's critique of Thalheimer's work opens Chapter 5.

1   The 'German October'

The 'German October' was preceded by what a later commentator characterised as the 'March madness' of 1921: 'Its significance historically lies in the fact that the Communist Party leadership completely misjudged what was happening, reacted wrongly and nearly wrecked their new-born party. They decided that this was a great "revolutionary", "offensive" action'.[2] Basically, as Harman describes it, 'the class would not move. In some places party members who had more determination than sense tried to move for it'. The 'theory of the offensive' indicated a new turn, a doctrine, Harman writes, 'which was propagated by Bukharin in Moscow and accepted to varying degrees by Zinoviev, Kun, Radek, the new German Central and the Berlin left of Friesland, Fischer and Maslow'. Amongst those supportive of this doctrine were Brandler and Thalheimer. On the Soviet side Lenin and Trotsky were little involved with this adventure, but afterwards Lenin wrote to Zinoviev: 'Levi [the deposed KPD leader] was politically right on many points. The theses of Thalheimer and Bela Kun are radically false'.[3] 'The "theory of the offensive"', he added, 'was nonsense: It is an illusion ... We will listen more to Marx than Thalheimer and Bela'.[4] Both Lenin and Trotsky 'decided', Harman writes, 'to fight together to "throttle" the "theory of the offensive" at the Third Congress of the International'.[5]

At the time of the 'German October' many of the same figures were to be involved: on the German side the now more cautious Brandler and Thalheimer; on the Soviet side a more present Trotsky and Stalin but also a now terminally ill Lenin. The KPD had recovered numbers lost as a result of the 'March Action', and circumstances seemed more advantageous against a deteriorating economic background and dramatic inflation, together with the rise of fascism.

---

2   Harman 1982, p. 201. This is a very accessible, widely informed account of the complex and fast-changing circumstances in Germany between 1918 and 1923.
3   Harman 1982, 214. Clara Zetkin wrote to Lenin for Levi's reinstatement: 'Levi lost his head', Lenin replied, 'but at least he had a head to lose'.
4   Ibid.
5   Harman 1982, p. 215.

Militant activity was greatest in Saxony and Thuringia, where 'proletarian hundreds' operated to secure food supplies and price controls, particularly from July onwards. In both states, also the KPD, on the advice of Moscow, entered government with a more left-leaning SPD.[6] A national strike brought down the Cuno government but also led to a decrease in activity, except in Saxony where, Brandler claimed, 'the Saxon comrades were entering not into an economic strike but a political strike, which signified the beginning of the armed rising'.[7] Cautioned by the mistake he made in 1921 'in launching a premature action', Brandler was determined not to repeat it, but, as Harman pointedly writes, 'he repeated his other mistake of 1921 – he turned to men who were isolated from detailed knowledge of German events to decide upon a tactical question'. He telegraphed Moscow for advice, 'seeking the opinions of leaders who did not even have second-hand knowledge of the political situation in Germany'.[8] By mid-August, however, Zinoviev wrote: 'The crisis is approaching ... A new and decisive chapter is beginning in the activity of the German Communist Party and the Comintern'. Trotsky now outlined a view that 'the time was approaching for a decisive struggle for power in Germany: Stalin thought they needed to wait until spring 1924'.[9] Radek was 'convinced of the unreality of all these decisions', as was Brandler, but as he would later write, 'I did not oppose the preparations for a rising in 1923. I simply did not view the situation as acutely revolutionary. But in this affair I regarded Trotsky, Zinoviev and the other Russian leaders as more competent'.[10] At the end of August, the party's leading theoretician, Thalheimer, wrote: 'It is necessary to travel a long road, as much on the political as on the organisational plane, before arriving at the conditions necessary for ensuring victory for the working class'.[11] Throughout September the KPD made military preparations – the arming of the proletarian hundreds – for the seizure of power. As Harman writes, Stalin was now enthused as can be seen from a letter to Thalheimer: 'The revolution approaching in Germany is

---

6   Karl Korsch was a member of the Thuringian government. For Korsch's wider involvement as a dissident Marxist and his friendship with Brecht, see Chapter 6 below.

7   Harman 1982, p. 272. The Berlin comrades to the contrary had engaged in an economic strike.

8   Harman 1982, p. 262. Zinoviev and Bukharin were for an 'offensive tactic', Stalin insisted that the 'German party would have to be held back', whilst Trotsky was honest enough to admit 'that he had not the faintest idea of the situation on the ground in Germany and could say nothing'.

9   Harman 1982, p. 273.

10   Harman 1982, pp. 273–4.

11   Harman 1982, p. 276.

the most important international event of our time. The victory of the German
revolution will be still more important for the proletariat of Europe and America than was the Russian revolution of six years ago. The victory of the German
revolution will transfer the centre of world revolution from Moscow to Berlin
…'.[12] Meanwhile, the Reichswehr under General Müller crossed into Saxony: as
Harman realistically comments, Müller rather than Trotsky set the date for the
outbreak of revolution, but against this threat it was not to happen. A general
strike was called off. The day after Müller entered Chemnitz, Radek, who had
just arrived from Moscow, 'agreed with the cancellation of the rising, accepting
that the party did not have enough arms in Saxony – and that with a divided
class defeat was inevitable'.[13] In his summation of the lessons of October, Harman points to the 'increasing bureaucratisation in Russia which was drowning
rational discussion there', writing: 'In the row over Germany, Brandler, Thalheimer and Radek defended the tactics of the German party with rational and
generally factually based arguments, even if these were often confused and
self-contradictory. But most of those who attacked them did so out of personal
animosity, factual bitterness and bureaucratic intrigue, picking up and discard-
ing arguments, even inventing facts, as it suited them'.[14]

As a result of these experiences, Thalheimer was to write a number of critical
responses including 'The Fifth Congress of the Communist International and
its Results' (1924), 'The Strategy and Tactics of the Communist International'
(1928), 'A Missed Revolution?' (1931).[15] Too detailed and wide-ranging for a study
more narrowly focused on cultural politics, they will be read for what light they
can throw on this arena. In his introduction to 'The Fifth Congress' article, the
translator succinctly summarises the moment. It followed upon the failure of
the 'German October' and the death of Lenin: 'The consideration of the two
factors was to become intertwined as the various contenders for power in the
Soviet leadership and their allies in the parties of the Communist International
used their particular interpretations of the failure of the "German October" to

<hr>

12   Cited in Harman 1982, p. 284. This was originally published in *Die Rote Fahne* on 10 October
      1923.
13   Harman 1982, p. 290. Cities like Berlin and Hamburg were not ready to participate, al-
      though 'the Hamburg rising was later mythologised by the German Communist Party –
      chiefly because of the role played by the future Stalinist leader Thälmann'.
14   Harman 1982, p. 294.
15   An English translation of all three is available in *August Thalheimer and German Com-
      munism* (Thalheimer 2004). From the translator's introductions, it appears that only one
      of the three appeared in English translation before 1993 (the 1931 article): the other two
      were retrieved from East German archives in the early 1990s and were translated for this
      volume.

bolster their own organisational positions and political standpoints within the Soviet party-state apparatus and the international communist movement'.[16] Thalheimer details the trajectory of the interpretation of the 'German October': 'The retreat in October had originally been considered as unavoidable, it later turned out to be dubious, and it finally became a grave error', the result of the 'opportunism of the rightist Brandler leadership'.[17]

In Thalheimer's questioning of what he characterises as an emerging 'organisational theory' we see his critical evaluation of the role of the Soviet party: 'This Bolshevik Old Guard will rightly be preserved as the most precious property of the party and the highest value will rightly be placed on the continuity of this leadership precisely through this Old Guard'.[18] This Old Guard was formed through years of struggle, the experience in the west is otherwise: the 'Russian Old Guard has primarily accumulated Russian revolutionary experience. That constitutes its strength but also its weakness ... This leadership must quite consciously work to make its superiority redundant ... If it in practice attempted continually to maintain *the* role of the Russian party, which can only be a temporary one, the inevitable march of history will work against it, instead of working with it'.[19] The starting point in the West is different, so too must be the means. As a claim to the type of perspective he would wish to establish, Thalheimer writes: '[we] have also indicated both at the congress and beforehand, with all clarity, that our evaluation of October [1923] coincides just as little or even less so, with that of Comrades Trotsky and Radek, as with that of comrade Zinoviev'.[20]

The congress had brought no new factors on the 'German October' to light, no real criticism emerged: 'that will have to await a future occasion when the necessary distance, and with it the necessary impartiality has been gained, then the criticism no longer follows a certain grouping but the facts, the complete and real facts'.[21] This Thalheimer would do in his 1931 article. In conclusion,

---

16   Thalheimer 2004, p. 125. The text was translated by Mike Jones. As part of this interpretation was the removal of Brandler and Thalheimer and their replacement by the 'ultra-leftists' Ruth Fischer and Arkadi Maslow. Jones provided a mini-history of events to the late 1920s, which will be explored further: the bare outline is this lurch to ultra-leftism, the retreat a year later 'followed by a lurch into the virulent ultra-leftism of the Third Period', the last of which would see the establishment of proletarian artists and writers groupings in Germany.

17   Thalheimer 2004, p. 129.

18   Ibid.

19   Thalheimer 2004, p. 132.

20   Thalheimer 2004, p. 142.

21   Thalheimer 2004, p. 143.

writing of the 'organisational and political leadership' of the Communist International and the sense of a possible crisis, he ascribes this sense as being traceable to one thing: 'the inadequate understanding of the necessary adaptations and alterations for the Western European milieu of the organisational and tactical routes to the proletarian dictatorship that were tested in Russia'.[22]

When Thalheimer wrote 'The Study and Tactics of the Communist International' in 1928, the Stalinisation of the KPD was well advanced and 'a secret agreement was concluded between the leaderships of the Soviet and German Communist Parties in order to fight the "right danger"'.[23] Thalheimer knew of the Soviet agreement and with Brandler and others set out to establish an intra-party opposition (KPD-O) to this ultra-leftist turn. As with the critique of the Fifth Congress addressed above, this critique of the Soviet Congress is also wide-ranging and will be considered only from the more narrow concerns of this text. He makes clear his unease with the inadequate formulations and gaps in theoretical research '… [which] for the most part tend to accumulate where the investigation of postwar capitalism has not been adequately carried out in advance, or carried out at all'; a less-than-veiled reference to the different conditions obtaining in Germany. A major part of his critique is concerned with Fascism (Section IV). 'Today', he writes, 'it is easy for anyone to see that in the theoretical evaluation as well as the practical treatment of fascism in Germany during 1923 … both the German Party and the Communist International made grave blunders'.[24] Amongst these was 'a false extension of the term "fascism" to other phenomena and forms of reaction. Fascism became the representative for the "one reactionary mass …"'. Their analysis lacked 'sufficient exposure of the social or class-based roots of fascism, its *political* manifestations …'. His third point questions 'certain incorrect historical analogies, above all from the experiences of the Russian Civil War [which] played a role – 1923: Seeckt-German Kolschak'.[25] This critique is being articulated at the moment when the SPD are being characterised as 'social fascists', the beginning of 'the Third Period'. He turns to Marx's *Eighteenth Brumaire*: on Louis Bonaparte's politics as a model, examining it at great length: 'From the above I draw the

---

22   Thalheimer 2004, p. 145. As mentioned in Chapter 2 above, the writer and co-founder of the KAPD Franz Jung also claimed that writers like Jack London and other Western authors were more relevant to struggle in the West than writing from Soviet sources, particularly Proletkult. Returning from exhibiting in Russia in 1925, Georg Grosz rejected the machine romanticism of Soviet artists as holding little interest for Western artists.

23   Thalheimer 2004, p. 147. The translator described it as 'a response to the programme drafted mainly by Bukharin for the Communist International Sixth Congress'.

24   Thalheimer 2004, p. 158.

25   Ibid. Seeckt was Commander-in-Chief of the Reichswehr.

conclusion that a more precise and profound analysis of fascism and the forms and conditions of the open dictatorship of capitalism is necessary, than that which is given in the corresponding section of the draft programme'.[26]

In Section Six 'The Transitional Period from Capitalism to Socialism and the Proletarian Dictatorship', Thalheimer writes: 'The transition must be presented more sharply than is done in this chapter as a dialectical process occurring through *contradictions*': 'Only in this way', he continues, 'can one initiate a deeper understanding of the contradictory phenomena of the transitional period in Soviet Russia'.[27] The Russian experience of the construction of socialism is obviously central but for the wider development '[o]*ne must be completely clear that this task cannot at all be completely resolved by means of the theoretical analysis of the present-day Russia nor by means of abstraction*'.[28] The Russian experience is only 'provisional and conjunctural'; if 'strict dialectical-materialist method' is not applied, it is 'easy to end up in the morass of scholasticism, verbiage without connection to reality'.[29] In a passage directly relevant to the cultural aspect of the transitional phase, Thalheimer calls for clarification in the document: the subject is the perception of the cultural backwardness of Soviet Russia in the West. It must make clear '[t]hat also in the highly developed and "most civilized" capitalist countries "culture" and "civilisation" are only a thin varnish on the widespread lack of culture of the popular masses, which is determined by the rule of capital and that here also the socialist revolution is the precondition for the cultural development of the millions-strong masses of the people'.[30] Thalheimer here takes for granted that proletarian culture as such is not possible before the 'socialist revolution', a position which allows Wittfogel to place him alongside Trotsky. He challenges rumours in which 'some comrades have accused me of a frightful theoretical misunderstanding of the transitional slogans of Marx and Engels' and rebuts the rumours by setting out the distinctions they had made in the Communist Manifesto between slogans that could only be *realised after* the conquest of power by the working class and those prior to it. Lenin's demands, he reminds his critics, for thorough preparation of the revolutionary requires 'finding the concrete forms of the transition to the proletarian revolution'.[31]

---

26   Thalheimer 2004, p. 173.
27   Thalheimer 2004, p. 174.
28   Thalheimer 2004, p. 176.
29   Thalheimer 2004, p. 177.
30   Thalheimer 2004, p. 180.
31   Thalheimer 2004, p. 196.

Thalheimer's 1931 article on the 'German October' of 1923 analyses the role of the Russian Party and the Comintern with regard to the KPD to cast light on the same relationship in 1931. Again only those aspects which had some effect on cultural politics will be focused on here: for example, the setting up of artists' and writers' unions and associations and related journals like *Die Linkskurve* in the late 1920s. The source of another aesthetic practice can be located within this 1923–31 development. In his report on the Fifth Congress, 1924, Thalheimer refers to 'a current in the West' which seeks to make Marxism 'more profound through badly-understood and even more wretchedly utilised old Hegelianism, that is, *idealism*'. It is sustained 'exclusively by young intellectual elements within the party, and clad in leftism …'. The reference appears to be to a group of which Karl Korsch was a prominent member.[32] Having detailed the various moves made on the Russian side on their leadership struggles, Thalheimer concludes by claiming that '[t]he ultra-left policy in the Communist International and Communist Party of Germany still prevails. So this lesson on the erroneous nature of this policy is always useful as the bogey of October 1923 raised its head again … The left legend of 1923 has already attained a venerable status … It must be liquidated as unquestionably as the revolution in Germany will be carried out by a communist party that had mentally mastered the task beforehand'.[33]

2   Intellectuals and 'the Second Culture'

Two interrelated strands of thought inform cultural developments from the middle of the 1920s: the appeal to intellectuals to seek common cause in the revolutionary movement, and the development of the 'second culture' concept articulated by Lenin. Both processes were haphazardly ongoing from the aftermath of the November revolution.

The political background for the first strand was being formed from 1923. Thalheimer has been characterised as the 'theoretical exponent of the united front *par excellence*', a concept that 'was a product of that group of old Spartacists moulded politically by Rosa Luxemburg', arising from her 'interpretation of Marxism'.[34] The Central Committee of the KPD in August 1923 set out guidelines for such a programme of engagement: 'Already during the prepar-

---

32   Korsch's relationship to Brecht and Benjamin gives on to a materialist aesthetic practice
        and theory very different from the proletarian impulse obtaining within the KPD-based
        organisations and will be considered below in Chapter 6.
33   Thalheimer 2004, p. 122.
34   Thalheimer 2004, p. 95.

atory stages in the struggle for power the proletariat must attempt to draw the middle class to its side or at least to neutralise it. The middle class is the only well-founded alliance that the proletariat can gain in its struggle against monopoly capital': included are 'the so-named intellectuals'.[35] In July 1924 Clara Zetkin addressed the Fifth Congress of the Comintern on 'Die Intellektuellen-frage' (The Question of the Intellectuals). This is a wide-ranging and objective historical account of the role of the intellectuals at various stages: the transition from the feudal to bourgeois society, their depreciation as that society developed, their endangered livelihoods in postwar society, 'particularly in Germany where it reached its greatest effect because the fall-out from war was sharpest'. This was a challenge: 'Comrades! The crisis of the intellectuals brings to a head an exceptional issue: the politicisation of the intellectuals' ('Genossen und Genossinen! Die Intellekuellenkrise zeitigte eine besondere Folge: die Politisierung der Intellektuellen').[36] Presently 'the strongest expression of their politicisation is Fascism'. Intellectuals wishing to be of assistance to the proletariat and historical development 'can organise themselves in supportive organisations in order to become socially active' ('Intellektuelle, die dem Proletariat, die dem geschichtlichen Werden dienen wollen, können sich in Organisationen Sympathisierender zusammenschliessen, um sich sozial zu betätigen'). Very impressed with the politicisation of intellectuals in Russia, she, like Pannekoek and Lenin, also points to differences between the tasks there and in the West: 'native bourgeois ideology in the old Russia was not so strongly rooted, had not exercised such powerfully binding influence as in the coun-

---

35   Kramer 1975, p. 175. 'Bereits während des Vorbereitsungsstadiums des Kampfes um die Macht muss das Proletariat versuchen, den Mittelstand auf seine Seite zu ziehen oder mindestens zu neutralisieren. Der Mittelstand ist der einzige Verbündete, den das Proletariat im Kampf gegen das Grosskapital gewinnen kann. ... und die sogenannten intellektuellen Berufe bilden ...'. An eight-page typed document 'Erste kulturpolitische Massnahmen nach Ergreifung der Macht' ('First Cultural-Political Measures After the Seizure of Power') exists in the Bundesarchiv, Berlin. Undated, it was probably written *circa* 1923. Much concerned with education, including that of art and design, it also advocates the seizure of all private museums and libraries, bringing all artefacts including private holdings into public ownership, thus enabling greater access to these. It proposes particular cultural sections in comrades associations. It is signed by Hermann Duncker, who would found the important Marxist School (MASCH), Gertrud Alexander and K.A. Wittfogel on behalf of the 'Agitpropabteilung der Zentrale der KPD' ('Agitprop Sector of the Central of the KPD'). I am greatly indebted to the generosity of Grant Mandarino for supplying a copy of this document. My thanks also to Grant for making available to me the document he discovered in the Staatsarchiv Berlin, concerning the establishment of the KPD Committee for the Arts in 1923.

36   Zetkin 1960, pp. 9–54, 26.

tries of Western Europe'.[37] Quoting Wagner but standing him on his head, she concludes: 'the strength of the revolution precedes the beauty of art and is her forerunner. From this point of view we must also consider the crisis of the intellectuals and spiritual work'.

In an essay titled 'Revolution Kunst und "Zweite Kultur"', the former East German historian Ullrich Kuhirt writes that during and after the November revolution, 'many of the artistic intelligentsia' ('... grosse Teile auch der künstlerischen Intelligenz'), previously unpolitical, became engaged and 'undoubtedly this powerful impetus changed much in the concrete relationship of the "two cultures"'.[38] Kuhirt quotes Lenin in the latter's polemicising against the 'great Russian nationalism' ('... gegen den grossrussischen Nationalismus ...'): 'The watchword of a national culture is a bourgeois deception ... In every national culture there are – be they also undeveloped – elements of a democratic and socialist culture because in every nation there is a working and exploited mass, whose living conditions inevitably produce a democratic and socialist ideology ... In every nation there is also a bourgeois (and in most extremely reactionary and clerical) culture and clearly one not rudimentary in form but dominant'.[39] Lenin's theory, Kuhirt continues, 'establishes the two principal sites of class opposition in the cultural context' ('... fixiert die beiden Hauptpole des Klassengegensatzes auf dem gebiet der Kultur'): 'it cannot be used as a template but must be considered as a foundational orientation in the analysis of all levels of cultural life, proceeding with the most concretely precise analysis possible of the most contradictory situations in the cultural sphere of the contemporary developmental phase of imperialism, of contemporary nations'.[40] Kuhirt emphasises the demands of this conceptualising for art history: the 'second culture' thesis is not restricted to 'what we today designate as spiritual, or more narrowly defined as artistic culture' ('... was wir heute

---

37   Zetkin 1960, p. 53. 'Die eingefleischte bürgerliche Ideologie ist in alten Russland nie so fest verwurzelt gewesen, hat nie einen so mächtig bindenden Einfluss ausgeübt, wie dies in den Ländern des europäischen Westens ...'.

38   Kuhirt 1979, pp. 101–19, 108. 'Dieser zweifellos machtvolle Aufschwung veränderte vieles im konkreten Wechselverhältnis der "zwei Kulturen"'.

39   Kuhirt 1979, pp. 102–3. 'Die Losung der nationalen Kultur ist ein bürgerlicher Betrug ... In jeder nationalen Kultur gibt es – seien es auch unentwickelte – Elemente einer demokratischen und sozialistischen Kultur; denn in jeder Nation gibt es eine wertkätige und ausgebeutete Masse, deren Lebensbedingungen unvermeidlich eine demokratische und sozialistische Ideologie erzeugen. In jeder Nation gibt es aber auch eine bürgerliche (und in den meisten Fällen noch dazu erzreaktionäre und klerikale) Kultur, und zwar nicht in Form von "Elementen" sondern als herrschende Kultur ...'.

40   Kuhirt 1979, p. 104. 'Man kann sie nicht als Schema fassen, sondern muss sie vielmehr als grundlegende Orientierung betrachten in der Analyse der Struktur jeder Ebene des kul-

als geistige oder, noch enger gefasst, als künstlerischen Kultur bezeichnen'), but is more broadly concerned with the social aspects of proletarian life and 'accordingly with the artistic inclination to the real' ('… und somit auch der künstlerischen Aneignung der Wirklichkeit').[41]

At this point it is worth pausing to consider briefly the complex development of thinking on culture in its aesthetic dimension before moving on. The theory of the 'second culture' was not consciously articulated as a concept per se during the period, but it was beginning to happen in practice. Rhetorically, Kuhirt asks, 'what does the "second culture" represent if not precisely the culture of the progressive class which struggles for the overthrow of the existing class of exploiters?' If 'we were to ask what a culture with such pronounced ideological and political objectives as that of a Grosz or Heartfield was it is clearly that "second culture"'.[42] At this moment, c. 1923–24, a number of politically aesthetic discourses co-exist: Mehring's concept of the role of 'das Erbe', the classic bourgeois 'heritage'; a 'spontaneist' practice (Dada, early Proletarian Theatre plays, including those of Franz Jung) in decline, and an emerging programme of practice still not concerned with 'das Erbe', which can be characterised as the 'second culture', containing artists like Grosz and Heartfield, who were originally central to the 'spontaneist' moment of the immediate post-revolution phase. The theory of the 'second culture' criticises the bourgeois claim for a 'national' culture, a position which was also central to Mehring's critique of the bourgeoisie's attempt to appropriate the work of Lessing, Schiller, and Heine for a national canon, in which strongly republican impulses which opposed the Hohenzollerns from Frederick II (the Great) through to his successors were repressed. The difference between the non-materialist conceptualised understanding of bourgeois criticism and the above position could not be more clearly marked.

---

    turellen Lebens, die einhergehen muss mit einer konkreten möglichst präzisen Analyse der widerspruchsvollen Situation in der kulturellen Sphäre der jeweiligen Entwicklungsphase des Imperialismus, der jeweiligen Nation u.s.w'.

41   Kuhirt 1979, p. 105.

42   Kuhirt 1979, p. 103. 'Proletarisch-revolutionäre Kunst – eine Kunst, die mit so prononcierter ideologischer und politischer Zielsetzung aggressive gegen die Fundamente der bürgerlichen Geselleschaft anging wie, sagen wir, die eines Grosz oder Heartfield – sie *ist* doch eben jene "Zweite" Kultur'.

3   Practice: From 'Die Rote Gruppe' to the 'Assoziation revolutionärer
       bildender Künstler Deutschlands'

The more open-ended type of experimental work produced by the Dadaists, including Franz Jung at the Proletarisches Theater, and supported by Lu Märten to an extent, diminished after the insurrectionary 'March madness' of 1921. Spearheaded by the KAPD, and in which Jung participated, its defeat led to the disintegration of the Party. In June 1924 the 'Rote Gruppe' of communist artists was founded, with former Dadaists George Grosz and John Heartfield as Chairman and Secretary respectively, but also including more traditional artists like Conrad Felixmüller, Otto Griebel, Wilhelm Lachnit, and Otto Nagel, some of whom would later affiliate with the Association of German Revolutionary Artists (ARBKD) in 1928. Many were already contributors to the satirical workers' paper *Der Knüppel* (cudgel), 1923–27. The Manifesto was published in *Die Rote Fahne* in June 1924. This may have been a response to Herzfelde's call in his 1922 brochure *Gesellschaft, Künstler und Kommunismus* for left-leaning artists to organise themselves within the KPD, a call reinforced by the above address to intellectuals: Zetkin's appeal was delivered in July 1924.[43] The opening passage in their Manifesto suggests that: 'Organised and activist painters and graphic artists within the Communist Party have formed a "communist" artists' group'.[44]

They shared the consciousness 'that a good communist was firstly a communist and then a specialist' ('... dass ein guter Kommunist in erster Linie Kommunist und dann erst Facharbeiter'), 'an instrument in the service of class struggle' ('... ihm nur Werkzeuge sind in Dienste des Klassenkampfes'). They will liaise closely with local centres of the Party to realise more strongly 'the effectivity of communist propaganda'. As against the former too-often anarchic production of communist artists ('noch zu sehr anarchistischen Produktionsweise der kommunistischen Künstler'), a plan of action must be established. There was a ten-point programme, including practical assistance with all revolutionary events; artistic education in localities, designing wall paintings, preparation of demonstration placards, 'support for the still amateurish efforts of

---

43   A Comintern decision of 1924 issued a call for establishing 'in all countries centralised associations of such writers, who with their work organise the thoughts and feelings of readers in the direction of Communism'. '... [In allen Ländern einheitliche Assoziationen proletarischer Schriftsteller ... mit ihrem Werk Gefühle und Gedanken der Leser in der Richtung zum Kommunismus organisieren ... geschaffen werden'. Fähnders and Rector 1974a, p. 295.

44   Schneede 1979, p. 106.

party members', through word and image to testify to the revolutionary will; organisation of travelling exhibitions; contact with students at art schools to revolutionise them. All of these artists had committed themselves to the communist cause since the revolution as members of one group or another – the majority in 'Die Novembergruppe' set up in the immediate aftermath of the revolution but who split from it as it moved towards the majority SPD. The 'Rote Gruppe' now brought many of these together after the defeats on the left in the 1921 'March Days' and 1923 'October', as mentioned above. These are artists unconcerned with that particular strand in Marxist cultural thinking around 'das Erbe', the cultural heritage, whether through Mehring or Lenin, but working as activists with conditions as they existed in their immediate situation. Points 7, 8, and 9 in their manifesto commit to 'countering counterrevolutionary cultural manifestations', 'the undermining or neutralising of bourgeois artists', 'using bourgeois exhibitions for propaganda purposes', signalling an engagement with rather than an ignoring of elements within levels of the bourgeoisie.[45]

At two subsequent party conferences in 1925 and 1927, both held in Berlin, this line was further emphasised. In 1925 party members were encouraged 'to raise the influence of the party in non-party environments with communist factions', whilst in 1927 the call was for 'the broad mass of manual and non-manual workers to join a red culture fighting front' against the powerful cultural and educational reactionary forces.[46] It also instructed individual party cadres to strengthen red culture fighting fronts in all cultural and educational organisations.

The founding of the 'Assoziation revolutionärer bildender Künstler Deutschlands' (ARBKD, also simply known as 'Asso') in 1928 incorporated the programme of the 'Rote Gruppe' and extended its scope. The first item in its statute indicates the developing relationship with Russia.[47] However, at the second full meeting of both German and Russian organisations in Berlin, dissension arose over the understanding of clause two in Asso's statute, concerning its invitation to all of those artists who 'stand on the ground of the proletarian class struggle' ('... die auf dem Boden des proletarischen Klassenkampfes stehen'). The Rus-

---

45   Schneede 1979, pp. 106–7.

46   Kramer 1977, p. 176. 'Der Parteitag der KPD ruft ... die breiten Massen aller Hand und Kopfarbeiter zur roten Kulturkampffront gegen die Machtgelüst der Kultur und Schulreaktion auf'.

47   Schneede 1979, pp. 146–9, 148. '... ist eine Bruderorganisation ...'. The ACHRR was the Association of Russian Revolutionary artists, founded in 1922. The founding of Asso, as reported in *Die Rote Fahne*, appears to have been suggested by the Russian group.

sian group argued for a more open invitation, for a more effective alliance to accept artists 'who only partially stand in the trajectory of our work ... [and to] attempt to exercise our influence to attract their contribution. We must continue further to enlarge this circle'.[48] Differences between German and Russian conditions again raised difficulties. The Germans responded that the Russians were mistaken in comparing Russian and German experiences: in Russia 'the dictatorship of the proletariat already exists – one can therefore draft specialists into artists' organisations' ('... machen Fehler in dem sie Deutschland mit Russland verwechseln. In Russland ist die Diktatur des Proletariats, wo man auch Spezialisten für die Künstlerorganisationen heranziehen kann ...'). The German artist Tichauer states Asso's policy: 'but we must not seek in the first instance to appeal to prominent artists, rather we must take care of proletarian and revolutionary strengths and draw on them' ('... sondern wir müssen uns um die proletarischen und revolutionären Kräfte kümmern und sie heranziehen'). Only by these means could their aims be achieved. This leftist turn found justification in developments in Russia.

In January 1929 the feuilleton editor of *Die Rote Fahne* Alfred Durus wrote a comprehensive account in Asso's paper, *Die Front*, on emerging cultural politics in Russia, on the AChR and the newly-founded Oktjabr group. 'In 1928', he wrote, 'the ideological and formal crisis of the AChR clearly came into view: it relates to the crisis of the fellow-traveller in the whole trajectory of Soviet art'.[49] Kurella, Berlin-born and trained at the Munich art academy, the leading theoretician of the newly-formed Oktjabr group, formulated clearly the ideological demand of contemporary Russia: 'not the art of revolutionary Russia, not the art of the masses but proletarian art! The fraternal German group of the AChR, the ARBKD, fulfils this demand under the conditions of capitalist Germany, in the same proletarian-revolutionary manner as the Oktjabr group under the conditions of the first proletarian-revolutionary state in the world'.[50] The Oktjabr manifesto declared its objective as raising 'the cultural ideological level of the working masses to that of the avantgarde of the most aware sec-

---

48   Kramer 1977, p. 180. '... die nur teilweise in der Linie unserer Arbeit stehen ... und ihr Dienste leisten könnten. Diesen Kreis müssen wir immer mehr vergrössern'.

49   Kramer 1977, p. 181. 'Im Jahre 1928 tritt die ideologische und formale Krise der AChR ganz deutlich in Erscheinung: sie hängt mit der Krise des ideologischen Mitläufertums auf der ganze Linie der Sowjetkunst zusammen'.

50   Ibid. 'Nicht Kunst des revolutionären Russlands, nicht Kunst der Massen, sondern proletarische Kunst! Die deutsche Brudergruppe der AChR, die ARBKD erfüllt diese Forderung unter den Bedingungen des kapitalistischen Deutschlands ebenso in proletarisch-revolutionären Sinne, wie die Oktjabr-Gruppe unter den Bedingungen des ersten proletarisch-revolutionären Staates der Welt'.

tion of the industrial proletariat'.[51] In a 'declaration' by the group in June 1928, it proposed to further the aims of the revolution by raising 'the backward levels of the working class and those of present workers still under hostile class influence' ... 'these principles are in agreement with the socio-economic structure of our state and in this relation art is until now being left behind'.[52] This is the Third Period and the radical shift to the left: the Oktjabr Declaration found official approval in its publication in *Pravda*. Kurella addressed Asso in Berlin in 1929. The Oktjabr programme is highly ambitious and wide-ranging, multi-disciplinary, supported by experienced practitioners, based on a decade of organised work in Russia, far in advance of what Asso could undertake. What it could undertake, however, was the undermining of the AChR 'fellow-traveller' and the accompanying leftward shift with an interventionist agenda. On the first of January 1929, Kemeny published a review of the art scene in Berlin during the previous year under the title 'Zwischen "neuer" und revolutionärer Sachlichkeit' (Between 'new' and revolutionary objectivity). The opening sentence sets the tone; '1928 – the sharpest separation of class boundaries also in the arena of art. On the bourgeois side: the "new" objectivity; this typical "art" of the relative stabilisation [of the economy]: on the proletarian side, revolutionary reality, political agitation and propaganda through the means of art'.[53] 'New' objectivity artists' representations 'are an attempt to sustain the stabilised bourgeoisie against the disruptive flow of history powered by capitalism, through their despairing imagery of a frozen world'.[54]

There are exceptions, with transitional potential, oscillating between 'new' objectivity and proletarian-revolutionary art, chief among them are Georg Scholz and Georg Schrimpf.[55] Grosz's drawings and designs for Piscator's pro-

---

51 Gassner and Gillen 1979, pp. 179–80. '... mit dem Ziel, das kulturell-ideologische Niveau der werktätigen Massen auf den Stand der Avantgarde des am meisten bewussten Industrieproletariats zu heben'.

52 Gassner and Gillen 1979, p. 180. 'Diese Prinzipien liegen auch der gesamten sozial-ökonomischen Struktur unseres Staates zugrunde, und nur die Kunst ist bislang in dieser Beziehung zurückgeblieben ...'.

53 Brauneck 1973, pp. 365–8, 365–6. '1928 – schärfste Abgrenzung der Klassenfronten auch auf dem Gebiet der Kunst. Bürgerlicherseits: die "neue Sachlichkeit", diese typische "Kunst" der relativen Stabilisierung: auf proletarischer Seite, als revolutionäre Tatsächlichkeit: politische Agitation und Propaganda mit Mitteln der Kunst'.

54 Ibid. '... als wollten die Künstler der stabilisierten Bourgeoisie den reissenden – den Kapitalismus in den Abgrund reissenden – Strom der Geschichte mit einer krampfhaft konstituierten Unbeweglichkeit – ihrer "Kunstwerke" aufhalten'.

55 Ibid. 'Natürlich gibt es Ausnahmen, Übergangserscheinungen, Künstler, die zwischen "neuer Sachlichkeit" und proletarisch-revolutionärer Kunst schwanken, Georg Scholz und Georg Schrimpf'. Interesting in terms of the major Bloch-Lukács exchanges on Expres-

duction of 'The Good Soldier Schweik' is 'amongst the most important revolu-tionary-political exhibitions' ('Doch am wichtigsten die revolutionärer-politi-sche Ausstellung ...').[56] Kemeny's 'balance-sheet': 'decisive the founding of the ARBKD'; '1928 was, amongst other things, the year of the birth of the artist, also of his death'.[57]

4   Wittfogel's Aesthetic Programme[58]

Between the end of May and the third week of June 1925, Wittfogel wrote a series of three articles on proletarian culture in *Die Rote Fahne* under the title 'Über proletarische Kultur'.[59] In contrast with much of the theoretical positions

sionism in the 1930s is Kemeny's very positive evaluation of their work, 'noch immer interessante und wertvolle Ausstellungen'.

56   Brauneck 1973, p. 368.

57   Ibid. '1928 war u.a ein Jahr der Künstlergeburts – und todestage'. Although not being pur-sued here, Kemeny's distinction between bourgeois-photomontage, the montagist as a type of photographer-engineer ('... eine Art von Photoingenieur'), fetishising the capa-city of the apparatus, and the proletarian photomontagist, the montagist as a dialectical materialist engaged in 'the experimental project of disclosing *reality*' ('... und Methoden des dialektischen Materialismus immer grössen Experimentierlust die *Wirklichkeit* zu enthüllen'), relates Heartfield's practice to that of Ottwalt and Brecht (März 1981, pp. 178–9). Lukács concedes that photomontage 'can on occasion even become a powerful polit-ical weapon', but discounts its 'claims to give shape to reality ... to a world of relationships ... of totality ... the final effect must be one of profound monotony' (Adorno et al. 1979, p. 43).

58   Wittfogel was a major figure on the cultural left. Initially a member of the USPD, he joined the KPD in 1920. He met the leading KPD theoretician Karl Korsch in the same year. He was invited by Korsch to the 1923 Frankfurt Conference that established the Institute for Social Research, of which he was a member from 1925 to 1933. In 1922 he published a book on the economics of bourgeois society (*Die Wissenschaft der bürgerlichen Gesell-schaft*) and in 1924 *Geschichte der bürgerlichen Gesellschaft* (*History of Bourgeois Society*), both through Malik Verlag. But he also wrote short plays, the first of which was staged by Piscator on the opening night of the Proletarisches Theater, others were published by the Malik Verlag. *Der Gegner* published his contribution 'Grenzen und Aufgaben der revolutionären Bühnenkunst' ('The Limits and Problems of Revolutionary Theatre Art'). Together with Gertrud Alexander, cultural editor of *Die Rote Fahne*, Hermann Duncker, director of MASCH (1926), he was appointed by the KPD in 1923 to draft its cultural pro-gramme, *Erste kulturpolitische Massnahmen nach Ergreifung der Macht*.

59   The Tenth Congress of the KPD in July 1925 voted for the organisational 'Bolshevisation' of the Party. A resolution called for the 'creation of a strong, unified, clear Marxist-Leninist foundation for general praxis and the relentless championing of the purity of theory against all deviation'. Wittfogel's articles can be seen as a first move towards the Proletkult-ism which became more pronounced with increasing Stalinisation towards the end of

encountered in the first two chapters, the tone of the address here is directed towards readers not overly familiar with more complex writings on culture. The purpose is didactic in a positive sense as section headings indicate: 'Was Kultur ist', 'Gibt es eine proletarische Kultur?', 'Der Charakter der proletarischen Kultur'. Lenin is quoted in the first paragraph: culture is '[e]verything that has been created by human society' ('All das, was von der menschlichen Gesellschaft geschaffen wurde'), 'material, social, political and spiritual'.[60] It is therefore 'onesided and consequently unmarxist' ('... daher unmarxistisch ...') to portray the economy and class position as the culture of a specific epoch: even more 'onesided' and 'unmarxist' to portray the spiritual life of an epoch and its culture. Representatives of the bourgeoisie particularly err on the second. The next paragraph, 'historical phases – cultural phases' ('Geschichtsstufen'), succinctly presents five historical stages and their related cultural manifestations. Paragraph Three, 'Gibt es eine proletarische Kultur', introduces what was the most contentious cultural issue on the agenda: what would such a culture look like?; in principle can there be such a thing? Here Wittfogel introduces the opposing positions of Trotsky and Lenin: 'Comrade Trotsky has, to much approval in the international bourgeois press, denied the possibility of a proletarian culture in principle', whilst 'Lenin, to the contrary, had assented to the possibility'.[61] In Trotsky's concept of world revolution, the dictatorship of the proletariat is only a brief transitional phase ('... *kurzbefristete Übergangsperiode*', Trotsky's own emphasis). Lenin, on the other hand, spoke of the dictatorship as a 'world-historical epoch' ('... von einer ganzen weltgeschichtlichen Epoche'). It is obviously clear then that 'Lenin and Trotsky must have thought very differently over the possibility of proletarian culture' ('... durchaus verschieden denken müssen').[62]

---

the 1920s. Gerhard-Sonnenberg 1976, p. 65. '... eine feste einheitliche, klare marxistisch-leninistische Grundlage für die gesamte Parteipraxis zu schaffen und die Reinheit der Theorie gegen jede Abweichung mit unerbittlicher Konsequenz zu verfechten'.

60   Brauneck 1973, pp. 194–206, 194. Not all of Lenin's works were available in translation – the Party Congress of 1927 made the decision to publish all. Gerhard-Sonnenberg 1976, p. 84.

61   Brauneck 1973, p. 195. 'Genosse *Trotzki* hat in mehreren, von der internationalen bürgerlichen Presse beifällig zitierten Formulierungen die Möglichkeit einer proletarischen Kultur ürberhaupt verneint. *Lenin* dagegen bejahte diese Möglichkeit'. As set out in Chapter 2, Lenin supported tradition (das Erbe) against Proletkult, which he reined in. The issue was really one of temporality; before, during or after the proletarian seizure of power. Trotsky's *Literature and Revolution* had been published in German in 1924 in abbreviated form; Lu Märten reviews it positively in *Internationale Presse-Korrespondenz*, 1924, no. 56, pp. 682–4. Copy in the Märten Archive, IISG, Amsterdam. By this time, as indicated in above passages on Thalheimer, Trotsky was under attack within the Soviet Party.

62   Brauneck 1973, p. 196.

In *Literature and Revolution* Trotsky had written that one could not speak of any art of any consequence during the transitional phase. Wittfogel quotes Trotsky that 'not only has a proletarian culture not existed but one will not exist' ('... eine proletarische Kultur nicht nur nicht existiert, sondern auch nicht existiern wird'). Lenin stressed, in his great speech to Russian youth, that 'a proletarian culture did exist and the laws by which it is formed' ('... nach welchen Gesetzen sie sich bildet'). Lenin's greater dialectical insight into the varying transitional conditions internationally allowed him to acknowledge unconditionally not just the possibility but the necessity of proletarian culture ('auch die Frage nach der Möglichkeit, ja Notwendigkeit ...'). This difference was a defining moment in the cultural politics of the KPD, pursued 'by us, as Leninist-Marxists, following the foundational theses of Lenin' ('... die wir, als leninistische Marxisten, der grundlegenden These Lenins folgend ...').[63] But at the present moment, within bourgeois society, proletarian culture 'is only one partly of structuring, more *one* of pure struggle' ('... wenigstens teilweise, bereits eine Aufbaukultur ... ist *eine* reine Kampfkultur'). Russia provides 'the classic example where the transition of Kampfkultur to Aufbaukultur' is taking place.

His second article is titled 'Proletarische Kampfkultur'. It will develop prior to the dictatorship, in bourgeois society. As with Mehring, 'das Erbe' is the treasure from which the revolutionary working class draws, 'measuring its living value for the present struggle, developing in practical working with the materialist dialectic' ('... in praktisch betätigter materialistischer Dialektik').[64] Lenin's address to Russian youth is again invoked in two sections. Lenin drew a parallel with the lesson of Marx, who familiarised himself with what was to be known from history: similarly with culture, where exact knowledge of the whole cultural development of mankind was to be established. Nor will proletarian culture be produced by people who 'call themselves specialists for proletarian culture' ('... die sich Fachleute für proletarische Kultur nennen'). With this speech Lenin refers to two opposing mistakes: firstly, the apparently radical point of view that proletarian culture can be produced based on nothing ('... man könne die proletarische Kultur aus dem Nichts schaffen') and, secondly, the 'Marxist' philistine in uncritical thrall to the heritage – the heritage is to be critically evaluated, to be tested by the workers' movement ('... an der Arbeiterbewegung zu prüfen'), appropriation through transformation ('Aneignung

---

63   Ibid. Towards the end of the 1920s, proletarian associations of artists and writers would be
         formed, with Wittfogel on the board of the writers' journal, *Die Linkskurve*.

64   Brauneck 1973, p. 200. As a footnote he provides a concise explanation of the mode of
         operation of the dialectic.

durch Umbildung').[65] So long as the proletariat does not grasp these secure class principles, it will 'remain politically and ideologically helpless between reformism and illusionary radicalism' (Scheinradikalismus).

The third article is titled 'In Kampf mit welchen Elementen entwickelt sich die proletarische Kultur?' ('In struggle with which elements does proletarian culture develop?'). Proletarian culture is made ('gemacht') by self-conscious producers from their own forms of life ('... eigene *proletarische* Lebensformen') – unions, party, cultural organisations, proletarian science, morality, in opposition to existing bourgeois structures, tenaciously and laboriously. The second section is called 'Wie sehen die "bisher herrschenden" Lebensformen aus?' ('How do the prevailing dominant life-forms appear?') The opening passages briefly set out what Marx has to say about the co-existence of different life-forms within capitalism, residual and emerging. Bukharin's *Theory of Historical Materialism* is then quoted, that 'impure capitalism' ('... "unreine" Kapitalismus ...') brings with it a 'blending of ideas' ('Ideenvermischung'): conjointly with 'the intertwining of *economic* forms there inevitably occurs an intertwining of *ideological* forms' ('Zugleich mit verflechtung der *wirtschaftliche* Formen wird unvermeidlich auch eine Verflechtung der *ideologischen* Formen'): 'Just as little as there is no absolutely unitary (einheitliche) form of production, there is no unitary form of imaginary projection'.[66] But this situation does not cancel out the predominance of one mode of production and of its consequent ideological form. Proletarian culture does not develop from 'a struggle with a unified reactionary cultural mass' ('erwächst nicht im Kampf mit einer einheitlichen reaktionären Kulturmasse ...'), but rather with 'a *predominant*, multidimensional one totally based on bourgeois principles', ('gegen eine vielfältig gegliederte, allerdings im ganzen von den Prinzipien der Bourgeoisie *beherrschte* Kultur'). It is with this that the proletariat grapples: as Wittfogel writes in the third section, 'it has much, indeed almost all, to learn from the bourgeoisie' ('... hat es von der Bourgeoisie viel, ja fast alles zu lernen'). The model: 'The Marxist system developed from the critical supersession of Hegelian philosophy and the Smith-Ricardo economic theories'.[67] Only by critical use of the bourgeois-controlled heritage, to reference Lenin ('... nach einem Worte Lenins'), can the working class move forward. In a passage reminiscent of Wieland Herzfelde on the necessity of involving bourgeois artists in proletarian

---

65   Brauneck 1973, p. 201. This was also Mehring's programme.

66   Brauneck 1973, p. 203. 'Ebensowenig wie eine absolut einheitliche Produktionsweise gibt es eine absolut einheitliche Vorstellungsweise'.

67   Brauneck 1973, p. 204. 'Aus der kritischen Aufhebung der Hegelschen Philosophie und der Smith-Ricardoschen Ökonomie ist das System des Marxismus erwachsen'.

ranks, Wittfogel writes that 'the working class must attract in large numbers educated "deserters" from the bourgeoisie' (*before* the seizure of power: revolutionary intellectuals as comrades in the struggle – *after*, until the formation of red directors, general staff, etc.).[68] The 'outstanding work' of Bukharin's *Proletarische Revolution und Kultur* (1923) is invoked, in which he addresses the possible dangers of this accommodation with bourgeois specialists and how to overcome them.[69] Concluding, he quotes Lenin from 'What Is To Be Done?', that workers must not constrict themselves to 'literature for workers but that they learn increasingly to engage with literature in general'. That may appear 'heretical' (ketzerisch) and, like every active tactic, dangerous ('... wie jede aktive Taktik, seine Gefahren ...'), but nobody understood such risks more than Lenin. The way mapped out by Lenin, as things stand, is the only one which makes possible 'the spiritual and therewith the organisational and political emancipation of the working class' ('Der von Lenin gezeigte Weg ist der einzige, der die geistige und damit die organisatorische und politische Befreiung der Arbeiterklasse wirklich ... vermag').

These articles by Wittfogel can be seen as a marker stage in the evolution of a more organisational step towards greater integration of cultural politics within the political. Alexander and Märten, in the early 1920s, were turning to the work of Marx to gain some purchase on aesthetic practice in the context of an historical-materialist understanding. Whilst Lenin was a marginal point of reference for Alexander, Trotsky, for example, was not on the horizon and only probably became known to Märten when she reviewed his *Literature and Revolution* in its German publication in 1924. When Wittfogel wrote these *Rote Fahne* articles, the political had changed dramatically: the 'German October' had failed, Lenin was dead, and Trotsky was being ousted by the Stalinist faction in the Soviet party. His deployment of Lenin's position on culture as against that of Trotsky, on the art, duration, and geopolitical reach of the transitional period and the possibility of a proletarian culture, can be seen as an indication of the increasing influence of Stalin on the KPD – at its Tenth Congress it had called for organisational 'Bolshevisation'. Another such stage would be marked by Wittfogel's next major contribution to *Die Rote Fahne*, to be considered in Chapter 5, when he reviewed two volumes of Mehring's essays, edited by August Thalheimer, who had formed the KPD Opposition (KPD-O).

---

68   Brauneck 1973, p. 205.

69   Ibid. 'auf die daraus entstehenden Entartungsgefahren und auf die Mittel zur Unschädlichmachung dieser Gefahren hat N. Bucharin in seiner vorzüglichen Schrift über *Proletarische Revolution und Kultur* ... in ausführlicher Untersuchung hingewiesen'.

5   Thalheimer's Introductions to Mehring's Oeuvre

5.1   *Literature*

Reference has been made in Chapter 1 to Thalheimer's introductions to Mehring's work. As one of these, for the 1929 volumes, would be the catalyst for Wittfogel's elaboration of a more scientific, i.e. Hegelian, aesthetic, they will be considered here. There is a particular dynamic to the mode of evaluation of Mehring's achievement. Both writers are very positive about Mehring's contribution to Marxist cultural thinking and to the working through of historical materialism in literary studies, but they occupy very different political sites – Wittfogel articulating the current official KPD line against the Right-Oppositionist Thalheimer.[70] Rather than a general overview of Thalheimer's introductions, the focus here will be on those aspects which Wittfogel would attend to in attacking Thalheimer's position. Wittfogel concentrates on the introduction to the collection of Mehring's writings on literature.[71] Thalheimer's introduction to Mehring's contributions to the history of philosophy (*Zur Geschichte der Philosophie*) did not appear until 1931, where it complements criticisms raised in the earlier introduction, no doubt because of the different discourse; no doubt either that these ideas were also available to Thalheimer in 1929. The general background to Wittfogel's critique was the wider availability of Marxist material published since Mehring's death in 1919, particularly relevant for him being Lenin's *Notes* on Hegel, and the consequent development of theory, which he censured Thalheimer for ignoring. Amongst particular issues were assertions that Thalheimer's understanding of capitalist development was deficient, that he shared Mehring's error in promoting an idealist aesthetic (Kant) in privileging form over content, and that his position on the art of transition to proletarian dictatorship was Trotskyist. Thalheimer positions Mehring's mode of practice as comparable with that of Marx and Engels: as with them there is little reference to method as it is being used, but it is rather worked through the material as presented ('sondern in diesen Arbeiten selbst'), the historical-materialist method as 'the critical overthrowing of the ideological bourgeois concept of history, the full mastery of actual historical

---

70   Thalheimer had been both a founding member of the KPD in 1919 and of the KP-O in 1929. Following the failure of the 'German October' he went to Moscow, where he taught philosophy at the Marx-Engels-Institute. Against the wishes of the Comintern he returned to Germany in 1928, where, with Brandler and others, he founded the KP-O, in opposition to the relapse into 'linke Kinderkrankheiten' ('left infantilism', Lenin's term of 1920) of Thälmann and the Stalinist line being pursued. He remained a Leninist and a defender of the Soviet state.

71   Published 1929, reviewed 1930.

material'. Thalheimer advances a similar claim in his introduction to Mehring's history of philosophy. 'The dialectical materialist', Thalheimer writes, 'is to be as little sought in the work of Mehring as in that of Marx, Engels, Rosa Luxemburg or Lenin except where they expressly address questions of dialectical material-ism or philosophy of history: much more it is with Mehring in his general and practical work, in which he reveals himself as a dialectical materialist and from which one can learn of dialectical materialism'.[72] He quotes from Mehring's *Nachlese* of 1899 that the 'laws of the dialectic will be learned', one who does so will 'penetrate more the dialectical relations of the real than those who have been knocking their heads against hard facts for so long'.[73] He provides a long outline analysis of the Schiller biography as example.[74]

On the questions of the materialist basis of the origins of middle-class culture of Lessing's era, Thalheimer quotes Mehring in his exchange with Paul Ernst, 'who played a brief guest role in the German worker's movement'. Based on arbitrary quotations from eighteenth-century writers, Ernst disputed Mehring's thesis that Lessing could have been 'the most advanced represent-ative of bourgeois class consciousness in Germany' because 'there was no sig-nificant bourgeoisie at that period'. A scientific history of the period, Mehring responds, will only be possible when economic facts become more widely avail-able, but at the time of writing the archives were not accessible: nevertheless, despite their comparative socio-economic backwardness, the German bour-geoisie were culturally approximating equal status with their Western coun-terparts. Thalheimer agrees with Mehring's position on the need to establish the more detailed economic background, additionally emphasising the need to articulate 'the stratifications within the bourgeois and the other classes', to establish 'the various ideological currents' of the period. In a later passage Thalheimer summarises the classical bourgeois revolutionary moment: in its preparatory stage, the bourgeoisie is already 'the decisive economic power' ('... bereits die ökonomische ausschlaggebende, herrschende Macht'), by virtue of which they will increasingly become dominant in the cultural sphere. During

---

72   Mehring 1931, p. 7. '... vielmehr ist es bei Mehring seine gesamte theoretische und prakt-ische Arbeit, in der sich der materialistische Dialektiker offenbart und an der man materi-alistische Dialektik lernen kann'.

73   Mehring 1931, p. 11. '... und wer die dialektischen Denkgesetzt kennt, wird in die dialekt-ischen Zusammenhänge der Wirklichkeit ganz anders eindringen, als wer sich an den harten Tatsachen so lange den Kopf zerstösst ...'.

74   See Chapter 1 above. On this Wittfogel would later concur: 'The political-social content of Schiller's work has never before been presented with such clarity'. See Chapter 5 for his contribution to the Soviet Literary Encyclopedia on Mehring in 1931.

the early phase, this culture will embrace proletarian struggle – Thalheimer refers to Heine and Freiligrath. These positions appear quite orthodox although Wittfogel would question Thalheimer's understanding.

Mehring's unwillingness to construct an aesthetic theory per se left him open to charges of Kantianism in his articulation of the relationship between form and content, the subjective and objective, in his work, reinforced by his scant references to Hegel. In his introductions Thalheimer addresses this issue. Mehring took a critical attitude to Kant (as set out in Chapter 1), but Thalheimer writes that 'he was right in considering Kant as the founder of scientific aesthetics' ('Mit Recht betrachetete Mehring Kant als den "Begründer der wissenschaftlichen Ästhetik"'), by which he meant no more than that Kant had established the phenomenon of art as a particular field for study, quoting Mehring that Kant 'ignored the historical condition of his aesthetic laws'. Thalheimer rejects, as did Mehring, the concept of 'subjective taste' as a basis for aesthetic understanding: a 'new Copernican' revolution was and is needed, 'from idealism to materialism, from subjectivity to objectivity', not only for Kant but for all aesthetic engagement. But Thalheimer elaborates on Mehring's assertion that historical materialism is the 'only key' to overcoming subjective taste: 'the foundation for such a solution arises from the judgement that "the productive means of material life" also condition and determine the "artistic life process"'. 'Here', Thalheimer continues, 'one must guard against a dangerous false conclusion'.[75] The precepts of aesthetics are subject to historical context and are thus variable but '[t]hat character does not at all abolish the particularity of the aesthetic, rather it demands that it be recast, revolutionised in accordance with the historical evolution of art'.[76] Therefore 'it is obvious to the dialectical materialist' ('... materialistischen Dialektiker'), he writes, 'that the aesthetic is not primary relative to art but secondary', as Mehring repeatedly emphasised ('... was Mehring immer wieder hervorhebt'). Central to this thinking is the issue of the dynamic relationship of content to form. Thalheimer draws a parallel between this way of considering the operation of the aesthetic and the laws of development of the capitalist economy: 'when the specificities of its historical development are stripped away there remains a more general

---

75   Mehring 1929, p. 23. 'Hier muss man sich vor einem gefährlichen Fehlschluss hüten'. All quotations from p. 23.

76   Ibid. 'Dieser Charakter der ästhetischen Gesetze hebt aber die ästhetische Gesetzmässigkeit überhaupt nicht auf. Er fordert nur, dass die jeweils entsprechend dem historischen Wandel der Kunst umgeformt, revolutioniert wird'. Mehring had written that Kant failed to recognise the time-bound nature of his theorising.

type of economic regularity which will still have a role in socialist society'.[77] 'Contrast', he writes, 'also always includes similarity' ('Der Gegensatz schliesst immer auch Gleichheit'), and refers to Marx's development of the laws of capitalist accumulation as 'a specific historically-transient form of an assured more general law' ('... eine spezifische, historischvergängliche Form gewisser allgemeiner Gesetze ...'), by which expansion of provision in whatever form it takes place secures material goods for society. 'So it is', he continues, 'that classical aesthetics contain a definite core of aesthetic theorising that extends beyond this or that art epoch. Mehring's exposition's indicate this'.[78] This entire passage is not a criticism of a 'deterministic' Mehring but a recovery of the unstated presence of dialectical thinking in Mehring's texts.

The form/content dynamic, the prioritising of the former over the latter, raised the most contentious issue. The idealist prioritising was most clearly articulated in Schiller's statement that 'the object of aesthetic consideration should not be the content but the form; the master's particular artistic secret consists in destroying the content through the form'.[79] Thalheimer quotes Mehring on Hauptmann's play 'Florian Geyer': 'the renewal of German drama does not lie in the overturning of dramatic form, or surely only to the extent that it is to a purpose. The disregard of customary dramatic forms is a major advance when new dramatic content can be seized ...'.[80] 'Kant und Schiller', he writes, 'only separate out form and content, without also taking into account their interrelationship' ('die Form und Inhalt nur trennten, ohne auch ihre Wechselbeziehungen in Betracht zu ziehen') and summarises Mehring's position: 'ultimately new artistic content also demands new artistic form; new content in old form is deficient, an incomplete artistic advance; new form without new content is artistic regression'.[81]

---

77   Ibid. '... wenn dies Spezifische abgestreift wird, einen bestimmten Kern von ökonomischer Gesetzmässigkeit allgemeiner Art, der auch in sozialistischer Wirtschaft noch seine Geltung haben wird'.

78   Ibid. 'Auf einige dieser Dinge mag hier an der Hand der Mehringischen Darlegungen hingewiesen werden'.

79   Wittfogel 1977, p. 59. 'dass der Gegenstand der ästhetischen Betrachtung nicht der Inhalt, sondern die Form sei, dass des Meisters eigentliches Kunstgeheimnis darin besthehe den Stoff durch die Form zu vertilgen ...'.

80   Mehring 1929, p. 25. 'Die Wiedergeburt des deutschen Dramas liegt nicht in der Umwälzung der dramatischen Form oder doch nur soweit darin, als diese Umwälzung Mittel zum Zwecke ist. Die Missachtung der überkommenen dramatischen Formen ist ein grosser Fortschritt wenn durch sie ein neuer Inhalt des Dramas erobert werden kann ...'.

81   Ibid. '... ein neuer künstlerischer Inhalt erfordert letzen Endes auch eine neue künstlerische Form; der neue Inhalt in alter Form ist ein Mangel, dass heisst ein unvolkommener

Thalheimer recognises the absence of Hegel in Mehring's 'Aesthetic Excursions'. The historical materialist must engage with Hegel despite the idealism of his philosophy, both to address the inadequacies of Kant's thinking but also to develop a more thoroughgoing materialist aesthetic than either of these. Hegel develops his theory of the evolution of art within the general schema of his philosophy of history, motivated by the 'Absolute Idea', subjugating art to the schema of his Logic rather than developing the logic and objective dialectic from the actual development of art itself. A particular problem is the religious dimension (... dass das Ideal und die Kunstformeln wurzeln in den religiösen Grundanschauungen der Zeiten und Völker ...). But despite the many violations of the real development of art, one also finds there original and profound individual insights concerning 'social interrelationships and, in the final analysis, class relationships and modes of production with reference to the forms and contents of art'.[82] Hegel's class-related characterisation of Cervantes' *Don Quixote*, the knightly epic ... of Dutch painting can 'with only slight alterations', Thalheimer proposes, 'be carried over into a historical-materialist history of art or aesthetics'.[83] He sets out a number of points where Hegel contributes, giving the issue of Tendenzkunst as an example, where, because of a lack of mediation, 'the artwork is essentially fractured, where form and content no longer appear as having been fused'.[84] He quotes Hegel on the ideal of art, 'the recovery of the real from the particular and contingent to the extent that the inner appears, in the generality of the external subsumed, as living individuality'.[85] But Thalheimer concludes on this Hegel passage that the historical-materialist aesthetic 'cannot therefore avoid Hegel nor can it naturally remain with him', but as Marx said 'to put it on its feet', and 'simultaneously free itself from the system'.[86]

---

    künstlerischer Fortschritt; neue Form, die keinen neuen Inhalt enthält, ist vom Übel, dass heisst sie führt zu einem künstlerischen Rückschritt'.

82   Mehring 1929, p. 26. '... so geniale und tiefe Blicke in einzelnen finden sich bei ihm über den Zusammnenhang der gesellschaftlichen Verhältnisse, letzen Endes der klassen Verhältnisse und der Produkionsweise mit den Formen und den Inhalten der Kunst'.

83   Ibid. 'Seine klassenmässigen Charakteristiken von Cervantes' "Don Quijote", des Ritterepos ... der holländischen Malerei könnten mit nur leichten Änderungen in eine historisch-materialistische Kunstgeschichte oder Ästhetik übernommen werden'.

84   Mehring 1929, p. 27. '... das Kunstwerk ein in ihm selbst Gebrochenes, in welchem Form und Inhalt nicht mehr als ineinander verwachsen erscheinen'.

85   Ibid. '... die Wirklichkeit zurückgenomonen aus der Breite der Einzelheiten und Zufälligkeit insofern das Innere in dieser der Allgemeinheit entgegengehobenen Äusserlichkeit selbst als lebendige Individualität erscheint'.

86   Ibid. '... kann also nicht an Hegel vorbeigehen, sie kann natürlich nicht bei ihm stehenbleiben, sondern muss ... zugleich vom Zwang des Systems befreien'.

Finally, Thalheimer concurs with Mehring's pre-war perspective on the possibility of a proletarian art prior to the seizing of power, writing that the conditions that Mehring observed still applied at present ('... dass sie heute noch genau so richtig sind wie jemals'). He compares Mehring's attempt at the Freie Volksbühne to foster proletarian drama with the current state of the Piscator theatre: 'the hitherto fortune of the Berlin Piscatorbühne from the point of view of the artistic and economic is a pertinent example of the plain truths established by Mehring'.[87] Thalheimer asks, despite the success of the proletarian revolution in Russia, did a proletarian art develop? He answers in the negative: 'The dispute over its characterisation, whether there is proletarian art or not, whether "proletarian art" is after all possible, appears to us to be richly scholastic and undialectical'.[88] The new content, arising from the great convulsive events of the revolution and civil war, 'has not yet found new forms adequate to that content' ('Die neue Formen, die dem neuen Inhalt gemäss sind, sind noch nicht gefunden'). They will be discovered, but not arbitrarily contrived or constructed ('... nicht willkürlich ausdenken oder konstruieren'). Mehring's Marxist-informed writings provide both a positive and negative compass: positive in that new forms do not arise from nowhere; negative in that neglect of content in pursuit of new form leads nowhere. Again, in his concluding passage, Thalheimer takes the opportunity to emphasise the unstated dialectical dimension in Mehring's writing.

5.2   *History of Philosophy*

As with his assessment of Mehring's achievement in the first introduction, Thalheimer is again very positive here. Mehring is 'unsurpassed', bordering on the unique, in his uncovering of the historical roots of individual philosophies and philosophers in the class struggles and economic bases of their eras, but against that 'his systematic interest in the generality of questions on dialectical materialism were not equally strong ...'.[89] Rather than articulating it systematically, 'he deployed it in his historical and political work' ('... als es in der Praxis der historisichen und politischen Arbeit anzuwenden'), acknowledging from

---

87 Mehring 1929, p. 31. 'Das bisherige Schicksal der Berliner Piscatorbühne, in künstlericher wie in ökonomischer Hinsicht, ist eine zutreffender Beleg für die von Mehring festgestellten einfachen Wahrheiten'.

88 Ibid. 'Der Streit um ihre Bezeichnung, ob das neue proletarische Kunst sei oder nicht, ob "proletarische Kunst" überhaupt möglich sei, scheint uns reichlich scholastisch und undialektisch'.

89 Mehring 1931, p. 7, 'war sein systematisches Interesse an der Gesamtheit der Fragen des dialektischen Materialismus nicht ebenso stark ...'.

first to last in his writings 'the methods and principles of the dialectic or, as he himself preferred, historical materialism'.

As noted above Thalheimer had returned to Berlin in 1928 from Moscow where he had been teaching at the Marx-Engels-Institute, an experience which informed him *inter alia* of the publishing situation with regard to the work of the major Marxist theoreticians. But the study of Mehring's contribution to the materialist history of philosophy must be brought into correspondence with related work by Marx, Engels, Plekhanov, and Lenin; 'we point above all to the advantage of the extremely important publications of previously unpublished work of Marx and Engels on the subject of dialectical materialism by the Moscow Marx-Engels-Institute, to the unfortunately sparse appearance of Plekhanov's works in German translation and the foundational work of Lenin in this area'.[90] 'This exercise', he writes, 'will not only produce a necessary systematic completion but to some extent correction' to Mehring's work, whilst also allowing Thalheimer to present his own understanding of where the studies were at that moment.[91]

He addresses the completion and correction on four points. Mehring had considered philosophy as ideologically-driven mental fabrication ('Hirnweberei'). Thalheimer modifies this by adding that 'the history of philosophy is not merely a history of ideology but simultaneously within certain boundaries and for individual classes at historically decisive moments, the development of a real science, of formal logic and dialectic' ('... Entwicklung wirklicher Wissenschaft, der formalen Logik und der Dialektik'). The history of philosophy does not comprise the totality of dialectical materialism but a section: the rest is formal logic and dialectic ('Der andere Teil ist die formale Logik und die Dialektik').[92] Dialectical materialism 'is not only method but also world view' ('... ist nicht nur Methode sondern auch Weltanschauung' ...), with systematic interrelationships and developmental stages as in science. It is not therefore a closed system in the manner of previous philosophies but a developing one. Finally, dialectic is not only a formal logic ('formale Denklehre'), a theory of

---

90   Ibid. 'Vor allem verweisen wir zu diesem Behufe auf die höchst wichtigen Veröffentlichungen bisher ungedruckter Arbeiten von Marx und Engels auf dem Gebiete der dialektischen Materialismus durch das Moskauer Marx-Engels-Institut, aud die leider sehr wenigen bisher in deutscher Übersetzung von Lenin auf diesem Gebiet'. The KPD had begun publishing work by Marx, Engels, and Lenin in 1927 on dialectical materialism.

91   Mehring 1931, p. 7. '... das nicht nur notwendige systematische Ergänzungen, sondern auch teilweise Korrekturen ergibt'.

92   Mehring was actually aware of this, quoting from Engels to that effect (see Chapter 1, n. 60 above). The charge of 'Hirnweberei' may apply to the work of Kant, Dietzgen, Mach and others, as Korsch proposes in support of Mehring (see Chapter 1, n. 37 above).

the laws of thought, but at the same time a theory of the general laws of movement in nature and history, the latter being primary, the former deduced from them ('... von denen die beiden letzeren die primären, die ersteren die davon abgeleiteten sind').[93]

The above completions and corrections of Mehring's position on dialectical materialism form the basis for a concise history of the dialectic from Hegel through to Feuerbach, Marx and Engels, to Plekhanov and Lenin; 'the materialist dialectician under whose leadership the working class established its first dictatorship in the Soviet Union' ('... unter der Führung des materialistischen Dialektikers Lenin ...').[94]

Thalheimer's two introductions are important contributions at this juncture in the context of Mehring's continuing presence in mainstream KPD thinking on cultural politics and the increasing pressure, through the recently formed Bund proletarische revolutionäre Schrifsteller (BPRS, Association of proletarian revolutionary writers), for a proletarian art. The above introduction on literature (1929) would be the starting point for Wittfogel's series of articles.

---

93 Mehring 1931, p. 15. All quotations from this page. A more recent commentator on Mehring's contribution, Thomas Metscher, re-addresses aspects of his work and its continuing relevance in his essay 'Franz Mehrings philosophische Schriften'. Writing of Mehring's theorisation of the scope of the practice of historical materialism, Metscher claims that: 'Such a concept of the relationship of historical process and idea, of being and consciousness, can really be designated dialectical' ('Ein solcher Begriff des Verhältnisses von historischem Prozess und Idee, von Sein und Bewusstsein kann ein wahrhaft dialektischer heissen'). Viewed overall 'Mehring's concept of Marxism is *historical* and *critical*, whereby the concept of critique is combined with deduction and proof'. 'The last word on Methode and Welantschauung', he continues, 'has not yet been said' ('... zu dem das letzte Wort noch nicht gesagt ist'). Requisite for his materialist concept is 'an ethical existential moment that till now has unfortunately been neglected'. Mehring's Marxism finds its place 'as a challenging presence in the framework of a Marxism which in fact must be pluralist if it is going to satisfy today's demands' ('... als spannungsvolle Ergänzung im Rahmen eines Marxismus, der in der Tat plural sein muss, will er heutigen Anforderungen genügen') (Metscher 1996, pp. 76–7).

94 Mehring 1931, p. 21. Thalheimer also writes an Appendix on contemporary bourgeois philosophy, focusing on neo-Hegelianism.

Wittfogel's Critique of Thalheimer's Introduction

In the opening passage of the first chapter, 'A Portrait', we have encountered the high appraisal of Mehring's political and cultural contribution to the proletarian movement in the words of Rosa Luxemburg and Clara Zetkin. When Wittfogel wrote his review of the two volumes of Mehring's work published in 1929, edited by Thalheimer, much had changed. Nevertheless his appraisal of Mehring's achievement can only adequately be described as an encomium. His review is titled: 'Die Pionier der marxistischen Literaturkritik in Deutschland'. Before considering the review in detail, its pivotal point should be established: 'Our confirmation of the extraordinary quality of Mehring's writings on literature should naturally not allow us to remain blind to the limits'. Just as it would be 'unacceptable to allow a great achievement by Mehring to remain unknown or unused', similarly it would be no less acceptable 'should we be uncritically satisfied with Mehring's heritage, without also consequently subjecting it to Marxism-Leninism'. The introduction of Leninism in this context is a very clear indication of change of orientation in critical assessment.[1]

Mehring's achievements in general are set out. This present two-volume publication finally allows 'every revolutionary worker and Marxist to form a vibrant image of this significant side of Mehring's contribution'. It is not a completely integrated history of German literature but it 'deals with a vast amount of the essential manifestations of the German literary world' ('... einen sehr grossen Teil der wesentlichen Erscheinungen der deutschen literarischen Welt'). Mentioned also are Mehring's few but 'encompassing and far-reaching investigations on language and style' ('... ausser den weniger umfassenden und tiefgreifenden Untersuchungen über Sprache und Stil ...'). Wittfogel picks up on Mehring's disavowal of any attempt to construct a Marxist aesthetic theory per se in his introduction to his 'Aesthetic Excursions' (see above, 'The Question of an Aesthetic', Chapter 1). As Mehring emphasised, 'there is no

---

1 Brauneck 1973, pp. 391–6, 393. 'Diese unsere Feststellung des *ausserordentlichen Wertes* der Mehringschen Schriften zur Literatur darf uns naturlich nicht blind machen gegen *die Grenzen* ... Frevelhaft wäre es, auch nur eine einzige der grossen Leistungen Mehrings unanerkannt und unausgenutzt zu lassen. Nicht minder frevelhaft aber wäre es, wenn wir uns kritiklos mit dem Erbe Mehrings zufriedengeben würden, ohne es am konsequenten, d.h. am *leninistischen* Marxismus zu prüfen'.

Marxist model per se presented here, rather it is thought of as ground rules (Prolegomena) for such'.[2]

In his passage 'Literaturkritik im Lichte des Marxismus', Wittfogel highlights Mehring's pioneering role 'almost without a model' ('.... fast ohne Vorbild'). He succeeded 'in making newly accessible in a Marxist sense a whole sphere of spiritual life' ('... eine ganze Sphäre geistigen Lebens marxistisch neu zu erschliessen'), seeking its 'grounding through historical materialism' ('mittels des historischen Materialismus ...'). In contrast to bourgeois criticism he brought to the attention of the reader an immense number of core issues that threw a searchlight on the class meaning of works, as in the Schiller biography how the social and political questions found their place, or as in the case of Heine or Freiligrath, amongst others, developing representations of how the working-class movement played a role. Not only does Mehring introduce a Marxist dimension to literary studies, but at the same time his work constitutes 'an original contribution to the deepening of our scientific insights into the class struggle as it has developed within the political and ideological husk of late feudal-bourgeois Germany'.[3] At this point he introduces the caveat with which I began the passage – an acknowledgement of his great achievement but also an awareness of certain limitations. His following passage 'Kant oder Hegel' indicates the tendency of his reservation.

He begins with a reference to Lenin and his comment on how 'the old German left' had gradually detached itself from the 'so-called Marxist centre' ('... langsam erst vom sogenannten marxistischen Zentrum losgelöst'), both to 'complete' dialectical materialism through Kant, to factually 'correct' it.[4] Unlike the Russian Marxists, the German left did not stand aside from this revisionism despite qualifications; they could not fully withdraw from Kantian influences. 'This manifests itself particularly', Wittfogel writes, 'in Mehring's conceptions in the arena of art theory, the aesthetic'.[5] Wittfogel takes Kant's claim that that which pleases outside of all interest is alone beautiful, and considers Mehring's

---

2   Brauneck 1973, p. 392. 'Also hochwichtig müssen endlich ... Mehrings "Ästhetische Streifzüge" genannt werden. Allein als grundlegende Vorbemerkungen (Prolegomena) zu einer solchen sind sie doch offenbar gedacht'.

3   Brauneck 1973, p. 393. 'Sie stellen zugleich ein einzigartiges Hilfsmittel dar zur Vertiefung unserer wissenschaftlichen Einsicht in die Klassenkämpfe, die sich politisch und in ideologischer Hülle im spätfeudal-bürgerlichen Deutschland abgespielt haben'.

4   Brauneck 1973, pp. 393–4. 'Auf philosophischen Gebiete war es der Austromarxismus, der den dialektischen Materialismus durch Kant "ergänzen", d.h. faktisch "korrigieren" wollte'.

5   Brauneck 1973, p. 394. 'Das zeigt sich insbesondere auch bei Mehrings Auffassungen auf dem Gebiet der Kunsttheorie, der Ästhetik'.

responses to that claim on two grounds. Unlike Kant's ahistorical position, Mehring certainly historicises the artwork: 'only ever in its historically conditioned manner, only in its continuous infringement', can it be understood. But this form of the weakening and violation of Kant's position still leaves Kant's core tenet in place, Wittfogel insists.[6] The second claim is that the aesthetic judgement does not at all extend to the object ('gar nicht auf das Objekt geht'), but rather that 'the form of the appropriateness of an object' is solely what matters ('... sondern rein der *"Form* der Zweckmässigkeit eines Gegenstandes" gelte'). This claim formalises the consideration of the artefact. Mehring, again, has fully criticised this Kantian principle but 'nevertheless has not superseded it' ('... jedoch nicht aufgehoben'). Had Mehring set out from Hegel instead of Kant, then he would have found a very different starting point ('... dann hätte er für sein Beginnen einen andersartigen Fusspunkt gefunden'). He quotes Hegel: 'because the content is what ... decides in art. Art ... has no other pursuit but to provide adequate sensuous presence for its replete content'.[7] In the Hegelian aesthetic, 'form must express the content, which is determinate, in an appropriate manner', but in the aesthetic of Kant and Schiller, 'form must eradicate content, annihilate it'.[8] Wittfogel's judgement is that Mehring, despite the many materialist qualifications he raises ('... so starke materialistische Einschränkangen er auch erhebt ...'), follows the Kant-Schiller position; consequently his fundamental formulations must remain 'insufficient from a Marxist position' ('... doch marxistisch unbefriedigend bleiben ...'). His pioneering materialist analyses disturbingly validate Kant's formal principle.[9] He is quick to assert that 'our criticism detracts nothing from Mehring's significance' ('Unsere Kritik nimmt den Arbeiten Mehrings nichts von ihrer Bedeutung'): it would be folly to accuse Mehring for a position he shared in general with Rosa Luxemburg and Karl Liebknecht. Such indulgence is not, however, permitted to Mehring's

---

6   Ibid. '... [A]ber in Gestalt dieser Abschwächung und Durchlöcherung *doch faktisch "durchgesetzt"'.*

7   Ibid. 'Denn der Gehalt ist es, der ... in der Kunst entscheidet. Die Kunst ... hat nichts Anderes zu ihrem Beruf, als das in sich selbst Gehaltvolle zu adequäter, sinnlicher Gegenwart herauszustellen'.

8   Ibid. '... soll die Form den Inhalt der das Bestimmende ist, in angemessener Weise *ausdrücken.* In der Ästhetik Kants und Schillers, soll die Form den Inhalt *vertilgen,* ihn zunichte machen'. Lukács initially held the same opinion but in his essay on Schiller (1935), published two years after his major essay on Mehring, he found Schiller's position to be more complex and nuanced than the 'eradication' of content.

9   Brauneck 1973, p. 395. Wittfogel here refers to a coming article in which he will address this issue more fully. This would be a series in *Die Linkskurve* under the title 'Zur Frage der marxistischen Ästhetik', to be considered below.

editor, Thalheimer, the section on whom is titled 'Thalheimer as Gravedigger' ('Totengräber').

Ignoring all the events (October and November revolutions) and changes that had occurred since Mehring's activities, 'the readership is offered a highly uncritical account of his work' ('... in diesem Sinne höchst unkritisch Mehrings Werk darbieten'). Of course he had to acknowledge that Mehring ignored Hegel's aesthetics ('... an Hegels Ästhetik "vorbeiging"'), but failed to see that more profound principles were at stake, regarding its absence as an 'undoubted omission' ('... als ein "gewisser Mangel" schien ihm hier vorzuliegen'). Little wonder that Thalheimer himself fully takes on board Kant's aesthetic formalism ('... *sich die Kunstformel Kants vollinhaltlich zu eigen macht*'). In his introduction to Mehring's texts, Thalheimer quotes a number of passages from Hegel's aesthetics which he feels could mediate between Mehring's concrete analyses based on historical materialism and the dialectic.[10] Wittfogel sees these quotations as being little concerned with the core problems of materialism but rather that Thalheimer 'pays lip service to Lenin's demand for a materialist study of Hegel' ('... legt Thalheimer als Lippenbekenntnis zu dem von Lenin geforderten materialistischen Studium Hegels ab').[11] Further to this charge of opportunism Wittfogel claims that 'in reality Thalheimer seeks to reconcile materialism with Kant' ('In Wirklichkeit sucht er den Materialismus mit Kant zu "versöhnen"').[12] Thalheimer fails to understand 'Lenin's philosophically structured principles of Marxism' ('gegenüber den von Lenin ausgebildeten philosophischen Prinzipien des Marxismus'), a failure repeated relative to 'ongoing questions of the revolutionary workers' movement'. The importance of Mehring's oeuvre for the movement stands, *not because of* Thalheimer's contribution but *in spite of* it ('Beides freilich nicht *dank* der Tätigkeit der Herausgeber. Sondern *trotz* ihrer').[13]

In these two *Rote Fahne* interventions – 'Über proletarische Kultur' (1925) and the present one – Wittfogel, as a member of the KPD cultural committee, has mapped out a number of positions which also correspond to changing

---

10   Brauneck 1973, p. 395. These quotations refer to passages in Mehring 1929, pp. 25–7.

11   Kevin B. Anderson throws light on the currency of Lenin's study of Hegel in Germany at the time, writing that 'while Lenin's Hegel notebooks were not published until 1932 in German, some of his other post-1914 writings on Hegel and dialectics had begun to appear in German by the early 1920s'. *A propos* of Wittfogel's exculpation of Mehring vis-á-vis Hegel, Anderson quotes Bloch that 'Hegel was never so pushed aside as in Germany after 1850' (Anderson 2007, pp. 122–3). Wittfogel ignores the fact that Thalheimer had been teaching at the Marx-Engels-Lenin Institute in Moscow between 1923 and 1928.

12   Brauneck 1973, p. 396.

13   Ibid.

political relationships both within the KPD and between it and the Soviet party, in which the influence of Lenin is evident. In the earlier series, he rejects 'spontaneism' as Lenin had done in his 1920 booklet on 'left-wing infantilism', but he also rejects Trotsky's negative position on the possibility of a proletarian art during the transitional period towards proletarian dictatorship. In his review of Mehring's work, Thalheimer, as a founder-member of the KPD-O (Opposition), replaces Trotsky as a target figure, but Wittfogel refines his criticism by advancing the importance of Lenin's reading of Hegel both for a revolutionary politics and for confronting any residual Kantianism in cultural thinking. The demands for a changed set of cultural practices, institutionalised in the party-based associations of writers and artists in 1928 would see Wittfogel develop the above positions in *Die Linkskurve*, the journal of the revolutionary writers' association. This would be the series 'Zur Frage der marxistischen Ästhetik'.[14]

1   **Zur Frage der marxistischen Ästhetik (On the Question of Marxist Aesthetic)**

Roughly contemporary with his *Rote Fahne* review of Mehring's writings as introduced by Thalheimer and his publishing of the above-named series in *Die Linkskurve*, Wittfogel contributed an entry on Mehring to the Soviet Literature Encyclopedia in 1931. This was republished in the journal *Die Rote Aufbau* ('Red Structuring') early in 1932 with a brief but very politically indicative introduction by the editorial board (Die Schriftleitung). The particular aim of the Encyclopedia entry was 'to discuss the position of the leading pre-war German Marxist historians on the problem of the superstructure, especially in the field of literature'.[15] The enquiry was initiated by 'the foundational letter of Comrade *Stalin*' ('Der grundlegende Brief des Genossen *Stalin*'), concerned with 'certain questions on the history of Bolshevism' ('... über einige Fragen der Geschichte des Bolschevismus ...'). This concern was that 'the wholly particular achievement of Lenin and Leninism might not be understood if one did not provide with full clarity not only the ideas and contributions but likewise the limits and serious errors of the non-Russian left, above all the German'.[16] Comrade Wittfo-

---

14   Brauneck 1973, p. 395.

15   Wittfogel 1977, p. 50. 'Er behandelt eine Spezialfrage: die Stellung des führenden marxistischen deutschen Vorkriegshistoriker zum Problem des Ueberbaus, insbesondere zur Literatur'.

16   Ibid. '... dass die ganz spezifische geschichtliche Leistung Lenins und des Leninismus nicht verständlich wird, wenn man sich bezüglich der Auffassungen, der Verdienste, aber auch

gel's article is 'the start of a comprehensive critical analysis of the position of the pre-war German left in all areas of Marxist theory and praxis'.[17] As against the more discursive dimension of his review, where Thalheimer is heavily criticised for not discussing failures in Mehring's theoretical position, Wittfogel is here more scientific, more Leninist, in undertaking that task himself.

The assessment of Mehring's overall contribution is again very positively evaluated. 'His *Lessing-Legende* is a most imposing achievement' ('Am grossartigsten aber hat Mehring Lessing dargestellt'), the result of his capacity to apply historical-materialist method to the richness of his historical knowledge and achieve a highly politicised outcome. The Schiller biography is similarly evaluated ('... in die Nähe der "Lessinglegende"'), 'the socio-political content of Schiller's production has never before achieved such clarity'.[18] His biographical-introductory essay to Heine's *Collected Works* in 1911 'belongs to his most outstanding achievements' ('über *Heine* gehört zu seinen Glanzleistungen'). His work on the poet's political stance to the bourgeois revolution and communism is 'widely documented, scientifically demonstrated' ('... wiederum mit sehr breiter Dokumentierung wissenschaftlich dargetan'). His work on the political nature of Romanticism is commended, as is also that on Naturalism. But it is in the arena of the aesthetic and critical theory that problems arise, stemming not from a tendency towards reformism as such but from the historical situation in which he happened to be: for example, the unavailability of Lenin's writing on party literature when Mehring was forging his own approach, or his inclusion of Lassalle in his aesthetic consideration, a sympathy he shared with Rosa Luxemburg, as may be seen from her 1913 commemorative piece, 'Nach 50 Jahren' ('After 50 Years').[19] His shortcomings were by-and-large ascribed to factors he shared with other 'leftist' colleagues during the period, including Luxemburg. Lenin had outlined 'the origins and mode of operation of Opportunism before 1914' but the German left failed to split from the Reformists to form a new party, opting instead to try 'to efface the difference between

---

die Grenzen und teilweise schweren Fehler der nicht russischen Linken, vor allem der jenigen Deutschlands, keine volle Klarheit verschafft'.

17 Lukács's biographical-length essay on Mehring (1933), to be considered below, would also be a contribution to this enterprise. Thalheimer's challenge over the interpretation of the roles of the Soviet and German parties in the 'German October', set out above in Chapter 4, provides a broader background.

18 Wittfogel 1977, p. 54 (both quotations). 'Der politisch-gesellschaftliche Gehalt der Produktion Schillers ist in einer vorher nie erreichten Klarheit ins Licht gesetzt'.

19 Luxemburg 2009 [1913], pp. 26–30. This was published in the 'Leipziger Volkszeitung' of which Mehring was editor. Not without reservation she nevertheless writes 'Lassalle and Marx led the working class up to the peaks of science' (Luxemburg 2009 [1913], p. 30).

a Lassallean Reformism and the revolutionary lineage of Marx and Engels' ('... Reformismus eines Lassalle und der revolutionären Linie von Marx und Engels zu verwischen'.) Despite the greatness of his achievement Mehring was a typical representative of the inconsistent left-wing of the old SPD, 'which did not yet possess an understanding of Marxist-Leninist practice and theory' ('... die noch nicht marxistisch-leninistischen Züge seiner politischen Praxis und seiner Theorie ...').[20]

Wittfogel cites two instances where Mehring's sympathy towards aspects of Lassalleanism were subject to criticism, both ascribed to Lenin. He writes:

> The error established by Lenin in Mehring's judgement of Lassalle also intrudes in ... ideological analysis. The historical materialism which Mehring in his foundational principles has most definitively made his own is permeated with *elements of an idealist aesthetic* which damage his impressive, audacious and comprehensive literary research in a number of ways as his attempt to conserve the politician Lassalle's reputation becomes sharper and more pronounced.[21]

In an earlier passage Lenin's response to the Lassalle issue is described as 'a rebuke' ('... von Lenin gerügten ...'), where Mehring is considered to be supporting specific Lassallean *aesthetic* views against the founders of historical materialism, if 'of course, qualified'.[22] This tendency Wittfogel also notes in Mehring's 1911–12 'outstanding work, *Freiligrath und Marx in ihrem Briefwechsel (Freiligrath and Marx in their Correspondence)*', which includes an exchange on the nature of the party and the writer's relationship to it, at its pinnacle or outside it, the latter position being Freiligrath's decision.[23] This exchange long preceded Lenin's 1904 article on party literature, but at the moment of Wittfo-

---

20 Wittfogel 1977, p. 52. This was literally so as the texts were not yet available.

21 Wittfogel 1977, p. 55. 'Der von Lenin festgestellte Fehler M[ehring]s in der Beurteilung Lassalles wirkt sich auch in der Ideologieanalyse störend aus. Der historische Materialismus den M. in seinen Grundprinzipien aus entschiedenste aufgenommen hatte, durchsetzt sich im gleichen Masse, in dem M.s Bemühungen am die Ehrenrettung des Politikers Lassalle bestimmter und schärfer werden – mit *Elementen einer idealistischen Ästhetik*, die den grossartigen, kühnen und umfassenden Literaturuntersuchungen Ms an einer Reihe von Punkten Abbruch tun'.

22 Wittfogel 1977 p. 54. '... gegen Marx und Engels auch bestimmten ästhetischen Meinungen Lassalles gegen die Begründer des historischen Materialismus seine freilich bedingte Zustimmung gegeben'.

23 Wittfogel 1977, p. 55. '... hat M. in einer besonderen Arbeit, "Freiligrath und Marx in ihrem Briefwechsel ..."'.

gel's article it was now being pursued more rigorously than before, particularly within the BPRS and *Die Linkskurve*, where any derogation would be subject to criticism.[24]

1.1 *Die Linkskurve*

As both Wittfogel and Lukács were to contribute major theoretical articles to *Die Linkskurve*, it is important to establish briefly the cultural politics of the BPRS (Association of Proletarian-Revolutionary Writers). It was not founded by the KPD but on the initiative of the International Association of Revolutionary Writers (Internationale Vereinigung Revolutionärer Schriftsteller: IVRS), in discussion with the writer Johannes Becher and other German Communist writers, and established in 1928 as the German Section of the Moscow International Association. Helga Gallas, whose history of *Die Linkskurve* is being drawn on here, notes 'the reservation on the side of the KPD ('Die Reservierheit auf Seiten der KPD ...'), nor was it initially financed by it, and its first number complained about 'the lack of understanding shown by the KPD', ('... Klagen des Bundes über das mangelnde Verständnis von Seiten der KPD ...').[25]

Although the greater number of members were communist, there were problems with the deployment of Marxism-Leninism in the field of literature. Gallas quotes from an account of developments from the BPRS to the Central Committee of the KPD in 1929: 'As we put the finalised programme of the association to the communist fraction for discussion it became very clear that even with our own comrades the application of Marxism-Leninism to the field of literature produced the greatest difficulties. We had to abandon the programme debate'.[26] The problem was the base-superstructure relationship which was initially 'solely mechanically perceived and in most articles of the early period remained totally unclear'.[27] The role of the Arbeiterkorrespondent as the authentic source of the new literature gave rise to divisive debate within the BPRS. The 'spontaneist' position was represented by the slo-

---

24   Related to this was Mehring's failure to articulate a 'proletarian aesthetic' as such.

25   Gallas 1974, pp. 29, 45, 46. The party retained a similar type of distance from MASCH, the Marxist Workers' School. The 'lack of understanding' complaint echoes that of Herzfelde in his 1922 'Gesellschaft, Künstler und Kommunismus' (see the passage in Chapter 2 above).

26   Gallas 1974, p. 35. 'Als wir das endgültige Progamm des Bundes in der kommunistische Fraktion zur Diskussion stellten, zeigte es sich krass, dass auch bei unseren eigenen Genossen die Anwendung des Marxismus-Leninismus auf das Literatur-Gebiet auf die grössten Schwierigkeiten stösst. Wir mussten die Programmdebatte fallenlassen ...'.

27   Gallas 1974, p. 32. 'dass das Basis-Überbau-Verhältnis in der LINKSKURVE [sic] vorerst bloss

gan 'Von der ersten Arbeiterkorrespondenz zur ersten Kurzgeschichte' ('From
the first worker correspondence to the first short story').[28] The counter-slogan
'Gegen den Ökonomismus in der Literaturfrage' ('Against economism in the
question of literature') reflects the concern with the danger of reductivism or
non-mediation. Joseph Winternitz, elected to the Central Committee of the
KPD in 1929, wrote under the above title in *Die Linkskurve*:

> We don't need 'the excessive literary language of professional writers' ...
> But the proletarian writer must understand his craft, the art of words,
> exactly, as we demand from the proletarian painter that he understands
> how to use stylus or brush. An awkward report on a strike for the factory
> paper can be more useful for class struggle than a masterwork of pro-
> letarian literature. Notwithstanding, we do not choose to designate this
> report 'proletarian literature', and the reporter a 'proletarian writer'.[29]

Winternitz quotes Lenin in support: 'only some poorly equipped intellectuals
think it is sufficient for the workers if one writes about events in the factory and
"repeats over and over again the well-known"'.[30] Paraphrasing Lenin, he writes:
'The literature we need must reflect the whole life of society, of all classes from
the viewpoint of the revolutionary proletariat' ('das Leben aller Klassen vom
Standpunkte des revolutionären Proletariats widerspiegeln'). The Marxistische
Arbeiterschule (MASCH), founded in 1925, would be a resource for addressing
some of these issues: it provided an array of courses for workers compatible
with the purposes of the KPD, including detailed courses on Marxism, the capitalist economy, culture, literature, and fine arts. Members of ASSO and the BRPS
lectured there.[31]

---

    mechanisch aufgefasst wurde und in den meisten Aufsätzen der ersten Zeit überhaupt
    völlig unklar blieb'.

28   *Die Linkskurve* 1976, 2, no. 3, pp. 18–20.

29   *Die Linkskurve* 1978, 2, no. 3, pp. 10–12. 'Wir brauchen nicht "halsbrecherische Wortkunsts-
    tücke berufmässiger Literaten" ... Aber proletarische Literaten müssen ihr Handwerk, die
    Kunst des Wortes, genau so verstehen, wie wir von einem proletarischen Maler verlangen,
    dass er mit dem Griffel oder Pinsel umzugehen versteht. Ein ungelenkener Bericht über
    einen Streik kann für die Betriebszeitung für den Klassenkampf nützlicher als ein Meister-
    werk der proletarischen Literatur. Deshalb wollen wir diesen Bericht jedoch nicht zur
    "proletarischen Literatur" und den proletarischen Berichterstatter nicht zu einem "pro-
    letarischen Schriftsteller" ernennen'.

30   *Die Linkskurve* 1978, 2, no. 3, p. 12. '... Nur einige (schlechte) Intellektuelle denken, für
    die Arbeiter genüge es, wenn man von der Fabrikordnung erzählt und "längst Bekanntes
    wiederkäut"'.

31   See Gerhard-Sonnenberg 1976. Its director was Hermann Duncker, a member of the Cent-

Although not the only problem raised by 'spontaneist' tendencies within the
BPRS one such instance gives an indication of ensuing debates. Maxim Vallentin, director of the agitprop group 'Das Rote Sprachrohr' ('Red Megaphone'),
submitted a draft to the editorial board, which amended it. He resisted the
interpolated 'Hegelian vocabulary' and insisted that new forms could not result from this 'organic' context of theatre from 'Aristotle to Mehring', but from
the interaction of author, director and the 'open form' of staging. Fitness for
struggle (Kampfwert) was the only criterion for assessing the 'political' and
'aesthetic' quality of the troupe. The editorial board, of which Wittfogel was a
member, strongly rejected this argument according to which 'we are no longer
on the *stage* of class struggle but present to the actual economic and political class struggle itself. If this melding of the one with the other is right for
the stage, then Comrade Vallentin must simply plant a machine gun on his
stage. Its fitness for struggle is not to be doubted'.[32] The board's response was
resolute: 'Only Tendenz (fitness for struggle) and no art. With that we have
lowered our ostensibly blood-red flags in the face of the despised bourgeois aesthetic'.[33] Gallas notes that on the conclusion of that debate, the next issue, May
1930, contained Wittfogel's first contribution, the articulation of an aesthetic
markedly indebted to Hegel's highly mediated dialectical aesthetic system. She
also remarks on 'the same indifference to Brecht's [epic] theatre as to agitprop',
a subject that will be considered later.[34] Wittfogel, Johannes Becher, a founding member, and others formed an anti-leftist group which, as Becher reported,
was the object of 'an intense hatred' from that fraction, being described as being

---

      ral Committee of the KPD and responsible for the party's education and propaganda sec-
      tion.

32   *Die Linkskurve* 1978, 2, no. 4, pp. 16–17, 16. 'Wenn diese Gleichsetzung des Klassenkampfes
      mit seinen ideologisch-bewussten künstlerischen Ausdruck auf der Bühne richtig wäre,
      dann müsste Genosse Vallentin einfach Maschinengewehre auf seiner Bühne aufpflan-
      zen. Deren Kampfwert ist nicht zu bezweifeln'.

33   Ibid. 'Nur Tendenz (Kampfwert) und keine Kunst! Damit haben wir vor der verachteten
      bürgerlichen Ästhetik alle unsere angeblich blutroten Fahnen gesenkt'. Later, in Septem-
      ber, Wittfogel writes that 'the achievements of a good Agitproptruppe are art' ('... die
      Leistungen einer guten Agitproptruppe sind Kunst'), but that the practice which equates
      'Tendenz' with non-art ('... Tendenz, also nicht Kunst ...') would be 'opportunistic capit-
      ulation to bourgeois values' behind which 'the ultra-left' hides ('das wäre eine oppor-
      tunistische Kapitulation vor bürgerlichen Wertsetzungen, die durch die ultralinke Geste
      hinter der sie sich vorbirgt'). *Die Linkskurve* 1978, 2, no. 9, pp. 22–6, 26, n. 6. This is the fifth
      in his series 'Zur Frage der marxistischen Ästhetik'.

34   Gallas 1974, p. 109. 'Die gleiche Indifferenz wie gegenüber der Agitprop zeigte Die LINK-
      SKURVE [sic] Brecht gegenüber'. In a 1931 review of 'Die Massnahme', there is no mention
      of epic theatre, of the 'non-Aristotelian theatre'.

'far worse than the right' ('... weit schlimmer als die Rechten ...'). As a result
Wittfogel's ideas were not taken up in that leftward shift. But with the increasing influence of Lukács in 1932 their more mediated thinking was to prevail.
Describing the series as the first attempt in Germany to set out a more accurate
Marxist aesthetic ('... Ansätze darzustellen, genauer'), Gallas makes the interesting observation that 'Lukács, who would slightly later become the spokes-
man for this direction in the Marxist aesthetic, was dependent on Wittfogel in
some elements'.[35]

Mehring, it will be remembered, refused to elaborate a merely speculative
aesthetic, preferring a more applied approach, of making available for contemporary use the best from the revolutionary past. Although Wittfogel and Lukács
would elaborate a more theoretically informed aesthetic, it is still one directed towards application, guidelines for contemporary production. Wittfogel, for
instance, extrapolates from Hegel's 'a chain with three links' and substitutes
them with his own, including 'the artistic arrangement of themes' and 'their
mode of realisation' (July 1930 article below). In his critique of Bredel's novels,
Lukács sets out what the successful proletarian-revolutionary novel has to do
and how: the concluding sentence in his 'Tendency or partisanship', the latter
is proposed as 'an important point at which we can break through to the full
use of Marxism-Leninism for our creative method'.

2   Wittfogel's Series

> We are ... for a proletarian-revolutionary aesthetic founded on dialectical
> materialism. For a Marxist aesthetic that is as little inseparable from com-
> munist politics as is Marxist philosophy.[36]
>
> KEMENY

Wittfogel's articles in *Die Linkskurve*, 'Zur Frage einer marxistischen Ästhetik',
were, as Gallas remarks, 'really the first in Germany to present more precisely the tendencies and principles of a Marxist *aesthetic*' ('... erste Versuch in
Deutschland überhaupt, Ansätze und Prinzipien einer marxistischen *Ästhetik*

---

35   Gallas 1974, p. 111. '... derjenigen Richtung der marxistischen Ästhetik, deren Wortführer –
      sich in einzelnen auf Wittfogel stützend – wenig spätere Lukács wurde'.
36   *Die Rote Fahne* 1931, September, p. 10. 'Wir sind ... für eine proletarisch-revolutionäre
      Ästhetik auf der Grundlage des dialektischen Materialismus. Für eine marxistische Ästhe-
      tik, die von der kommunistischen Politik ebensowenig zu trennen ist, wie die marxistische
      Philosophie'.

darzustellen, genauer ...'). The series ran from May to November 1930, with a final article in June 1931, a response to Lu Märten's criticism.

These articles, published in the proletarian-revolutionary journal, *Die Linkskurve*, cover the aesthetic thinking of Kant and Hegel, its critique by Marx, and in light of Lenin's reading of Hegel (and his encouragement that Hegel's *Logic* be read and discussed in party journals). He moves quickly from a rehearsal of his earlier critique of Mehring and Thalheimer to a detailed engagement with Hegel's idealist dialectic and to its materialist inversion. For example: in the July article he presents Hegel's idealist 'chain with three links' in the realisation of art and then substitutes his own materialist three 'links'. The September article addresses the art of the proletariat in struggle followed by the art of the proletarian dictatorship. The October article sets out in detail the 'formal-idealist' and 'dialectical-materialist' determinations of form and content. In the November article the tone shifts from a general philosophical-aesthetic discourse to an instructive guideline one, the recognition of textual elements and their application, schematic in its presentation. His theorising is set out in fuller detail below.

In his introductory remarks, he mentions the political turmoil against which the series is written and the need for the 'Kulturfront' to participate in these struggles. The more particular motive was the publication of Mehring's work and Thalheimer's introduction, but, in contrast to Thalheimer, 'to uphold with all strength Lenin's elaboration of the core structure of Marxist philosophy'.[37] He is a sympathetic reader of Mehring but his ascription to him of a Kantian orientation is questionable. The second heading, 'Mehrings Ausgangspunkt: Kant' ('Mehring's point of departure: Kant') overstates the case to a considerable extent. Mehring, as stated above, accorded Kant the role of founder of an aesthetic science in that he had separated out the phenomenon of art for specific study, but apart from that Mehring was highly critical of him – Kant's concept of the 'Ding-an-Sich' was 'a major retrogressive step against materialism' ('Allein mit dem "Ding-an-Sich" machte Kant ... einen gewaltigen Rückschritt gegen den Materialismus'): he rejected subjective taste as the basis for an aesthetic science, and Mehring criticised him as the least historically concerned of the Enlighteners – Kant took for the absolute what was only relative – and, as Wittfogel writes here, 'Kant's theory of beauty is historically conditioned' ('... freilich nur in historisch-bedingter Weise'), an exculpation trope Wittfogel uses on a number of occasions to detach Mehring from charges of idealism. Mehring

---

37   *Die Linkskurve* 1978, 2, no. 5, pp. 6–7, 6. '... wenn in Gegensatz zu Thalheimer, die von Lenin herausgearbeitete Kernstruktur der Marxschen Philosophie mit aller Schroffheit aufrechterhält'.

never subscribes to a theory of beauty in his writings. Thalheimer is more correct in his characterisation of Mehring as practical aesthetician and dialectician (the dialectic of form and content as found in his work on Schiller and Hauptmann, for instance). Wittfogel's ascription here seems to be one based on strategy: the displacement of Kant by Hegel and the greater deference to Lenin: likewise, outside Russia the increasing support for Lenin's Marxist conceptions ('... auch ausserhalb Russlands immer stärker an Boden gewinnende Leninische Marxauffassung ...').

The June article is titled 'Kant oder Hegel – der Ausgangspunkt einer marxistischen Ästhetik'. The subjective dimensions of Kant's philosophy in general and the aesthetic in particular are outlined with a quotation from Engels 'on the philosophical whim' ('philosophische Schrulle') of Kant's subjective theory of knowledge. Due regard is accorded the progressive nature of idealism vis-à-vis mechanical materialism during its period, as acknowledged by Marx, Engels, and Lenin, but that has now been superseded by the active and the dialectic, by dialectical materialism. We are again reminded that Mehring did not hold all of Kant's aesthetic in high regard, his judgement based on his 'materialist instinct' ('materialisticher Instinkt'). Hegel wrote that Kant in countering the 'objective dogmatism' ('objektiven Dogmatismus') of his predecessors had substituted for it a 'subjective dogmatism'. 'Hegel's philosophy', Wittfogel writes, 'unites the two, the mechanistic dominance of being and the equally mechanistic consciousness, in a higher unity, if admittedly also with metaphysical idealist symptoms'. Whilst in Kant's thinking 'being and consciousness were externally and superficially connected ... Hegel's philosophy of totality shows the world indeed as a self-contradictory unity (and in the final analysis conceptually sustained)'.[38] Consequently, 'forms of thought and forms in art are no longer accidentally and externally bound with their subject matter but necessarily so' and, contra Kant and Schiller, 'the form of the artwork does not function to efface the content, to cause its disappearance, but in a fitting manner to bring to expression the essence of the event'.[39] Thus, Wittfogel claims, 'the subject matter of the work of art will no longer stand outside the great and crucial interests of the time but will express vividly in the language particular to art

---

38   *Die Linkskurve* 1978, 2, no. 6, pp. 8–11, 10 '... zeigt Hegels Totalitätsphilosophie die Welt als eine, freilich widerspruchsvolle (und letzen Endes vom Begriff getragene Einheit'). All references are from this page.

39   Ibid. 'Die Formen des Denkens – und der Kunstproduktion – sind also nun nicht mehr zufällig und äusserlich mit ihrem Stoff verbunden, sondern auf eine notwendige Weise. Die Form des Kunstwerks ist nicht dazu da, um den Gehalt zu vertilgen, ihn verschwinden zu lassen, sondern um ihn in der dem Wesen der Sache angemessenen Weise zum Ausdruck zu bringen'.

their material nature'.[40] Unlike Kant, who saw only the play of beauty ('nur ein schönes Spiel getrieben'), Hegel saw the people 'deposit their richest inner intuitions and ideas in art', very often 'the key to understanding of their wisdom and religion'.[41] Despite his inherent idealism his aesthetic marks a massive step forward ('einen ungeheuren Fortschritt') from Kant. For this reason Lenin called for 'a systematic study of Hegel's dialectic interpreted in materialist terms'.[42]

The July article focuses on the essence of the artwork (Wesen des Kunstwerks). The opening paragraph briefly summarises the difference between Kant's and Hegel's positions on nature: Kant's ascription to the deity, nature as passive, Hegel's still retaining the religious dimension but nature as freely active, engendering change. The latter informed Marx's thinking on the active role of man in nature and the consequences for the organisation of society from particular modes of production. As a result of his dialectical mode of thought, still metaphysical, Hegel saw the concept unfolding to a higher level in society than in nature ('... den Begriff sich in der Gesellschaft höher entfalten als in der Natur'). He further asserted that not only natural beauty 'but also the processes of human society are aesthetically more incomplete than artistic beauty' ('... sondern auch die Vorgänge in der menschlichen Gesellschaft ästhetisch unvollkommen seien, als das Kunstschöne'). Only occasionally and accidentally 'did the essence of phenomena come to light in the prose of life' ('... in der Prosa des Lebens das Wesen der Erscheinungen anschaulich klar zutage'), normally the whole (das Ganze) appeared only as a manifold, separate particulars ('... eine Menge von Einzelheiten ...'). But, Wittfogel continues, this situation relates to earlier social formations, including late monopoly capitalism ('... im monopolistischen Spätkapitalismus'): under 'the systematically planned society of socialism, despite certainly not losing its validity, this perception will undergo fundamental condensing down of which Hegel had no presen-

---

40   Ibid. '... aber steht wiederum nicht ausserhalb der grossen und wesentlichen Interessen der Zeit, sondern er drückt gerade anschaulichen Sinnlichkeit aus'.

41   *Die Linkskurve* 1978, 2, no. 6, p. 11. '... haben die Völker ihre gehaltreichsten inneren Anschauungen und Vorstellungen niedergelegt ... und für das Verständnis der Weisheit und Religion macht die schöne Kunst sie allein den Schlüssel aus'.

42   Ibid. '... hat Lenin aufgefordert ... zur Organisation eines systematischen, von materialistischen Geschichtspunkten geleiteten Studium der Dialektik Hegels ... nach allen Seiten hin ausarbeiten ... in unseren Zeitschriften aus den wichtigsten Werken Hegels Auszüge publizieren und ... diese Hegelsche Dialektik in die Sprache der Materialisten übersetzen'. Lenin's programme seems to be what Thalheimer suggested in his introduction to Mehring's literary studies (see above Chapter 4), although Wittfogel disputes this – 'not as Thalheimer does in his study of Mehring' ('... wie das Thalheimer in seinem Vorwort zu den Mehringbänden tut, dürfen wir natürlich nicht').

timent'.[43] The phenomena of life, the contemporary relations to his time and class position, which the struggling human attempts to grasp through scientific insight expects to see in a similarly exact historical manner their vivid artistic representation. 'Just as the realm of science', Wittfogel continues, 'aspires with the instrument of abstraction to uncover the laws of motion of natural and social processes, so the artist shows us vividly, through his particular means, their sensuous reflection'.[44] He briefly lists how the various media, including film, achieve this effect. He references Hegel: 'the beautiful appearance which the artwork produces is not the play of subjective capacities of consciousness, that even the worst dissembling appearance (heuchlerisch Schein) is, as with every true appearance, the presence of the inner law of the event itself for another'.[45] 'Far therefore from being pure appearance', Hegel wrote, 'the representations of art are, relative to customary reality, endowed with a higher reality and a more truthful existence'.[46] Wittfogel comments that 'that is fully dialectically thought through' ('Das ist vollständig dialektisch gedacht'): what Marx had stated in the economic context 'we find here, despite the idealistic husk, similarly firmly established for the realm of art' ('... trotz der idealistischen Hülle, ähnlich tief für das Bereich der Kunst festgestellt'). Wittfogel here introduces the form/content relationship as articulated by Hegel: fine art cannot, from the point of view of content, allow free rein to phantasy ('... in wilder Fessellosigkeit der Phantasie umherschweifen, ...') because the interests of Spirit set precise limits for their objectives ('... diese geistigen Interessen setzen ihr für ihren Inhalt bestimmte Haltpunktefest ...').

Hegel, Wittfogel continues, envisaged a 'chain with three links': 1. the interests of the time ('... die Interessen der Zeit'), mystified as 'geistigen Interessen'; 2. the regular, and in accordance with theoretical principles, emergence of the content of art from these interests; 3. through these contents, again in accordance with theoretical principles, specific forms, through which alone contents

---

43   *Die Linkskurve* 1978, 2, no. 7, pp. 20–4, 20. All above quotations taken from p. 20. 'Für die planmässig organisierte Gesellschaft der Sozialismus erfährt sie, ohne freilich ihre Gültigkeit überhaupt zu verlieren, eine tiefgreifende Einschränkung von der Hegel nichts ahnte ...'.

44   *Die Linkskurve* 1978, 2, no. 7, p. 22. 'Wird in der Region der Wissenschaft mit dem Werkzeug der gedanklichen Abstraktion die Blosslegung der Bewegungsgesetze der natürlichen und gesellschaftlichen Vorgänge erstrebt, so zeigt uns der Künstler jene Gesetzmässigkeiten mit den ihm eigentümlichen Mitteln sinnenmässiger Anschaulichkeit'.

45   Ibid. '... ein Erscheinen des inneren Gesetzes der Sache selbst für Andere'.

46   Ibid. 'Weit entfernt also, blosser Schein zu sein, ist den Erscheinungen der Kunst, der gewöhnlichen Wirklichkeit gegenüber, die höhere Realität und das wahrhaftigere Dasein zuzuschreiben'.

achieve representation in their appropriate manner.[47] Wittfogel rejects the
first, replacing it with the social and political informed by historical materialism and proposes his own tripartite formula:

1.   Social-political struggle, conditioned in turn by the prevailing state of pro-
      ductive forces and the appropriate type of material production;
2.   The artistic arrangement of themes ('Die künstlerische Themenstellung'),
      the content ('der "**Inhalt**"'), the material ('der "**Stoff**"') of artworks;
3.   The mode of realisation of the theme, the form ('die "**Form**"'), the config-
      uration ('die "**Gestaltung**"').

It is through the elements of this model, Wittfogel claims, 'that class struggle in
the sphere of art is conducted' ('Ausdruck ... des Klassenkampfes in der Sphäre
der Kunst'), even if not always directly ('... keineswegs immer direkt und hand-
greiflich in der herrschenden Kunst kundgeben ...'). Obviously Hegel's aesthetics could raise none of these issues, addressing as they do the subject of class
struggle in art. Here he refers to the work of the art historian Wilhelm Hausenstein, 'who has done in the area of visual art what Mehring had done with
his concrete analysis in literature', and 'that for the first time, by way of Marx's
theorised concept of historical conjuncture, a higher form of thinking the aesthetic becomes possible'.[48]

The heading of the first section of his August article is 'Thalheimer's vulgar-
Marxist "Analysis"'! He quotes Marx on the historically conditioned relationship between material and spiritual production, 'for example a different type
of spiritual production conforms to the capitalist mode of production than
to the mode of production of the middle-ages'. He ascribes to Thalheimer a
three-stage model of the relationship between capital and art, based on the

---

47   Ibid. 'die gesetzmässig, nicht regellos, aus diesen Interessen hervorwachsenden Inhalte
      der Kunst ... die durch diese Inhalte wiederum in gesetzmässiger Weise bestimmten For-
      men, durch die jene Inhalte allein in der ihnen angemessenen Weise zur Darstellung
      gelangen'.
48   *Die Linkskurve* 1978, 2, no. 7, p. 24. '... dass erst und nur mittels der von Marx konstituierten
      Geschichtspunkte eine höhere Form ästhetischer Betrachtung möglich wird'. Wittfogel
      references the book in footnote 17: *Der nackte Mensch aller Zeiten und Völker*, Munich, 1911.
      'The first attempt to create a Marxist history of art' ('Der erste Versuch der Schaffung einer
      marxistischen Kunstgeschichte'). In 1912, Hausenstein published *Bild und Gemeinschaft.
      Entwurf einer soziologie der Kunst* (*Image and Society: A Sociological Outline of Art*). In 1914,
      his *Die bildende Kunst der Gegenwart* (*The Art of the Present Day*) was published: Chapter 9
      is titled 'Das soziale Element in der Kunst der Gegenwart' ('The Social Element in the Art
      of the Present'). These publications constituted an early corpus of socially informed art
      history. Lu Märten was part of Hausenstein's circle; he reviewed her play 'Bergarbeiter'
      ('Miners') very favourably, and as her archive shows, he discussed contemporary art with
      her. See above Chapter 2. For Hausenstein's work, see the Appendix below.

theory of surplus value (Mehrwert): early capital was niggardly relative to the 'unproductive' and, thus, artists: with the absolute growth of surplus value ('mit dem absoluten Wachsen des kapitalistischen Mehrwertes') greater generosity to art, but in the imperialist stage, encountering constriction, capitalism cuts back, placing the quality of art in danger ('... qualitativ werde die Kunst jetzt gefährdet'). He describes Thalheimer's model as 'a barbarous truncated conclusion' ('... barbarische Kurz-Schluss') of the relationship between surplus value and the condition of art and is 'wholly false for the stage of early capitalism' ('... ist für die Zeit des Frühkapitalismus völlig falsch'), as the bourgeoisie of that period, with a few exceptions, were not in a position to be the dominant class vis-à-vis the Absolute Courts.[49] In addition to the amount of wealth available for this courtly type of art and the themes cultivated, there are essentially other social conditions not addressed by Thalheimer. The increasingly social and associated cultural, self-consciousness of the young revolutionary bourgeoisie curbed this state of affairs but could not abolish it. The law of motion of art ('... das Bewegungsgesetzt der Kunst ...') 'within bourgeois society', he writes, 'must be more concretely grasped' ('... konkreter gefasst ... werden') and in a manner different from Thalheimer. Marx had identified clearly capitalism's unpropitious (Kunstfeindlichkeit) relationship to art at an earlier stage and Hegel had recognised that 'bourgeois society was not advantageous to art' ('... dass die bürgerliche Gesellschaft der Kunst nicht günstig sei ...'). Calling upon Marx's method and deploying Hegel's theory of history, 'we can seek to grasp the requisite principle, around which Thalheimer moved helplessly in circles'.[50] Writing in the 1820s, 'Hegel gives as ground, above all, the strongly emerging scientific thought' ('... nennt Hegel zunächst das In-den-Vordergrund-Dringen wissenschaftlichen Denkens').[51] Hegel sang the praises of the 'heroic age', whose qualities provided Homer's greatness, and noticed their absence in contemporary bourgeois society but could not give an account of that ('Erklären konnte er sie nicht'). 'For this', Wittfogel writes, 'he would have needed a class-based analysis, which from his bourgeois position he could not advance'.[52] 'We will see', he concludes, 'that employing the above means given

---

49   Although 'technically' correct, Wittfogel's judgement seems restrictive. Mehring's *Lessing-Legende* deals with exactly the imbalance Wittfogel refers to, and as Thalheimer refines Mehring's reading, it is not clear how Wittfogel is reading Thalheimer.

50   *Die Linkskurve* 1978, 2, no. 8, pp. 15–17, 15. 'In Anwendung seiner Methode und unter heranziehung Hegelscher Geschichtspunkte werden wir das Prinzip selbst zu erfassen suchen, um das Thalheimer sich hilflos im Krise herumgedreht'.

51   *Die Linkskurve* 1978, 2, no. 8, p. 16.

52   Ibid. 'Dafür hätte es einer klassenmässigen Analyse bedurft, zu der von seinem bürgerlichen Standarte aus nicht vorstossen konnte'.

to us by Hegel and Marx a fundamental answer to the question of proletarian art can be determined, a dialectical answer, that is, an answer that looks totally different from what Trotsky – and in a much weaker and stunted manner Thalheimer – have expressed on this issue'.[53]

The September article discusses issues related to proletarian art, with its title 'Die Kunst des um die Macht kämpfenden Proletariats' ('The art of the Proletariat in its struggle for power') indicating its content. Its first section is headed 'Die Tendenzproblem', a vexed issue, as may be seen above in the exchange between Max Vallentin, leader of the agitprop group 'Das Rote Sprachrohr', and the editorial board of *Die Linkskurve*. As the truth of bourgeois art declines within the increasing contradictions of capitalism, proletarian art will become the only site 'from which the truth can be spoken, what is' ('... wo ansgespochen werden kann, was ist'). 'Does proletarian art therefore require a particular tendency?', he asks, and defines Tendenz 'as the intention to call forth a definite effect'.[54]

The intention – particular to the proletariat – is the overthrow of the bourgeois state, the establishing of the dictatorship and the building of socialism. 'How does genuine, profound representative art stand relative to this intention?', he asks. The dialectical mode teaches us something other than Kant's subjectivism: through it the genuine artwork speaks in its intuitive, sensuous means, the deepest accessible truths of its epoch. He quotes Hegel: 'From this perspective it may be affirmed that the higher art's standing the more such (instructive) content it has to take up ... Art has in fact become the first teacher of the people'.[55] Only the proletarian artwork can articulate the contradictions of bourgeois society, can become 'the truthful artwork' ('ein wahres Kunstwerk werden'): 'to that extent it is also Tendenz' ('In sofern auch ist es Tendenz'). This is not the unmediated Tendenz of which Vallentin (above) was accused in his controversy with the editorial board of *Die Linkskurve* but the highly mediated Tendenz informed by Hegel and dialectical thought. [As we shall see below, Lukács used 'Tendenz' in a reductive sense.] Capitalist accumulation also implies 'the accumulation of misery' ('verbundene Akkumulation

---

53   *Die Linkskurve* 1978, 2, no. 8, p. 17 '... auf die Frage nach der Möglichkeit einer proletarischen Kunst ermittelbar wird, eine dialektische Antwort, d.h. eine Antwort, die grundsätzlich anders aussieht als das, was Trotzki – und, in abgeschwächter und verkümmerlicher Form, Thalheimer – zu diesem Punkte geäussert haben'.

54   *Die Linkskurve* 1978, 2, no. 9, pp. 22–6, 22. 'Bedarf dafür die proletarische-revolutionäre Kunst einer besonderen "Tendenz" ... Tendenz ist die Absicht, eine bestimmte Wirkung hervorzuruffen'.

55   Ibid. '... dass die Kunst, je höher sie sich stellt, desto mehr solchen (belehrenden) Inhalt in sich aufzunehmen habe ... Die Kunst ist in der Tat die erste Lehrerin der Völker geworden'.

des Elends') but includes too the heroism of class struggle. 'Elendsmalerei', the painting of immiseration, is only a half-truth: 'the relation of these two moments produces the real truth of the representative artwork of our time'. Through this the proletarian artwork seeks to be 'that notable artwork' ('jenes hochstehende Kunstwerk zu sein') of which Hegel spoke. In contrast to the bourgeois concealment of Tendenz, the proletarian artwork honestly declares it. Wittfogel, in line with the editorial board policy, insists on the art in the artwork: content is suspended 'always in the sphere of sensuous intuition' ('immer in der Sphäre der sinnlichen Anschauung'). No criticism being raised here, he writes, of the 'non-developed proletarian artists and writers' ('unfertige proletaraische Künstler, Schriftsteller ...'), but 'it is the large mountains that are difficult to scale, not the small'.

The second half of the article carries the title: 'Die Kunst der proletarischen Diktatur'. The protagonists are Trotsky and Lenin: 'the former, "as is well known", bluntly took up a negative position', the latter a positive one. For Lenin it was a question of how this was to be achieved: he sharply rejected any attempt 'to falsely "conceive" a proletarian culture rather than developing it dialectically from a deconstruction of the cultural heritage', but 'that such a culture must be established was not up for discussion'.[56] Thalheimer is accused of siding with Trotsky's ideas, based on an excerpt from his introduction to Mehring's literature studies: a new great art will emerge 'when the socialist construction is so widespread, that the springs of social riches flow freely'.[57] Trotsky's and Thalheimer's positions are characterised as a 'fully mechanical conception' ('Eine völlig mechanische Auffassung'). Although the proletariat has the political strength to defend itself against internal and external enemies, only in the cultural field, according to this theory, is it still stuck in chaotic beginnings. As though the heroic period of construction itself were not chaotic in places: as though the magnificent social revolutionary storm itself did not offer the most colossal impetus to a great art. 'For the dialectician Hegel', he notes, 'the heroic ages are the ages of great art' ('... sind die heroischen Zeitalter die grossen Zeitalter der Kunst'). Subject to Marxist critique such a concept could be adapted for the heroic art of recent socialist achievement – ten years

---

56   *Die Linkskurve* 1978, 2, no. 9, p. 24. '... dass aber eine solche Kultur sich herausbilden müsse, stand für ihn ausserhalb jeder Diskussion'. The difference was based on conceptions of the duration of the transitional phase, as Wittfogel set out.

57   Wittfogel modifies his criticism by acknowledging that Thalheimer's terms 'as one knows' ('Wie man weiss') are from Marx's 'Critique of the Gotha Programme', and are applied to the 'higher phase of communist society', a stage which Lenin designates 'in a narrower and proper sense' ('... im engeren und eigentlichen Sinne nennt').

after the end of the civil war in the Soviet Union, novels and film achieve the heroic epic ('das Heldenepos'). We separate ourselves from Trotskyist discouragement and pessimism. We see in contemporary Soviet art the early form of very great art in the epoch of the dictatorship ('... während der Epoche der Diktatur') before the higher phase of communism develops. What follows is a paean to Soviet film in this Hegelian context (but complicated by a need to criticise Thalheimer for a position he did not hold): 'one who simply perceives in Soviet film new contents, who is not capable of sensing that from the new contents already a complement of new forms have unfolded, who despite the flood of films new in content and form still awaits "the artistic genius who will ultimately bring the new forms", has perhaps fervidly studied Kant's theory of genius'.[58] The quotation is from Thalheimer's concluding passage to his introduction to Mehring's writings on literature, where his opinion on the question of the art of the transitional phase is consonant with that of Lenin. Wittfogel has quoted Lenin above as rejecting the attempt 'to falsely [artificially, künstlich] conceive a proletarian culture rather than developing it dialectically'. In this passage Thalheimer writes that the new forms for the new contents have not yet been found, 'but they will be found and they will not allow themselves to be arbitrarily thought or constructed' ('... aber sie lassen sich nicht willkürlich ausdenken oder konstruieren'), hardly a Kantian position. Wittfogel's position here is more directly politically motivated: 'The right-oppositionist scepticism concerning the creative powers of the revolutionary proletariat finds in such a theory its specific cultural politics expression'.[59]

Wittfogel's October article is titled 'Formal-Idealistische und Dialektisch-Materialistische Auffassung der Kunstformen', with the subheading 'Auffassungen und ihre Vorgeschichte' ('Two conceptions and their prior history'). A diagram links Kant-Schiller/Lassalle/Mehring (Rosa Luxemburg) as one source and Hegel/Marx-Engels/(Plekhanov) on the other, but significantly cross-referencing Mehring and Luxemburg to Marx and Engels. Wittfogel comments that whilst Mehring had absorbed so much of the materialist sources, he had not fully let go of the idealist. Building on the July and September material, the outlining of structural transformations of theme and truth content ('... der struk-

---

58   *Die Linkskurve* 1978, 2, no. 9, p. 25. 'Wer nicht im sowjetrussischen Film lediglich neue
       Inhalte bemerkt, wer nicht wahrzunehmen vermag, dass sich hier aus den neuen Inhalten
       heraus bereits eine Fülle neuer Formen entfaltet haben ... wer angesichts der Flut "künst-
       lerischen Genius wartet, der endlich die neuen Formen bringen soll" der hat – vielleicht –
       Kants Genietheorie mit heissem Bemühen studiert'.
59   *Die Linkskurve* 1978, 2, no. 9, p. 26. 'Der rechts-opportunistische Unglaube an die schöp-
       ferische Kräfte des revolutionären Proletariats findet in solcher Theorie seinen spezifis-
       chen kultur-politischen Ausdruck'.

turwandlungen von Themenstellung und Wahrheitsgehalt ...') of bourgeois and proletarian art, it is now time to address 'what the motives are through which the relationship between forms in art and artistic contents are determined'.[60]

'Significant for Kant's formalist conception', Wittfogel writes, 'is his aversion to the experiential dimension of artistic content' ('Bezeichnend für Kants formalistische Denkweise ist seine Scheu vor der Lebensnähe des künstlerischen Inhalts'). Just as the older Kant had capitulated to Absolutism on the question of religion, 'so too in this text had he capitulated to Absolutism in the realm of the aesthetic' ('... er kapitulierte in dieser Schrift vor dem Absolutismus auch auf dem ästhetischen Gebiet'). The 'classical' Schiller conformed to Kant's formalist idealism. Before his conversion to enlightened Absolutism, the young Schiller had been a disciple of a revolutionary way of thinking about art espousing the thematic and subject matter. 'He had once', Wittfogel comments, 'challenged the theatre that it become a guide through bourgeois life, hold authority to account, to speak truth to power', a position he abandoned.[61] Now 'the most serious material must be so handled that we have the capacity immediately to transform it into the lightest type of performance', an attitude culminating in the definitive 'in a true work of art content should be nothing, form everything' ('In einem wahrhaft schönen Kunstwerk soll der Inhalt nichts, die Formal alles sein'). 'Why this trivialisation of content', Wittfogel asks, 'why such devaluation of substance?' 'Because', he continues, 'this earlier advocate of revolutionary-bourgeois tendencies, who now politically became the messenger of white terror against the bourgeoisie, simultaneously switched in his classical poetry from material of concern to the bourgeoisie to that of enlightened Absolutism'. To the extent that Schiller directed all attention to the apparently novel forms emerging from the new range of material, 'he veiled the socio-political orientation of his changed stance'.[62] Mehring correctly noted 'the basic counter-revolutionary tendency of Schillerian-idealism' but because of Lassalle's influence could not fully, despite many reservations, reject it, placing himself on this issue at odds with Marx and Engels. Rosa Luxemburg is also brought to book on Schiller for recognising him as 'the dramatist of great style ... embodying tragedy to its greatest power and effect', placing her here

---

60 *Die Linkskurve* 1978, 2, no. 10, pp. 20–3, 20. '... welches die Bestimmungsgründe sind, nach den das Verhältnis der Kunst-Formen und des künstlerischen Gehalts sich regelt'.

61 *Die Linkskurve* 1978, 2, no. 10, p. 22. 'Der junge Dichter war Anhänger einer vom Thema, vom Stoff her orientierten revolutionären Kunstbetrachtung gewesen ... Hatte er einst von der Bühne gefordert, sie solle ein Wegweiser durch das bürgerliche Leben sein, sie solle die gesetztgebende Macht zur Verantwortung ziehen, solle den Grossen der Welt die Wahrheit, die sie sonst nie oder selten hören, ins Gesicht sagen'.

62 Ibid. '... verschleierte er den gesellschaftlich-politischen Sinn seines Frontwechsels'.

in the idealist camp, where 'the material is deduced from the formal requirements of the genre' ('... der Stoff aus den formalen Bedürfnissen der Kunstgattung abgeleitet').[63] The opposing line of thought, which Mehring approached, 'leads from Hegel, by way of the materialist inversion of Marx and Engels to Plekhanov' ('... führt von Hegel – unter materialistischer "Umstülpung" – über Marx und Engels zu Plekhanow'), a line which fundamentally declared 'form as the derived, not as the moment of derivation' ('... die Form für das abgeleitete, nicht für das abgleitende, Moment'). 'With this', he concludes, 'the materialist principle is preserved, securing the dialectic'.[64]

The November article continues the subject being developed in October, under the title 'Die Gestaltung des Stoffs' ('The Forming of Subject Matter'). Thoroughgoing idealism proposes 'that it is form which seeks its material' ('... dass es die Form sei, die sich ihren Stoff suche'). Even before his Mehring introduction, Thalheimer had shown that 'the dialectical-materialist relationship between content and form was a sealed book'.[65] Briefly restating the Hegel/Marx-Engels/Plekhanov line, he writes: 'accordingly we wish to set out concisely in the following paragraphs what the dialectical-materialist position seems to us' ('... was uns der dialektisch-materialistische Standpunkt zu sein scheint ...').

The first passage is titled 'Der Stoff – der Ausgangspunkt der Kunstgestaltung' ('The Subject Matter – the Starting Point for Form in Art'). 'Existence-subject-matter-forming', he begins, 'compose a unity in the artwork which permeate each other in contradictory fashion, and obviously so as the subject matter emerges from a socially class-based existence'.[66] The unity of the three moments is also upheld in the Hegelian aesthetic, including that of contradiction, but 'the third element', Wittfogel writes, 'is essentially other than in Hegel, where allegedly the spirit or concept expresses the content (Gehalt): In the Marxist conception the Hegelian idealist structure is destroyed and replaced by a materialist foundation'.

---

63 Quotations are from her review of Mehring's biography, Chapter 1 above.

64 *Die Linkskurve* 1978, 2, no. 10, p. 23. 'Damit ist das materialistische Prinzip gewahrt ... dessen dialektische Gestaltung ... sicher-gestellt wird'.

65 Ibid. '... das ihm das dialektisch-materialistische Verhältnis von Ihalt und Form ein versiegeltes Buch ist'. Wittfogel footnotes his source as 'the Thalheimer Deborin book on Spinoza', Wien-Berlin 1928, an indication of the level at which this issue was pursued.

66 *Die Linkskurve* 1978, 2, p. 9. 'Leben-Stoff-Gestaltung bilden im Kunstwerk eine Einheit, die sich in widerspruchsvoller Weise durchsetzt, und zwar so, dass der aus dem (gesellschaftlich-klassenmässigen) "Leben" hervorwachsende Stoff den Ausgangspunkt der künstlerischen Gestaltung bildet'.

At this point, Wittfogel introduces the term 'Motiv', not unambiguous in its employment in the art context, into the context of the other terms used, "Stoff" (subject matter), 'Leben' (existence), and illustrates their interrelationship with reference to the concrete example of Zola's *Germinal.* In a somewhat cryptic passage, the dynamic is set out: 'Subject matter is not the "motif", as little as "existence" is the subject matter. But as the subject matter is contained in "existence", so too is the motif. The duty of the artist is to develop the second from the first, to discover and extricate it'.[67] Wittfogel concludes the passage: 'The same relationship between motif and forming persists but at a higher stage'.[68] His example:

> a specific form of existence: capitalism, experienced from the proletarian position; subject matter, need and the struggle of the working class, decomposition of petit bourgeois elements, exploitation and extravagance of the bourgeoisie; theme in a narrower sense, a concrete slice of life – the fate of a miner. Motif: a young worker enters mining life, a major strike develops. With the selection of this double-motif (Doppelmotiv), indebted to Zola's *Germinal,* it is possible to indicate a powerful range of subject matter in its essential forms of motion. The young worker experiences in the pit and in spare time the characteristic events that mark the everyday of the coalminer. In the strike movement, the fate of the miner is raised to the height of an as yet immature but already heroic political manifestation of strength. What holds good for the action equally does so for the activists: 'the deeper, more richly they are stirred in the expressions of their conditions, the artist has so much stronger formed what represents human concerns, that is, has creatively extracted and formed what possibilities inhere in the subject matter, the decisively crucial aspect'!'[69]

Although no artistic (or scientific) truth is absolute truth, 'there is nevertheless an objective real, "absolute" world: what in Lenin's formulation holds true

---

67   Ibid. 'Der Stoff ist nicht das "Motiv", so wenig wie das "Leben" der Stoff. Aber wie im "Leben" der Stoff, so ist in diesem das Motiv enthalten. Die Aufgabe des Künstlers ist es, das Zweite aus dem Ersten zu ent-wickeln, herauszu-wicklen, heraus zu-finden'.

68   Ibid. 'Zwischen Motiv und Gestaltung endlich besteht das gleiche Verhältnis auf höher Stufe noch einmal'.

69   Ibid. 'Je tiefer und reicher die Menschen in ihren wesentlichen Lebensäusserungen ergriffen sind, desto starker hat der Künstler, was die Menchendarstellung angeht, den Stoff "geformt", d.h. die in Stoff ruhenden (dies ist entscheidend wichtig!) Möglichkeiten schöpferisch "herausgeholt", gestaltet'.

for scientific truth applies equally so to artistic truth'.[70] Lenin writes: 'The dialectical materialism of Marx and Engels implicitly includes relativism but not reductively so, that is, it concedes the relative nature of all our knowledge but not in the sense of denying objective reality, rather in the sense of the historical restrictions of the boundaries in the advance to our knowledge of that truth'.[71] 'As approximation to knowledge proceeds in an historically regulated manner', he writes in conclusion to this section, 'so too does it in artistic production (Kunstschaffen)'. Subject matter and selection of motif, together with form-giving, relate to social class positions at a given time.

The following short section is titled 'Formänderungen-Ausdruck realer Aenderungen' ('Changes in Form – the Expression of Changes in the Real'). Thalheimer is again the figure of critique, being accused of an idealist concept of form: 'Marxism does not recognise such self-movement of form'.[72] Wittfogel quotes Marx in the context of form in the organisation of labour, namely that changes in form only follow objective changes – that is right also for art forms. Except for changes in minor details, art forms only change in response to changes in motif, generated by social change. Essential changes in conception, in forming, indicate that essential transformations in the art-creating class have already preceded them. 'Either forward development (Vorwärtsentwicklung) has taken place: thereupon form must follow. Or the general prospect, the themes have become deformed, shrivel up, decline, because the supporting class ... is at a loss, because its authorities unravel, disintegrate, decay'. A concrete reference is of assistance here; he is writing of the social foundation of the Expressionist dissolution of bourgeois German art from the end of the war: 'But German Expressionism itself disappeared from poster and exhibition soon after the stabilisation of the mark. As the bourgeoisie openly entered the fore-

---

70   Ibid. 'Mag keine künstlerische [wie keine wissenschaftliche] Wahrheit absolute Wahrheit sein. Es gibt trotzdem eine objektive, reale, "absolute" Welt, Lenins Formulierung, die der wissenschaftlichen Wahrheit gilt, trifft auch für die künstlerische Wahrheit voll zu ...'.

71   Ibid. 'Die materialistische Dialektik von Marx und Engels schliesst unbedingt den Relativismus ein, reduziert sich aber nicht auf ihn, d.h. sie gibt die Relativität aller unserer Kenntnisse zu, aber nicht im Sinne der Verneinung der objektiveren Wahrheit, sondern im Sinne der geschichtlichen Bedingtheit der Grenzen der Annäherung unserer Kenntnnisse an diese Wahrheit'.

72   *Die Linkskurve* 1978, 2, no. 11, p. 10. 'Der Marxismus erkennt solche Selbstbewegung der Form nicht an'. In his Introduction to Mehring's writing on literature above, Thalheimer wrote *a propos* the new Soviet art that the great events had not yet found new forms adequate to them, but they would 'not be arbitrarily contrived or constructed' in line with Lenin's position.

ground, with its capitalist stabilisation and reconstruction efforts, bourgeois artists began to see the world with the eyes of New Objectivity'.[73]

He ends the article and the series with three conclusions, the first of which is 'the recognition that subject matter is the central bond between existence and form and signifies a powerful weapon for our critique of artistic production'.[74] A list of works in which this principle has been falsified, includes Shakespeare's Jack Cade (*Henry VI*, Part II). Goethe's idyllic representations of contemporary German peasants are not only objectively wrong but subjectively consciously false, as his letters display his awareness of their still feudal exploitation; similarly with his own contemporary Arnold Zweig's depictions of the 'noble German soldiers and officers'. 'Conscious falsification', Wittfogel continues, 'destroys fully the worth of art' ('Die bewusste Fälschung zerstört den Kunstwert völlig'). The naive narrowmindedness of the petit bourgeois we can place socially. We therefore maintain a criterion which allows judgement of how far the artistic truth of a particular class and period was approximately objective 'in representing the reality of its era, and where distortion and curtailment began'. His second point concerns recent (junger) proletarian-revolutionary art, some of which he strongly condemns for 'neglecting form in the context of new material' (he had earlier quoted Engels's response to Mehring on his own neglect of form but the responsibility to be concerned with it), a situation he describes as 'inimical to development, to revolution, capitulating opportunistically to bourgeois standards'.[75] His third point reinforces the second, warning against the retention of old forms, impeding the stages through which development must occur ('... hemmt die Entwicklung, die zwar diese Phase durchlaufen ... muss ...'). The requirement is difficult but it is nev-

---

73   The two most important critics on this transition are the unorthodox Marxist critics Siegfried Kracauer and Ernst Bloch. Lukács's 'Expressionism: Its Significance and Decline' (1934) is a major contribution to an engagement with this moment, particularly its central section 'Expressionism and the Ideology of the USPD (German Independent Socialist Party)', proposing crucial relationships between the economics of imperialism, the politics of the USPD, and their representations in the cultural work of Expressionist writers (Lukács 1981, pp. 76–113). Richard Hamann and Jost Hermand address the visual much later.

74   *Die Linkskurve* 1978, 2, no. 11, p. 11. 'Die Erkenntnis, dass der Stoff das zentrale Zwischenglied zwischen "Leben" und Form darstellt, bedeutet eine mächtige Waffe für unsere Kritik künstlerischer Schöpfungen'.

75   Ibid. '... die über dem neuen Inhalt noch die Form vernachlässigt ... entwicklungsfeindlicher, revolutionsfeindlicher, bürgerlicher oder opportunistisch vor bürgerlichem Wertmass kapitulierender Standpunkt'.

ertheless 'our obligation as dialectical materialists to recognise the problem and not to avoid by way of a permanent explanation the certain transitional stages'.[76]

Summing up, he writes: 'Marxism provides us with powerful tools to critically evaluate class art of the past and hostile class art of the present, to engage in proper self-critique of our own production, to provide appropriate self-consciousness, to drive forward the path of development'.[77] 'Based on Marx's materialist adaptation of Hegel's dialectic, we have, following Lenin's precept', he continues, 'sought to elaborate this dialectic in the realm of art'.[78] He quotes Lenin: 'Certainly such a study, such an elucidation, such a propagation of Hegel's dialectic is no easy task, and the first attempts will without doubt be subject to errors. But freedom from error is only for him who does nothing'.[79] Any criticism which openly or secretly opposed this dialectical approach, an approach until now not engaged in the cultural field in Germany, would be sharply repulsed, but 'those who wished to develop the mode further would be rightly greeted' ('... die über das von uns Entwickelte hinaus vorwärts geht, begrüssen wir aufrichtig'). 'We have taken the first step, no doubt not error-free: the second step, the consolidation of the principles elaborated, superseding these, will stride forward' ('... ihn "aufhebend" hinausschreitet').

3   Becher: 'Unsere Wendung' (Our Turning Point)

Between the last contribution by Wittfogel in his series and the beginning of Lukács's first contribution to *Die Linkskurve* there is a major account of the current state of revolutionary-proletarian writing by one of its editors, Johannes R. Becher.[80] He surveys the current situation in light of the recent resolution

------

76   *Die Linkskurve* 1978, 2, no. 11, p. 12. '... die Aufgabe anzuerkennen und ihrer Lösung nicht durch eine Permanenzerklärung gewisser Durchgangsstadien auszuweichen'.

77   Ibid. 'So liefert uns der Marxismus machtvolle Werkzeuge, die Klassenkunst der Vergangenheit und die klassenfremde Kunst von heute kritisch zu bewerten, sowie in richtiger Selbstkritik unserer eigenen Produktion das ihr zustehende Selbstbewusstsein zu geben und sie auf ihrem Entwicklungsgange vorwärts zu führen'.

78   Ibid. '"Gestützt auf die von Marx befolgte Anwendung der materialistischen erfassten Dialektik Hegels" haben wir, dem Gebote Lenins folgend, diese Dialektik nach der Richtung der Kunstanalyse auszuarbeiten gesucht'.

79   Ibid. '"Gewiss", sagt Lenin, "ist ein solches Studium, ein solches Erläutern, eine solche Propaganda Hegelscher Dialektik keine leichte Sache, und die ersten Versuche in dieser Richtung werden zweifellos mit Fehlern behaftet sein. Aber fehlerfrei ist nur der, der nichts tut"'.

80   Becher was initially an Expressionist in orientation but joined, via the USPD, the KPD in the

at the Kharkov All-Union Conference on the literature of the world revolution (Literatur der Weltrevolution) and the report of the plenum of the Russian group RAPP (Russian Association of Proletarian Writers) on the hegemony of proletarian literature ('Die Hegemonie der proletarischen Literatur') as reported in *Pravda*. Although no individuals are named, a number of positions may be extracted which provide an informative context for Lukács's criticism, which first appears a month later in November, 'Willi Bredels Romane'.

'Our literature', Becher writes, 'grew not only in theory but also in practice', but referring to the resolutions at Kharkov, he points to the emphasis on the latter, the possibility of proletarian-revolutionary literature before the seizure of power 'would be determined in the first instance not through theory but through practice'.[81] Writers should now be confident enough to withstand relentless criticism being directed towards their weaknesses and failures (an opportunity of which Lukács would avail himself in his critique of Bredel), that such criticism is now being seen 'not as hindering but as stimulating' ('... nicht mehr hemmend sondern weitertreibend'). He was against complacency and points to their 'lack of inventiveness in the use of new small formats – broadsheet short stories, poems, wall posters' ('... wir sind nicht erfinderisch genug in der Anwendung neuer kleiner Kunstformen – Flugblattkurzgeschichten, Flugblattgedichte, Klebestrophen u.s.w').[82] The BPRS must make 'the transition from the struggle around the existence of our literature to the struggle for its development'. A method of working must be established so that 'the incidental and the arbitrary vanish from our ranks' ('... das Zufällige und Willkürliche muss noch Möglichkeit aus unseren Reihen verschwinden'). The elaboration of this method is not directly pursued but two crucially important issues are raised which indirectly address it: mass literature and what is designated (by RAPP) as 'the theory of raw/unwrought material' ('Theorie des Rohmaterials'), the practice ascribed to Tretyakov and his comrades.

---

early 1920s and espoused the revolutionary-proletarian position, becoming a major presence. He later became Minister of Culture in the German Democratic Republic. 'Wendung' is ambivalent; it can also denote 'crisis', here one which may occur if some present practices do not change, for example, in the method of criticism.

81   *Die Linkskurve* 1980, 3, no. 10, pp. 1–8, 1. '... und den Charkower Beschlüssen heisst es mit Recht: die Möglichkeit einer proletarischen Literatur vor Eroberung der Macht durch das Proletariat ist in erster Linie nicht durch die Theorie, sondern durch die Praxis entschieden worden'.

82   *Die Linkskurve* 1980, 3, no. 10, p. 3. One might see here a momentary crossover point between the BPRS and the more experimental stance of the non-BPRS writers, Brecht in particular.

The observation was made at the Kharkov conference that 'bourgeois literature in Germany was understood almost exclusively in terms of such "representative" figures as Thomas and Heinrich Mann, Döblin, Wassermann etc. But this is only part of bourgeois literature and not the essential bourgeois mass literature'.[83] 'We must', he proposes, 'consider the whole gamut – middlebrow, Heimat- and Volksliteratur', even the trash literature ('... das Schmutz- und Schundschriften'). The turn to mass literature, the creation of mass-literature writers is 'the decisive link in the chain' ('... auf dem literarischen Gebiet das entscheidende Glied in der Kette') in Germany.[84] But in so doing they must from the outset guard against two conceptions of mass literature. The first damaging conception lies in 'the limited evaluation of mass literature, which is nothing other than a presumptuous underestimation of mass readership itself, doubting the possibility of achieving mass effectiveness other than through "quality" literature, holding fast to a concept of quality taken from the lumber room of bourgeois aesthetics'.[85] This attitude, he claims, 'leads to exaggerated avantgardism' ('... führt zu einem überspannten Avantgardistentum'), to the idea of the specialist who is cut off from the revolutionary movement. This tendency also manifests the over-evaluation of the experimental, confusion of form, the playing off of one position against another: Agitation-Propaganda. To this belongs the nonsense about 'the end of literature' ('Hierher gehört der Unfug vom "Ende der Literatur"'). The representative figure here is Tretyakov, recently in Berlin, mistakenly identified by 'linksbürgerlichen' (leftist bourgeois writers, no doubt including Brecht, Benjamin, Döblin and others) as representing an 'official' Soviet position.[86] Becher quotes from the *Pravda* report of the

---

83   *Die Linkskurve* 1980, 3, no. 10, p. 4. 'Wir verstanden unter bürgerlicher Literatur z.B. in Deutschland beinahe ausschliesslich solche "representative" Erscheinungen wie Thomas und Heinrich Mann ... Aber das ist doch nur ein Teil der bürgerlichen Literatur und nicht die eigentliche bürgerliche Massenliteratur'.

84   The 'representative figures' were those central to Lukács, bourgeois mass literature most probably 'terra incognita'. After the war Becher, as GDR Minister of Culture, promoted the work of Hans Fallada, one of the most popular German writers, anti-Nazi but politically non-aligned, admiring his capacity to create characters with whom his readers could identify. He made available to Fallada the Gestapo files on Otto and Elise Hampel, whose personal resistance campaign to the Nazis became the core of Fallada's *Jeder stirbt für sich allein* (English title: *Alone in Berlin*). See Williams 2012.

85   *Die Linkskurve* 1980, 3, no. 10, p. 5. '... als eine überhebliche Unterschätzung der Lesermassen selbst, in dem Zweifel, mit "qualitativer" Literatur überhaupt Massenwirkungen erreichen zu können, in dem hartnäckigen Festhalten an einem Qualitätsbegriff, der der bürgerlichen ästhetischen Rumpelkammer entnommen ist'.

86   Tretyakov does not fit Becher's description of such a writer: 'the literary engineer who, from his atelier, montages and provides for the revolutionary movement a training ground'

RAPP plenum against this tendency: 'The struggle for a great bolshevist art is at the same time a struggle against the remarkable theory of the ready-to-hand [unrefined] material' ('Der Kampf für eine grosse bolschewistische Kunst ist zugleich ein Kampf gegen die Merkwürdige Theorie des "Rohmaterials"'). Its representatives say they are for the great bolshevist art, but later, for at present there is no time. This leftist theory 'accords fully with Trotsky's literary conception' ('… vollständig übereinstimmt mit der Literaturauffassung Trotskis'). It is clear that this is a theory which leads to 'the liquidation of proletarian literature'. Behind this 'Rohmaterial' theory is concealed the renunciation of quality and 'a petit-bourgeois anxiety of being incapable of surviving in the complex reality of the period of construction' ('… das Unvermögen, sich in der komplizierten Wirklichkeit der Aufbauperiode zurechtzufinden').

'The second, no less greatly damaging conception', he writes, 'which would isolate us equally from the masses, exists in a frivolous approach to the production of mass literature' ('… bestünde in der leichtfertigen Produktion von Massenliteratur'). 'Mass literature is not a broadly based swindle', he adds, 'not a bauble but a many-sided opportunity to be seriously thought through'.[87] Blame cannot be ascribed to readers because of their ignorance but to the writer's inability 'above all to give living shape to subject matter' ('vor allem lebendig gestalten zu können'), a RAPP principle, also central to Lukács's critique: only that which 'stirs, convinces, that which is given form, lasts' ('Recht behält in der Literatur auf die Dauer nur das, was erschütternd, überzeugend, was gestaltet ist').[88] 'It is not sufficient for the writer to be familiar only with the political moment; they must also be familiar with the whole gamut of the proletarian everyday, with all its nuances, contradictions, variations, and above all with the

<hr>

('eines Literaturingenieurs, der aus dem Atelier heraus montiert und für die revolutionäre Bewegung ein Uebungslände abgibt'). Tretyakov's practice was more participatory, as Benjamin's brief but informative summary of his activities shows: 'The Author as Producer' (1934), in Benjamin 1977, pp. 88–9.

87 *Die Linkskurve* 1980, 3, no. 10, p. 6. '… eine nach allen Seiten hin ernsthaft zu durchdenkende Angelegenheit'.

88 In a long footnote Becher sets out RAPP thinking on this: a literature of high artistic quality ('von hoher künstlerischer Qualität'), ideas-driven ('die in hohen Masse ideendurchdrungen ist'), informed by bolshevistic consciousness of reality ('bolschewistische Bewusstmachung der Wirklichkeit'), in which the questions of the thematic are inseparable from a world conception, where for the dialectical-materialist proletarian writer the question of the 'What' is inseparable from that of the 'How' ('… wo doch die Fragen der Thematik von der Weltanschauung untrennbar sein, da für proletarischen dialektisch-materialistischen Schriftsteller die Frage des "Was" mit der Frage des "Wie" untrennbar verbunden ist').

language of the class' ('mit der Sprache der Klasse'). The writer must learn the language of the masses 'in order to make themselves intelligible to them'. He must draw close to worker cadres, worker correspondents, to factory life. But the real does not coincide with the amassing of detail, quoting Marx 'that all science would be unnecessary if appearance and essence coincide in an unmediated manner'.[89] Writers must be prepared to learn and adjust ('zum Lernen und Unlernen'). He again returns to the need for rigorous critique, noting that 'many comrades readily become impatient at literary theory discussions', including those on 'das Erbe' (the heritage), as left to us by 'a Lessing and a Mehring'.

Concluding, he writes that the Wendung (turn) can only become a crisis if they fail to translate their programme into practice, to produce their own writers and literature, to become 'the pioneers of the great bolshevist art' ('die Vorkämpfer der grossen bolschewistischen Kunst'). 'When our literature stirs the masses', he continues, 'it will become a material force and contribute an important component to changing the world'.[90]

4   Lukács and *Die Linkskurve*

As Gallas's history of the journal shows, there were rapid changes in policy in response to political circumstances. One such change in 1931 saw top echelons of the KPD, including Willi Münzenberg, support the 'anti-sectarian line' in the arguments and 'as Lukács reported … guaranteed protection to himself and Wittfogel'.[91] The BPRS policy now espoused 'the necessity of theoretical clarity and rejected curtailment to so-called literature of the moment' ('… die Notwendigkeit theoretischer Klärung und lehrte die Beschränkung auf die sogennante Tagesliteratur ab'). Wittfogel had addressed the former, Lukács would address the latter. Between November 1931 and November 1932, Lukács published a number of book reviews in theoretical articles: 'Willi Bredels Romane'; 'Gegen die Spontaneitätstheorie in der Literatur' ('Against the Theory of Spontaneity in Literature'); 'Tendenz oder Parteilichkeit?' ('Tendency or Party Liter-

---

89   There is a side-swipe at unnamed comrades who 'take flight, for example, into Chinese or American material' ('… z.B. in chinesische und amerikanische Stoffgebiete flüchten'). Tretyakov's 'Roar China' had been produced in Berlin in 1926; Brecht was working on 'St. Joan of the Stockyards' at the end of the 1920s.

90   *Die Linkskurve* 1980, 3, no. 10, p. 8. 'Unsere Literatur kann, wenn sie die Massen ergreift, zur materiellen Gewalt werden und ein bedeutendes Teil dazu beitragen, die Welt zu verändern'.

91   Gallas 1974, p. 60. '… wie Lukács berichtet, und gewährten Lukács … Wittfogel Schutze innerhalb der KPD-Spitze'. Gallas interviewed Lukács (Gallas 1974, p. 16).

ature?'); 'Reportage oder Gestaltung' ('Reportage or Formation'); and 'Aus der Not eine Tugend' ('A Virtue from Necessity').[92]

Lukács reviewed two of Willi Bredel's novels in the November 1931 *Linkskurve*.[93] The review is both an evaluation of Bredel's achievement and the opportunity for a major theoretical statement. Both novels, he writes, mark a significant moment in the development of proletarian-revolutionary literature in Germany. Their thematic material – the effects of the incipient economic rationalisation subsequent to the American Dawes Plan for stabilisation, the everyday life and struggles of workers seen from the point of view of the proletariat, subjects which lie at the centre of the interests of all workers – offers 'all readers new content' ('... ein Neuland an Inhalt ...'). His handling of individual events in factory life are seen only as moments in the overall class struggle, of a movement in process, epic in scale ('echt episch'). He seeks to depict the life of workers in concrete interaction with other classes, particularly the petit bourgeoisie, in contrast to the 'economistic' approach of other proletarian writers, who pitch factory owners against workers or workers against the bourgeois state. In both novels, Bredel has constructed the framework, the schema, for a good proletarian-revolutionary novel, but no more than that, the finished novel is not far from a first draft.

'If we want to give a precise account of the basic failure of artistic form in Bredel's novel', Lukács writes, 'it is this: an artistically unresolved contradiction between the essentially epic dimension of his story and his mode of narration, at times a type of reportage, other times an account before an assembly'.[94]

---

92   These titles do not translate readily from their context with the contested positions they carried. The terms 'spontaneity', 'tendency', and 'reportage' carry material overtones, for example, the argument over 'agitprop' between Vallentin and the BPRS editorial board, and the criticism of the Arbeiterkorrespondenten (both above). Wittfogel stressed 'Form', quoting Engels, not 'Gestaltung' most often in his Hegelian model.

93   *Die Linkskurve* 1980, 3, no. 11, pp. 23–7. These were *Maschinenfabrik N & K. Ein Roman aus dem proletarischen Alltag* and *Die Rosenhofstrasse*: the first the machine factory of Nagel and Kaemp in Hamburg where he had worked as a turner; the second a working-class block in the same city. Born in 1901 he had an intense engagement with the left: a Spartacus member, later KPD, he participated in the Hamburg rising in 1923 and was sentenced to two years for that. He became a worker-correspondent and editor of the *Hamburger Volkszeitung*. Found guilty of 'the preparation of literary high treason' ('Vorbereitung literarischen Hochverrats') in 1930 during Bruning's emergency decree administration, he was sentenced to two years and wrote his first novels there. When Lukács reviewed them, they were 'hot off the press'. Bredel was the archetypal model for the BPRS programme.

94   *Die Linkskurve* 1980, 3, no. 11, p. 24. 'Wenn wir den Grundmangel der künstlerischen Gestaltung Bredels auf eine knappe Form bringen wollen, so müssen wir sagen: es besteht ein künstlerisch ungelöster Widerspruch zwischen den breiten, alles wesentliche umfas-

Social intercourse between living characters is lacking, his humans do not develop. 'This must be prepared for artistically', Lukács continues, 'sudden, unprepared change rings untrue' ('... aber nur, wenn es künstlerisch vorbereitet wird ...'). A novel demands other means for forming than reportage: a mode of characterisation which suffices for the latter is for the novel thoroughly unsatisfactory ('Ein Roman erfordert eben andere Gestaltungsmittel als eine Reportage ... ist für jenen durchaus ungenügend'). This inadequacy is at its most blatant in speech patterns, almost without exception, in the language of the press report. Even where required, for example in political discourse (here Lukács mentions speeches by Thälmann, KPD leader and the high-ranking Naumann), it lacks nuance. 'Linguistically', Lukács writes, 'it lags behind the reality it should represent artistically' ('Er bleibt also sprachlich hinter der Wirklichkeit, die er künstlerisch gestalten sollte ...').

It would be very obvious to conclude from what has been said that Bredel 'only lacks the technical side of writing but that is not the case' ('... zu schliessen: Bredel fehlt eben die "Technik" des Schreibens. Das Naheliegende ist aber auch in diesem Fall nicht das Richtige'). Of course, Bredel lacks the technical but the critic would do him no good should he say 'your novels are fine, from the point of view of content, ideology, Marxism and the political: you must just master the technique of writing and of form, then the great proletarian novel is to hand' ('... du musst nur die "Technik" des Schreibens, nur das Beherrschen der Form erlernen, dann ist der grosse proletarische Roman schon da'). Not so. 'Form and content interrelate closely, their reciprocal dialectical interweaving is ... considering the dominance of class subject matter' ('... bei allem Vorherrschen des Klasseninhalts'), 'much more intimate, mediated, intricate, as though the answer to this question could turn out to be mechanically simple' ('... als dass die Beantwortung dieser Frage so mechanisch einfach ausfallen könnte'). In the first instance, the forming of human beings is not a technical question 'but above all the use of the dialectic in the field of literature' ('... sondern vor allem die Frage der Handhabung der Dialektik auf dem Gebiet der Literatur'). 'Dialectical thought on our courses show how reified thinking can become process' ('... dass das dialektische Denken die starr scheinenden Dinge auch im Denken in Prozesse was sie wirklich sind, auflöst').[95] 'Does this fundamental tenet not also hold good for literature?', he asks ('Gilt dieser Elementarsatz der Dialektik nicht auch für Literatur?') 'Should not literature at

---

senden epischen Rahmen seiner Fabel und zwischen seiner Erzählungsweise, die teils eine Art von Reportage, teils eine Art vor Versammlungsbericht ist'.

95   The reference to courses here is most probably those at the Marxist School (MASCH), mentioned above.

least achieve the level achieved by party functionaries in everyday praxis?' ('... das in der Tagespraxis der Klassenkämpfe sich weitgehends ...'). 'I even believe that we are justified to make a higher demand', he adds ('dass wir berechtigt sind, höhere Forderungen zu stellen ...'), to achieve the level of the highest achievements of revolutionary praxis and theory of the KPD and Comintern.

'This lack of dialectic in form also interferes with content' ('... dieser Mangel am Dialektik in der Gestaltung schlägt auch ins Inhaltliche um'). 'In consequence of our depicted manner of representation', Lukács writes, 'Bredel – completely against his wishes – must obviously blot out the difficulties with which the development of the revolution has to struggle'.[96] Lukács describes the general scenario that proletarian writers have not yet managed to represent – the obstructions which keep good workers at a distance from the revolutionary movement, which drive the proletarianised petit bourgeoisie to counterrevolution; 'how difficult the path to be trodden is before the masses achieve ideological clarity'. Bredel – and not only Bredel – precisely fall short here. 'He gives us the outcomes', Lukács writes, 'not the process, with its obstructions, difficulties, reverses, which falsifies the representation' ('Das aber verfälscht auch inhaltlich das Bild'). To depict the truth Bredel must represent 'the ascending trajectory of the revolution' ('... die aufsteigende Linie der revolutionären Bewegung gestalten'). Lukács admits that 'some comrades may find this criticism harsh', but the writers must not lag behind the movement in general. On the contrary, 'through unsparing self-criticism they must familiarise themselves with what impedes them' and 'through acquiring knowledge of how to employ the materialist dialectic to eradicate them as quickly as possible' ('... durch Erlernen der Handhabung der materialistischen Dialektik im literarischen Schaffen so rasch wie möglich liquidieren').[97] But this is also autocritique; Bredel is not the only one to fail to achieve the highest level: 'All of us, in our creative or critical activity, have failed'.[98]

Bredel responded to Lukács's review under the title 'Einen Schritt Weiter' ('A Further Step'), picking up on the latter's demand in his concluding paragraph. He recognises 'the fundamental justification and correctness of such criticism and the necessity for the further development of our literature'.[99] He criti-

---

96   *Die Linkskurve* 1980, 3, no. 11, p. 25. 'Infolge der von uns geschilderten Darstellungsweise muss nämlich Bredel – ganz gegen seinen Willen – die Schwierigkeiten, mit denen die Entwicklung der Revolution zu kämpfen hat, verwischen'.

97   *Die Linkskurve* 1980, 3, no. 11, p. 26.

98   *Die Linkskurve* 1980, 3, no. 11, p. 27. 'wir können und müssen es fordern, weil wir der Ueberzeigung sind, dass er imstande ist, diese Forderungen zu erfüllen'.

99   *Die Linkskurve* 1971, 4, no. 1, pp. 20–2, 20. '... die Erkenntnis der grundsätzlichen Berechti-

cises proletarian writers for being concerned with the [recent] past – the Kapp Putsch [1920], the 'March Days' [1921], inflation [1923] – and not the present – the dangers of Fascism, the latent civil war, the desire for a revolutionary united front, and advocates a 'step forward, forward to our working method'.[100] All the particular criticism that Comrade Lukács raises must be conceded as fitting the facts ('... alles, das muss jeder Genosse, der unsere Literaturerzeugnisse kritisch prüft zugeben, entspricht den Tatsachen'). 'Comrades', he demands, 'to current problems of the working class'. A further step, 'we have repeated the language of class struggle but mostly disjointedly, undialectically, therefore unconvincingly. Where are the connective nuances?'[101] We must not just concentrate on the heroic episodes (... die heldenhaften Episoden ...) but with the aid of Marxism-Leninism study and analyse the proletariat and the class enemy, 'as well as all levels between' ('... sowie alle Schichten, die zwischen beiden liegen ...'). He espouses the confidence expressed by Lukács: 'we are convinced that we will master the difficulties'. As to how to proceed, he quotes a long passage from Lenin's 1920 address to young workers on the task of the communist: 'you must not just assimilate knowledge from the past but examine it critically ... work over it in consciousness ... enrich all matters through this knowledge. One must find one's way through those things one must critically confront. Marxism is an example of how communism develops from the sum of human knowledge'.[102]

The April 1932 issue of *Die Linkskurve* published, under the title 'Neue Bücher', two separate contributions: the first, by Otto Gotsche, on the left of the BPRS, was a critique of Lukács's review of Bredel's novels, 'Kritik der Anderen – Einige Bemerkungen zur Frage der Qualifikation unserer Literatur' ('The Criticism of Others – Some Remarks Concerning the Right to Comment on Our Literature'): the second, Lukács's response to Gotsche ('Gegen die Spontaneitäts-theorie in der Literatur').[103] The 'others' on Gotsche's title were fellow workers whom he interviewed. Lukács's review had 'raised a series of questions which should not remain unanswered'. Bredel in response to Lukács, Gotsche felt,

---

gung und Richtigkeit solcher Kritik und der Notwendigkeit der qualitätiven unserer Literatur'.

100   *Die Linkskurve* 1971, 4, no. 4, p. 21. 'Einen Schritt vorwärts, Genossen, and die aktuellen Probleme dessen Klassenkampf. Einen weiteren Schritt vorwärts in der Methodik unserer Arbeiten'.

101   Ibid. 'Wir haben bisher ... die Parolen im Klassenkampf wideregegeben, aber meistens unzusammenhängend, undialektisch und daher unecht. Wo blieben die verbindenden Nuancen?'

102   *Die Linkskurve* 1971, 4, no. 4, p. 22.

103   *Die Linkskurve* 1971, 4, no. 4, pp. 28–33. Gotsche, a sheet metal worker, was to publish his first novel in 1933, *Die März-Stürme* (*March Storms*), on the March Days of 1921.

should have defended himself more positively. Healthy self-criticism is useful when it is not excessive, becoming then criticism only. Lukács had pointed to the positive in Bredel but had deployed in his criticism of the weaknesses an undermining approach ('... eine zersetzende Methode der Kritik ...'). Gotsche acknowledges the absence of dialectical analysis, of the Marxist-Leninist science, in the characterisation of the interrelated lives of the most different social levels, but doubted that Bredel lacked writerly technique; 'his novels live, they are not concocted' ('... seine Romane wirken nicht gemacht, sind Leben'). Does the weapon of Marxism-Leninism operate uniformly across all social sectors? There is an issue of temporalities: the 'maturation of pure proletarian knowledge and its outcomes proceed at a much slower tempo than the tempo of the acceleratingly inevitable collapse of the capitalist order'.[104] Thälmann has, with bolshevistic clarity, uncovered the origins of this failure: should the most recent link in the chain, proletarian literature, be free from it?

He then introduces his mini-sociological survey: 'as a consequence of Lukács's review I have spoken to a number of comrades', including one from Bredel's depicted factory, N/K. He had chosen critical extracts from Lukács: the unlifelike characterisation; the newspaper-article feel of the writing, the role of party speech; the kitschy unrealistic psychology. None of these found agreement; Bredel's representations were seen as successful – 'let the critic do better' ('... soll selbst Besseres leisten') was the reaction.[105] Responses having accorded with his expectations, he sums up: 'the spontaneity of practical work is brilliantly depicted. And what was one to take exception to in the dialogue? – only that it was not always realistic enough'. To meet demands, 'our literature must interrelate with our daily experience', then the mass character of our literature

---

104   *Die Linkskurve* 1971, 4, no. 4, p. 28. '... noch langsamere Tempo als der sich in immer schnelleren Tempo vollziehende unaufhaltsame Zusammenbruch der kapitalistischen Gesellschaftsordnung'.

105   A short note on reception at this point: Fähnders, Rector, and Gallas had interviewed surviving members of *Die Linkskurve* circle. The former base their information on the word of Georg W. Pijet, a leader of the BPRS, who said of Lukács's lectures on theory that 'at least within the BPRS many of the members could not follow such expositions, so that Lukács's contributions to discussion regularly remained a monologue'. Fähnders and Rector 1974b, p. 299, n. 776, '... das hohe theoretische Niveau und Abstraktionsvermögen von Lukács dazu führte, dass zumindest auf internen Bundes-Versammlungen viele der Mitglieder kaum solchen Ausführungen folgen konnten, so dass die Diskussionsbeiträge von Lukács's regelmassig Monologe blieben'. Gallas notes, based on discussion with former members, that Wittfogel's 'expositions were not discussed' ('Seine Ausführungen wurden nicht diskutiert') and found no resonance in the journal ('... ohne eine Resonanz in der Zeitschrift'). Gallas 1974, p. 196, n. 64. They were, however, praised at the 1931 Kharkov conference on proletarian literature.

becomes a fact. Our writers will attain the higher levels more quickly 'when a real mass self-criticism demands a higher standard'. We lag behind because we are not under 'sufficient supervision of the masses'. But 'we have learned much from Bredel, not from Lukács – tomorrow Bredel will learn from us. Our literature must become mass literature, our criticism mass criticism'.[106]

Lukács's critique of Gotsche's article gives him the opportunity to set out, briefly but succinctly, his opposition to the theory of spontaneity and its practical consequences, here within the more immediate field of literature. He politely but firmly rejects Gotsche's endorsement of spontaneity. 'Comrade Gotsche's remarks', he writes, 'certainly show that he is not clear about the demands of criticism. To him criticism means criticism by the masses. That is the point of view of spontaneism, one of the not-few Luxemburg remnants of the German working-class movement'.[107] If a worker responds 'let the critic do better' (a response in Gotsche's article), Comrade Gotsche must say 'that is not the task of the critic' ('... müsste ... darüber aufklären, dass dies nicht Aufgabe des Kritikers ist'), an infantilism (Kinderkrankheit) also found in early bourgeois literature. It could happen, he continues, 'that a good Marxist critic could also be a good proletarian ... revolutionary writer', adding that 'it might be desirable if our proletarian revolutionary writers worked with that type of developed Marxist consciousness, so that they were in a position to subject the principles of their creative method to criticism'.[108] Criticism has its role to play in our proletarian-revolutionary movement, its special tasks: 'that of employing the materialist dialectic in the field of literature, to assist in accomplishing the creative modes which answer, disclose and clarify the problems of class struggle, daily and epochal: if necessary, also to oppose a particular practice'.[109]

---

106   *Die Linkskurve* 1971, 4, no. 4, p. 30. '... von Bredel haben wir unendlich gelernt – nicht von Lukács – und morgen wird Bredel von uns lernen. Unsere Literatur muss Massenliteratur, unsere Kritik, Massenkritik werden'.

107   *Die Linkskurve* 1971, 4, no. 4, p. 31. 'Freilich zeigen die Bemerkungen der Gen. Gotsche dass er über die Aufgaben der Kritik selbst nicht im Klaren ist. Ihm scheint, Kritik ist gleich: *Massenkritik*. Das ist der Standpunkt der Spontaneität, einer der nicht wenigen Luxemburgischen Ueberreste in der deutschen Arbeiterbewegung'.

108   *Die Linkskurve* 1971, 4, no. 4, p. 30. 'Obwohl es wünschenswert wäre, wenn unsere proletarisch-revolutionären Schriftsteller mit derart entwickelter Bewusstheit arbeiten würden, dass sie imstande wären, die Prinzipien ihrer schöpferischen Methode auch kritisch darzulegen'. He lists the earlier writers who were also great critics, including Diderot, Lessing, and Heine.

109   *Die Linkskurve* 1971, 4, no. 4, pp. 30–1. '... durch Anwendung der materialistischen Dialektik auf dem Gebiete der Literatur, jene schöpferischen Methoden die den Problem des Klassenkampfes (der Tageskämpfe wie dem grössen Kämpfe ganzer Perioden) jeweils am besten entsprechen, aufzudecken, klarzumachen, ihre literarische Geltung durchzuset-

Lukács is not totally dismissive of spontaneity; it facilitates an expanding and deepening of the contacts between literature and the masses, is important for their literary education, provides a check on whether our literature gives expression to what moves them, and if not does so in the correct and most effective way, not lagging behind the development of the masses. 'But it is not criticism' ('Sie ist aber keineswegs die Kritik'). Certainly he does not want that but 'What does Comrade Gotsche bring concretely against my criticism?', Lukács asks. 'His article shows that he is very uncertain in his terminology. Comrade Gotsche has simply not thought the issue through to its conclusion. Can he claim that Bredel's books, if lacking dialectical-materialist understanding, could be complete works of art' ('... wenn sie in der Anwendung der materialistischen Dialektik mangelhaft sind, vollendete Kunstwerke sein können?') 'Bredel agreed with my criticism', Lukács writes, and Gotsche argues with that but resists its concrete application. 'Is this consistent, is it dialectical?': his answer is 'no'. The difference Gotsche draws between artistic forming and direct impact on class struggle is simply bourgeois. Through spontaneity, as Lenin had shown in 1902, bourgeois ideology flourishes in the workers' movement; it retards our literature rather than advancing it. 'Or does he mean', he continues, 'that if Bredel had Gorki's powerful creative energy that his works would not be as penetrating and because of that more effective for class struggle?' What must be discussed is whether an account or report ('Bericht oder Reportage') can replace 'artistic forming' ('die Gestaltung ersetzen'). Is perhaps reportage 'the correct contemporary method?' ('die richtige zeitgemässe Methode') 'But with Comrade Gotsche's spontaneism', he asserts, 'we cannot even pose the question properly'. 'I would have liked', he concludes, 'to have addressed more burning issues with regard to literature, but unfortunately the question of spontaneity took up much space'. Until this is solved there will be no progress. The remnants of petit-bourgeois ideology still persist in working-class readers and writers. Our duty is 'to pursue energetically the struggle against the ideological heritage of the Second International, also concretely in the field of literature, not to reinforce the workers in their false perception, their perseverance with the theory of spontaneity'.[110]

---

zen zu helfen ... wenn nötig, auch gegen die gegebende Praxis der Schriftsteller zu kämpfen'.

110   *Die Linkskurve* 1971, 4, no. 4, p. 33, 'den Kampf gegen das ideologische Erbe der II Internationale auch auf dem Gebiet der Literatur konkret und energisch aufzunehmen, nicht aber die Arbeiter in ihrer falschen Auffassung, in hrem Beharren auf dem Boden der Spontaneitästheorie noch zu verstärken'. Michael Löwy provides a very succinct account of Lukács's position at this moment as reflected in his contributions to *Die Linkskurve*,

Consonant with the outlines of the Stalin letter, quoted above in the opening paragraph of Wittfogel's *Linkskurve* series, 'the bourgeois baggage handed down by the Second International' is the major focus in the Lukács's second contribution, 'Tendency or Partisanship?'[111] Even Mehring himself, 'the most significant German literary theorist of the nineteenth century', failed to identify correctly the problematic status of 'tendency'.[112] Lukács ascribes this to Mehring's inability to transcend the Kant-Schiller form-content complex, even though he rejected the 'timelessness' or 'time-transcending' character of art central to it.[113] Once worn as a badge of honour at an earlier period, 'we referred to our literature with pride as a "tendency" literature'; it has now become a debased term in the polarisation of 'pure art' (bourgeois and 'tendentious', i.e. proletarian), a struggle between what is proper to art (the aesthetic) and what is imported, from what is 'foreign to art', the social and political. This non-negotiable stand-off Lukács characterises as 'eclectic idealism'; we are confronted by 'the ideological relocation of the capitalist division of labour'.[114] The obstructive pressure is 'the false and undialectical view of the objective facts' and he quotes from Marx and Engels, 'who repeatedly gave the dialectic of subjective and objective factors in social development a correct formulation'.[115] 'Knowledge of social necessity', he writes, 'determines the correct (and important) place of the subjective factor in the development, contrary to both the mechanistic and idealist conceptions'.[116] The proletariat is the only class

---

including this one: 'Nevertheless, this defence of the cultural heritage of the past, of Balzac and Goethe, against the sectarian divagations of the Third Period neo-Proletkult did of course have a justifiable side to it; it was, moreover, related to the wing of the KPD that had most reservations about the Stalinist doctrine of "social fascism" – Heinz Neumann and Willi Münzenberg' (Thalheimer could also be included in that list). He goes on to remark that Lukács's position with regard to traditional culture 'had affinities with the theses defended by Trotsky in *Literature and Revolution*' (Löwy 1979, p. 202, n. 23). The complexity of that moment becomes manifest when one adds in Wittfogel's positions on Mehring, Thalheimer, and Trotsky, as set out above.

111   Lukács 1980, p. 43.

112   Lukács 1980, p. 37.

113   Lukács ascribes to Mehring a position he did not hold, that he subscribes to Schiller's 'destruction of the material by the form' (Lukács 1980, p. 36). Engels, above, had drawn to Mehring's attention the danger of neglecting form in his literary studies. Wittfogel does not make that accusation, but rather points up Mehring's comparative neglect of Hegel. In keeping with the demands of the moment (the Third Period), the 'uncritical acceptance of Mehring's writings in our literary and cultural theory has given a boost to Trotskyism' (Lukács 1980, p. 39).

114   Lukács 1980, pp. 36, 37.

115   Lukács 1980, p. 39.

116   Lukács 1980, p. 40.

unburdened by false consciousness, able to understand the role of the subjective factor in social development: 'both the determination of this subject factor by the objective economic and historical development and the active function of the subjective, in the product of the transformation of the objective conditions'. This knowledge of social being has to be produced, 'is both a product of the internal (material and ideological) disposition of the proletariat, as well as a factor promoting the development of the proletariat from "a class in itself" to a "class for itself"'.[117] The proletarian revolutionary writer 'with a command of dialectical materialism' must view the development in this manner, thus overcoming the problems of tendency in rejecting 'the dilemma between "pure" art and "tendency"'. The class struggle, dialectically understood, culturally dispenses with the 'pure art'/'tendency' polarity. Proper partisanship grasps the totality of the social processes, the 'true driving forces, as the constant and heightened reproduction of the dialectical contradictions that underlie it'. Contemporary practice, including the literary practice of Trotskyism in all its varieties, 'manifests' that 'even its best product is still full of "tendency"'. Partisanship as defined above is the pathway 'for our creative method'.[118]

5   Reportage or Portrayal

Lukács's first two contributions to *Die Linkskurve* – the first being his critique of Bredel's novels and the issue of spontaneism in politics and literature, and the second that of the prioritising of partisanship over tendency, defined as a bourgeois mode – were both somewhat sophisticated theoretical instructions to writers from a proletarian background on how to write a proletarian-revolutionary novel. His next two, 'Reportage or Portrayal? Critical Remarks *à propos* of a novel by Ottwalt', and 'A Virtue of Necessity', the second a response to Ottwalt's own response to Lukács, '"Tatsachenroman" und Formexperiment, eine Entgegnung an Georg Lukács', address a very different issue.[119] The focus now was the challenge to the traditional novel form espoused by Lukács and the Soviet cultural bureaucracy, by the experimental form of the factual novel, whose leading exponents were the Russians Tretyakov and Ehrenburg, an aesthetic practice favoured by Ottwalt and Brecht.

---

117   Lukács 1980, p. 41.

118   Lukács 1980, pp. 42 and 43.

119   The initial Lukács critique was published across two issues, July and August 1932, the Ottwalt in September, and the second Lukács piece in November–December.

'For the creative writer', Lukács writes, 'does not create in perfect freedom, simply out of his own mind ... He is on the contrary closely tied to the reproduction of reality in a manner faithful to its true content'. The guarantor of the production of this truth is the operation of dialectical materialism which enables him 'to reproduce the overall process (or else that part of it, linked either explicitly or implicitly to the overall process) by disclosing its actual and essential driving forces'.[120] This premise in the field of literature is given a wider context in a later passage on how Marx, Engels, and Lenin criticised an 'ideological product'. Rhetorically, Lukács asks, 'Do these general considerations apply also to literature? Or is literature rather a special field on its own, in which the lessons we have drawn from the way that Marx, Engels and Lenin worked in the fields of economics, philosophy etc., no longer apply?'[121] Hegel's concept 'the truth is the whole' underpins Lukács's theory.

The origins of the style represented by Ottwalt, Tretyakov, Ehrenburg and others Lukács traces to the rejection of the psychological novel by writers like Zola, Hugo, Sue 'close to the workers' movement'. But the rejection did not go deep enough into the reasons. 'Psychologism', Lukács argues, 'must be grasped in terms of the social being of the bourgeois class, the capitalist division of labour and commodity fetishism ... the reification of consciousness experienced by those not directly connected with material production'. The response was inadequate, the highlighting of social facts, a mechanical not a dialectical process, 'the same inability as the psychological novelist to see relations between people (class relations) in the "things" of social life'. The 'new school' (Ottwalt and others) 'commit the typical mistake of the old school materialism and do not recognise the dialectic through which the "driving forces" of society and history operate in the brains of the actors' – quoting Engels on Feuerbach. They want 'the object to be purely objective, the content to be pure content without any dialectical interaction with the subjective and formal'. They fail 'to grasp and give adequate expression to both objective and content' thus producing 'a one-sided exaggeration of content [which] leads to an experiment in form, the attempt to renew the novel with the means of journalism and reportage'.[122]

In the field of art, the form-content relationship is crucial and is governed by the operations of dialectical materialism, some of which were referred to above in the writings of Hegel, Marx, Engels and Lenin. For this practitioner, content

---

120   Lukács 1980, pp. 51, 52.
121   Lukács 1980, p. 64.
122   Lukács 1980, pp. 47, 48, 50.

is privileged over form and 'ultimately determines form'. But form is not a passive participant, having its own 'dialectically, necessary activity, autonomy and inherent dynamic', nevertheless it 'is only the essence of the content become visible, palpable and concrete'. He quotes Hegel on the 'revulsion' of form and content, where the two are constantly changing places, but only 'if the dialectically dynamic whole is concretely portrayed with all its determinations'.[123] This then is the outline of the critical armoury Lukács deploys in his critique of Ottwalt's novel, *Sie wissen was sie tun* (*They Know What They Do*). The novel depicts the operations of the legal system in Weimar Germany.

Ottwalt opens his response by claiming that 'an uncontested acceptance of Lukács's theory would have serious consequences for our proletarian-revolutionary literature' ('... auf die bedenklichen Folgen hinweisen ... für unsere proletarish-revolutionäre Literatur ergeben muss'). He holds 'Comrade Lukács's critical method to be one-sided and false' ('Ich halte die kritische Methode des Genossen Lukács für einseitig und falsch'). Philosophical investigation of a literary work can produce important outcomes but 'in the sense that Lukács only and exclusively relies on this method is, in my opinion, a definite defect' ('In dem Lukács aber nur und ausschliesslich eine schöpferische Methode analysiert, begeht er meines Erachtens einen entscheidenden Fehler'). Lukács 'suppresses or ignores all those interrelationships that exist between the literary work and reality' ('... unterdrückt und vernachlässigt aber alle diejenigen Wechselbeziehungen, die zwischen einem Literaturwerk und der Wirklichtkeit bestehen').[124] Ottwalt relates the instance when he was invited by factory workers to speak but not just on literature. They agreed on a lecture on 'Class justice in Germany'. He comments that for the class-conscious worker in the era of fascism, that discussion of a book had purpose and only made sense 'when it led to the real and not to a literary-aesthetic real' ('... wenn sie in der Wirklichkeit und nicht in einer literatur-ästhetischen Wirklichkeit geführt wird').[125] 'Lukács', Ottwalt counters,

> who always raises the claim for the grasping of the totality of dialectic interrelationships with regard to the proletarian-revolutionary novel contradicts his own demand, as reality – except as a word – is only presented

---

123   Lukács 1980, p. 60.

124   *Die Linkskurve* 1971, 4, no. 10, pp. 21–6. All quotations from p. 21.

125   *Die Linkskurve* 1971, 4, no. 10, p. 23. Lukács endorses the nineteenth-century Russian tradition, but Ottwalt objects that the tradition (das Erbe) plays a different role in Germany, where it is a 'living element of reaction' ('lebendige Elemente der Reaktion'), struggled against daily. For Ottwalt, Lukács neglected the particularity of the German situation.

in connection with aestheticising values. The doubtless unintended consequence is as though Lukács wanted a book, a novel, which should be a weapon in class struggle, detached and separated from all real factors and valued and considered on the projected plane of philosophical-aesthetic axioms.[126]

'I fear', Ottwalt writes, 'that strict regard for the critical stipulations will ultimately harm proletarian-revolutionary literature'.[127] Against the organicist implications of closed form, generated in accordance with the theoretical positions outlined above, Ottwalt writes that 'proletarian-literature is not an end in itself but should help to change reality ... its purpose is not to stabilise the consciousness of the reader but to change it'.[128]

The level of achievement of literary forming ('Grad dichterische Gestaltung') cannot be the exclusive criteria of judgement; rather its functional significance ('funktionelle Bedeutung') in the context of 'a reality structured by specific economic and political influences'. Lukács's ascription of the factual novel to petit-bourgeois rejection of the psychological novel is 'not dialectical, but mechanical' ('... sei aber kein dialektischer, sondern ein mechanischer'). The popularity of factual novels, recognised by Lukács, 'derives from the social environment'. The form is not innocently imported into the proletarian-revolutionary novel by authors whose class basis is narrow (a suggestion of Lukács's), 'but meets the requirement of the proletariat, it complies with the demands of class struggle' ('sondern sie kommt einen Bedürfnis des Proletariats entgegen, sie entspricht den Erfordernissen des Klassenkampfes'). He rejects Lukács's characterisation

---

126   *Die Linkskurve* 1971, 4, no. 10, pp. 21–2. '... also wolle Lukács ein Buch, einen Roman, die Waffe im Klassenkampf sein will und sein soll, losgelöst und abgesondert von allen realen Faktoren lediglich auf die Ebene philosophisch-ästhetisches Axiome projiziert werten und betrachten'.

127   *Die Linkskurve* 1971, 4, no. 10, p. 22. 'Ich befürchte, dass die strenge Berüchsichtigung der kritischen Festellungen des Gen. Lukács letzen Endes die Prodkuktion proletarish-revolutionärer Literatur hemmen wird'. Ottwalt's fear would be later articulated in the GDR *Lexikon sozialistischer deutscher Literatur*, which began publication in 1959. Michael Rohrwasser, in his 1975 book on proletarian mass literature, *Sauber Mädel-Starke Genossen*, quotes from it: 'Lukács's influence inflicted considerable ideological damage on socialist literature and above all on literary science in Germany'. 'Lukács "Einfluss hat besonders der Entwicklung der sozialistichen Literatur und vor allem Literaturwissenschaft in Deutschland beträchtlichen ideologischen Schaden zugefügt"' (Rohrwasser 1975, p. 125). The 1953 Hungarian Rising and Lukács's presence may have had something to do with that opinion.

128   Ibid.

of Tretyakov as 'petit-bourgeois' and notes that Tretyakov's style has been iron-
ised in the Soviet Union recently as 'Tatsachenfetischismus' (fact fetishism):
this he ascribes to the presence of 'Udarniki-Literatur' (the literature of the
shock-brigade worker), underlining social change and the demands of the Five
Year Plan. He points out that the best representation of the Five Year Plan in
Germany is Becher's *Grosser Plan*: a 'thoroughly "Formexperimente"' (Becher
was also founder and Committee member of *Die Linkskurve*, a circumstance
which indicates the state of the debate). The old form is being exploded by
the immensity of the present. For Ottwalt this makes the concept of 'Totality'
highly problematic, the Balzacian encyclopaedic work is not possible. 'I readily admit', he writes, 'that I find this ambiguity in the question of Totality an
awkward one' ('Ich gestehe offen, Zweideutigkeit in der Frage der Totalität als
peinlich empfinde'). It is only 'partial challenges' ('Teilforderungen') that 'we
can supersede' ('erheben können'). The drive towards Totalität, the grasping of
the totality of dialectical interrelationships, must not induce one to reject the
forming of a 'factual complex' ('Tatsachenkomplexe'), whose operation 'on specific political, not literary grounds, would appear to be necessary in a definite
situation'.

Lukács's response, 'A Virtue of Necessity', appeared in the last issue of *Die
Linkskurve* (November–December 1932). His objective is 'the great proletarian
work of art ... to create works that encompass ... the basic developmental tendencies of the period as a whole, works which, without neglecting the immediate here and now, also take into consideration the persistent, longer-term and
genuinely typical features of the period'. Ottwalt, on the other hand, 'restricts
the "functional" significance of literature to the most immediate level', failing to recognise that 'the present stage of development of the class struggle
sets higher tasks for proletarian revolutionary writers'.[129] Ottwalt's approach
is widespread today 'but it is neither Marxist nor correct'. His functionalism:
'Our literature does not have the task of stabilising the consciousness of its
reader'; it seeks to alter it, is an anti-portrayal theory that reveals 'its undialectical character'. 'Every class is continuously changing, and for this reason every
class is constantly forced, on pain of disappearance, incessantly to change the
consciousness of both its own members and of the members of other classes
that it influences'. (Brecht's 'new theatre' is also included in this critique.) He
ascribes this aspiration to a vulgarisation of Marx's revolution on Feuerbach,
the counterposing of 'interpreting' to 'changing', as though prior to Marx there
was not 'both a "changing" of reality and necessarily also of consciousness, i.e.

---

129   Lukács 1980, p. 65.

a praxis', with the vital difference that 'it was based on a false consciousness'. Lukács stresses the role of abstraction in achieving correct praxis, quoting from Lenin:

> Thought proceeding from the concrete to the abstract – provided it is *correct* ... does not get away *from* the truth but comes closer to it. The abstraction of *matter*, a *law* of nature, the abstraction of *value*, etc, in short *all* scientific (correct, serious, not absurd) abstractions reflect nature more deeply, truly and *completely*. From living perception to abstract thought, and from **this to practice** – such is the dialectical path of the cognition of truth, of the cognition of objective reality.[130]

Lacking dialectic, abstraction, and totality, Ottwalt's activity is not praxis but mere 'practicism', confusing totality with the sum of facts.

6   From the Second to the Third International: Lukács's 'Franz Mehring, 1846–1919'

Lukács, in response to Ottwalt's rejoinder to the former's assessment of his novel *Sie wissen was sie tun*, sets out what can be read as his governing theory of cultural production. 'Any critique that Marx, Engels or Lenin made of an ideological product', he writes,

> no matter in what field, will show that they saw the effect as a necessary result (even if complexly mediated, and 'uneven' in expression) of the determinate class factors in its development, i.e. that for them the central object of investigation is always the method with which a specific kind of ideological product is produced. This in no way means, as Ottwalt objects to me, that 'they remained stuck in "aesthetic", "philosophical", "economic", etc., investigations of a specialist character, being in this way divorced from "reality"'.

To the contrary: 'the objective class base reveals itself in the method', and 'the method of treating the material is also a uniquely important link in transmitting a work's effect ...'. Rhetorically, he asks, 'if these considerations also apply to literature', or is literature 'a special field of its own, in which the lessons we have

---

130   Lukács 1980, pp. 66, 72.

drawn from the way that Marx, Engels and Lenin worked in the fields of economics, philosophy etc., no longer apply'. 'The masters of materialist dialectics', he concludes, 'themselves used this very same method in questions of literature; it needs only proper application to the specific field in question'. Mehring's achievements were to be re-assessed in the light of this comprehensive theorisation, with its demands for the recognition of the complex interconnected discursive fields set out above.[131]

The subject matter will be addressed under the following two broad aspects: the positive assessment and lasting importance of Mehring's contribution; the necessity for the augmentation and intensification of the level of Mehring's contribution in light of limitations becoming apparent in the later 1920s, particularly with the greater presence of Lenin's work, especially his reading of Hegel. Lukács's critique is informed by the concept of totality as set out in the Ottwalt essay, in the section 'Fact, Totality and Portrayal': '... Marx and Lenin have precisely shown us the way in which it is possible, despite the incompleteness of our knowledge, to meet this demand that we should understand the totality'.[132] For the sake of clarity, it seems best to deploy Lukács's categories as set out in the previous quotation, 'the fields of economics, philosophy etc.' to examine his critique of Mehring.

The first area of interest may be established quickly. The criticism of Mehring's contribution ('des Mehringschen Erbes') is not to disregard his achievement, which remains unchallenged, a great historical service, the first after Marx and Engels to examine literature systematically, 'who has achieved in many and not unimportant subjects the proper outcomes' ('sondern auch in vielen und nicht unwichtigen Punkten zu richtigen Resultaten gelangt ist').[133] His Lessing study, into which he was able to pour, unrestricted, his 'revolutionary energy' on the side of that 'indefatigable fighter', was his most significant achievement, on Schiller he stumbled, but on the less comprehensive and detailed study of Heine, he produced a work of considerable importance based as it was on Mehring's own 'experience of the transition from a bourgeois to proletarian-revolutionary stance'.[134] Mehring's 'revolutionary energy' is

---

131 Lukács 1980, p. 64.
132 Lukács 1980, p. 73.
133 Lukács 1954, p. 320.
134 Lukács 1954, p. 372. '... von Mehring selbst erlebten Übergangs zwischen bürgerlich-und proletarisch-revolutionärer Haltung doch eine beträchtliche Höhe'. There is a passage in Mehring's *Zur deutschen Geschichte*, quoted by Friedrich Mülder in his essay 'Schiller und Heine in den Büchern Franz Mehrings', which reflects Lukács's statement: 'Heine had always fought for bourgeois freedom, and certainly cauterised all supineness and disunity of bourgeois Liberalism with glowing metal' ('Heine hat immer für die Iddee der

a trope frequently invoked by Lukács, which is deployed to bolster his 'eclectic dialectic', where his 'Praxis as literary historian and critic is often better than his theory'.[135] In his criticism of Lessing, Goethe, and Schiller, 'Mehring raised the subjective factor largely ignored by Second International writers, an antidote to fatalism': 'his revolutionary activism, his stressing of the active element of revolutionary subjectivity in art is an important developmental step in our literary theory'.[136] Although Mehring's heritage must be sharply criticised ('diese aller schärfste Kritik'), it must not be renounced ('nicht verzichtet wird').[137] Mehring's work on German literature is unavoidable 'for anyone who wishes to study literature from a Marxist-Leninist point of view' ('der sich mit den Problemen der deutschen Literatur vom marxistischen-leninistischen Standpunkt auseinandersetzen will'): they will 'find his mistakes and limitations equally as instructive as the results of his brilliant literary investigations'.[138]

Lukács frequently refers to Mehring's inadequate treatment of the economic: 'the inadmissible simplification in the analysis of economic fundamentals', 'often schematic and scant', and its consequent negative impact on his theorising.[139] The reader is reminded that Mehring got Rosa Luxemburg to write the chapter on Marx's economics in his highly regarded biography of Marx. Some of the charges are general: 'he adopted Marxist economics as guidelines for historical research without the slightest interest for the theoretical problems raised by it'.[140] The root cause for Mehring's failure to follow through on his basic economic understanding Lukács ascribes to his inability

---

bürgerlichen Freiheit gekämpft, und doch hat er alle Halbheit und Zwiespältigkeit des bürgerlichen Liberalismus mit glühenden Eisen gebrannt') (Mehring, quoted in Mülder 1996, p. 94).

135   Lukács 1954, p. 369. 'Dass die Praxis Mehrings als Literaturhistoriker und Kritiker sehr oft viel besser ist als diese Theorie, kann die theoretische Grundlegung selbstverständlich nicht retten. Denn Mehrings Praxis ist in diesen Fällen nicht aus seiner Theorie heraus richtig, sondern trotz seiner Theorie'.

136   Lukács 1954, p. 403. 'Der revolutionäre Aktivismus Mehrings, seine Betonung des aktiven Elements der revolutionären Subjectivität in der Kunst ist eine wichtige Entwicklungstufe unserer Literaturtheorie ...'.

137   The fact that a 12-volume collection of Mehring's work was published in the Soviet Union in 1934, the year following this essay, confirms that it was not renounced.

138   Lukács 1954, p. 403.

139   Lukács 1954, pp. 372, 374. 'Die unzulässige Vereinfachung in der Analyse der ökonomischen Grundlage', 'bei Mehring die ökonomische Analyse selbst oft schematisch und dürftig ist'.

140   Lukács 1954, p. 326. '... und sich die marxistische Ökonomie als Leitfaden zu der historischen Forschung angeeignet, ohne dabei das geringste eigene theoretische Interesse für die theoretischen Probleme der marxistischen Ökonomie zu zeigen'. The Rosa Luxemburg reference is on p. 326.

as editor of the young Marx's writings on the subject to recognise their signi-ficance: as for instance *The Economic and Philosophic Manuscripts of 1844* and *The German Ideology* ('... dass er bei seiner Herausgabe der Marxschen Jugend-schriften an den grundlegenden philosophischen Manuskripten, *Ökonomisch-philosophische Manuskripte von 1844, Die deutsche Ideologie* achtlos vorbei-ging').[141] Lukács is factually correct in that Mehring edited some early Marx work: *Aus dem literarischen Nachlass von Karl Marx, Friedrich Engels und Fer-dinand Lassalle (From the Literary Legacy of Karl Marx ...)* in 1902, and the Marx-Freiligrath correspondence (*Freiligrath und Marx in ihrem Briefwechsel*) in 1912: as the *Economic and Philosophic Manuscripts 1844* and *The German Ideo-logy* were only available in the 1930s, Mehring could not have had access to them.[142] Lukács provides no examples of authors who have met such criteria.[143] The theoretical problems were those presented by the ramifications of the dia-lectic ('... und sie inbesondere nicht auf alle ideologischen Probleme in ihrer ganzen dialektischen Verzweigheit angewendet hat').[144]

There are also a number of specific instances: here I am heavily indebted to the wide-ranging research of Mehring's biographer, Hans Koch. Lukács asserts that Mehring failed to comprehend the particulars of 'capitalist development in Germany as brilliantly established by Marx and Engels time and again' ('... die Besonderheit der kapitalistischen Entwicklung in Deutschland von 16 Jahrhunderts ... in der glänzenden Weise dargestellt haben').[145] In a long note Koch counters with Mehring's class analysis and economic structure in sixteenth-century Germany, as found in his *History of German Social Demo-cracy*, as also set out in his collected lectures at the Party School ('wie sie in den Vorlesungen an der Parteischule zusammengefasst sind'). Mehring wrote: 'The knightly landowning class, as formed since the sixteenth century ... in the Prus-sian provinces east of the Elbe, owed their origin to the economic upheavals of

---

141 Lukács1954, p. 328. At a much later conjuncture Althusser is very positive about Mehring's study of Marx's early works: 'whose history and significance were well enough described by Mehring'. Althusser is writing of 'young Marxists ... caught out, ill prepared for a struggle they had not foreseen', '... and no doubt because they had not grasped the true value of Mehring's classic work'. Althusser 1977, p. 51.

142 Maynard 1979, p. 12, writes: '*The German Ideology* (but for a brief excerpt) remained in obscurity until 1932'. Larrain writes that 'the first two generations of Marxist thinkers did not have access to *German Ideology*, which remained unpublished until the mid-1920s' (in Bottomore 1991, p. 250). Lenin, presumably, was in a similar position to Mehring.

143 In his essay 'Lenin as a Literary Theorist', Stefan Morawski deals at length with Lenin's essays on Tolstoy. Lenin's focus, Morawski writes, was on the political and the 'artistic-cognitive' dimension of the work, 'the ideological content of what Tolstoy wrote'.

144 Lukács 1954, p. 333.

145 Lukács 1954, p. 384.

the Reformation era. The warrior-knight became the producer of goods. But he accomplished fully the restoration of his feudal legal titles'.[146] Although Mehring integrated the capitalist/feudal lordship, Lukács sees this 'most significant critic of Prussianism' as 'juxtaposing undialectically the two different productive orders: capitalism and feudalism'.

Lukács is also critical of Mehring's account of the Romantic movement, again on grounds of 'schematic simplification of economic fundamentals' ('Die schematische Vereinfachung der ökonomischen Grundlagen ...'), simplifying the question of 'the difference between feudalistic Romantics and progressive bourgeois writers' because he uncritically accepted bourgeois critics of the Romantics. 'Here', Lukács wrote, 'he stood in sharpest contrast to Marx's view' ('... im schärfsten Kontrast zu der Auffassung von Marx über die Romantik'). The specific charge is that Mehring's understanding of the social origin of the Romantics was deficient as he failed to understand the East Elbean economy, particularly as set out in Lenin's theory of the 'Prussian road to capitalism'. Schleifstein defends Mehring against the charge: 'Mehring had not opportunistically considered the capitalisation process of the rural economy and specifically that of the Junker-Prussian form of the process, but rather represented it concretely, fundamentally and graphically' and not in the 'generally abstract phrases emanating from Lukács' ('nicht die abstrakt-allgemeine Phrase von der Lukács ausgeht').[147] Kleist and other Berlin Romantics 'were closely connected with the reactionary Junker circles ... Mehring by no means denied the at-times bourgeois contents of Romanticism'.[148] Mehring could be right on the Romantics, as Lukács comments on his quotation from Mehring. 'Never was "pure art" more exuberantly celebrated than by the feudalistic Romantics ...

---

146   Koch 1959, p. 367. 'Die ritterliche Gutsherrschaft, wie sie seit dem 16 Jahrhundert ... in den preussischen Provinzen östlich der Elbe enstanden war, verdankte ihren Ursprung den ökonomischen Umwälzungen im Zeitalter der Reformation. Aus dem Kriegsmanne war der Ritter ein Warenproduzent geworden. Aber auf feudale Rechtstitel hin vollzog er seine Wiedergeburt'. A more recent commentator, Jairus Banaji writes approvingly of Mehring's *Absolutism and Revolution in Germany* on this particular issue: 'Revolutionary merchant capital *not only created modern absolutism* but also transformed the medieval classes of society' (Banaji 2018, p. 154).

147   Schleifstein 1959, p. 148. 'Mehring hat den Kapitalisierungs Prozess in der Landwirtschaft und die spezifisch junkerlich-preussische Form dieses Prozess nicht nur, wie Lukács meint, gelengtliche gesehen, sondern ihn auch konkret gründlich und auschaulich dargestellt'. Schleifstein refers to a number of sources in Mehring's writings where he addresses the issues.

148   Ibid. '... aufs engste Verbunden ... dass Mehring die teilweise bürgerliche Inhalte der Romantik gar nicht geleugnet hat'. In Schleifstein's judgement, based on Mehring's writings, it is Lukács who stands in 'sharpest contrast' to Marx and Engels on the Romantics.

with them is not only mingled the "least interest" but also the most brutal of all interests: the conscious or unconscious opposition of declining classes against historical progress'. 'Without doubt', Lukács responds, 'that is ... a correct critique of the artistic theory of Romanticism'. Mehring is here rescued from his alleged Kantian dependency by his 'revolutionary instinct'.[149]

The role of the economic in Lukács's theorising of totality is clearly stated but, in his criticism of Mehring, no models with their processes of mediations are presented. Despite the presence in Mehring's work of his engagement with the economic in his responses to Paul Ernst and Jean Jaurès on the *Lessing-Legende*, of his understanding of the East Elbean Junker economy, as established by Koch and Schleifstein, work of which Lukács appears to have been ignorant, the latter finds fault with this aspect of Mehring's work related to the Romantics (and Naturalists), of failing to locate their social sites.[150] The levels of generality or particularity Lukács invokes relative to the aesthetic arena are left unstated, their mediatory processes unaddressed, their potential accommodation unclear. Koch, in *Marxism und die Ästhetik*, subjects Lukács's theorising to a searing critique. He writes:

> Lukács invents within the compass of his aesthetic theories an extraordinary amount concerning the 'general' dialectic, of the connections between base and superstructure. Preferentially he dwells on the 'general' dialectic, which ostensibly should be at the root of the 'general' asymmetry of development of material and artistic production. But almost never does one find concrete historical-economic investigations of social reality ... the specific, historical determinate of the base remains in darkness.

Consequently, 'his aesthetic-historical investigations often bear a very strong "idealist-geistesgeschichtlichen" character that are merely decorated with some materialist trimmings'.[151]

---

149   Lukács 1954, pp. 366–7. 'Niemals ist die "reine Kunst" überschwenglicher gefeiert worden als von der feudal Romantiker ... in sie "mengt" sich nicht nur das "mindeste Interesse" sondern soger das brutalste aller Interessen: der bewusste oder unbewusste Widerstand niedergehender Klassen gegen den historischen Fortschritt'. '... Das ist ohne Zweifel richtig gesagt ... eine richtige Kritik der Kunsttheorie der Romantik ...'.

150   Again, without counter-examples, Lukács writes that Mehring clearly saw ideological and cultural problems in relation to the proletariat 'but not as an ideological consequence of its social being' (1954, p. 347), a lack of 'a deeper understanding of economic problems' being a root cause.

151   Koch 1962, p. 118. 'Er fabuliert im Rahmen seiner ästhetischen Theorien ausserordent-

The second discursive practice listed by Lukács in his components towards a theory of totality is philosophy. A comment by Schleifstein summarises how much this was the intellectual terrain of the Third International: 'For the first time, through the philosophical works by Lenin, the conscious and comprehensive deployment of dialectical materialism was made possible in the aesthetic field and with that the understanding of the original nature of the thinking of Marx and Engels in this field was disclosed'.[152] Lukács's critique of Mehring's position is succinctly posited here. 'The representation of Kant's philosophy is a remarkable web of correct historical perceptions and fundamentally false philosophical ones'.[153] Mehring recognised the historical relationship between Kant's philosophy and eighteenth-century French materialism, the superiority of that materialism, based as it was on the greater sociopolitical development of the French bourgeoisie: 'In France the powerful aspiring bourgeoisie used it as its sharpest weapon against feudal legitimacy by divine right'. In Germany, 'philosophy could only develop through incessant compromises with clerical despotism'.[154] Despite this correct historical perception, 'Mehring did not recognise the superiority of the French materialists to Kant' ('erkennt Mehring nicht die philosophische Überlegenheit der französischen Materialisten Kant gegenüber').[155] To clarify Mehring's problem with his understanding of Kant's position on idealism and materialism, Lukács introduces the example of Lenin, who also proceeds from the 'compromise character of Kant's theory of knowledge' ('Auch geht Lenin von Kompromisscharak-

---

lich viel über die "allegemeine" Dialektik der Beziehungen zwischen Basis und Überbau. Er hält sich mit Vorliebe bei der "allegemeinen" Dialektik auf, die der angeblich "allegemeinen" Ungleichmässigkeit der Entwicklung von materieller und künstlerischer Produktion zugrunde liegen soll. Aber fast nirgends finden sich konkrete historisch-ökonomische Untersuchungen der gesellschaftlichen Wirklichkeit ... dass das Spezifische, historisch Bestimmte dieser Basis in Dunkeln bleibt. Damit hängt dann zusammen, dass ästhetisch-historische Untersuchungen oft einen sehr stark idealistisch-geistesgeschichtlichen Charakter tragen, die lediglich mit einigem materialistischen Aufputz verziert sind ...'.

152   Schleifstein 1959, p. 124. 'Erst durch die philosophischen Arbeiten *Lenins* wurde die bewusste und allseitige Anwendung des dialektischen Materialismus auf dem Gebiete der Ästhetik ermöglicht und damit auch eigentlich erst das Verständnis für die genialen Gedanken von Marx und Engels auf diesem Gebiet erschlossen'. As noted above, this disclosure was augmented with the publication of the 1844 *Paris Manuscripts*, the complete *German Ideology*.
153   Lukács 1954, p. 356. 'Die Darstellung der Philosophie Kants durch Mehring ist nun ein merkwürdiges Gewebe von historisch richtigen und philosophisch grundfalschen Anschauungen'.
154   Ibid.
155   Lukács 1954, p. 356.

ter der Kantschen Erkenntnistheorie aus').[156] 'The fundamental disposition of Kant's philosophy is a reconciliation of materialism and idealism', Lenin says, 'a compromise between both ... When Kant assumes that our ideas answer something outside us, some thing in itself, he is materialist. When he declares this thing in itself as unknowable, transcendent, beyond, he appears as an idealist'.[157] Lukács concludes that Mehring 'could not have achieved this high level of dialectical-materialist theory of knowledge'. Mehring in his Kant essays (see above) rejected the suprasensible and although he would have been capable of understanding Lenin's brief exposition, his rejection could be seen as non-dialectical, not theorised in the manner of Lenin or Lukács. 'Mehring', Lukács writes, 'saw in Kant a type of founder of a dualistic-methodology of Nature and a science of history'.[158] He criticises the ground on which Mehring, in one of his essays on Kant, judges the relationship between Kant's social class and his philosophy, overly dependent on anecdotal material from Heine rather than on a class analysis of Germany in Kant's time: Lukács describes this process as 'a juxtaposition of mechanical "sociology" and mere biographical psychology', an expedient Mehring had to resort to in the absence of a more dialectical practice.[159]

To what extent Lukács's characterisation reflects Mehring's practice is open to question. The issue of Mehring's deployment of the discourse of psychology was first raised negatively by Paul Ernst in his critique of the former's *Lessing-Legende*: Ernst accused Mehring of ignoring the psychological dimensions and essentially producing an empiricist account of the socio-cultural world of Lessing. Rejecting Ernst's criticism, Mehring describes his procedure as 'seeking to understand the historical facts as they were and using the historical-materialist method as guide to discover their inner connections'.[160] Koch draws attention to the 'many biographical outlines Mehring had written, in which he used

---

156 Ibid.

157 Lukács 1954, p. 357. 'Der Grundzug der Kantischen Philosophe ist eine Aussöhung von Materialismus und Idealismus, ein Kompromiss zwischen beiden ... Wenn Kant annimmt, dass unseren Vorstellungen etwas ausser uns, irgendein Ding an sich, entspreche, ist er Materialist. Wenn er dieses Ding an sich, für unerkennbar, transzendent, jenseitig erklärt, tritt er als Idealist auf'.

158 Lukács 1954, p. 357. 'Er sieht also in Kant eine Art Begründer jenes Methoden-Dualismus von Natur und Geschichtswissenschaft ...'.

159 Lukács 1954, p. 375 '... ein Nebeneinander von mechanischer "Soziologie" und bloss biographischer Psychologie entstanden'. This criticism would also be applied to Mehring's study of Schiller.

160 Mehring 1975, p. 377. '... während ich die historischen Tatsachen zu erkennen suche, so wie sie gewesen sind, und die materialistische Methode als Leitfaden benutze, um ihre inneren Zusammenhänge abzufinden ...'.

fundamental Marxist principles'.[161] Koch rejects Lukács's judgement, that in Mehring there is a straight-line mechanical character of the relation between base and superstructure in his conception which he tries to overcome through 'the juxtapositioning of mechanical sociology' and 'simple biographical psychology'.[162]

Another criticism levelled against Mehring is his use of the Kantian term 'Gattung' (species, type) rather than Marx's 'Klasse'. In the following passage he criticises Mehring on grounds of Kantian idealisation, in this instance that of 'type' (Gattung) and the 'concept of type' (Gattungsbegriff), raising indirectly the issue of modes of representation. Lukács quotes Mehring:

> The type is in itself the concept. When we speak of a Junker – a bourgeois – a working class, *we thus speak from concepts that we have constructed for ourselves* [Lukács's italics] from ideas as individuals, ideals, and to transform these ideals into their natural appearances is the duty of the fine arts. A Junker, a bourgeois, a worker represented by poet and artist becomes in the aesthetic sense of the word so much finer and truer the freer he is from the inessential accidents of the individual, the more permeated he is by the essential qualities of the type.[163]

Koch in a note elaborates on Mehring's customary usage of both terms across his writings: 'Mehring frequently, in like manner, uses the Marxist established concept of class for the social stratum rather than that of "Gattung"'.[164] But he favours the 'Kant-derived concept of "Gattung", which he always intends to be understood in its socially conditioned sense, which is evident as soon as he uses it in relation to his concrete cultural analysis', a preference which is based on Mehring's perception that 'it appears more complex and compre-

---

161   Koch 1959, p. 89. '... vielmehr kommt es darauf an Mehring die marxistischen Grundsatze innerhalb diese Aufgabenstellung anwendete'.

162   Ibid.

163   Lukács 1954, p. 368. 'Er sagt: "Die Gattung ist an sich nur ein Begriff. Wenn wir von einer Junker-, eines Bürger-, einer Arbeiterklasse sprechen, *so sprechen wir von Begriffen, die wir uns gebildet haben* (von mir hervorgehoben – GL), von Ideen als Individuen, von Idealen, und diese Ideale in natürliche Erscheinungen zurückzuverwandeln, ist die Aufgabe der schönen Kunst. Ein Junker, ein Bürger, ein Arbeiter, den der Dichter oder Maler darstellt, wird im ästhetischen Sinne des Wortes um so schöner und um so wahrer sein, je freier er von den wesenloser Zufälligkeiten des Individuums und je durchdrungender er von den wesentlichen Eigenschaften der Gattung ist"'.

164   Koch 1959, p. 380. 'Mehring gebraucht des öfteren statt des Begriffes "Gattung" den marxistisch aufgefassten Begriff der Klasse, der gesellschaftlichen Schicht'.

hensive, because it should embrace the human being of a determinative social stratum or class'.[165]

Koch's comments on Mehring's use of both 'Gattung' and 'Klasse' can be related to his practice both as literary theorist and social historian. The presence of the fictional Junker ('a constructed concept') here is interesting in that Mehring has also written of the historical Junker, a situation which allows one to consider the transformative representational modes involved, where that of the fictional may be characterised as secondary (Mehring writes 'in the aesthetic sense of the word') in contrast to the objective first order of the historical. The research of Koch and Schleifstein (as set out above) established the rigour of Mehring's representation of the historical Junker enhancing its class status through newly developing economic power. Lukács uses the term 'concretisation' (Konkretisierung) many times throughout his essay to criticise Mehring for failing to found his social type in the economic sphere. The Junker is a concretised social type, historically situated by Mehring: as he indicates, it is also possible to represent him fictionally.[166] Do the processes Lukács criticises Mehring for using in the realm of the fine arts, 'concepts that we have constructed for ourselves', not also operate for the historical Junker, if also impelled by a different demand? In the latter the various registers in which the dialectic operates become discernible in their separateness and connections, capable of being empirically investigated and tested. Given that Mehring was committed to such investigation, it was inconceivable that the 'concept of the type' referred to in Lukács's italicised passage could be a retreat to an idealist category. Lukács ignores the possibility that Mehring's characterisation of the representational mode of the fictional might be informed by the acknowledged achievement of his representation of the historical Junker. Mehring's theoretical practice may have been a more distributive system than Lukács was aware of.

Coupled with this apparent dependence on Kant was Mehring's neglect of Hegel, not uncommon during the period of the Second International. Koch is in general agreement with Lukács here. In a long passage on the 'Ensemble der gesellschaftlichen Verhältnisse' ('Social relations', the term is Marx's) and the

---

165   Ibid. 'Aber er bevorzugt den von Kant übernommen Begriff "Gattung", den er immer in seiner gesellschaftlichen Bedingtheit verstanden wissen will (das zeigt sich, sobald er ihn in Zusammenhang mit konkreten künstlerischen Analysen gebraucht). ... weil er ihm komplexer, umfassender erscheint, weil er das ganze Menschsein einer bestimmten gesellschaftlichen Schicht oder Klasse umfassen soll'. Koch references specific texts for his observation.

166   The present intention is not to draw some absolute distinction between the two modes – the creative power of language in the shaping of an 'ideological product' (Lukács's term) has been established since the work of Voloshinov in the late 1920s.

relationship between 'Individuum' and 'Gattung' (species being), Koch imputes Mehring's 'central aesthetic category' to read: 'Agreement between individual and species, in contrast to Marx's unity of Individuum und Gesellschaft' which can only be a 'dialectical unity of contradictions' ('dass sie immer nur als dialektische Einheit von Widersprüchen ...'). 'But Mehring's shortcoming in dialectical materialism', Koch continues, 'does not allow him to consistently define the category. He derives it from pre-Hegelian classical German aesthetics and attempts to give it an exclusively historical materialism turn'.[167]

There can be no doubt that Mehring did not articulate the expansive theorising of the processes of dialectical movement in the manner of Marxism-Leninist practice, concentrating instead on the concrete practice which found support later from Korsch (see Chapter 6 below).[168] The workings of social contradiction, however, were not unknown to him, as set out in his Lessing and Schiller studies, in the work of Romantic and Naturalist writers, where Lukács nevertheless recognised his 'eclectic dialectic' and Koch his inconsistency in defining his 'central aesthetic category' as achieving positive results. But this did not fully meet the theoretical level demanded by Third International requirements. However, as one may see, scattered throughout his writings, Mehring was very aware of the importance of Hegel. In his Appendix to the *Lessing-Legende* he writes that 'what annoys them', the bourgeoisie, 'is Hegel's scientific conception of history as a process of human development ... whose inner laws must be proved through all apparent contingencies'. It is not Hegel's 'arbitrary historical constructions', but 'his dialectical method ... that dances the dance of death for the bourgeoisie'.[169]

---

167   Koch 1959, p. 254. 'Mehring's "ästhetische Zentralkategorie" lautet: "Übereinstimmung von Individuum und Gattung". Aber Mehrings Mangel an dialektischen Materialismus gestattete ihm nicht, diese Kategorie konsequent dialektisch-materialistisch zu bestimmen'. 'Er entlehnte Sie aus der vorhegelschen klassischen deutschen Ästhetik und versuchte, ihr auf eine eigentmüliche Weise eine historisch-materialistische Wendung zu geben'.

168   'Mehring', Lukács writes, 'sought to derive from historical materialism an integral method for the historicising of philosophy' (1954, p. 326). Korsch would defend Mehring's position vis-á-vis that of Lukács, approving that of the former.

169   Mehring 1975b, pp. 17–19. First published in 1893 as an Appendix to *Die Lessing-Legende*, establishing Mehring's understanding of Hegel's importance at this relatively early stage in his major output.

7   'Nur-Kampfkultur oder positive Kultur'?[170]

In *Die Linkskurve* of January 1931, Wittfogel wrote a report on the recent proceedings of the Interessengemeinschaft für Arbeiterkultur (Society for the Consideration of Working-Class Culture) under the title 'Entwicklungsstufen und
Wirkungskraft proletarisch-revolutionären Kulturarbeit' ('Stages of Development and Efficacy of Proletarian-Revolutionary Cultural Work'), a report which
also reads somewhat like a summary of the material covered in this study.[171]

In the opening paragraph he juxtaposes simply, in two sentences, the core
concerns of the left in its investment in theorising and producing culture: 'Naturally overall the immediate prosecution of the economic-political struggle
remains our central duty. Nevertheless the effective contribution of revolutionary cultural work, as experience shows, should not be undervalued'.[172] However,
as his article makes clear this was not an uncontested terrain, and it contains an informed locus for considering the varied expectations of the participants, rehearsing as it does the sharp divisions on the left. More pressing,
as he emphasises, 'the frightful growing crisis' ('Die engeheuer anwachsende
Krise') of National Socialism creates more offensive opportunities for cultural
work. His arguments in this article will be considered before a more general
account of the left's cultural engagement across the period being dealt with in
this text is set out.

Central to his exposition here are the positions taken at the conference on
the status of 'Nur' Kampfkultur, the culture in struggle before the seizure of
power, and 'positive' Kultur, the culture developed and established on achieving power. He notes that doubt was voiced over the 'Nur' Kampfkultur relative
to 'positive' Kultur. He quotes a number of times from Lenin on culture, from
the more general as practices present across the everyday to the 'revolutionising of the spiritual life-processes of the proletariat' ('Die Revolutionisierung
des geistigen Lebenprozesses des Proletariats ...'). Against what he characterises as 'the mechanistic nodal-point theory' ('Die mechanische Knotenpunk-
theorie'), essentially the argument around the cultural maturity of the pro-

---

170 Wittfogel is assessing the status of proletarian culture – as a culture only for the struggle
  or one in its own right, 'positive', on the eve of this 'frightful growing crisis', the surge in
  National Socialism.
171 Wittfogel 1980, *Die Linkskurve* 3, no. 1, pp. 17–23.
172 Wittfogel 1980, *Die Linkskurve* 3, no. 1, p. 17. 'Natürlich bleibt überall die unmittelbar
  ökonomisch-politische Kampfführung unsere zentrale Aufgabe. Gleichwohl darf die Hil-
  fwirkung der revolutionären Kulturarbeit, wie die Erfahrung beweist, nicht unterschätzt
  werden'.

letariat before the access to power, 'Nur' Kampfkultur or 'positive' Kultur, he again quotes Lenin from 1913 on the possibility that, given their particular life experiences, 'even if in undeveloped form elements of a socialist culture could be established' ('erzeugen wenn auch in unentwickelter Form, Elemente einer ... sozialistischen Kultur'). Marx and Engels are invoked to support this dialectical process: 'According to Marx and Engels the proletariat prior to their victory transverse different developmental stages'.[173] The exemplar is the dialectical infiltration of bourgeois cultural norms through the cultural world of the feudalist-absolutist stage before their access to power.[174]

Wittfogel claims authorship of the category 'Kampfkultur', which he deployed against Trotsky in his 1925 series in *Die Rote Fahne* (see Chapter 4) where he criticised the latter for rejecting the possibility of a positive culture before the *Übergangzeit*, the transitional period. The SPD and Mehring were criticised by Lukács for holding a similar position, thus separating Second- from Third-International cultural politics and their ideological implications. But the designation 'Nur' Kampfkultur (only art-in-struggle) signified something different, its contrast (at the conference) with 'positive' Kultur (a term he does not elaborate on here) is again characterised by Wittfogel as 'a mechanistic formula'.[175] This was not only a downgrading of Kampfkultur, but it also placed those 'who hold this position as entering into questionable closeness to the theoretical views of Korsch, Lukács and Sternberg'. 'All of these', he continues, 'see the process of Marxist struggle as somewhat mechanistically negative, uncreative, whereas it is a question of a dialectically negative procedure, a procedure in that whilst it destroys through criticism itis simultaneously creatively active'.[176] The presence of Korsch and Sternberg is not unexpected as they were both in Berlin and taught a non-orthodox dissident Marxism. Lukács, a future fellow-worker on *Die Linkskurve*, was still in Moscow.

---

173   Wittfogel 1980, *Die Linkskurve* 3, no. 1, p. 19. 'Nach Marx und Engels durchläuft das Proletariat vor seinem Siege "verschiedene Entwicklungsstufe"'. The Lenin quotation is from the same page.

174   The work of the art historian Wilhelm Hausenstein on the Baroque is important in its tracing of the bourgeois presence in the culture of the Absolutist courts and through the transitional phase of [French] Rococo to full bourgeois access to its own culture. Hausenstein cites these transitions as related to the economic stages of mercantilism, physiocracy, and agiotage, speculative financialisation on French colonies in North America. See the Appendix below.

175   Wittfogel 1980, *Die Linkskurve* 3, no. 1, p. 20. 'Die Zweite von unseren mechanistischen Freunden vorgebrachte Formel lautet "Nur" Kampfkultur'.

176   Ibid. 'Sie allen sehen den marxistischen Kampfprozess als etwas mechanisch Negatives, Unschöpferisches, während es sich doch um einen dialektisch negativen Vorgang handelt, der, indem er kritisch zerstört, zugleich schöpferisch tätig ist'.

Wittfogel provides very brief introductions to their various 'deviations'. Thus with Korsch 'the idea that Marxism could be "critique" only, that it was incapable of achieving anything with regard to the "centuries old(!)" separate branches of science'.[177] He references two passages from Korsch's 1922 *Kernpunkte der materialistischen Geschichtsauffassung (Core Concerns in the Materialist Concept of History)* as evidence. In the first Korsch writes in context to disabuse SPD members and others of the idea that 'in the accepted bourgeois sense of "science" Marxism has never been a "science" and so long as it remains true to itself never can be'.[178] It is, he continues, 'neither "economics" nor "philosophy", nor "history", nor some kind of "intellectual history of ideas". It is, as the title of his economic masterpiece, and every page confirms, from beginning to end a "Critique" of political economy, written from the interest of the proletariat'.[179] Further on Korsch rejects the many 'completions' of Marxism: The Marxist system does not require this completion 'as little as it requires a specific Marxist philology or mathematics'. Marx and Engels, who had 'an encyclopedic knowledge', 'did not indulge in such mad conceits'.[180] Somewhat simplified by Wittfogel, Korsch opposed the focus on the concrete particular to the elaboration of a Weltanschauung and the contemporary Soviet 'renaissance' of what he termed 'a pseudo-philosophical dialectic'.[181]

Lukács is accused of 'separating Marxism as a means of struggle from Marxism as the site of pure scientific knowledge'.[182] Wittfogel's criticism is not unlike Koch's above, where Lukács is criticised for dwelling on the 'general' dialectic between base and superstructure, but 'almost never does one find concrete historical-economic investigations of social reality ... the specific, historical

---

177   Ibid. 'Daher dann bei Korsch die Meinung, der Marxismus sei nur "Kritik", auf den "jahrtausendalten"(!) einzelnen Wissenschaftsgebieten vermöge er nichts'.
178   Korsch 1973 [1922] p. 7. '... dass gerade im wohlständigen, gutbürgerlichen Sinne des wortes "Wissenschaft" der Marxismus eine "Wissenschaft" niemals gewesen ist und, so lange er sich selbst treu bleibt, auch niemals werden kann'.
179   Ibid. 'Vielmehr enthält das "ökonomische" Hauptwerk Marxens, wie sein Untertitel ausdrücklich besagt, und sein gesamter Inhalt und jeder Seite bestätigt, von Anfang bis zu Ende eine "Kritik" der politischen Ökonomie ...'.
180   Korsch 1973, p. 11. '... solchen törichten und grössenwahnsinnigen Einbildungen hingeben'.
181   Korsch's position is elaborated in Chapter 6 below, in his relationship with Brecht. A recent reviewer of Korsch's 1938 *Karl Marx* writes: 'But there is no denying the impact of the challenging perspectives associated with his stark and lean analyses'. Le Blanc 2017, p. 1.
182   Ibid. 'Aehnlich trennt Lukács den Marxismus als "Kampfmittel von Marxismus als dem Mittel" der reinen wissenschaftlichen Erkenntnis'. The source is *Geschichte und Klassenbewusstsein*, Berlin, 1923, p. 231.

determinate of the base remains in darkness'.[183] Sternberg's position trumps both ('übertrumpft'), declaring with ultra-mechanistic emphasis that 'culture and class struggle exclude each other ... culture shatters in class struggle. The great epochs of German philosophy and German music preceded the class struggle'.[184] The Sternberg quotation is from his widely regarded book *Der Imperialismus* and in its non-contextualised presence here stands very much at odds with his recorded discussions with Brecht from 1928 (see Chapter 6 below).

The value of the Wittfogel article is that, *in nuce*, it contains the contending Marxist cultural politics at this moment, one of crisis when 'Marxism was under attack by fascism of all stripes' ('vom Faschismus aller Schattierungen angegriffen ...'), one for which 'success in pursuit of political struggle' ('mit vollem Erfolge im Dienste des politischen Kampfes') will only be achieved 'if we are clearly aware of the strength and particularity of our weapons' ('wenn wir uns der Kraft und Eigenart unserer Waffen klar bewust sind').

Conclusion

There is a passage in the *Introduction to a Critique of Political Economy*, from the section on 'The Method of Political Economy', which may with advantage be introduced here, where Marx charts the progression from 'imaginary concrete terms to more and more tenuous abstractions' before returning to real concrete elements, 'a totality comprising many determinations and relations'.[185] Of this progression he writes: 'The totality as a conceptual entity seen by the intellect is a product of the thinking intellect which assimilates the world in the only way open to it, a way which differs from the artistic, religious and practically intelligent assimilation of the world'. The difference is that 'the concrete-subject remains outside the intellect and independent of it – that is so long as the intellect adopts a purely speculative, purely theoretical attitude. The subject, society, must always be envisaged therefore as the precondition of comprehension even when the theoretical method is employed'.[186] The parallel between

---

183 See Koch above, this chapter.

184 Ibid. 'Er erklärt mit einer schon geradezu ultramechanistischen Massitivität: "Kultur und Klassenkampf schliessen sich aus ... Kultur zerbricht in Klassenkampf. Die grossen Epochen der deutschen Philosophie und der deutschen Musik liegen vor dem Klassenkampf"'.

185 Marx 1974, p. 141. In this passage Marx moves from an immediate perception, 'population', through various social, economic, political, etc. mediations to arrive at the 'real concrete' population.

186 Ibid.

the processes of assimilation of the world and terms used in the brief passage may not be exactly congruent with those of the proponents of a Marxist aesthetic practice but they are suggestive: the implicit demand for the dialectical relationship between the conceptual and non-conceptual modes, and the associated process, through 'tenuous abstractions', from 'imaginary concrete terms' to 'real concrete elements'. The range would stretch from Lukács's elaboration of a Weltanschauung theorising to the Korsch/Brecht pursuit of the concrete real.

Two conceptions of Marxist aesthetic practice informed by two contending versions of Marxist theory have been outlined in the text. The first can be considered an orthodox one, stretching from the work of Mehring through to that of Lukács, sustained initially by an orthodox reading of the available Marxist texts, later elaborated towards the end of the 1920s by the availability of recently recovered texts by Marx, and informed by a Lenin-influenced re-engagement with Hegel. This practice was mostly based on Marxist interpretations of established writers on their texts: Mehring on Lessing and Schiller, Lukács (and Lenin) on Tolstoy. The intention was to disclose the revolutionary impulse animating these texts, to identify the traces of class struggle, and to provide an intelligibility for these representations of social conflict. The later complex theorising of Wittfogel and Lukács was essentially in the service of informing proletarian writers, here members of the BPRS, of the requirements for the production of revolutionary texts. Lukács may have been elaborating theory but he was also holding contemporary writers to account for failing to understand the import of the theory and thus failing their class. The second conception was unorthodox, certainly from the official KPD point of view, ideologically spontaneist in its early phase – Lukács ascribed it to remnants of Luxemburgism amongst radical workers and unions – productivist in aesthetic practice, that is, interventionist in contemporary struggle, and consequently experimental in responding to that struggle, using *inter alia* the new media of film and montage, agitprop, street theatre, 'living' newspapers, etc. Inevitably it was a practice based on open rather than closed textual form, the former heavily criticised by Lukács. The experimentation promoted by this tendency reached its maturity in the work of Heartfield, Piscator, and Brecht.[187]

A number of references in passages from the text may be brought together here to indicate how these positions were theorised and what was at stake.

---

187   Lenin did not reject spontaneism entirely, recognising its potential to develop into class self-consciousness. Brecht can be seen as an end point for certain Dadaist and agitprop activities.

For Lukács there was no doubt that literature should be analysed as were economics, history, philosophy, etc. by Marx, Engels, and Lenin in their analyses of 'an ideological product', that is, with the concept of a Weltanschauung. He is responding to Ottwalt's criticism to such an approach that these investigations remain stuck in 'aesthetic', 'philosophical', 'economic' categories. Lukács rejects Ottwalt's position as he bases his own practice on the Weltanschauung conception, originating in Hegel, transformed by Marx and Lenin. Yet, as set out in Chapter 5, Lukács's own practice in the literary field was severely questioned by Hans Koch. He writes: 'Lukács invents within the compass of his aesthetic theories an extraordinary amount concerning the "general" asymmetry of development of materialist and artistic production. But almost never does one find concrete historical-economic investigations of social reality, the specific historical determinate of the base remains in darkness'. Koch concludes that 'consequently his aesthetic-historical investigations often bear a very strong "idealist-geistgeschichtlichen" character that are merely decorated with some materialist trimmings'.

In the final passages of Chapter 5, Wittfogel singled our Brecht's Marxist 'teachers', Korsch and Sternberg, for particular criticism. Both rejected Marxism as a Weltanschauung. Korsch had argued that Marx and Engels, in the *Critique of Political Economy*, abandoned their previous philosophical outlook: 'From then on the purpose of their polemics on philosophical questions is only to enlighten or annihilate their opponents (such as Proudhon, Lassalle and Dühring): it is no longer intended to "clarify their own position"'.[188] There is a passage in *The German Ideology* which may provide a generalised framework for Korsch's position, under 'Philosophy and Reality', it is a critique of 1840s German philosophy: 'One has to "leave philosophy aside" ... one has to leap out of it and devote oneself like an ordinary man to the study of actuality, for which there exists an enormous amount of literary material, unknown of course, to philosophers'.[189] Whilst this may not be a call to abandon philosophy absolutely, as in Korsch's understanding of Marx's position, Marx's thinking here is richly suggestive; the knowledge status of philosophy, the engagement with actuality, enhancement through literary material (as this last was for the historical understanding of Marx and Engels in the case of Balzac).

General overarching structures – Weltanschauung (Lukács) or its displacement (Korsch), the relationship of the cognitive to the non-cognitive mode of assimilation of the world – bore within them two particular important

---

188 Korsch 2012, p. 48, n. 19. He also argued that this was Lenin's position too.
189 Marx and Engels 1974, p. 103.

issues: the author's revolutionary subjectivity and the stimulation to class self-consciousness; and the relationship of form to content. Lukács paid tribute to Mehring's 'revolutionary activism' and 'his emphasis on the role of revolutionary subjectivity in art is an important developmental step in our literary theory'. Koch examines Mehring's concern with this dimension in the study of his subject's contribution to Marxist literary theory: the section is titled 'Über die ästhetische Bedeutung der revolutionären Subjectivität' ('On the Aesthetic Significance of Revolutionary Subjectivity'). In the historically present period Mehring proposed that 'the author's revolutionary subjectivity was an essential prerequisite for achieving the highest outcome in literature' ('... dass die revolutionäre Subjectivität des Schriftstellers in der neuen geschichtlichen Periode eine wesentliche Entwicklungsstufe eines hohen künstlerisch-ideellen Wertes ...'). This was necessary 'in order to properly represent the dialectical and revolutionary developing reality being governed by the proletarian struggle for freedom' ('um die sich dialektischund revolutionäre entwickelnde Wirklichkeit, die vom proletarischen Befreiungskampf beherrscht wird ...'). Revolutionary subjectivity was also 'a necessity to produce social consciousness from the specificity of artistic-literary form'.[190] Koch then established the deployment of this approach across a number of Mehring's articles and reviews, confirming Lukács's assessment.

Lukács is more negative in his assessment of Ottwalt's and Brecht's practice concerning revolutionary subjectivity. He is initially referring to Ottwalt's response to his criticism: 'Our literature does not have the task of stabilising the consciousness of its readers: it seeks to alter it'; Lukács then refers to Brecht, who 'counterposes the "unchangeable human being" of the old theatre to the "changeable and changing human being" of the new'. The old theatre 'confirms the spectator's opinions whereas the new "forces him to make decisions": "only aesthetic conclusions are drawn in a literary reality, and not practical ones"'. Lukács dissents from this view.[191] For Lukács, Ottwalt and Brecht mistakenly believe their ambitions find support in

> the last of Marx's 'Theses on Feuerbach', where the well-known counterposing of 'interpreting' and 'changing' reality is presented as the line of separation between previous philosophy and dialectical materialism. The idea that before Marx reality was only 'interpreted' and that since Marx

---

190   Koch 1959, p. 271 '... als eine Notwendigkeit, die sich aus der Besonderheit der künstlerisch-literarischen Form des gesellschaftlichen Bewusstseins ergibt'. All quotations from p. 271.
191   Lukács 1981, p. 66.

we merely want to change it, is a superficial vulgarisation of Marx's views in which not only does the dialectic disappear, but materialism as well.[192]

Lukács deploys the theorising of the form/content relationship against both Mehring and Ottwalt/Brecht; in the case of the former on grounds of idealism, of endorsing the Kant-Schiller proposition that form be prioritised over content, particularly as embodied in Schiller's claim that artistic mastery was manifested in the annihilation of content through form; in the case of the latter that a 'mechanical and one-sided exaggeration of the content leads to an experiment in form: to attempt to renew the novel with the means of journalism and reportage', a rejection of the dialectical concept that 'form and content belong causally together'.[193]

The Marx-derived aesthetic conceptualising of the form/content relationship can be traced from Kant through Hegel to Marx, where it was given its materialist reading in the context of the socio-economic process. For Kant, 'form is the organising synthesising principle of matter, defined as a given sensory diversity', introducing to 'the traditional problem of the relation between matter and form' a new aspect, 'the content and form of thought'.[194] 'Hegel', it continues, 'introduced the category of content, of which form and matter are moments. Content consists of both form and matter ... the relationship between content and form is an interrelation of dialectical opposites, a mutual transformation'. Marx and Engels developed this further, writing that

> content constitutes not the substratum per se but its internal state, the totality of the processes that characterise the interaction of the constituent elements of the substratum with each other and with the environment and that determine their existence, development and replacement. In this sense content is a process. Dialectical materialism conceptualises form as a structure that develops and comes into being.

---

192   Lukács 1981, p. 67.

193   Lukács 1981, p. 46. In a section 'Über Inhalt und Form in der Literatur' ('Concerning Content and Form in Literature'), Koch disputes through many examples this criticism of Mehring and refers to Lukács's own essay 'Zur Ästhetik Schillers' in which Lukács had interpreted Schiller's 'destruction of content' statement in 'a more dialectical manner' ('dialektischer interpretiert'), further that 'it had very different, very contradictory meanings' ('habe sehr verschiedene, sehr widerspruchsvolle Bedeutungen'). Koch 1959, p. 284. The Schiller essay was published two years after the Mehring (1935).

194   Entry in *The Great Soviet Encyclopedia* (1979) via *The Free Dictionary*, https://encyclopedia 2. thefreedictionary.com(Content+and+Form). This passage is indebted to the succinct account of Kant, Hegel, and Marx on this subject.

In the process, content transforms into form and form into content and 'the filling of the old form with new content'. Lukács transfers this process from the socio-economic to the cultural, from the cognitive to the non-cognitive, suggestive if nevertheless open to question, and uses it as a criterion against both Mehring and Ottwalt/Brecht. Apart from Lukács's own oscillation on Schiller's claim for form (see footnote 193), Mehring had clearly rejected the priority of form in his very clear statement on Hauptmann's 'Florian Geyer', that pouring new content into old form was retrogressive, new content demanded new form. The charge against Ottwalt was that the exaggeration of content led to formal experimentation, lacking the internal interactions set out by Marx, introducing what he referred to as alien material into the work of art.

Lukács's theorising addressed the closed textual form of the classical novel. Mehring wrote on the more open form of drama. More experimental artists like Ottwalt, Brecht, and Piscator embraced the creative potential of the open text, often collaboratively – Piscator with Brecht and George Grosz on the staging of the 'montaged' picaresque novel of Hasek, *The Good Soldier Schweik*; Brecht and Ottwalt on the film 'Kuhle Wampe'. The production of Brecht's 'Die Massnahme' was broadly welcomed by *Rote Fahne* and *Linkskurve* critics for its striking formal innovations, seen as the way forward, if also censured for some ideological failures.[195]

What the text has rehearsed are two antagonistic claims to a Marxist aesthetic on the German left, their ambitions to furnish, in a different register, knowledge of class conflict and thereby provide occasion for and stimulation to a revolutionary class consciousness capable of engaging with that conflict. History, of course, had to be the arbiter of how successful these positions turned out to be, determined as they were by the overwhelming events in Germany and the USSR. Despite these calamities they must be judged on the extraordinary challenge they offered to traditional modes of theorising culture. This was a fundamental questioning of why cultural products merited the attention that was claimed for them: the theorists and practitioners considered in this text provided the evidence as to why this attention might or might not be warranted, that culture be made answerable for its social status. Art might not be exactly congruent with the world, but the sophisticated pathways they opened up through dialectical-materialist reasoning led to otherwise undisclosed interactions with the socio-economic and political spheres. It may not structurally constitute a 'third pillar' of socialism, but its objective of mediating the interactions between the cognitive and non-cognitive provided the crucial foundation

---

195   See Chapter 6 for a range of responses to it.

for the most profound understanding of how this level of culture contributes to our knowledge of the social totality.

In 'The Uses of Cultural Theory', Raymond Williams wrote 'of what might be called the road from Vitebsk', a reference to the late discovery in Western cultural circles of the work of the Bakhtin School, and bemoaned the time lost to postmodernist ideas.[196] The work of the above theorists has not been superseded and could be carried forward in the context of the materialist linguistics of Volosinov and the materialist psychology of Vygotsky (Brecht sought out his work), both Soviet contemporaries from the 1920s and 1930s, and the later work of Ilyenkov.

196   Williams 1986.

CHAPTER 6

Crisis and Critique: Continuity and Conflict

Roughly contemporary with the founding of *Die Linkskurve* (1929) Benjamin and Brecht were canvassing opinion for the founding of another journal, *Krise und Kritik*, that did not get beyond the planning stage. Nevertheless the correspondence surrounding the proposal discloses interesting insights into how thinking about a Marxist aesthetic practice was developing, an outline of which can only be delineated here.

Amongst names pencilled in were those of Lukács and Wittfogel, both contributors to *Die Linkskurve*, a surprising inclusion given their very different concepts of an aesthetic practice.[1] Brecht was sceptical of the revolutionary-proletarian writers of the BPRS, whom he described as 'proletarian literary proprietors', out 'to corner the proletarian market', 'as literature owners they regard "their" readers purely as customers ...', 'Should we blame them for not learning how to write, when they are guilty of the far greater crime of not teaching people how to read'. Brecht dismisses this proletarian culture, 'a hideous little superstructure, an ornament, bourgeois in character', and 'for us consequently not an aim but a field of operations'.[2]

Interesting too is reference to the work of Franz Mehring and Lu Märten. Erdmut Wizisla, in his study of *Krise und Kritik*, writes that 'Benjamin thought a "debate" was necessary on "what has until now been brought to us from the materialist side about literary criticism (Franz Mehring, Merten [i.e. Lu Märten] etc.")'[3] Märten's work has been seen as anticipating ideas further developed by Brecht and Benjamin. A propos of Brecht's criticism of BPRS writers not teaching their readers how to read, Märten had noted in her 1921 'Die revolutionäre Presse und das Feuilleton' that the party press provided its readers with criticism but not the critical tools through which they might develop their own critical practice (Chapter 2). In her 1920 brief introduction to her bro-

---

1 See Wizisla 2009.
2 Brecht 1990, p. 119 (all quotations from this page). This letter to Bernhard von Brentano, who was attending the inaugural Congress of the BPRS, is dated July 1928. This letter would appear to contradict the information contained in Gallas 1974, p. 225, n. 64, that Brecht had wanted to join the BPRS but that his application had been thwarted by Becher and Lukács, 'dieser Beitritt sei jedoch von Becher und Lukács verhindert worden'.
3 Wizisla 2009, p. 79.

chure *Historisch-Materialistisches über Wesen und Veränderung der Künste*, she describes it as 'an orientation for co-thinking and co-work', for which Erhard H. Schütz claims that

> Lü Märten's theory seems particularly appropriate, because her positions signify an important step towards Brecht and Benjamin ... as she not only saw 'art as nothing other than history', but, simultaneously, the aesthetic itself as an historical problem, in that she raised the question of the alteration of sensuous perception and of aesthetic forms as arising through the political struggles of the masses.[4]

She was an early advocate of film, as shown in a short section of her 1914 study of the economic situation of artists, *Die wirtschaftliche Lage der Künstler*. She rejects a purely reproductive role for film: 'The cinema', she writes, 'has nothing to do with fine art, as it exists', but 'the artist has something to do with cinema, with the film industry'. The cinema could presently be an important cultural phenomenon, 'where it could knowingly pursue its determination as a field of operation and workshop of inventive photography and technique', among which subjects would be 'scientific, technical, working-processes of great interest, social settings etc. ... situations which would allow the greatest possible perfection of the medium'.[5] A member of the SPD at the time, she was critical of their advocacy of 'Grossekunst' (great art): her interest in design and the everyday (as set out in Chapter 2) disposed her towards the technical: 'One who perceives the consequence of a socialist aesthetic should discover its specific temporal and technical problems'.[6] Märten continued to speculate and write on the potential roles of radio and film for left-wing culture, articles which preceded those of Benjamin and Brecht. In her 1924 book she writes of film as one of the most important coming forms of pleasure, a new art form,

---

4   Schütz 1973, p. 72. 'Lu Märtens Theorie scheint besonders geeignet, weil ihre Positionen eine entscheidenden Schritt an Brecht und Benjamin heran bedeuten ... Märten fasst hier nicht nur Kunst als "nicht anderes denn auch Geschichte, sondern gleichzeitig Ästhetik als Problem der Geschichte", in dem sie die Frage nach der Veränderung der sinnlichen Wahrnehmung und der ästhetischen Ausdrucksformen durch den politischen Kampf der Massen aufwirft'.

5   Märten 1914, pp. 59–61. 'Der Künstler hat mit dem Kino, mit der Filmindustrie zu tun ... wo es sich seiner Bestimmung als Arbeitsfeld und Betrieb ingeniöser Photographie und Technik bewusst würde' ... 'um den echten Charakter einer natürlichen, d.h. gegebenen Situation in möglichster Volkommenheit der Mittel erscheinen zu lassen'.

6   *Die Neue Zeit* 1912, p. 792. Her positive espousal for film's potential developed at a time when the left was highly suspicious of film, mostly seeing it as irredeemably capitalistic.

an alignment in which science as a practical essential will be freed from the secret cabinet of the professional, that 'the scientific experiment and even its incomplete result carries pleasure in itself'.[7] Although there is no further elaboration here, Schütz has suggested that 'in these as yet unsystematic remarks from 1924 one finds the central concepts – pleasure, experiment, science – of the film discussion of the following years, as they were particularly marked by Brecht, Benjamin and Kracauer'.[8]

In an article of 1928, 'Arbeiter und Film', she focuses on the technical potential for the production of qualitatively different images, 'the apprehension of things and movements invisible to our normal capacity for seeing. Because the film camera is armed with slow motion camera and microscope'.[9] Benjamin would later develop such a perception into the 'optic unconscious' ('das optisch Unbewusste'). The technical possibilities of radio are discussed in a contemporary piece, 'Die Eigengesetzlichkeit des Rundfunk' ('The Particular Possibility of Radio'), where, following Marx, she writes there is the potential 'to discover the reason that has always existed in things and to produce their rational forms'.[10]

Märten's theorising did not achieve the developed sophistication of either Brecht or Benjamin but in its opposition to the 'Spielfilm' ('movie') it was exploring the possibility for production. She consistently contributed to that cultural left which rejected the prioritising of the party ideological demand, characterised by Brecht as 'the enemies of production', over the more open-ended promptings of a practical aesthetic which was not afraid to discover something on the way. Rainhard May's account of Märten's contribution is balanced: he recognises her failure to 'uncover the real dialectic between the technical-economic and social-factors' ('Damit gelang es ihr nicht die reale Dialektik von technisch-ökonomischen und sozialen Faktoren zu entdecken'), but also the importance of her contribution 'as one of the few to have established a systematic initial assessment of the relations between new forms

---

7   Märten 1924, p. 71. '… das wissenschaftliche Experiment und Selbst sein unvollkommenes Resultat – eine Genusspotenz in sich trägt'.

8   Schütz 1973, p. 96. 'Bereits in diesem noch unsystematischen Bemerkungen von 1924 finden sich die zentralen Befriffe-Genuss, Experiment, Wissenschaftlichkeit – der Filmdiskussion der kommenden Jahre, wie sie besonders durch Brecht, Benjamin und Kracauer'.

9   May 1982, p. 118. 'Die Ergreifung auch des unserm gewöhnlichen Sehvermögen unsichtbaren Dinge und Bewegungen. Weil die Filmkamera bewaffnet ist mit Zeitlupe und Mikroscop'.

10   Quoted in Schütz 1973, p. 98. '… die Vernunft die immer existierte in den Dingen zu entdecken und die ihr venüftigen Formen zu schaffen'.

and media, their potential ... the significant contributions on film and radio are an example of the theoretical consistency of her model'.[11]

The presence of Franz Mehring's name is possibly more surprising than that of Märten. It occurs in an exchange between Benjamin and another prospective contributor, Rychner, in which the former declares his preference for 'the clumsy rough-and-ready analyses of Franz Mehring' to the 'most profound circumlocutions of the realm of ideas emanating from the Heidegger school, because the former seemed to him methodologically better suited to solve the problems of aesthetics, indeed of philosophical thought in general'.[12] Benjamin's assessment of Mehring's contribution is most interesting in light of the reservations expressed by Wittfogel and Lukács in their *Linkskurve* articles, even if their ideas are not coming from Heidegger. Brecht more clearly identifies the source in a frank letter to Lukács on the proposed new journal: Lukács's definition of what the journal could be is opposed as 'too over-abstract', it 'would be ineffectual', making 'Brentano and myself only too well aware of your superiority'. Brecht adds the note: 'It is undoubtedly a mistake to suppose that because intellectuals have been jolted by the crisis the slightest push will send them toppling like ripe pears into the lap of communism'.[13] Although in no way directly connected with the journal, the name of Karl Korsch is of interest here because of the close relationship between Brecht and himself since the late 1920s when Brecht attended sessions taught by Korsch. There is a passage in Korsch's 'Why I am a Marxist', admittedly later than the attempt to found the journal but probably known to Brecht much earlier, which gives a context to Benjamin's surprising statement on Mehring. Korsch is criticising 'the renaissance of this pseudo-philosophical dialectic in the writings of "modern" Marxists' and comments 'how sober, clear and definite was the standpoint adopted by such old revolutionary Marxists as Rosa Luxemburg and Franz Mehring, who saw that the principle of materialistic dialectic as embodied in Marxian economics means nothing more than the specific relation of all economic terms and propositions to *historically* determined objects'.[14]

There is more evidence of this 'rough-and-ready analysis' (Benjamin) in an unpublished nine-page typescript in the Korsch Archive in the International Institute for Social History, Amsterdam, titled 'Dialektik des Alltags' ('Everyday Dialectic') from 1931, the subject matter of which, one may speculate, must have been familiar to Brecht. The dialectic is basically a very simple process and of

---

11   May 1982, p. 90.
12   Wizisla 2009, p. 82.
13   Brecht 1990, pp. 127–8. Dated to 'end of 1930–beginning of 1931'.
14   Korsch 1971, p. 64.

the everyday, its operations are ordinary, unnoted.[15] It is manifested through conflict, contradiction, paradox, irony, sarcasm, aphorism, all, in effect, literary tropes.[16] It is preserved in the 'original dialectical nature of human thinking and affairs, in its complete living quality': as 'it ostensibly goes into decline in formal science, philosophy, and politics, it thrives as the dialectic of the everyday'.[17] In conflicts between the 'great social groups and classes', it becomes more indispensable in grasping and dealing with contradiction and conflict as essential elements of the real.[18]

With these references to the work of Märten and Mehring we are in the context of a different aesthetic practice, one that is concerned more with the exploration of the technological as a source for innovatory leftist cultural practices and concerned less with party orthodoxy on the formal structure of the dialectic but not the effectiveness of its operations. Korsch provides a legitimising context for Brecht's refined 'plumpes Denken' ('clumsy thinking', to repeat Benjamin's term); for instance, to make the 'unnoted' noted by 'way of the practice of distanciation; Verfremdung'. I now want to consider briefly the product of such 'plumpes Denken'.

The concentration will now be on Brecht, as well as Fritz Sternberg and Karl Korsch, whose teaching sessions Brecht attended, and their contributions to his aesthetic practice.[19] Like Thalheimer (see Chapter 4), they were highly critical of the Stalinisation of the KPD and the distortion of Marxist thinking. They

---

15   Korsch Archive 76/1, p. 1. '... dass das Dialektisches in Grund etwas ganz Einfaches und Alltäges ist ... dass man es gar nicht mehr merkt'. It has been noted above (Chapter 4) that the committee of the BPRS had to suspend its seminars on the operation of the dialectic due to problems of reception with its participants. Lukács refers to these sessions in his criticism of Bredel's novels.

16   A context for such a formulation is provided indirectly by Mehring's article on Marx's style, 'Marx und das Gleichnis' (Chapter 1 above). Korsch refers to Mehring's 'interesting study of Marx's style', quoting from it. Korsch 1971, p. 58.

17   Korsch Archive 76/1, p. 9. 'Die in der offiziellen Wissenschaft und Philosophie und Politik scheinbar ausgestorbene Dialektik lebt als "Dialektik des Alltags" fort'.

18   Ibid. '... desto notwendiger wird auch die Dialektik, die den Gegensatz und Widerspruch als wesentliche Bestandteile der Wirklichkeit begreift und behandelt'. There is a similar desacralisation of philosophic language in a passage from *The German Ideology*, in a section titled 'Language and Thought', Marx writes: 'the philosophers would only have to dissolve their language into the ordinary language from which it is abstracted, to recognise it as the distorted language of the actual world, and to realise that neither thoughts nor language in themselves form a realm of their own, that they are only *manifestations* of actual life'. Marx and Engels 1974, p. 118.

19   Brecht presented Sternberg with a copy of 'Mann ist Mann' with the dedication 'Meinem ersten Lehrer' (to my first teacher). In his letters he constantly acknowledges Korsch as his 'teacher'.

were both critical of democratic centralism and espoused the Council's (Räte) idea – Sternberg had been a member of the Soldatenrat in his native Breslau in 1919, whilst Korsch's work on industrial socialisation in 1919 in Berlin inclined him towards the council system. Korsch, who had been expelled from the KPD in 1926, formed 'Die Plattform der Linken' ('Korsch Gruppe') in 1926: Sternberg joined the SAPD (Socialist Worker's Party) in 1931.[20] Noticeably absent will be that elaboration of Hegelian philosophy and the accompanying aesthetic elaborated in the theorising of Wittfogel and Lukács in response to Lenin's advocacy of the dissemination of Hegel's contribution to Marxism. Absent also, the result of 'normalisation' or 'democratisation', were the concepts of 'dialectic' or 'Weltanschauung' as used by Wittfogel and Lukács: for Sternberg, as a commentator wrote, 'Marxism was a method which could through analysis embody the empirical within the theoretical; he did not see in Marxism a Weltanschauung or a dogma'.[21] Korsch had situated the dialectic in the 'everyday' in an unpublished essay (see above).

Brecht and Sternberg first met in Berlin in 1926, shortly after the publication of the latter's *Der Imperialismus*, based on his research as political economist and sociologist, a text which, according to the Sternberg scholar Helga Grebing, 'was the initial basis for the discussions between Brecht and Sternberg'.[22] Sternberg, incidentally, had a wide cultural background: his first wife was an actress; upon her early death, he married the daughter of one of the most eminent contemporary art historians, Wilhelm Worringer. His discussions with Brecht were wide-ranging, particularly on drama: in 1932 he wrote an essay 'Soziologische Dramaturgie. Shakespeares Julius Cäsar' for *Die Literarische Welt*, a subject he had discussed with Brecht and Piscator. Sociology, politics, and drama formed the core of their long and frequent discussions – Sternberg's courses were on

---

20   Details of their programmes are given in Fowkes 2015. Amongst SAPD policies was the building of the State 'based on the Soviets of the working masses ...'. An indication of Sternberg's standing may be seen from his 'Conversations with Trotsky', the outcome of a week spent with the latter in France in 1934, concerned with setting up the Fourth International. Trotsky wanted him to draw up an economic memorandum. A fellow visitor Jean van Heljenoort wrote: 'incidentally, the only persons with whom Trotsky contemplated a literary collaboration were economists ... Sternberg in St Palais' (p. 56). The memorandum was not written.

21   Hermann Weber, *Die Zeit Online*, http://www.zeit.de(1982)o6/ein-vergessener-theoretiker. p. 2. 'Denn für Sternberg war Marxismus eine Methode, die den empirisch zu erforschenden Tatbestand in die Analyse einordnen konnte; er sah in Marxismus keine Weltanschauung und kein Dogma'.

22   Sternberg 2014, p. 146. 'Die Ausgangsbasis für die Gespräche zwischen Bertolt Brecht und Fritz Sternberg ...'. All of the following material is based on Sternberg's reminiscences.

Marxism and Geisteswissenschaften (the arts). The major topic of discussion over the years 'was the poet in our time'.[23]

The level of interest and intimacy is established by Sternberg's statement that Brecht brought him almost everything he wrote ('fast alles was er schrieb …') much that was as yet unpublished ('… sehr vieles, was zunächst nicht veröffentlicht wurde …'). Sternberg in turn lent him books on Marx and Engels. In an exchange on Brecht's play 'Trommeln in der Nacht' ('Drums in the Night'), the issue of sociological context, intuition and the rational was raised. Sternberg gives as an example modern industrial society

> in which one cannot just simply see the various social levels. Go into a factory, see what the employers, the directors, the employees do. When you have seen all this you know almost nothing! Analysis of contemporary society must be undertaken, which can only be achieved through the rational and then deal only with your great intuitive resources.[24]

In an exchange of opinion with Brecht published in the *Berlin Börsen-Courier* (1927) based on previous discussions, Sternberg writes that the 'decline of contemporary drama is no historic accident, rather completely the opposite, an historical necessity': 'When classes become personae dramaticae', he continued, 'Thomas Mann no longer writes *Buddenbrooks* … Individualism has died and confronted by collective powers poets become writers'.[25] 'The content of the drama', he wrote, 'models conflicts of human beings themselves, conflicts in their relationships with institutions'.[26] In an earlier dialogue, Brecht had criticised his own 'Trommeln in der Nacht' (1922), as it had placed a man/woman

---

23   Sternberg 2014, p. 12. '… über den Dichter … in der heutigen Zeit, über den Dichter in Deutschland vor 1933'.

24   Sternberg 2014, p. 15. '… kann man die verschiedenen sozialen Schichten nicht einfach mit den Augen sehen. Gehen Sie einmal in eine Fabrik, sehen Sie, was die Unternehmer, was die Direktoren, was die Angestellten, was die Arbeiter tun. Wenn Sie all dies gesehen haben, wissen sie gar nichts. … Das Sehen allein führt zu keinem Resultat und ebensowenig die Intuition. … die nur durch die Ratio und nicht durch die Intuition geleistet werden kann … wieder versuchen, die Ratio zurückdrängen und Ihre grossen intuitiven Quellen auszuschöpfen'. Later in a radio discussion in 1929 with the theatre director Ihering and Sternberg, Brecht will use the trope of the factory (Ford) which 'technically, a Bolshevist organisation, suits better a Bolshevist society rather than that of bourgeois individualism'. Sternberg 2014, p. 113.

25   Sternberg 2014, p. 69. 'Wenn die Klassen personne dramatique werden … Thomas Mann nicht die *Buddenbrooks* schreiben … Das Individuum ist gestorben, und vor den Kollektivkräften verhüllen die Dichter ihr Haupt und werden zu Literaten'.

26   Sternberg 2014, p. 108. 'Den Inhalt des Dramas bilden Konflikte von Menschen unterein-

dynamic at its core, something no longer sustainable: it was at this point that Sternberg introduced the sociological and Marxism. Brecht responded to the anonymous 'Herr X' (Sternberg): 'When I invited you to look at the drama from the sociological point of view I did so because I was hoping that sociology would be the death of existing drama', going on to state that 'yours is the only branch of knowledge that enjoys sufficient freedom of thought ...'. The sociologist's 'scale of judgement', he continued, 'runs not from "good" to "bad" but from "correct" to "false"'. 'The sociologist is the man for us', he declares.[27] This thinking ushers in the era of the epic drama.

The Hegelian concept of totality as articulated by Lukács in his *Linkskurve* reviews and articles is absent from Sternberg's work. As a political economist his focus was more concrete – as Weber noted above, Sternberg saw Marxism as a method, not as a Weltanschauung. The overcoming of capitalism is only possible Sternberg writes 'when the working class achieves the correct class consciousness through knowledge of the totality', one to be structured on the concrete.[28] In a wide-ranging review of Sternberg's work, published and unpublished, in 1985 the reviewer Michael Schneider quotes from Iring Fetscher's 'Fritz Sternbergs Beitrag zur Weiterentwicklung des Marxismus', who describes him as 'unorthodox', 'as close to Marx as a Marxist could be' ('aber eng an Marx gebundener Marxist sei'), foremost among whose concerns was 'the hypothesis that all political and cultural phenomena, as Engels said, relate back to the socio-economic'.[29] 'The Marxist historian', Sternberg wrote, 'can distinguish the necessary from the unlikely direction, but the living, against that on the other hand – because she cannot know all factors – can only ever indicate an unfolding' ('Der jetzt Lebendige dagegen kann – da er nicht alle Faktoren kennen kann – immer nur die Möglichkeit einer Entwicklung aufweisen').[30]

---

      ander, Konflikte von Menschen in ihren Beziehungen zu Institutionen'. In the 1929 round-table discussion, Brecht promotes the roles of science and the sociological, Sternberg's 'teaching'.

27   Sternberg 2014, pp. 72–3. 'Wenn ich bat, das Drama von Standpunkt des Soziologist aus zu beurteilen, so geschah dies, weil ich von der Soziologie erwartete, dass sie das heutige drama liquidiert ... Keine andere Wissenschaft als die Ihre besitzt genügend Freiheit des Denkens ... Die Skala seiner Schätzungen liegt nicht "gut" und "schlecht", sondern zwischen "richtig" und "falsch"'.

28   Sternberg 2014, p. 80. '... wenn die Arbeiterschaft durch Erkenntnis der Totalität zum richtigen Klassenbewusstsein kommt'.

29   Schneider 1985, p. 684. 'Die Hypothese, dass alle politischen und kulturellen Phânomonie sich "in letzter Instanz", als Engels sagte – auf sozioökonomische zurückführen lassen'.

30   Schneider 1985, pp. 678–86, 685. This is a quotation from Sternberg's review of Henryk Grossman's 1930 book on accumulation and imperialism.

Had Sternberg articulated a theory of totality it might have sounded like Ottwalt's response to Lukács; Ottwalt, who collaborated with Brecht at this time (c. 1930–32) and shared his aesthetic practice, wrote that the 'craving for totality, for the seizing of the totality of dialectical interrelationships should not henceforth – and that must be said, because Lukács's expression here is misleading – prevail in the general renunciation of those complexes of data, whose treatment on particular political – not literary – grounds, in specific situations, appear necessary'. He then applies this to his own novel, which Lukács has criticised: 'it is self-evident that the justice system cannot be encompassed as a general process'.[31] Sternberg would have agreed.

In 1929, Brecht wrote: 'The theatre's future is philosophical'.[32] This was at the time he was in close contact with his 'teachers', Fritz Sternberg and Karl Korsch, both of whom introduced him to Marxism in general and to the dialectic in particular. Sternberg was in a position to discuss both Marxism and drama with him (see above), but his discussion with Korsch, as his correspondence shows, was more focused on Marxism.[33] Both Sternberg and Korsch would have raised doubts about the adequacy of the philosophical per se, arguing that Marxism was based on the concrete and was not a Weltanschauung, a totalising world view in the Hegelian sense, even if put back on his feet. In *Marxism and Philosophy* Korsch writes: 'The emergence of Marxist theory is, in Hegelian-Marxist terms, only the "other side" of the emergence of the real proletarian movement, it is both sides together that comprise the concrete totality of the historical process'.[34] For Korsch, Marxism 'eschews every attempt to force all experience into the design of a monistic construction of the universe in order to build a unified system of knowledge. Marxist theory is not interested in everything, nor

---

31   Ottwalt, *Die Linkskurve* 1971, 4, no. 10, p. 25, 'Der Drang zur Totalität, zur Erfassung der Totalität dialektischer Wechselbeziehaugen darf nun nicht – und das muss gesagt werden, weil Lukács' [sic] Ausdrucksweise hier missverständlich ist – dazu verführen, generell auf die Gestaltung jener "Tatsachenkomplexe" zu verzichten deren Behandlung aus bestimmten Situation notwendig erscheint. Es ist eine Selbstverständlichkeit dass das Justizwesen nicht als Gesamtprozess gestaltet werden kann'.

32   Brecht and Willett 1964, p. 24.

33   Brecht seems to have come to Hegel much later and in a manner different from Lukács. He 'umfunktioniert' Hegel, as Gerd Irrlitz wrote: 'he read his *Philosophy of History* as drama'; 'The dialectic-comic connection with Brecht's Hegel interest is well-known' ('Die Dialektik-Komik-Verbindung bei Brechts Hegel-Interesse ist bekannt'). He mistrusted Hegel's metaphysics, he saw his dialectic as 'the negation of experience' ('als die Negation von Erfahrung'). In this 20-page essay on Brecht's philosophical sources ('Philosophiegeschichtliche Quellen Brechts'), only one page is concerned with Hegel (Irrlitz, in Brecht-Zentrum der DDR 1983, pp. 148–67. All quotations from p. 167).

34   Korsch 2012, p. 45.

is it interested to the same degree in all the objects of its interests'.[35] From his reading of the *Critique of Political Economy* Korsch asserts that Marx 'did not remotely intend to turn his new principle [historical materialism] into a general philosophical theory of history that would be imposed from the outside upon the actual pattern of historical events'; his conception of history was 'that it was not meant to be a dogmatic principle but merely an original and more helpful approach to the real, sensuous, practical world that presents itself to the active and reflective subject'.[36] The following passages will attempt to trace what the radically innovative playwright sought and received from the theorists.[37]

In his essay 'Bertolt Brecht and Karl Korsch: Questions of Living and Dead Elements within Marxism', Heinz Brüggemann mentions 'Brecht's short theses on the "Derivation from Dialectics of the Three Propositions in Korsch's *Why I am a Marxist*"', a text which contains 'the most vital, if not indeed, the most essential elements of Brecht's conception of Marxism'.[38] The Korsch text was published in 1935, when both he and Brecht were in exile. But there are earlier texts, from the period when the playwright attended Korsch's lectures in the Karl-Marx-Schule, in the working-class district of Neukölln, Berlin, which, because they were current, would have provided material for ongoing discussion between the two.[39] Many of the ideas contained in these texts would be reprised in 'Why I am a Marxist'.

His 'Introduction to *Capital*' reads like a primer on how to read *Capital*: to begin with Chapter Seven, 'The Labour Process and the Process of Producing Surplus-Value' as it 'refers directly and immediately to palpable realities and in

---

35   Korsch 1971 [1934–35] p. 68. This text, 'Why I am a Marxist', was of greatest interest to Brecht, and will be considered below.

36   Korsch 1971 [1932], p. 59. This is from his 'Introduction to Capital'. Provocatively in a text from the previous year, 'The Present State of the Problem of Marxism and Philosophy: An Anti-Critique', he couples Lenin with Kautsky on defending the idea 'that socialism could only be brought to the workers "from outside"'. In a recently edited biographical outline of Karl Kautsky, Ben Lewis notes (2017, p. 165, n. 50): 'This passage provides a pithy summation of what Lars T. Lih calls "the merger formula" or "the merger of socialism and the worker movement" common to both Kautsky and Lenin'.

37   Korsch's general status and controversial role in the Marxist canon will not be addressed.

38   Brüggemann 1974, pp. 287–96, 291. The latter part of Brüggemann's title refers to a series of Korsch's lectures 'Living and Dead Elements in Marxism', 1928–29.

39   Brüggemann recounts a fellow student recalling that following Korsch's lectures, Brecht pushed for 'a new revolutionary formula for dialectics' (1974, p. 289). These texts included *Die materialistische Geschichtsauffassung* (*The Materialist Concept of History*) 1929, 'Thesen zum Vortrag "Hegel und die Revolution"' ('Notes for a Lecture ...'). Others will be referenced in the text.

the first instance to the palpable reality of some human work process'. More abstractly *Capital* presents itself as 'an artistic whole' or 'a scientific work of art' and 'this aesthetic attraction will help the beginner to overcome both the alleged and genuine difficulties of the book'. Volume One achieves 'as a whole ... artistic form' in spite of 'a style that often seems stiff and unnecessarily constrained'.[40] There are phrases here which would accord with Brecht's practice – his concern with the palpable, the concrete, the human work process, the perception of the text as 'a scientific work of art', an oxymoronic characterisation resonant with Brecht's aspiration. In a 1934 letter to Korsch, he reinforces this commitment to the concrete: '... it shows where my sole hope lies, namely, in a strictly concrete study of our situation'.[41] Brecht's interest in what Korsch could provide was more wide-ranging than that, as Brüggemann suggests, based on their correspondence: 'Hence, in the first letters written during the period of exile, Brecht's repeated intention is quite clearly to persuade Korsch to reconstruct the revolutionary, critical and subversive content of Marxist theory'.[42] Korsch had been working on just such a project since the mid-1920s.

Korsch's 1923 'Die Marxische Dialektik' emphasises the activist dimension of Marx's thinking, the crucial element which would appeal to Brecht. Marx neither created 'the proletarian class movement' nor 'proletarian class consciousness', rather 'he created the theoretical-scientific expression adequate to the new content of consciousness of the proletarian class and thereby at the same time elevated this class consciousness to a higher level of its being'. 'Only by taking the form of a strict "science"', Korsch continues, 'could socialism become the "theoretical expression" of revolutionary proletarian class action'. In cutting out 'the practical meaning of the scientific form of modern or Marxian socialism we have at the same time also described the meaning of the *dialectical method* which Karl Marx applied ... a proletarian dialectic ... that form in which the revolutionary class movement of the proletariat finds its appropriate theoretical expression' – here Korsch quotes Marx: 'Form has no value if it is not the form of its content'.[43]

Korsch develops his position on the dialectic in his 1924 article 'Über materialistische Dialektik', where he discusses the effects of Lenin's suggestion 'to organise a systematic study of Hegel's dialectic from a materialist standpoint' –

---

40   Korsch 1971, pp. 39–59, 46–7. On the question of style, Korsch refers to Mehring's 'interesting study of Marx's style' (see above Chapter 1, 'Karl Marx und das Gleichnis').

41   Willett 1990, p. 167.

42   Brüggemann 1978, p. 291.

43   Korsch 2009 [1923], pp. 1–5. 'Proletarian dialectics was a term Brecht would later use, as in the incomplete essay titled "Proletarian Dialectics"'.

he also references misgivings in *Die Rote Fahne* concerning the dangers of misunderstanding the source. Korsch settles on a brief article by August Thalheimer, a leading KPD theoretician. In this article he writes: 'Comrade Thalheimer links up with Franz Mehring's thesis – which I share and hold tenable – that from the Marxist dialectical-materialist standpoint it is no longer and factually not even possible to deal with this "material dialectical" method separated from a concrete "matter"'. Thalheimer concedes that 'although Mehring's rejection of an abstract treatment of the dialectical represents as such a correct nucleus, it nevertheless "oversteps its goal"'.[44] As well as the presence of the particular concrete, 'Thalheimer', Korsch writes, 'claims the need arises to create a comprehensive and orderly world view (!) something that lies beyond the practical demands of the struggle and the building of socialism, and this ... contains within itself "the demand for a dialectic"'. In *Marxism and Philosophy* Korsch writes: '... modern materialism is essentially dialectical and no longer needs any philosophy standing above the other sciences. As soon as each individual science is bound to make clear its position in the great totality of things, a special science dealing with this totality is superfluous'.[45] He dismisses the 'idealist dialectician' Thalheimer and sets out 'what in our conception constitutes the essence of materialist dialectic, that is, *Hegel's dialectic applied materialistically by Marx and Lenin*'. But the transition from Hegel to Marx and Lenin cannot be simply effected 'by a mere "overturning"'. Marx may have used the term but 'one needs to delve into Marx's theoretical practice to see that this "transition" in method, like all transitions, represents not a mere rotation, but rather has a rich concrete content'. In conclusion, he writes that '[t]he "materialistic dialectic" of proletarian class cannot be taught as a practical "science" with its own particular abstract material, nor by so-called examples. It can only be applied *concretely* in the practice of the proletarian revolution and in a theory which is an immanent real component of this revolutionary practice'.[46] 'Marx', Korsch writes in 'Introduction to *Capital*', 'could not have grasped these questions theoretically and incorporated them in his work, had they not already been posed, in some form or other, as actual problems in the real life of his own epoch'.[47]

---

44   This 'discourse' on Mehring, whilst brief, references a wider range of issues: Thalheimer, in his introduction to Mehring's collected works, tries to ward off criticism by supplementing him with Hegel (Chapter 1): Lukács criticised Mehring for lacking a Weltanschauung (Chapter 5). Korsch, critical of both, agrees with Mehring.

45   Korsch 2012, p. 50. n. 23.

46   Korsch 2009 [1924], pp. 1–5.

47   Korsch 1971, p. 39.

There are a number of issues here that could attract the playwright Brecht's attention: the re-emphasising of the concrete, that the materialist dialectic of the proletariat cannot 'be taught as a practical science, with its own particular abstract material, nor by so-called examples', that 'theory is an immanent real component' of revolutionary practice.

Both Korsch and Brecht thought that the original Marxian dialectical practice had deteriorated into being merely an ideology which, unlike the original, neglected the concrete. Brüggemann writes that 'Brecht read Lenin with the intention of turning the practical and activist tendencies within the texts against a Leninism that had deteriorated into an ideology with their grotesque inconsistencies and crying contradictions'.[48] Again this intention may be ascribed to a passage in Korsch's 1931 'Anticritique', in which he contrasts Lenin's position with those of his 'epigones': 'Lenin himself when alive did not base this philosophy [Marxism-Leninism] on any essentially theoretical formulations. Instead he defended it on practical and political grounds, as the only philosophy that was beneficial to the revolutionary proletariat'. 'The real importance of Lenin's work', he claimed, 'rests in the extreme rigour in which he tried to practice to combat and destroy these philosophical trends' [neo-Kantianism, Machism], regarding them as 'ideologies that were incorrect from the standpoint of party work ... Lenin decided philosophical questions *only* on the basis of non-philosophical considerations'.

In 'Why I am a Marxist' Korsch set out the 'essential points of Marxism'; even those which appear general are *specific*; Marxism is not *positive* but *critical*; the primary purpose is not *contemplative enjoyment* of the existing world but its active transformation (*praktische Umwaelzung*).[49] He criticises the current Soviet Union 'renaissance of this pseudo-philosophical dialectic [contemporary Marxism-Leninism]' and contrasts it with the 'sober, clear and definite standpoint adopted by such old revolutionary Marxists as Rosa Luxemburg, and Franz Mehring, who saw that the principle of materialist-dialectic as embodied in Marxian economics means nothing more than the specific relation of all economic terms and propositions to *historically* determined objects'.[50] He quotes Marx on uneven development in the sphere of art, of material production and artistic creation, 'the relation between different forms of art within the domains of art itself', as well as the 'relationships between the whole field of art and the whole field of social development': 'The difficulty consists only in the general way these contradictions are expressed. Just as

---

48 Brüggemann 1974, p. 289.
49 Korsch 1971, p. 61.
50 Korsch 1971, p. 64.

soon as they are made specific and concrete, they are therewith clarified'.[51] His exposition of 'Marxian theory' again has much to offer to the reflective cultural producer: 'It includes from the point of view of the *object* an empirical investigation "conducted with the precision of natural science", of all its relations and developments, and from the point of view of the *subject* an account of how the impotent wishes, intuitions and demands of individual subjects develop into an historically effective class power leading to "revolutionary practice" (Praxis)'.[52] Brecht notes in his 'Derivation from Dialectics of the Three Propositions in Korsch's *Why I am a Marxist*': 'when you are talking about what determines a process, do not neglect yourself as one of the determining factors'.[53]

Brecht provides a very specific concrete as locus for dialectical thinking:

> Dialectical thinking corresponds to a differentiated society with powerful productive forces which develop quickly in catastrophic form amid wars and revolutions. The intensification of the class struggle, the laws of competition, the free run given exploitation, the accumulation of capital through the accumulation of misery – the result of all this is that dialectics becomes ever increasingly the only means of finding one's bearings.

'Such perceptions and experiences', he continues, 'develop dialectics. It's high time that dialectics be derived from reality rather than from the history of ideas, and that reality cease to be merely a source of examples of dialectical laws'.[54] The specific locus is pre- and post-war industrial Germany. Brecht's claim that dialectical thinking corresponds to a differentiated society resonates with other claims already encountered for an objectively based type of German 'exceptionalism' (i.e. non-ideological), including Dadaists Grosz, Herzfelde, Jung in the cultural arena, Thalheimer, Sternberg, and Korsch in the theoretical and activist sphere.

Brecht's 1930 Lehrstück (learning piece) 'Die Massnahme' ('The Decision', or 'The Measures Taken'), a collaboration with the director Slatan Dudow and composer Hanns Eisler, envisaged an event from current revolutionary activity in China undertaken from a generalised communist party position. This was at an early stage of Brecht's engagement with Marxism (Sternberg and Korsch) and the politics of the Communist Party. As the piece represented possible communist activities, it also drew the attention of some leading supporters

---

51   Korsch 1971, p. 65.
52   Korsch 1971, pp. 65–6.
53   Brüggemann 1974, p. 289.
54   Brüggemann 1974, p. 283, quoting from Brecht's *Arbeitsjournal, 1930–1942*, p. 86.

of the cultural politics of the Association of Proletarian-Revolutionary Writers (BPRS). 'Durus' (Kemeny), Otto Biha, and Alfred Kurella were positive in their artistic evaluation but negative in their ideological appraisal.[55] The piece and the critical response succinctly manifest the differences between these two concepts of Marxist cultural practice and theory at this juncture of the Third Period.

The 'plot' may be summarised briefly. Five political agitators are sent from Moscow to assist with the preparation of revolutionary activity in China. One of them is impulsive, driven by emotion rather than observation of strict discipline. Amongst his errors were alienation of the bourgeoisie whose support was needed, interference in trying to prevent police injustice, premature disclosure of this presence and an attempt to lead a hopeless revolution. The work of his comrades was made impossible. As they cannot smuggle him out, they decide to kill him, a decision he agrees with. They present their argument to the Chorus, which agrees with their decision.

Die Rote Fahne published three reports on the performance. The first 'Anonymous', described it as an 'exceptional success' ('zu einem aussergewöhnichen Erfolg') but with an unacceptable text unmarxist ('... da unmarxistisch'). It is a successful experiment that once begun must be built on. The 'indirection of art' ('Umweg der Kunst') for the transmission of Marxist and political teaching is developing in unprecedented ways the possibilities for our agitational and propaganda work ('... steigert in bisher kaum geahntem Masse die Möglichkeiten unserer Agitation und Propaganda').[56] A questionnaire had been distributed at the performance: 'Had the performance of "Die Massnahme" political value ("politischen Lehrwert") for spectators and performers' with a follow-up session. Amongst the responders was Wittfogel (see Chapters 4 and 5 above): the collective working methods of agitprop groups 'here receives an essential expansion and enrichment' ('erhielt hier eine wesentliche Verberiterung und Bereicherung'). Although dealing with crucial contemporary political issues, its lesson was based on an imagined action ('auf der Grundlage einer konstruiereten Handlung') and was factually wrong from the point of view of

---

55   A German, Kurella had much intimate contact with Soviet culture. Between 1926 and 1928 he was deputy director of the Agitptop Department of the Executive Committee of the Communist International; 1928–29, director of the Fine Art Department of the People's Commissariat for Education. Accused of 'ultra-left and formalist errors' – he was critical of more acceptable art and supported the more avantgardist position of the newly formed 'Oktyabr' group – he returned to Germany and worked for the KPD. Brecht's dismissive comments on the cultural politics of the BPRS have been quoted above.

56   Brauneck 1973, p. 420.

concrete revolutionary practice; for example, the shooting of the young comrade, which 'contradicts the facts of revolutionary reality', or that 'an emotionally driven comrade would be drawn into increasingly dangerous and difficult illegal actions by experienced Bolsheviks'. Despite these errors, the consensus was that it was 'an extraordinary political and artistic success ... for the German revolutionary movement'. In keeping with Brecht's intentions and practice, the questionnaire reports, 'the authors had already been induced to undertake *political changes* to the text' ('hat die Autoren bereits dazu veranlasst, an den Text der "Massnahme" *politische Änderungen* vorzunehmen').[57] 'Durus' (Kemeny), who succeeded Gertrud Alexander as cultural editor of the paper, wrote a more detailed account. 'It is not the least merit of this innovative, formally outstanding artwork', he writes, 'that it elicits from all sides political standpoints, that it does not allow a passive, aesthetic reception'. Despite being the result of a 'purely conceptualised elaboration of revolutionary theory' ('aus der blossen gehirnlichen Verarbeitung der revolutionären Theorie ...') and 'not revolutionary Praxis' ('nicht aus der revolutionären Praxis ...'), 'we must say a decisive "Yes" to it' ('... ein entschiedenes Ja sagen'). Critical of the practice portrayed in the piece, 'Durus' nevertheless sees it as important because it places the Party above the individual, that without 'clarity of revolutionary theory one is only half a revolutionary' (a position Kurella will later dispute). But neither can Brecht's knowledge of Marxism-Leninism theory *alone* be sufficient ('die Kenntnis der Theorie des Marxismus-Leninismus *allein* nicht genug') to displace revolutionary experience and the detail of revolutionary movement. In order to fully grasp revolutionary theory, the next indispensable step is contact with *revolutionary praxis* ('ist als nächster Schritt das Hinein in die *revolutionäre Praxis*'). 'Durus' notes the 'dialectical exchanges between artistic form and the social content of the work' ('eine dialektische Wechselwirkung zwischen der künstlerischen Form und dem sozialen Inhalt des Kunstwerks') and expects that the 'half anarchic "Massahme" will incite many other revolutionary writers by its formal means to produce ideologically more perfect works'. Although 'epochal' in its artistic, literary, and musical elements 'Durus' assesses its standing as not yet that of some agitprop groups. Like all the commentators on the work, 'Durus' is most positive about Hanns Eisler's settings of Brecht's poetry and in particular its performance by three choirs from the workers' choral movement, 'to this point the ideologically most mature and artistically

---

57   Brauneck 1973, pp. 421–3, 421–2. Willett refers to a source that claims the 'changes were
      made at the suggestion of the Communist Party after the first performance' (Willett 1977,
      p. 39).

most accomplished evening of choral work' ('das bisher ideologisch reifste und künstlerisch vollendeste abendfüllende Chorwerk für Arbeitersänger ...').[58]

'Wherein lies the ideological value of this work?', Otto Biha asks in *Die Linkskurve*. For the first time, to his knowledge, in Germany or beyond, has the attempt been made to present in this form 'the great and selfless struggle of the working class under the leadership of the Communist Party'. It is of 'pioneering importance' ('eine bahnbrechende Bedeutung') in its formal achievements. But 'we must also speak about those things we are not in general agreement with ... despite our fundamental recognition of its great worth'. 'From the outset let it be said: The conception of this work is idealist' ('Die Konzeption dieses Stückes ist eine idealistische'). Although Brecht's grasp of theory is extremely strong, he falls short in his depiction of praxis. The real representation of the Party is 'as an alien, secretive, great power centre ... detached, almost isolated ...' ('Für Brecht ist sie eine fremde, fast geheimnisvolle Grossmacht ... der losgelöst, fast isoliert ... steht'). Having set out the various episodes, he writes: 'In all of them an abstract assumption confronts the complex and multilayered struggle and experiential knowledge of the Party'. The Party rather 'is you and me', under control of the revolutionary masses, which quickly recognise the mistakes and shortcomings of its leaders. These criticisms do not mean that the work be disavowed: 'In this piece the author is not a hostile observer, but a fellow comrade' ('In diesem Stück ist der Autor kein fremder Beobachter sondern ein Mitkämpfer'). 'Should we reproach him because the piece is not Marxist?': 'we had never until now thought to consider Brecht's production as that of a revolutionary comrade'. Now exceeding all expectations and deploying his language in class struggle, should we not recognise common ground in our positions, 'the position of the author himself as a step in his development towards the revolutionary proletariat' ('eine Stellungnahme des Autors selber, als einen Schritt seiner Entwicklung zum revolutionären Proletariat'). Only the proletariat will provide 'the space for creative experiment and great artistic perspectives', and the best of the bourgeois artists must make the move. 'The future will show whether Brecht is persistent in pursuing the path of the revolutionary writer', Biha conjectured.[59]

---

58   Brauneck 1973, pp. 423–5.

59   *Die Linkskurve* 1980, no. 1, pp. 12–14. Biha was on the editorial of *Die Linkskurve*. The Brecht/Ottwalt/Dudow/Eisler film collaboration 'Kuhle Wampe' had a somewhat similar, nuanced, sympathetic reception. Although hampered by a 'lack of practical experience in daily struggle' ('liegt ein Mangel an praktischer Erfahrung im täglichen Kampf') and over-reliant on 'acute theoretical study alone' ('noch so eifriges Studium allein ...'), the reviewer in *Die Rote Fahne*, Heinz Lüdecke, nevertheless seeks to 'offer our comrades our hand:

Kurella's title 'Ein Versuch mit nicht ganz tauglichen Mitteln' ('An Experiment with Not Quite Adequate Means') indicates the balance he intends. Kurella raises the issue of the concrete in a way not done by the others, central in the context of the emphasis Korsch and Brecht accorded it in their exchanges. His fictionalised context (Chinese revolution, etc.) should be identified with the realities, on the example for which it was selected. As the piece was intended for a 'concrete public' ('ein konkretes Publikum'), including performers who would have known 'concrete details' of the Chinese revolution, 'concrete associations' ('konkrete Assoziationen') should have formed the basis for the piece: 'indeed these associations *must* be a formative element if the piece is really to have meaning' ('diese Assoziationen *müssen* sich bilden, wenn das Lehrstück überhaupt einen Sinn haben soll'). To judge what behaviour was correct and what was in error, and consequently what is of value in the piece, 'we work on the supposition that this behaviour would proceed in a real, and of course the Chinese, revolution' ('von der Annahme aus, dass die Handlung in einer realen, und zwar in der chinesischen Revolution'). Contrary to all the previous commentators, he decides in favour of the young agitator: considering the behaviour of all five, 'there is much more ground to assert that *the young comrade actually represents the standpoint of the consistent revolutionary and Bolsheviks, whilst the others are examples of opportunistic behaviour, called in the language of the Third International, "right deviationists"*'.[60] For the sake of German readers, his (first) concrete example is set in the 'German October' of 1923. The 'right opportunists' are Brandler, Thalheimer, and Radek, the young comrade, one Hesse. Kurella sets out a little scene, providing the speakers with dialogue. Hesse urges immediate action, the workers cannot wait any longer, the other three urge caution; together with factory council congress, the Party has decided to delay armed action. The choice of concrete example is decided by the politics of the Third Period, as may be clearly seen from the late 1920s passages on Thalheimer in Chapter 4 above, where ascription for blame is still being contested. To approve of the action of the four who shot their young comrade, Kurella claims, 'would be to extol the standpoint of the

---

commit yourselves fully to us' ('Wir reichen ihnen als Kameraden die Hand: Kommt ganz zu uns'). 'It is', he continues, 'for your creativity, whose value we recognise and need, of fundamental importance'. Reprinted in Kühn, Tümmler, and Wimmer 1978, Vol. 2, pp. 162–5, 164.

60   Kurella 1979 [1931], pp. 383–99, 386, '... *so kommen wir zu dem Schluss ... der junge Genosse vertrete tatsächlich den Standpunkt des konsequenten Revolutionärs und Bolschewisten, während die Agitatoren Musterbeispiele für opportunistisches Verhalten seien*, für das, was man in der Sprache der Dritten Internationale "rechte Abweichungen nennt ..."'.

right-opportunists'.[61] Kurella provides other models of 'how the Bolsheviks and Lenin, under corresponding circumstances, represent the standpoint of the young comrade and carried it through'; he refers to the Moscow uprising of 1905, when Lenin opposed Plekhanov's position, and the July demonstration in Leningrad 1917. 'How is one to explain', he asks, 'that the authors intended to write a bolshevistic Lehrstück and produced an opportunists' text?'[62] In order to answer this question, 'we want to retrace the whole chain of the author's errors, to the ideological and philosophical origin of this mistake'.[63]

Kurella's requirements are severe: to exemplify their ideas the authors have chosen an artificial milieu, not the reality of a concrete revolutionary situation, consequently not meeting Lenin's demands on dialectical materialists to analyse from all sides in order to found the real, 'which is always concrete' ('die immer konkret ist'). They work with particles of the real. In brief they proceed with a philosophical idealist methodology which pervades the piece, most clearly in their conception of Communism and the Party. For them Communism is an idea, it exists in the teachings of the classic texts, the Party is not seen as the representative of the proletariat. The text only displays an apparently correct relationship between theory and practice, 'an idealist distortion' ('eine idealistische Entstellung') of Marx's conception of the role of theory, which becomes a force as soon as the masses grasp it. 'Brecht', Kurella claims, 'believes himself to be in possession of the teachings of Communism and that seems enough, to him, to be able to create, as a specialist in a laboratory, revolutionary art' ('und das scheint ihm zu genügen, um als Spezialist in Laboratorium revolutionäre Kunst zu schaffen').

But the real theme of the piece is not, as many 'superficial' critics propose, the pre-planned killing of the young comrade; rather, he asserts, 'the thesis of the primacy of intellection vis-á-vis emotion' ('die These von dem Primat des Verstandes über das Gefühl ...'). The whole structure of the piece rests on counterposing the correctness of acting on intellection against the error of acting on emotion, 'a fundamentally false, unmarxist formulation' ('grundfalschen unmarxistischen Fragestellung ...'): *intellection and emotion are presented here as autonomous, self-resourcing processes ... they are coun-*

---

61   Kurella 1979 [1931], p. 387. '... dass die Verherrlichung des Standpunkts der drei Agitatoren tatsächlich die Verherrlichung des Rechtsopportunismus ist'. First published in *Literatur der Weltrevolution.*

62   Kurella 1979, p. 389. 'Wie ist has nun zu erklären, dass die Autoren, dass sie ein bolschewistisches Lehrstück schreiben wollten und ein opportunistisches dabei herauskam'.

63   Ibid. '... wollen wir die ganze Kette der Fehler der Autoren bis zum ideologischen, philosophischen Ursprung dieses Irrtums zurückverfolgen'.

terposed metaphysically, not dialectically' ('Ihre Gegenüberstellung ist nicht dialektisch, sondern metaphysisch'), 'conceived of as abstract and general, instead of being in conflict as the struggle of opposites within the unity of revolutionary thinking and behaviour', a frequent phenomenon. This problem can only be resolved 'when one investigates the concrete circumstances' ('wenn man konkret die Umstände untersucht'), which means seeking out the concrete social origins which promote intellection in one revolutionary, in another emotion. He returns to his example of the 'German October' (above), and ascribes to the three party functionaries (Brandler, Radek, and Thalheimer) the false preference for intellection in determining non-action in the event, emotion, as offering more potential, to the worker Hesse. Kurella imputes a class basis to the behaviour of the 'right-opportunists' – 'kleinbürgerlich' (petit bourgeois), but the capacity to oscillate between intellection and emotion to 'roots in totally determinate class influences' ('seine Wurzeln in ganz bestimmten Klasseneinflüssen'). The history of the author's social background might disclose the roots: disappointed with the politics of the Independent Socialists (USPD) and by the decline of Expressionism, intellectuals 'made their way over the bridge of the understanding of revolutionary dialectics and materialism to us', but not without occasioning 'a conflict between the intellection and emotion' and a disavowal of the role of the latter.[64]

Though ideologically flawed, 'Die Massnahme' is nevertheless 'of great significance for the further development of proletarian art': 'in those places where simple, clear and correct thinking from the thought-world of the proletariat is poetically and musically presented the work is raised to the highest artistic level'.

Lukács comments briefly on 'The Measures Taken' in the context of his 1932 *Linkskurve* essay 'Reportage or Portrayal', more specifically in his response to Ottwalt, 'A Virtue of Necessity'. Ottwalt's novel, *Sie wissen was sie tun*, shares the same qualities as those of Tretyakov, Ehrenburg and others: 'for them these contents still remain abstract, despite a recognisable concretising tendency ... and not the objective driving forces of the revolution ... We could refer for instance to Brecht's play *The Measures Taken*, where the strategic and tactical problems of the party are narrowed down to "ethical problems". From the starting point of this world outlook, it is impossible to really recognise and portray the driving forces'.[65]

---

64 There is a 'pre-echo' in Kurella's suggestion of the ideas Lukács would explore in his 1934 essay, 'Expressionism: Its Significance and Decline'.

65 Lukács 1981, p. 71.

The reviews of 'The Measures Taken' provide an interesting index of trends within cultural production, of two very different conceptions from contending versions of Marxism. One follows the line of the Third Period, as theorised by Wittfogel and Lukács and subscribing to a totalising Hegelian philosophy and a totalising Marxist Weltanschauung, even if an inversion of Hegel. For Sternberg, Korsch, and Brecht, Marxism was not a Weltanschauung in that sense but a method based on the historical rather than on the philosophical *sensu stricto* – Korsch above quoted Marx on the uneven development between the social and cultural registers, that difficulty arises because of the manner in which 'contradictions are expressed', but 'when made specific and concrete', that is, by way of mediation, 'they are therewith clarified'. Brecht asserted that the dialectic should start from the concrete, not from the history of ideas. For Lukács, for whom the 'concrete' was established by way of the dialectic, Brecht's concrete had only the semblance of the concrete, but was essentially 'abstract', absent of mediation – Kurella criticised Brecht's concrete, an imagined episode from the Chinese revolution, as an insubstantial fictional projection, and selected one for him: the event of the 'German October' of 1923, providing him with four identifiable *dramatis personae* already to hand, the three party functionaries and a worker, together with dialogue. It was also one in the recent past of the struggle, by implication its closer study would have been a 'Lehrstück' for Brecht.[66] Unlike Lukács's concern with the concrete being 'abstract' in Brecht's conception, Kurella seems more concerned with seeking the event with most potential as an originating concrete for transformation, as did the various agit-prop groups, and *pace* Kurella, more successfully than Brecht to date. Again, unlike Lukács, 'an enemy of production' in Brecht's characterisation, Kurella, importantly involved with the leading progressive Soviet artists in the 'Oktjabr' group, may have been more tolerant of the experimental and less closed relationship between form and content.

This moment sees the re-emergence, through the figure of Brecht, of that dissident, experimental presence from the Dadaists, through Piscator, Märten, and others in left-cultural production, where 'concrete practice' was prioritised over the ideological, when concerns were being expressed about the course of Marxism-Leninism in the Soviet Union, of the degeneration of dialectical materialism into an ideology.

---

66   Kurella's own ideological position is transparent – the right-oppositionists frustrate the
      revolution by attempting to rein in the impetuosity of the worker.

Towards a Materialist History of Art

What a fascinating field art history is, and what scope for study it presents to a marxist![1]

LENIN

∴

In 1929 the Berlin artist and teacher Otto Greiner wrote 'Visual art is the Cinderella among the cultural activities of the German worker'.[2] Concern with the visual had not been a priority on the left in the earlier period for multiple reasons, including access to its sites, museums and galleries. Wieland Herzfelde noted in his 1922 brochure *Gesellschaft, Künstler und Kommunismus* that although literature had resolved issues concerning form and content in recent decades, nothing similar had been addressed or achieved in the visual arts (see Chapter 2 above). But by the time Greiner had made the above statement, some advances had been registered. This excursus tracks some of the sources available for the development of a comparable history and theory of the visual, from the marginal comments of Mehring to the more self-conscious Marxist theorising of Max Raphael in the early 1930s.

In his review of the major 1891 Berlin international exhibition, Mehring provides a basis for a socio-political-materialist conception of visual cultural production, reading the art on view in terms of the levels of capitalist development in the various countries. He allows aesthetic practice its own dimension of autonomy: 'where Impressionism has broken through the capitalist mode of thinking it is able to seize the beginnings of a new world in its essence, it has a revolutionary affect, it becomes a new form of artistic representation to which no earlier compares in its particular dimension and power', in the realm of the artistic arena 'they are a type of bourgeois socialism'. Their objective, however, is not a revolutionary overthrow of the system, but rather 'to cleanse, strengthen and uphold it as their inalienable right'.[3]

---

1 Hadjinicolaou 1978, p. 3, uses this quotation from Lenin in his Introduction to *Art History and Class Struggle*.

2 This quotation, which is here taken from Guttsman 1997, p. 1, was first published in *Sozialistische Bildung* (Culture).

3 One of Mehring's students at the SPD School in Berlin, Richard Hamann, was to become a

The presence of the trained art historian was not likely to be a constant in the publications of the left during this period for understandable reasons – amongst other considerations it was a discipline in formation. But the writings of Wilhelm Hausenstein did receive frequent mention and had much to offer. In addition his work was also published by the leading German publishers. As in the German tradition he studied not only art history but also philosophy, history, and national economy. In 1907 he joined the SPD and worked for their paper *Vorwärts*: he edited the reformist *Sozialistische Monatshefte*, for which he wrote articles on art. In 1919 he left the SPD to 'become a communist': 'it appeared to me to place me in an impossible compromise with the right', in Munich during the period of the Räterepublik.[4] He wrote an appreciation of Kurt Eisner, leader of the Council Republic, who was assassinated by right-wing extremists, in *Die Neue Merkur*, of which he was editor: 'Erinnerungen an Eisner' ('Remembering Eisner').[5] Mehring commissioned him to write on van Gogh, an artist more accessible and sympathetic to the readers of *Die Neue Zeit*.[6] Lunacharsky, Commissar for Enlightenment, translated his 1912 (extended in 1920) *Bild und Gemeinschaft. Entwurf einer Soziologie* (*Image and Society. Outline of a Sociology of Art*). A wide-ranging essay on the Baroque was published in the Soviet Encyclopedia in 1926.[7] In his series 'Zur Frage der marxistishen Ästhetik' published in *Die Linkskurve* (see above Chapter 5), Wittfogel quotes from Hausenstein's *Der nackte Mensch in der Kunst aller Zeiten und Völker* (*The Naked Body in the Art of All Eras and Peoples*), published in 1913 (extended in 1917) and refers to his work as 'Der erste Versuch der Schaffung einer marxistischen Kunstgeschichte' ('the first attempt at the creation of a Marxist art history').[8] Brecht quotes from Hausenstein's writings on Cézanne in his *Arbeitjournal* (1948): 'Cézanne

---

leading art historian, advocating a social history of art, although he did his dissertation under the leading idealist art historian Heinrich Wölfflin. A medievalist, he would later, in the GDR, co-author with Jost Hermand a five-volume history of art and literature: *Deutsche Kunst und Kultur von der Gründerzeit zum Expressionismus*. A two-volume *Geschichte der Kunst* was in Brecht's library.

4   Sulzer 1982 p. 15. '... weil sie mir in einem unmöglichen Kompromiss mit der Rechten zu stehen schien ... auf dem Sprung, Kommunist zu werden'.

5   An English translation is published in *The Weimar Republic Sourcebook* (Kaes, Jay, and Dimendberg 1994, pp. 52–3).

6   Lu Märten had sent an essay on Van Gogh to Mehring but he turned it down because of his commissioning from Hausenstein. It was later published in *Die Grenzboten* in 1913. She was a member of a circle which included Hausenstein, traces of whose approaches may be found in her work. She wrote to Kautsky in 1914 offering a review of Hausenstein's *Die bildenden Kunst der Gegenwart* but he rejected it on the grounds that *Die Neue Zeit*'s readership would lack access to such difficult material.

7   Walter Benjamin quotes approvingly from Hausenstein's *Von Geist des Barock* (1921) a number of times in his *Ursprung des deutschen Trauerspiels* (1924–25).

8   A more recent biographical entry, in the *Dictionary of Art Historians*, introduces him immediately as a 'Marxist art historian', https://arthistorians.info/hausensteinw.

weaves, highly differentiated in themselves, faces, landscapes, still-lives, but not sep-
arable within a striking painterly practice ... an uncanny estrangement between the
model and its representation has been effected ... a psychically charged face has been
transformed into a coloured architecture, a modulated complex (Hausenstein und Jed-
licka)'. Brecht summarises: 'did Cézanne deploy too much or too little distanciation
effects', adding 'the face as still-life'.[9] Although this is later Hausenstein, traces of this
way of thinking in relation to the visual can be found in his earlier work, for example,
Soziologie der Kunst der Gegenwart (1913). From the above references it can be seen that
his work had much to offer to an historical and materialist theory of visual culture in
a foundational phase. Some of the above referenced earlier material will be presented
in the following passages.

Hausenstein's training in national economy and history is plainly visible in the terms
he uses to frame developments in the visual arts across the period from the Gothic to
the contemporary: mercantilism, physiocracy, stock-jobbing (*Agiotage*), and capitalism amongst others.

In his first major publication, *Der Bauern-Bruegel* (*The Peasant Bruegel*), Hausenstein signals his practice as that of a materialist art historian: the 'peasant' Bruegel is
prioritised over the 'artist' Bruegel. 'From the people he spoke to them' ('Er war aus
dem Volk und sprach zum Volk').[10] His father worked the land 'silently bent over its
poor soil' ('... das sich wortlos über einen armen Boden beugte ...'). Bruegel was a participant in the great peasant weddings and their Kirmessen (fairs) he portrayed, not an
observer. As sites of possible socio-political unrest the Emperor Charles v had placed
restrictions, but not always observed, covering the numbers in attendance, the quality
of food served and the clothes worn.[11] Social class is examined. The burghers had not
totally lost their peasant origins: 'we see', Hausenstein writes, 'a trading and commercial country that preserves a healthy plebian dimension' but with a class which through
its 'aesthetic-philosophical pretensions' ('mit ästhetisch-philosophischen Ansprüchen
...') organised through its societies, 'separated itself from the more vulgar taste of the
general public', with its predilection for the burlesque. In his summary, Hausenstein
characterises Bruegel as a 'communist revolutionary' ('Bruegel ist kommunistischer
Revolutionär').[12]

---

9   Brecht 1983, p. 168. '... malerei cézannes verwebt, in sich selbst äusserst differenziert,
      gesichter, landschaften, stilleben unausgeschieden in eine einzige malerische formalität
      ... eine unheimliche entfremdung zwischen modell und bildnis vollzieht sich ... ein psych-
      isch belebtes gesicht wird in eine farbige architektur, in einen modulationskomplex ver-
      wandelt (hausenstein und jelicka): aber gebrauchte er zu viele oder zu wenige verfrem-
      dung? (das gesicht als stilleben)'.
10   Hausenstein 1909, p. 86.
11   Hausenstein 1909, p. 12.
12   Hausenstein 1909, p. 121.

The first image in the text, a copper engraving after Bruegel, is that of a fully armed merchant vessel sailing towards a city, most probably Antwerp: it is situated within the opening six-page passage which details the socio-economic development of that city, then the richest in northern Europe. Its wealth is celebrated, 'its disagreeable quarters' ('fatale Quartier') ignored, the latter partly as the result of ordinances by the Spanish colonial administrators, as sites of possible socio-political unrest.

Considering cultural representation, Hausenstein writes: 'A way of thinking that strives to see artistic achievements as part of a cultural whole ... cannot evade the detailed engagement with economic and social history'. Such an approach will incline towards achieving 'illustrative content' ('... neigt den illustrativen Gehalt ...'): 'The illustrative is always a cultural-historical document' ('... oder doch kulturgeschichtliches Dokument'). But these documents are not mere reflections of that which presents itself to immediate observation – the difference between reflection and representation, the former unmediated, the latter mediated, is crucial to a materialist aesthetic. Hausenstein's text sources elements which provide those mediations. Amongst these were resentment against Spanish rule, the roles of religion and superstition, a peasantry that had entered a money economy earlier than France or Germany but was still subject to extortion, and the search for a visual form of representation that was not dependent on the classical model of the Italian renaissance, an issue not merely of style but also a marker of social and national difference.

Bruegel's predecessor Bosch set a precedent. Bruegel recognised in him 'the master of the daemonic, of the didactic grotesque' ('... den Meister der Diabelerie, den Meister der didaktischen Groteske'). But Bruegel mediated that rich visual archive through 'intellectual engagement, through rationalist figures of the humanist rhetoricians of the sixteenth century'.[13] Hausenstein reads Bruegel's daemonic images through this lens: Bosch's 'didactic grotesque' is transformed into 'the field of social satire' ('... das Feld der sozialen Satire'), a transformation Hausenstein characterised as the 'secularisation of the devil' ('... ist ein Säkularisation der Teufelei'). The field of action is transferred to earth, the daemonic, hell, becomes an encyclopaedia of earthly burdens, 'morality supports psychological crises' ('... die Moralität erhält psychologische Wendungen').[14] Bruegel's homeland 'encircled the world with its extensive trading as far as the tropics, and with that engendered in the minds of his fellows the strangest phantasies, the result also of political fortunes – it was from time immemorial the classical theatre of war in Western Europe'.[15] Bruegel's imagination was inescapably socially structured.

---

13   Hausenstein 1909, p. 34. '... verband sich dem intellektuellen Ton, den rationalen Anzüglichkeiten der humanistischen Rhetorekenkammern des 16 Jahrhunderts'.

14   Hausenstein 1909, p. 77.

15   Hausenstein 1909, p. 120. '... durch einen riesenhaften Handels die ganze Welt bis in die

Hausenstein deals with a wide range of Bruegel's work (there are 67 illustrations) in terms of both form and content, but only a few will be referred to so as to indicate his practice as an art historian. Bruegel's biblical paintings are other than merely religious. The 'Carrying of the Cross' is more than biblical illustration, more than a moral narrative: 'it is the specific document of extraordinary historical circumstances. Informing this image is the practice of a criminal justice system which deploys terror in the service of political and religious persecution'.[16] Hausenstein points to stylistic disparities within the composition to establish his reading: colour coding differentiates the traditional grouping of mourners in their earlier muted Burgundian dress from the Spanish outriders accompanying Christ in their bright cinnabar uniforms. Incidents across the large composition refer to colonial impositions on his contemporaries.[17] *The Alchemist* (*Der Goldmacher*), here in a copperplate, addresses both the foolishness of their practice but also the consequences of the pursuit of gold – outside the window, children are being led into the poorhouse. His social criticism intensifies. His *Battle between fire-proof safes and money boxes* (*Der Krieg zwischen den Kassenschränken und den Sparbüchsen*) leads to 'a correlation of the material and the aesthetic in another satire on capitalism'.[18] This critique is confirmed in *Everyone seeks his gain* (*Jeder sucht seinen Profit*): 'the figures are the realised ciphers of the individual, of the individual in his socially destructive function, that of Antwerp bourgeois, the Antwerp large merchant who in pursuit of his own gain forgets social solidarity – unaware of the Spanish lances in the background who, in any case, he will oppose with the logic of his ledger'.[19] In these critical works Hausenstein, alert to the signifying role of artistic decisions, notes that form and content are equal in value ('Die Gewalt der Form ist der Gewalt des Inhalts ebenbürtig'). Here the figures 'grow out from the space', whilst, for instance, the allegories of virtue ignore this potential, the figures reside within the space.

Tropen … und damit umspannt die Phantasie der Heimatmenschen … die abenteurlichsten Vorstellungen, … aber auch ein Erzeugnis politischer Schicksale Belgien was von jeher der klassische Kriegsschauplatz des westlichen Europas'.

16 Hausenstein 1909, p. 89. 'Sie ist das spezifische Dokument aussergewöhnlicher geschichtlicher Umstände. … Hinter diesem Bild steht die Praxis einer Kriminaljustiz, die ihre Schrecken in den Dienst der politischen und religiösen Verfolgungen stellte'.

17 Other Bruegel paintings which represent harsh Spanish rule were *Census at Bethlehem* and *The Slaughter of the Innocent*.

18 Hausenstein 1909, p. 82. 'Von hier führt stofflicher und ästhetischer Zusammenhang zu jener anderen Satire auf dem Kapitalismus'.

19 Hausenstein 1909, p. 82. '… [Elck] ist die sinnliche Formel des Individiuums, des Individuums in seiner gesellschaftzerstörenden Funktion, des Individualismus. [Elck] ist im besonderen Fall der Antwerper Bourgeois, der Antwerper Grosshändler, der vor lauter Sorge um seine privates Wohl die soziale Solidarität vergisst und nichts von den spanischen Lanzen weiss, die am Horizont tauchen – die er allenfalls mit der Logik des Hauptbuch bekämpfen wird'.

As the title 'Der Bauern Bruegel' betokens, representation of the peasant is a central concern. 'In the representation of peasants, in the landscape', Hausenstein writes, 'in unconstrained study of the surrounding world of the everyday Bruegel experienced the splendid power of the real. ... But neither could his spirit let go of the disposition towards the didactic which the times had determined. From these two postulates grew his mature work'.[20] 'The acknowledgement of a chtonic spirit', Hausenstein continues, 'simultaneously engenders an acknowledgement of democracy ... a protest against the rich ... scorn for the plump clerical ... engaged support for the poor'.[21] But the democratic is not only a protest against the destructive impositions of the rich, it is also a protest against 'the aesthetic sophistry of urban writing and thinking'.[22] 'This fundamentally folk-prose' (perception of the state of affairs), Hausenstein continues, 'he embodied so realistically as well as symbolically in the bodily imaging of the peasants in their Kermessen (fairs). Bruegel recognises the communality of the peasantry, the source of its potential, the secret of its folk-poetry is that it is the language of experience' ('Es ist das Geheimnis der Volkspoesie, dass sie im Grunde Volksprosa ist').[23]

As quoted above, Hausenstein characterises Bruegel 'as a communist revolutionary', his response to his reading of the implications of the artist's work. In this text, his first major publication, he opens up the visual to the lineaments of a materialist discourse, producing a social intelligibility for an artistic practice. This was a radical departure in the practice of art history.[24]

Hausenstein's second publication, *Der nackte Mensch in der Kunst aller Zeiten* (*The Naked Body in Art Across the Ages*) from 1911, as its title indicates, is more wide-ranging than the Bruegel book. Its materialist concern is less immediately discernible, given the range of material covered, from the cultural products of the then-designated 'primitive' societies to late nineteenth-century European, in three and two dimensions, but Wittfogel was justified in claiming it as a 'materialist history of art', if not 'the first'

---

20   Hausenstein 1909, p. 38. 'In der Bauerndarstellung, in der Landschaft, in unbefangenem Studium einer alltäglichen Umwelt hatte Bruegel die herrliche Gewalt der Wirklichkeit erlebt'.

21   Hausenstein 1909, p. 121. 'Der Bekenntnis zur Animalität formt sich zugleich als ein Bekenntnis zur Demokratie. Die Demokratie ist ihm Hohn wider den feisten Klerikus ... Kampft für die armen'.

22   Ibid. 'Sie ist im ein Protest nicht nur gegen die verderbliche Last des Reichtums, auch gegen die ästhetische Spitzfindigkeit grossstädtischen Dichtens und Denkens'.

23   Both Mehring and Zetkin saw proletarian poetry as the successor to Volkspoesie. The unorthodox Marxist Ernst Bloch saw the KPD as abandoning this earlier source to its colonisation by the National Socialists.

24   Michael Podro's *The Critical Historians of Art* (Podro 1991) provides an instructive background on the interests of academic art historians roughly contemporary with Hausenstein, particularly Riegl and Wölfflin, from which one can see the radical nature of Hausenstein's concerns and his readings.

in his *Linkskurve* series on a Marxist aesthetic.[25] The trajectory outlined is from the constraints of priestly castes, through the humanism of the Renaissance to the liberal bourgeois individualism of the nineteenth century, from the sacral to the secular, of how representations of the naked body signified within the religious and socio-political formations at these historical moments. This passage will be concerned with the secular only.

The social perspective is introduced early in the text, when Hausenstein comments on the relativity of the aesthetic: 'Our age has for long been analytical, critical, specialist. The unflagging dialectic of history now tends towards synthesis, to totally integrated forms. As our society longs for new social bonds from the chaos of liberal individualism so it longs for clear symbols'.[26] The generator of changes in modes of representation is not internal to any artistic or aesthetic Kunstwollen (the will-to-art), but from changes in the socio-political register: 'Every art develops the technical competence it needs in order to facilitate expression ... Every age can technically satisfy its necessary stylistic requirements'.[27]

The Renaissance introduces a new moment in the history of art but it is one replete with contradictions. As against earlier art, it develops 'a reflective aesthetic consciousness. ... The problems of form burst forth with sharper outlines all at once'. But it also 'began the undermining of the collective and the separation of the individual'. The 'isolated work of art begins in the Renaissance' in contrast to the 'publicly shared concept of style' in the Middle Ages, the Renaissance began 'to privatise it'.[28] The painterly naked figure of Venetian Renaissance art possessed general cultural assumptions: 'it signified

---

25   This is a period when major ethnographic museums are being established to house collections of cultural artefacts expropriated from colonised peoples. Such museums were to provide resources for modernising European artists: the Dresden ethnographic collection provided this function for German Expressionist artists in their representations of the naked body.

26   Hausenstein 1911, p. 28. 'Unsere Zeit war lange analytisch, kritisch, spezialistisch. Die unermüdliche Dialektik der Geschichte gibt ihr nun den Drang zur Synthese, zu den ganz gebundenen Formen. Wie unsere Gesellschaft sich aus dem Chaos der liberalen Individualismen nach neuen sozialen Bindungen sehnt, so sehnt sie sich in der Kunst nach lapidaren Symbolen'.

27   Hausenstein 1911, p. 40. 'Jede Kunst erzeugt die Technik, deren sie bedarf, um sich zu äussern ... Jedes Zeitalter kann technisch genau so viel, als er nötig hat, um seine Stilbedürfnisse zu befriedigen'. This phrase from Marx was also quoted by Gertrud Alexander in her exchanges with Lu Märten on the subject of historical materialism (see Chapter 3 above).

28   Hausenstein 1911, p. 78. '... zu ästhetisch reflektierenden Bewusstsein ... Die Probleme der Form sprangen mit einem Mal schärfer umrissen hervor' (p. 97). '... Die Renaissance begann die Zersetzung des Kollektiven und die Vereinzelung der Individualitat ...'. '... Die Renaissance begann ihn zu privatisieren' (p. 98).

the absolute reawakening of Italian self-confidence vis-à-vis antiquity'.[29] It was 'an aesthetically constructed cult fired by a newly experienced passion, it was the discovery of a private reality'. These depicted women 'were not naked but unclothed. Consequently their forms also bore a monumental erotic charge'.[30]

Hausenstein covers immediate post-Renaissance developments but these will be referred to later.[31] His treatment of mid- to late nineteenth-century figures introduces more directly the vocabulary and terms for a progressing materialist conception. The great satirist Daumier, painter and draughtsman, 'represents almost all stylistic revolutions from 1815 to the present', pointing towards further development. Addressing a Daumier grisaille (grey monochrome) work of three non-idealised naked female bodies, he writes: 'In Daumier's naked figures there is something of a new age, like the overcoming of 1848: the essence of a period from whose womb an historically necessary big-boned unflinching heroism of the worker-movement will develop'.[32] Countering the academic defamation of Courbet, he draws on the great Courbet monograph by Georgs Riat, which deals with the artist's trial as a Communard 'with well-disposed

---

29   Titian's 'Venuses' also caught the eye of Heine, as Lukács recounts. The poet wrote that the emergence of Luther meant the end of the Middle Ages. Effective as the theses pinned on Wittenburg's Church door were, Lukács summarises Heine's perception, namely that 'there were other more effective theses against Catholic reaction at the time, and these were Titian's naked "Venuses"'. Lukács adds his own interesting observation: 'Heine was not only right because the existence of naked Venuses was a protest against the medieval Catholic ideology of the times. But also because art historians who examine this question correctly will discover Titian's stand in every stroke of the brush, in his conception of light and shade, in his composition of colour etc.' (Lukács 1952, p. 313).

30   Hausenstein 1911, p. 76. '… etwas wie bodenständiges Realismus. … Das Nackte … war Sache eines mit neuerlebter Glut inszenierter ästhetischen Kultur: es war die Entdeckung einer heimatlichen Wirklichkeit … Diese Frauen waren nicht nackt; sie waren entkleidet und darum hatten ihre Formen auch jenen monumentalen erotischen Überschwang'. His reading of Venetian painting was influenced by Feuerbach, whom he quotes relative to Rubens: 'Only one philosopher celebrated love, Ludwig Feuerbach' ('Nur einziger Philosoph hat die Liebe gefeiert – Ludwig Feuerbach') (p. 119). That context is ambivalently materialist. Engels recognises that Feuerbach 'preaches sensuousness, absorption in the concrete … [in] sex relations between human beings', but is 'elsewhere thoroughly abstract' (Engels 1946 [1886], p. 46).

31   For instance, the Baroque, but consideration of this subject will be focused on his 1926 major contribution the Soviet Encyclopedia on Culture, probably commissioned by Lunacharsky, Commissar for Enlightenment, who had translated earlier work by Hausenstein.

32   Hausenstein 1911, p. 162. 'In den Akten Daumiers ist etwas von einer neuen Zeit, etwas wie Überwindung des Vormärz: das Wesen eine Periode, aus deren Schoss sich der starkknochige, geschichtsnotwendig brutale Heroismus der Arbeiterbewegung hervorentwickelte'. Daumier's work was to be important on the German left. Eduard Fuchs, a publisher member of the SPD, gathered an extensive collection. Daumier's work was also admired by John Heartfield.

impartiality', a book whose cultural historical value does not rest only 'with its painstaking presentation of the political stance of the painter'. Of Rodin Hausenstein writes that 'he had developed Naturalism to its most extensive possibilities'. He distinguishes between two types of Naturalism – the subjective and the objective in a dialectical relationship, if not that of a more articulated Lukács-type accent. Subjective Naturalism 'wishes to be the double of nature', in an unmediated relationship to it and 'therefore rarely dialectically superseding itself – as happens with all impotent aspirations'.[33] But there is another Naturalism which 'excludes all evidence of individual human demand, be it ever so honourable. It appears with the force of the object: as a power which approaches from outside us and which sustains itself. It wants to embody the power of its objectivity. It is an act of self-affirmation'.[34] 'Subjective Naturalism', Hausenstein writes, 'moves towards the annihilation of the subject. The Objective raises it up – expands it into a force of nature'. He concludes: 'So Rodin's art is simultaneously an image of objective power but one with a highly personal dimension. It is the summit of objectivity, that is, of artistic Naturalism'.[35] Rodin's 'Turm der Arbeit' ('The Tower of Labour'), which Hausenstein designates 'a monumental decorative work' in the positive sense of addressing the public space, is situated in the context of a social culture 'which must individualise everything and is incapable of producing a broad collectivity, such as that of the medieval Gothic period'. 'Social eras', he concludes, 'have the most monumental arts; there the naked human form appears in its decorative monumentality at its best and most powerful'.[36] The Belgian Meunier, whom he treats at greater length later, 'seeks his forms where the naked body appears at work, in the miners of the Borinage and in the boiling temperatures of the casting furnaces of the glassworks'.[37] Hausenstein concluded that the naked form may continue to be significant but 'it must really be a part of lives, as something real originating from our experience'. However, it

---

33 Hausenstein 1911, pp. 140–3. '... er will zur Dublette der Natur werden. ... Er hebt sich darum dialektisch selber auf, wie alle strebsame Schwäche'.

34 Hausenstein 1911, p. 140, p. 143. 'der alle Zeugen menschlicher Bedürftigkeit – seien sie noch so achtbar – ausgestossen hat. Er erscheint mit der Wucht des Objekts: als eine Grösse, die von aussen an uns herantritt und durch sich selber wirkt. ... Er will die Macht ihrer Objektivität verkörpern. Es ist ein Akt der Selbstbehauptung'.

35 Hausenstein 1911, p. 146. 'Der subjektive Naturalismus zerquält das Subjekt zur Vernichtung. Der objektive hebt es empor – erweitert es zu einer Naturkraft. So ist die Kunst Rodins zugleich ein Bild von objektiver Gewalt und ein höchst persönliches Element'.

36 Hausenstein 1911, p. 150. 'Der Turm der Arbeit ist eine zum grösseren Teil sozial begründete Rückbildung der Organe dekorativer Begabung. Soziale Zeitalter haben die monumentalisten Künste: dort erscheint auch der nackte Mensch in seiner dekorativen Schönheit am reinsten und mächtigsten'.

37 Hausenstein 1911, p. 191. '... wo der nackte Körper in lebendigen Funktionen erscheint – in die Borinage zu den Kohlenhauern ... in die Siedehitze der Giessereien und der Glashütten'.

is not feasible to foretell how future social organisations will extend the possibility, but extend it they will.[38]

In the closing pages of his *Bild und Gemeinschaft. Entwurf einer Soziologie der Kunst* (*Image and Community. Outline of a Sociology of Art*), Hausenstein recognises its still underdeveloped state: 'The sociology of plastic art is as yet little more than chaotic half-insights. An initial effort of the deepening of realisation and classification remains a task still based on provisional hypotheses'.[39] Despite these reservations, Hausenstein has made an informed and structured contribution at this early moment to promoting a materialist conceptualisation of cultural production.[40] It is an attempt to extend the insights set out in *Der nackte Mensch in der Kunst aller Zeiten und Völker* (see above) and 'to establish the foundation for a new consideration of the history of art' ('... Zur Grundlage neuer Betrachtung der Kunsthistorie gemacht waren'). Hausenstein is critical of art historians who try to account for change in stylistic terms rather than socio-historical ones, as in stylistic 'reaction' or 'the neo-gothic in the Renaissance', and he refers approvingly to the work of Richard Hamann (student of Franz Mehring's), his *Die Frührenaissance in der italienischen Malerei*, since he writes of a 'sozialästhetischer Sinn' relative to the socio-economic patronage of Renaissance Italy.

Such an approach is non-reductivist: 'Sociology of art is not art itself nor unmediated conformity with the form' ('Soziologie der Kunst ist nicht die Kunst selbst noch unmittelbare Übereinstimmung mit der Form'); 'rather, it seeks the trace of the origin of styles' ('Aber sie geht in Spuren der Herkunft des Stils'). For the moment, 'it is nothing other than a demonstration of a decisive genetic hypothesis of art' ('... ist einstweilen nichts als Nachweis einer entscheidenden genetischen Voraussetzung der Kunst').[41] In its commitment to an examination of the social dynamics of both content (themes) and form, to a non-reductivist account of art, it bears a family resemblance, albeit

---

38   Hausenstein 1911, pp. 189, 191. 'Das Nackte müsste wahrhaft ein Teil unseres Daseins sein ... wie kunftige Gesellschaftsorganisationen diese Möglichkeit in einzelnen und differenzieren können. Es ist sicher, dass es geschehen wird'.

39   Hausenstein 1920, pp. 106–7. 'Soziologie bildener Kunst ist bis jetzt kaum mehr als ein Chaos halber Einsichten. Auch ein beginnender Versuch der Eintiefung, Durchführung und Ordnung bleibt vorläufig Kunststück mit Hypothesen'. This material was first published as a contribution to the 'Archiv für Sozialwissenschaft und Sozialpolitik' in 1913. In 1920, Hausenstein augmented the original, a text which was translated by Lunacharsky, and which received approval in the Soviet Union (Sulzer 1982, p. 101). Hausenstein uses the terms 'Gemeinschaft', 'Gesellschaft' and 'Kollektivismus' interchangeably throughout the text.

40   It was only later with the publication of previously unpublished texts of Marx that a more rigorously scientific work could be undertaken: *The Paris Manuscripts* were available to Mikhail Lifshitz for his 1933 *The Philosophy of Art of Karl Marx* in Moscow.

41   Hausenstein 1920, pp. 9, 10, 11.

less elaborated, to the theorising of Wittfogel and Lukács above on the relationship between content and form. 'Inasmuch as art is form', Hausenstein writes, 'the sociology of art only ultimately meets its obligation when it is a sociology of form. The sociology of material is possible and necessary but that is not specifically sociology of art in that such a sociology can have intrinsic meaning only as a sociology of form'.[42] Form, however, 'does not work in metaphysical freedom. It is much more at times the uppermost ideology of specific material conditions, those of lived experience'.[43] As with Wittfogel and Lukács, 'Tendency' art is opposed: 'Solches bekämpfen wir, wenn wir Tendenzkunst bekämpfen'. But just as Wittfogel distinguished between the socio-cultural achievements of different 'Tendenzkunst' productions (there could be effectively realised proletarian 'Tendenzkunst'), so too did Hausenstein. He is addressing the work of the late nineteenth-century graphic artist, Steinlen, many of whose works were politically critical: 'Their tendency is transformed through astonishing formal qualities. For that reason the work is remarkable'.[44] The dialectical play of content and form he describes in the following way: 'Every era authenticates its sense for form on specific material and this sense for form is at any given time bonded by the material to the specific social formation of an era'.[45] Hausenstein's 'sociology of form' is applied to a forming process in which, as with Wittfogel and Lukács, socio-political material is embodied to represent the concerns and experiences of social classes ('... Bereich der lebendigen Tatsächlichheiten ...'). Social material is available for general collective observation, consequently 'the selection of material in a transitional socio-historical era signifies an aesthetic act'.[46] The aesthetic is essentially social.

Having sketched a general outline of Hausenstein's theoretical positions, I will now consider a number of instances where he applies them. 'We naively apply the standards

---

42   Hausenstein 1920, p. 15. 'Da Kunst Form ist, kann eine Kunstsoziologie zuletzt nur dann ihren Namen verdienen, wenn sie eine Soziologie der Form ist. Soziologie des Stoffs ist möglich und nötig. Aber sie ist nicht spezifisch Soziologie der Kunst, da eben Soziologie der Kunst im eigentlichen Verstand nur Soziologie der Form sein kann'. In his criticism of the proletarian novels of Bredel, Lukács condemns the importation of material external to the formal embodiment of the content. Similarly, Hausenstein's understanding of form is not formalist.

43   Hausenstein 1920, pp. 17–18. 'Form wirkt ... nicht in metaphysischer Freiheit. Sie ist vielmehr jeweils die höchste Ideologie bestimmter Stofflichkeiten, die Leben genannt werden'.

44   Hausenstein 1920, p. 20. 'Ihre Tendenz ist in erstaunliche formale Qualitäten zurückübersetzt. Darum ist ihre Kunst merkwürdig'.

45   Hausenstein 1920, p. 22. 'Jedes Zeitalter bewährt sein Formgefühl an einem besonderen Stoff, und diese Vergegenwärtigung des Formgefühls ist durch den Stoff jeweils an die besondere gesellschaftliche Gestalt eines Zeitalters gebunden'.

46   Hausenstein 1920, p. 23. '... so, dass die Wahl eines Stoffes durch ein formendes Zeitalter der Gesellschaftsgeschichte einen ästhetischen Akt bedeutet'.

of the modern bourgeois descendants of the Renaissance', Hausenstein writes, 'if we wish only to discover the spiritual in art ...'.[47] With the supersession of the feudal and the onset of the Renaissance, new socio-economic and political conditions developed: 'The art of the Renaissance is the art of an age which stands under the sign of a victorious, onward driving bourgeois commodity culture'.[48] Where the prerequisites of economic and social life are struggled for 'there sooner the economic factor has claim on the attention of consciousness and its structuring of ideologies'.[49] Attention to the material becomes a dominant cultural disposition, 'the object in all its qualities is to be studied, assimilated, possessed and represented', an overturning of the feudal period downgrading of the object.[50] Apparently paradoxically but intelligibly, Hausenstein proposes that the 'starting point of the bourgeois world is not the subject but the object'. Representation based on resemblance, a step towards realism, began, 'persons were observed with objectivity'. 'It is in relation to the sought after object that bourgeois individualism is formed'.[51] Hausenstein references the first recognised art historian, Vasari: 'One must read Vasari in order to feel how the discovery of the nearness of objects, the "conversazione" between object and the human being immediately portended shock for contemporaries'.[52] The development of urban life with its greater proximity of citizens accelerated and intensified the role of the material. There is a new self-reliance on scientific observation: art shifts suddenly – initially with Signorelli, then Mantegna – to

---

47   Hausenstein 1920, p. 29. 'Wir legen naiv die Massstäbe der aus der Renaissance stammenden modernen Bürgerlichkeit an, wenn wir Seele nur in einer Kunst entdecken wollen ...'.

48   Hausenstein 1920, p. 30. 'Die Kunst der Renaissance ist die Kunst eines Zeitalters, das im Zeichen einer siegreich vordringenden bürgerlichen Warenwirtschaft steht'.

49   Hausenstein 1920, p. 31. '... da hat eher der wirtschaftliche Faktor Anspruch auf die Aufmerksamkeit des Bewusstseins und seiner dichtenden Ideologien'. It is interesting to compare the formalist art history conceptualisation with this; here Podro is summarising a passage in Wölfflin: 'the new temper transforms a bourgeois art of anecdotal interest and everyday subject matter into an aristocratic art of symbolic and reserved dignity' (Podro 1991, p. 114).

50   Ibid. '... das Ding in allen seinen Qualitäten zu studieren, zu erobern, zu besitzen und darstellen'. On pp. 76–8, he draws some socio-economic distinctions between the human being of the feudal world and that of the Renaissance.

51   Hausenstein 1920, p. 80. All quotations from this page. 'Der Ausgangspunkt der bürgerlichen Welt ist nicht das Subjekt, sondern das Ding. Erst im Verhältnis zu den umworbenen Dingen bildet sich die bürgerliche Individualität'. This again is an inversion of the subject/object hierarchy in feudal society's ideology, as Hausenstein persuasively proposes in his examination of visual art from the period.

52   Hausenstein 1920, p. 78. 'Man muss den Vasari lesen um nachzufühlen wie die Entdeckung der Nähe der Dinge, der "Conversazione" zwischen Ding und Mensch für die Menschheit der Renaissance geradezu eine Erschütterung bedeutet'.

optical and definitively scientific understanding.[53] The paradigmatic representative of this 'irreverent bourgeoisie' ('... pietätlosen Bürgerlichkeit ...') was Leonardo 'who only painted what he knew' ('... der nur malt, was er weiss').

The emancipation of the landscape as artistic theme, Hausenstein proposes, cannot be emphasised enough as a sociological phenomenon, connoting the increasing secularisation of painting from the late Renaissance to seventeenth-century Holland. 'A style based on the principle of resemblance, Dutch landscape painting', he claims, 'is the expression of bourgeois culture ... of a liberal world ... of an exalted Spinozean, pantheistic world but basically one of physiological materialism'.[54] The landscape manifests reason, which illustrates that 'one may trust to a monistic self-evolution of nature'. Holland was 'the most advanced commercial state of its era', driven by socio-economic determinants we designate 'Mercantilism' ('... den wir mit dem wirtschafts-geschichten Begriff des Merkantilismus bezeichnen'). This is the historical intersection of the feudalistic socio-economic imperative 'with incipient bourgeois physiocracy' ('... mit der beginnenden bürgerlichen Physiokratie'). 'Mercantilism is paradoxical, caught between older feudal forms and the new culture of Absolutism, consequently deprived of its internal development, but a fruitful paradox whose cultural articulation is the Baroque' ('... der Begriff des Merkantilismus steht hier in seiner universalisten kulturellen Bedeutung ... ist das Baroque').[55]

The sociology of art discloses the socio-economic and attendant political determinants of cultural production. Hausenstein's objective is a socialist art. 'Socialism', he writes, 'signifies the overcoming of the physiocratic, that is, bourgeois materialism – and the management of things through the formed energies of organised mankind'.[56] Art is in principle 'bound to social life'; without that, art cannot exist. The individual cannot produce a style, 'the mastery of existence' can only be mediated through society. Much later nineteenth-century art had become the preserve of the atelier, a specialism reflecting the division of labour, a private affair: 'With this division of labour art loses its former significance as a mediator of public communication'.[57] The artist must

---

53 Hausenstein 1920, p. 79. 'Die Kunst schlägt – etwa bei Signorelli, dann bei Mantegna – in optische und schliesslich in wissenschaftliche Intelligenz um'.

54 Hausenstein 1920, p. 27. 'Der auf das Prinzip der Ähnlichkeit gegründete Stil der holländischen Landschaftsmalerei ist Ausdruck bürgerlicher Kultur – einer liberalen Welt ... eines pantheistischen, spinozistisch erhöhten, aber im Grunde physiologischen Materialismus'.

55 Hausenstein 1920, p. 39, all quotations. This cultural phenomenon will be dealt with below in the context of his article in the Soviet Encyclopedia of 1926.

56 Hausenstein 1920, p. 100. 'Sozialismus bedeutet die Überwindung der Physiokratie – das ist des bürgerlichen Materialismus – und die Beherrschung der Dinge durch die formale Energie organisierter Menschheit'.

57 Hausenstein 1920, p. 59. 'Bei dieser Arbeitsteilung verliert die Kunst die alte Bedeutung eines öffentlichen Verkehrsmittel'.

'embrace socialism' ('... sich subjectiv zum Sozialismus bekennt'). Courbet is an artist who has done this in his 'Stonebreakers': 'he worked under the yoke of bourgeois materialism but he invested objective painting with the most personal tension. This strength remains both an objective and unintentional expression of bourgeois reality'.[58] 'We have begun to see', Hausenstein writes, 'fully social content' ('... vollen sozial Inhalt'), its 'social substance' ('... seine soziale Substanz ...') will follow. Van Gogh – who is, moreover, a socialist – and wanting to commit the new style to a Fourier-type series of paintings from communist life – has, 'as a painter of the future, pointed the way'.[59] In early 1919, the date of his foreword, this had to remain an open question.[60]

The Baroque[61]

Having set out the socio-economic and political developments within which this cultural phenomenon took shape, Hausenstein defines the core elements and their interrelationships: 'From these observations the economic-sociological style formula alone is no longer sufficient to produce the historical concept of the Baroque: the Baroque is the embodiment of the aesthetic ideologies of Absolutism and the Counter Reformation'.[62] Hausenstein's observations detail the origins and development of the Baroque cultural era, the interaction of the feudal-clerical tradition from the late Middle Ages and the free-thinking bourgeois ('bürgerlich-freisinnigen') departure of the Renaissance. The play of forces is complex, the initiative of absolutist princes. This initiative empowered the buoyant bourgeois money economy of the Renaissance cities ('... bemächtigt sich das geldwirtschaftlich bürgerlichen Auftriebs der Städte ...') vis-

---

58　Hausenstein 1920, p. 60. 'Er malt sie im Joch des bürgerlichen Materialismus. Er gibt der Gegenstandmalerei die persönlichste Spannung. Aber diese Kraft bleibt zugleich objektiv – unwillkürlicher'.

59　He concludes the text with a number of questions, summarised in the following: 'The question remains if today's art, which certainly manifests an organising and in many ways an associative spirit, will develop into being a truly collective form' ('... organisierenden und in mancherlei Sinn assozierenden Geist manifestiert, zu Reife einer wahrhaft kollektivierenden Form auswachsen wird').

60　Hausenstein 1920, p. 106. 'Van Gogh – der übrigens Sozialist und den neuen Stil fourieristischen Malereien von kommunistischen Leben unvertrauen will – hat als Maler der Zukunft einen Weg gerriesen'.

61　Hausenstein was commissioned to contribute an article on the Baroque to the Soviet Encyclopedia in 1926, probably by Lunacharsky. The original German was mislaid and only published in 1982, in Sulzer 1982, pp. 101–23.

62　Sulzer 1982, p. 103. 'Aus diesen Wahrnehmungen lässt sich für den geschichtlichen Begriff des Barocks nunmehr wohl die ökonomisch-stilsoziologische Formel gewinnen: Barock ist der Inbegriff der ästhetischen Ideologien des Absolutismus und der Gegenreformation'.

á-vis the lesser feudal aristocracy whilst simultaneously using the latter 'to curb the early urban capitalism in its energetic drive for freedom' ('... um die zur Emanzipation treibenden frühkapitaliststädischen Energien im Zaum zu halten').[63] The most powerful Absolutist states (France, Spain) and some German and Italian courts of the second order would exploit this rivalry. But for their major economic and political enterprises they needed political-spiritual ('... politisch-geistigen ...') support and this they found in the Counter-Reformation church. Hausenstein describes the energies unleashed as similar to those of the later bourgeoisie. 'The Baroque is the style of jobbers (von Gründern), operating with an organising activity which resembles that of the nineteenth century', erecting building upon building in an empty landscape – as an example he mentions the planned cities of Karlsruhe and Mannheim. 'Baroque productivity', he continues, 'had the accelerated, feverish tempo of the money-economy, one might say the spirit of industrial enterprise and a similar capitalist sense for large dimensions'.[64]

The culture of the Baroque is a highly contradictory phenomenon, reflective of the conflicts of social class experienced: 'the Baroque is dialectically riven by contradictory forces. ... It is the strength of the Baroque at its height to master these contradictions'. But this mastery could not be sustained: 'then it was torn asunder by its contradictions, the generative force of the French Revolution'.[65]

Despite its mobilisation by Absolutist states and the Counter-Reformation church to represent their authority, Hausenstein also discloses the presence of bourgeois taste ('... das erste abendländische Beispiel bourgeoisen Geschmacks ...') and of a recognisable

---

63   Ibid. This is how a contemporary formalist art history accounts for the transition from the Renaissance to the emergence of the Baroque: 'The development will only fulfil itself where the forms have passed from hand to hand long enough, or, better expressed, where the imagination has occupied itself with form actively enough to make it yield up its baroque possibilities' (Wölfflin, quoted by Podro 1991, p. 128).

64   Sulzer 1982, p. 104. 'Die barocke Produktivität hat das schnelle, ja fieberhafte Tempo der geldwirtschaftlichen Welt, einen sozusagen industriellen Unternehmungsgeist und einen gleichsam kapitalistischen Sinn für grosse Dimensionen'.

65   Sulzer 1982, p. 106. 'Auf diese mannigfache Weise also ist das Barock von entgegengesetzen Kräften dialektisch durchgespannt. ... Es ist die Kraft des Barocks in seiner grossen Zeit, alle diese Widersprüche in Eins zu bändigen ... dann wird es von seinen eigenen Widersprüchen zerrissen: es entsteht die französische Revolution von 1789'. The transition is not direct but mediated through the socio-cultural period designated the Rococo, on which Hausenstein had written a separate study. In *Bild und Gemeinschaft* he set out its dynamics. It is a cultural phenomenon which emerges from a socio-economic restructuring. It is the time of stock-jobbing (agiotage) on French colonial lands in America, of a young bourgeois Parisian plutocracy ('... junge Pariser Plutocratie ...'). A manorial aristocracy, versed in the role of modern finance ('finanzverständigen Seigneuradels ...'), transmitted to this newly enriched social level its elevated sense of form, which now becomes subject to the enthusiastic, 'naive naturalism of their drives' ('... naiv naturalstische Ursprünglichkeit

proletarian presence in its art.[66] Spanish and Dutch paintings are peopled with proletarians: Velázquez's 'Spinners' labour in the spinning works 'of the mercantilist era', Callot's work shows the proletarianisation of Europe during the Thirty Years' War, the 'menials' in Ruben's Passion scenes are Antwerp dockers, Teniers and Ostade painted expropriated peasants 'marginalised in their inns … not allegorical but a particularly exact reality, objectively presented and not seldom with concealed passion'. Poverty is not virtuous, as in the Gothic era, here it is 'already at times thematically substantive'. The Dutch republic is the exception co-existing with Absolutist rule. It is the most developed capitalist state – commercial, colonial and financial – of the Baroque era, its compromises with Spanish or other Absolutist states is based on economic strength. In its figure painting, the individual is displaced by the group portrait, landscape becomes a major genre.[67] Already the physiocratic bourgeois system of economic liberalism casts its shadow over the Baroque dynasties; 'already in these beautiful paintings there appears the impersonal-naturalistic spirit of "laisser aller", the anonymous fatalism of "laisser-faire"!'[68] It was an era which was striving to extend the experience of the senses, in which the developments in the study of optical light were reflected in luminist paintings, in which light was no longer symbolic, rather rationally observed. If one considers the intelligible dimensions of the Baroque, reflects on them sociologically, the element of bourgeois rationalism becomes apparent, certainly subject to dynastic and religious influence but nevertheless basically bourgeois. The insistently painterly quality of Baroque art, its experimental surfaces, its ex-centric, asymmetric compositions, also has 'an immediate socio-economic origin, one may see in it the principles of an indulgent bourgeois liberality … The bourgeois world is a mobile world. More, it is a world of the impetuous transformation of values'. Its painting style is 'an ideological co-ordinate of the mobility of bourgeois trade'.[69]

---

ihrer Triebe!'): 'So develops the Rococo social level, as the fusing of an immediate naturalism with a thorough-going conservative form' ('So entsteht die Gesellschaft des Rokoko als die Verschmelzung eines noch abstandslosen Naturalismus mit durchgebildeter konservativer Form') (p. 53).

66   Sulzer 1982 p. 105. ('… ein besonderes Auge für das Proletarische in einer eigentümlichen barockhöfischen Beziehung haben … ja Proletarischen mitunter schon Hauptwort und Thema').

67   It is again instructive to read an idealist account of such work, here that of Alois Riegl in Podro's characterisation: 'its development is in his account generated by the specific problems in the enterprise of painting a group portrait: the tension between, on the one hand, combining the members of the group in some dramatic way, which appears to the spectator as a self-contained fictive world, and on the other, retaining a sense of the individual portraits which are not absorbed into a story' (Podro 1991, p. 83).

68   Sulzer 1982, p. 107. '… schon erscheint in diesen schönen Bildern der unpersönlich Geist des "laisser aller", der anonyme Fatalismus des "laisser-faire"!'

69   Sulzer 1982, p. 112. 'Es hat auch eine unmittelbare sozialökonomische Ursache; man darf

In attempting to summarise this powerfully energetic and highly contradictory period in modern European history, culturally and otherwise, Hausenstein writes that 'the dialectical apparatus of this art, wholly unprecedented in its luxurious-erotic symbolisation of the supersensual, is sociologically founded: the extreme economic and social tensions which came together and form an astonishing unity bring forth, of necessity, the strongest dialectical excesses in the ideological sphere'.[70] 'Of necessity', he concludes, 'the Baroque was a dialectical deception which finally deluded itself'.[71]

Something should be briefly said about 'pre-war' and 'post-war' Hausenstein. The historical materialist who theorised the work of Bruegel and the Dutch painters of the Baroque, or the transition from the Gothic to the Renaissance and through to the Baroque and Rococo, the advocate of a monistic concept of the natural world, in the immediate post-war years began to conceive of a new 'dualism'. This was a complex world: the defeat of Germany, brutal suppression of the November Revolution on the orders of the Majority SPD-led government, his disillusionment with the SPD and his brief move towards the KPD. He became disillusioned with Expressionism, a movement he had espoused and defended, but which he now dismissed in a number of publication and lectures. In the 1923 edition of his *Die bildende Kunst der Gegenwart* [1913] he writes about 'a longing for a new dualism' ('... in der Sehnsucht der Zeit, nach einem neuen Dualismus') a longing based 'in the collectivist tendencies of society' ('... in der kollektivistischen Tendenzen der Gesellschaft'). But this is not the dualism of earlier periods. These tendencies 'impossible though it may seem, lie in the materialist politics of the masses' ('... so unmöglich dass aussieht, in der materialistischen Politik der Masse'). The masses drive on this materialist politics 'because they want the organisation of material existence', which 'rationally and speedily we will in the economic sphere relieve as soon as possible'.[72] Our energies will then be released to pursue 'spiritual matters' ('... geistige Angelegenheiten'). 'The consequences of a correctly con-

---

sie in den Prinzipien einer zum Luxuriösen drängenden bürgerlichen Liberalität ... Die bürgerliche Welt ist eine mobile Welt. Mehr: sie ist eine Welt des raschen Umsatzes der Werte. ... geschwinde Temperament barocken Malens ist eine ideologische Koordinate der Beweglichkeit des bürgerlichen Verkehrs'.

70   Sulzer 1982, p. 117. 'Der dialektische Apparat dieser Künste, der sich in Ganzen als ein unerhörtes Beispiel luxuriös-erotischer Versinnlichung des Übersinnlichen auswirkt, ist soziologisch substanziert: die extremen wirtschaftlichen und gesellschaften Spannungen, die im Barock zusammenkommen und zu erstaunlicher Einheit werden, bringen notwendig die heftigsten dialektischen Exzesse in der ideologischen Sphäre hervor'.

71   Ibid. 'Das Barock muss eine dialektische Verführung sein, die endlich sich selbst verblendet'.

72   Hausenstein 1923, p. 282, '... weil sie eine Organisation der materiellen Existenz will, die uns möglichst rasch der Sphäre der ökonomischen Notwendigkeiten enthebt ...'. All previous quotations from p. 282.

ceptualised socialism', he continues, 'is a new unheard of spirituality, a new religiosity', by which he does not mean an organised religion. Such a stage will only be achieved when 'the economic is somehow rationally organised' ('... wo das Ökonomische irgendwie rationell organisiert wird'). Hausenstein's thinking here is not unlike many of his contemporary left-leaning artists who struggled to find a representational language for fast-moving social and political events – for example, one finds the murders of Karl Liebknecht and Rosa Luxemburg represented in the visual language of Christian martyrology. By the time Lukács wrote his essay 'Grösse und Verfall des Expressionismus' ('The Significance and Decline of Expressionism') in 1934, sufficient time had elapsed for an historical perspective on the period, to apply concepts such as Lenin's 'imperialism', which provided a more structured analysis of the period Hausenstein was responding to: of particular interest is the second section on the ideology of the Independent SPD (USPD), relative to the cultural-political nexus.

What was important about Hausenstein was his objective, set out in a letter of 1910; 'with systematic one-sidedness to deal completely with the democratic content of art history'.[73] In the introduction to *Der nackte Mensch in der Kunst aller Zeiten und Völker* (1912), he quotes Marx's foundational phrase: 'It is not the consciousness of men that determines their existence, but conversely this social existence that determines their consciousness'. Because of his early commitment to socialism, an academic career was not open to him; instead he worked for and contributed to socialist papers (*Vorwärts*, *Sozialistische Monatshefte*, and *Die Neue Zeit* amongst others), so his thinking on culture was potentially available as a socialist resource. This potential was supplemented by publication with leading German publishing houses, including Wolff and Piper. Lu Märten, whose work was discussed above, brought Hausenstein's materialist concerns in a different direction, concerned with accommodating more contemporary experimental work addressing a proletarian culture. To that extent Hausenstein may be seen as on 'das Erbe' wing of leftist cultural politics, although he promoted no specific era within the culture he examined in pursuit of an authentic socialist collectivist style, one inhabiting the public arena.

'Max Raphaels kunsttheoretische Konzeption'

In her essay 'Max Raphaels kunsttheoretische Konzeption' ('Max Raphael's Concept of a Theory of Art'), Tanja Frank refers to the reception of Raphael's 1913 book *Von*

---

73   Sulzer 1982, p. 12. '... mit planvoller Einseitigkeit den demokratischen Gehalt der Kunstgeschichte auszuschöpfen'. Probably the only other figure to have such a programme was Franz Mehring.

Monet bis Picasso. Grundzüge einer Ästhetik und Entwicklung der modernen Malerei (*From Monet to Picasso: Characteristic Features of an Aesthetic in the Development of Modern Painting*). Richard Hamann, whose materialist analysis of Italian renaissance art was commended by Hausenstein, noted the 'essential weakness' ('... wesentliche Schwäche ...') of the book, that Raphael's conceptual model for art was construed from 'formal philosophical ideas' ('... aus formalen Begriffen der Philosophie heraus ...'), so that it 'on the one hand did not grasp the specificity of art, and on the other expelled religion from the system and substituted it with art'.[74] Of his second book *Idee und Gestalt. Ein Führer zum Wesen der Kunst* (*Idea and Form: A Guide to the Essence of Art*) from 1921, Frank herself comments that it still maintained the 'elite status of the artist' ('... von der elitären Stellung des Künstlers ...'), 'an idealist mode of thinking' ('... des idealistischen Gedankengutes'), and accordingly 'an inability to grasp art as a socially conditioned phenomenon' ('... seine Unfähligkeit, die Kunst als ein gesellschaftlich bedingtes Phenomenon zu begreifen'). Frank speculates that Raphael may first have encountered Marxist thought around 1925 when he taught art history at the Berlin Volkhochschule, mainly an SPD institute, where *The German Ideology* was on the curriculum. In 1931, he also came in contact with the more radical Marxist MASCH (Marxist Schule), established in 1926, whether as a student or a teacher is not clear. Here he could have met Heartfield, Brecht, Korsch, Lu Märten and many others closely involved in establishing the grounds for a materialist culture. Two essays on architecture – 'The Doric Temple' and 'The Work of Corbusier' (both of 1930) – manifest more pronounced socio-historical interest: in 1932, he published 'Zur Kunsttheorie des dialektischen Materialismus', the most detailed engagement with Marxism by a German art historian to that date.[75]

Frank records Raphael's attendance at university seminars in Berlin, on mathematics, physics, and scientific subjects to understand 'what a science was in order to be able to structure a scientific theory of art' ('... was eine Wissenschaft ist, um eine Kunstwissenschaft machen zu können'). By 1932, his science now was that of dialectical materialism. The two major elements of a study in this field – aesthetics and art history – are approached as follows: the former 'was unusable, consisting as it does of a mixture of metaphysical deductions and empirical findings which are determined by the requirements of the deductive method rather than by objective laws', whilst the latter 'was concerned with a host of external manifestations rather than with the phenomenon of art itself'.[76] The task of constructing a sociology of art is demanding: 'for it

---

74 Frank 1975, pp. 293–4. '... einerseits das Spezifische der Kunst nicht erfasst, andererseits die Religion aus dem System verdrängt und die Kunst als Ersatz für sie [anbietet]'.

75 This was published in *Philosophische Hefte* 3, 51, pp. 125–52. An English translation is available in Raphael 1981.

76 Raphael 1981, p. 75.

requires, to begin with, penetration and mastery of the materials of the history of art all over the world and, further, the joint collaboration of several special sciences (economics, sociology, psychology, theory of knowledge, history of religions, philosophy etc.'). As of now 'dialectical materialism has not been able to undertake more than fitful fragmentary investigations into specific artistic problems', but its deployment is necessary for a theory of art. This passage is informed by Marx on material and spiritual production as historical forms and by Engels's later letters to various correspondents on the comparative neglect of form by Marx and himself. Following Marx and Engels on the production of ideologies from a materialist base, Raphael describes the functioning of ideology: 'every ideological domain acts upon all other domains, and in the end reacts upon its own cause, the economic substructure'. What obtains for all other ideological domains 'are also valid for art, for artistic creation and theory'. 'The first fundamental task of a Marxist theory of art', he continues, 'is thus clearly to show the concrete manifestation of the most general laws of dialectical materialism in the domain in question'. The essential problem is posed: 'Under what concrete and limited forms are reality and consciousness opposed to each other in such a way that their relations are dialectical and thus constitute the domain of art, distinct from all other ideologies?'[77]

The question to be answered is: 'What are the relations between the relative independence of artistic creation (together with a scientific theory of art interpreting it) and economic conditions (together with a sociology of art elucidating these conditions)?' A science of art, although not applying the full rigour of natural science 'nevertheless applies their method ... such a science will be closely connected with the history and sociology of art'.[78] Raphael then unfolds the outlines of such a science, too detailed to rehearse here, 'according to the categories of element, relation, totality and concretisation, which govern the constitution of empirical science', combining his interest in natural science with that of dialectical materialism. The scope of the undertaking is demanding: 'a comparative study of works of art dating from all epochs in the history of all peoples, to abstract the most general elements, relationships, totalities and domains of concretisation: it constitutes the ideal work of art in its most typical aspects'.[79] But such a sociology does not address issues raised in art history or art criticism. Art history does not deal with the elements detailed for the sociology of art but with 'influences, dependencies, variations and changes of form, i.e. to temporary conditions'. Its method, the comparative study of works of art 'is not art as a faculty of artistic creation, but

---

77   Raphael 1981, p. 80.

78   Raphael 1981, p. 82.

79   The scope of ambition here can be contrasted with Korsch's claim 'that Marx's theory is not interested in everything, nor is it interested to the same degree in all objects of its interests'. See Chapter 6.

rather the technical means of production ... art history loses sight of its true subject – art – which the science of art put forward as the ideal subject, in a pure and abstract manner'. A history of art can only develop successfully within a sociology of art which reveals to it 'the conditions that have altered so pure and abstract a movement of historical spirit': the latter is found 'in a general science of society, more accurately, of its material production and reproduction'.[80]

The third element of the trinity, art criticism, which establishes norms for its own period ('the mistakes an epoch makes about itself') takes its place between art history, which 'demonstrates this by showing to what extent such predilections vary', and the sociology of art, 'which show the economic and social causes that account for each given selection, confirms it'.

At this point (norms, or taste), Raphael proposed a distinction related to class, of a declining class and the circulation of 'sham art' on the one hand, of a rising class and 'true artistic production on the other'. Only a science of art criticism alone can solve the question: 'What are the criteria that enable us to distinguish between factitious and true works of art, and within the latter, to assign various degrees of value'.[81] Amongst the distinguishing criteria for the 'true work of art' are 'the formal expression given to the immaterial idea, compositional logic etc., which must be both discovered empirically and justified theoretically'. These elements tend 'towards the goal of perfect congruence of form and content with what is concrete and abstract, relative and absolute *in every given epoch*'.

These three sciences – of essence (art), evolution (art history), and value (art criticism) – 'isolate their subject to the point of abstract purity and try to locate their foundation in an immanent manner'. The sociology of art, on the other hand, is extraneous to art, deals with 'the concrete particularity of each work, the interaction of ideologies with each other, and art's influence upon that basis'. This interrelationship between the immanent and the extraneous, the relative autonomy of art to social life, composes 'the dialectical interlocking of material and intellectual production', the grasping of 'all the facts of social life in terms of a single method'.[82] Having established 'a methodology of a materialist and dialectical sociology of art', Raphael moves on to specifics as to how this would be exercised. These would include social formations of feudalism, capitalism in its various stages of development, class relationship and struggles, relations between the art of the masses and that of the ruling class, patronage and markets, innovations in

---

80   This relationship between the sociological and the cultural was basic to Hausenstein's and Hamann's practice as materialist historians: absent was the idealist emphasis on 'art' for which Raphael's first two books were criticised (see Hamann and Frank above).

81   Raphael 1981, p. 84.

82   Raphael 1981, p. 85.

the materials and technical developments in the arts. He appends many sub-divisions of these categories to extend the coverage, for example, 'the sociological functions of genius and of the talents of various degrees down to the lowest'.[83]

In the final section of this passage, he turns to the 'the retroactions' of art, 'i.e. the influence of art on the social factors that determine it', including that of the 'economic substructure itself', the reciprocal effect of the ideological on the materialist base. Surprisingly he introduces '[a] problem of particular interest to Marxists, that of the industrial arts', in a manner reminiscent of Lu Märten, whom he may have got to know at MASCH, where she taught – her Amsterdam archive contains an annotated copy of Raphael's essay. 'Does the creative artistic faculty begin with such objects (i.e. with the most urgent material needs), or do these derive their forms from purely artistic objects? Are the industrial arts at the bottom or top of the ladder?' He concludes the passage: 'the creative faculty was applied at a far earlier date to objects related to the collectivity than to objects serving individuals or restricted groups'.[84]

Much of the remainder of this long essay is engaged with Marx's own writing on Greek art, on 'a historically determined and limited mythology, conceived as an intermediary between the economic substructures and art', but which, Raphael continues, 'leads to a series of other problems that Marx never thought to raise, let alone be solved'.[85] Only one will be considered here, namely the permanent value of Greek art as 'a standard and unattainable ideal'. In this 'concrete example', Raphael writes, 'the historical, materialist factor clashes with the dialectical, logical, absolute and general factor, and therein lies the great theoretical importance of the problem'; instead of discussing 'the "eternal charm" of Greek art, we shall inquire whether there is such a thing as a permanent norm valid for works of art regardless of the historical period in which they were produced'.[86] The question Raphael poses is: 'Why could Greek art repeatedly take on normative significance at various epochs of Christian art?' This then allows him to examine a number of revivals of Greek form across the ages, from Gothic sculpture to neo-Classicism, within their historical epochs. The framework for considering such an issue lies in 'the Marxist theory of knowledge [which] has established that truth is at once absolute and relative', absolute 'signifying a progressive development towards a

---

83   Raphael 1981, p. 87.
84   Raphael 1981, p. 88. Märten had rigorously argued for the priority of the technical in what she designated the 'so-called arts', as detailed above in her exchanges on historical materialism with Gertrud Alexander in the early 1920s. She welcomed the 'engineer-artist' of the early days of the Russian Revolution, a concept of art very different from anything encountered in Raphael, at odds with his terms 'the ideal work of art', 'the true work of art', 'the perfect congruence of form and content', as set out above.
85   Raphael 1981, p. 90.
86   Raphael 1981, pp. 103–4.

goal ever closer to reality'.[87] 'Materialist dialectics', he continues, 'implies, with respect to the total evolution of human thought in history, different degrees of approximation to an "absolute" final value. Within these limits, we may speak of a hierarchy of values'.[88]

This most consciously structured attempt at a Marxist theory of art was not afforded the opportunity for further development, discussion or application before the seizure of power by the Nazis. Further elaboration and application was only possible, initially in France, then in the United States. Raphael's framework alerts the art historian and theoretician to the demands of analysis, the existence of separate but independent elements, e.g. a science of art, of art history, of art criticism within the overarching concept of the sociology of art, all negotiated within the demands of dialectical materialism, the mediated interactions of the ideological and material base. Lodged within the essay, nevertheless, are indications of a continuing idealist thinking, the references to the 'ideal work of art', 'true art' (as against the 'factitious'), 'so pure and abstract a movement of historical spirit'. It would be difficult to argue with Tanja Frank's statement that 'one would look in vain in Raphael's work from the Berlin period for possible connections to the evolving proletarian-revolutionary art'.[89] In his theoretical work of the early 1930s, 'there is no formulation of the concrete social function of art, no including of the spectator in the effect of the work'. In this essay, she wrote, 'the concept of art appears theoretically to defer back to its own origin, a concept which could possibly have been outlined with a sharper sense of social applicability but with Raphael dissolves into a problem of taste or "private social relations"'.[90]

87 Raphael 1981, p. 108.
88 Lukács used this argument in his *Linkskurve* articles, contemporary with Raphael's essay.
89 Frank 1975, p. 401. 'Vergeblich sucht man in Raphaels Arbeiten aus der Berliner Zeit nach möglichen Verbindungen zu der sich gerade formierenden proletarisch-revolutionären Kunst'.
90 Frank 1975, p. 402. 'In dem Artikel "Zur Kunsttheorie des dialektischen Materialismus" erscheint dann auch theoretisch der Gedanke der Rückwirkung der Kunst auf ihre eigene Basis, ein Gedanke, der eventuell die gesellschaftliche Verwendbarkeit der Kunst hätte schärfer umreissen können, der aber bei Raphael im Problem des Geschmackes oder der privaten Sozialbeziehungen versickert'.

References

Adorno, Theodor W. 1986, *Aesthetic Theory*, trans. C. Lenhardt, London: Routledge and Kegan Paul.

Adorno, Theodor W. et al. 1979, *Aesthetics and Politics*, trans. and ed. Ronald Taylor. London: NLB.

Alexander, Gertrud (G.G.L.) 1973 [1920], 'Dada', in Brauneck (ed.) 1973, pp. 75–8.

Alexander, Gertrud 1973 [1920], 'Proletarisches Theater', in Brauneck (ed.) 1973, pp. 92–6.

Alexander, Gertrud 1973 [1920], 'Proletarisches Theater und der "Gegner"', in Brauneck (ed.) 1973, pp. 96–8.

Alexander, Gertrud 1973 [1920], 'Zur Frage der Kritik bürgerlicher Kunst', in Brauneck (ed.) 1973, pp. 109–10.

Alexander, Gertrud 1974b [1920], 'Herrn John Heartfield und George Grosz', in Fähnders and Rector 1974b, pp. 55–7.

Alexander, Gertrud 1974b [1920], 'Kunst, Vandalismus und Proletariat. Erwiderung', in Fähnders and Rector 1974b, pp. 60–5.

Alexander, Gertrud 1982 [1921], 'Historischer Materialismus und Kunstkritik', in May 1982, pp. 156–66.

Alexander, Gertrud 1982 [1921], 'Kunst und historischer Materialismus', in May 1982, pp. 166–9.

Alexander, Gertrud 1982 [1921], 'Noch einmal Kunst und historischer Materialismus', in May 1982, pp. 169–71.

alternative 1973, *Zeitschrift für Literatur und Diskussion*, Berlin: Alternative Verlag.

Althusser, Louis 1977, *For Marx*, London: NLB.

Anderson, Kevin B. 2007, 'Rediscovery and Persistence of the Dialectic', in *Lenin Reloaded: Toward a Politics of Truth*, edited by Slavoj Žižek, Stathis Kouvelakis, and Sebastian Budgen, Durham, NC: Duke University Press, pp. 120–47.

Arbeitskonferenz des Bereiches Kunstwissenschaft der Humboldt-Universität 1977, *Entwicklungsprobleme der proletarisch-revolutionären Kunst von 1917 bis zu den 30er Jahren*, Berlin: Humboldt-Universität.

Arbeitsprogramm der 'Roten Gruppe' 1981 [1924], in März 1981, pp. 131–3.

Arbeitstagung zur proletarisch-revolutionären Kunst, Akademie der Künste der DDR 1979, *Kunst im Klassenkampf*, Berlin: Humboldt-Universität.

Assmann, Georg (ed.) 1978, *Wörterbuch der Marxistisch-Leninistischen Soziologie*, 2nd edition, Berlin: Dietz Verlag.

Assoziation Revolutionärer Bildender Künstler Deutschlands (ARBKD, known as Asso) 1928, *Manifest*, in Schneede (ed.) 1979, pp. 146–9.

Banaji, Jairus 2018, 'Globalising the History of Capital: Ways Forward', *Historical Materialism*, 26, no. 3: 143–66.

Baxendall, Lee and Stefan Morawski (eds) 1977, *Karl Marx, Frederick Engels on Literature and Art*, New York: International General.

Becher, Johannes R. 1980 [1931], 'Unsere Wendung. Vom Kampf um die Existenz der proletarisch-revolutionären Literatur zum Kampf um ihre Erweiterung', *Die Linkskurve*, 3, no. 10 (October): 1–8.

Behne, Adolf 1981 [1921], 'Dada', in *März* 1981, pp. 44–5.

Benjamin, Walter 1977, *Understanding Brecht*, trans. by Anna Bostock, London: NLB.

Beutin, Wolfgang and Wilfried Hoppe (eds) 1996, *Franz Mehring (1846–1919)*, Frankfurt am Main: Peter Lang.

Bottomore, Tom (ed.) 1991, *A Dictionary of Marxist Thought*, 2nd Edition, Oxford: Blackwell.

Brauneck, Manfred (ed.) 1973, *Kritik, Theorie, Feuilleton: Die Rote Fahne, 1918–1933*, München: Wilhelm Fink Verlag.

Brecht, Bertolt 1990, *Letters 1913–1956*, trans. by Ralph Mannheim, edited with commentary and notes by John Willett, New York: Routledge.

Brecht, Bertolt 2019, *Brecht on Performance: Messingkauf and Modelbooks*, edited by Tom Kuhn, Steve Giles, and Marc Silberman, London: Bloomsbury.

Brecht, Bertolt and John Willett 1964, *Brecht on Theatre: The Development of an Aesthetic*, London: Methuen.

Brecht-Zentrum der DDR 1983, *Brecht und Marxismus. Dokumentation*, edited by Inge Jahn-Gellert, Berlin: Henschelverlag Kunst und Gesellschaft.

Bredel, Willi 1971 [1932], 'Einen Schritt Weiter. Ein Diskussionsbeitrag über unsere Wendung an der Literaturfront', *Die Linkskurve*, 4, no. 1 (January): 20–2.

Brüggemann, Heinz 1978, 'Bertolt Brecht and Karl Korsch: Questions of Living and Dead Elements Within Marxism', *Praxis*, 4: 287–96.

Campbell, Joan 1989, *Joy in Work, German Work: The National Debate 1800–1945*, Princeton, NJ: Princeton University Press.

Davies, Cecil W. 1977, *Theatre for the People: The Story of the Volksbühne*, Manchester: Manchester University Press.

Engels, Friedrich 1946 [1886], *Ludwig Feuerbach and the Outcome of Classical German Philosophy*, Moscow: Progress Publishers.

Fähnders, Walter and Martin Rector 1974a, *Linksradikalismus und Literatur: Untersuchungen zur Geschichte der sozialistischen Literatur in der Weimarer Republik*, Vol. 1, Reinbek: Rowohlt Taschenbuch Verlag.

Fähnders, Walter and Martin Rector 1974b, *Literatur im Klassenkampf. Zur proletarisch-revolutionären Literaturtheorie. Eine Dokumentation*, München: Fischer Taschenbuch Verlag.

Fitzpatrick, Sheila 1970, *The Commissariat of Enlightenment: Soviet Organisation of the Arts Under Lunacharsky*, Cambridge: Cambridge University Press.

Fowkes, Ben 2015, *The German Left and the Weimar Republic: A Selection of Documents*, Chicago: Haymarket Books.

Frank, Tanja 1977, 'Max Raphaels Auffassung zum Verhältnis des Proletariats zur Kunst', in *Entwicklungsprobleme der proletarisch-revolutionären Kunst von 1917 bis zu den 30er Jahre*, Arbeitskonferenz des Bereiches Kunstwissenschaft der Humboldt-Universität, Berlin, pp. 154–9.

Frank, Tanja 1978, 'Anfänge marxistischer Kuntsttheorie und Kunstkritik in Deutschland von 1920 bis 1933', in *Revolution und Realismus. Revolutionäre Kunst in Deutschland 1917 bis 1933*, Berlin: Staatliche Museen zu Berlin, pp. 82–96.

Frank, Tanja 1975, 'Max Raphaels kunsttheoretische Konzeption', in *Arbeiter, Kunst und Kunstler*, by Max Raphael, Frankfurt am Main: Fischer, pp. 391–410.

Frölich, Paul 1972, *Rosa Luxemburg: Ideas in Action*, London: Pluto Press.

Gallas, Helga 1974. *Marxistische Literaturtheorie*, Neuwied and Berlin: Hermann Luchterhand Verlag.

Gassner, Hubertus and Eckhart Gillen (eds) 1979, *Zwischen Revolutionskunst und Sozialistischen Realismus. Dokumente und Kommentare Kunstdebatten in der Sowjetunion von 1917 bis 1934*, Köln: DuMont Buchverlag.

Gassner, Hubertus and Eckhart Gillen 1979, *Oktjabr* – Vereinigung der Arbeiter in neuen Arten der Kunsttätigkeit, pp. 172–202.

Gaughan, Martin Ignatius 2007, *German Art 1907–1937: Modernism and Modernisation*, Oxford: Peter Lang.

Gegner, Der 1979 [1920], 'Blätter zur Kritik der Zeit, Fotomechanischer Neudruck mit einem Geleitwort von Wieland Herzfelde und einer Einleitung von Hans-Jörg Görlich', Berlin: Das Arsenal.

Gerhard-Sonnenberg, Gabriele 1976, *Marxistische Arbeiter-Bildung in der Weimarer Zeit (MASCH)*, Köln: Pahl-Rugenstein.

Goode, Patrick 1979, *Karl Korsch: A Study in Western Marxism*, London: The Macmillan Press.

Gotsche, Otto 1971 [1932], 'Kritik der Anderen – Einige Bemerkungen zur Frage der Qualifikation unserer Literatur', *Die Linkskurve*, 4, no. 4 (April): 28–30.

Grosz, George 1986, *Ein kleines Ja und ein grosses Nein: Sein Leben von ihm selbst erzählt*, Reinbek bei Hamburg: Rowohlt.

Grosz, George and John Heartfield 1920, 'Der Kunstlump', *Der Gegner*, I, nos. 10–12: 48–56.

Grosz, George and Wieland Herzfelde 1979 [1925], 'Die Kunst ist in Gefahr. Ein Orientierungsversuch', in Schneede (ed.) 1979, pp. 126–37.

Gumpertz, Julian 1974b [1920], 'Kunst, Vandalismus und Proletariat. Eine Antwort an G.G.L.', in Fähnders and Rector (eds) 1974b, pp. 57–60.

Guttsman, W.L. 1977, *Art for the Workers: Ideology and the Visual Arts in Weimar Germany*, Manchester: Manchester University Press.

Hadjinicolaou, Nicos 1978, *Art History and Class Struggle*, trans. by Louise Asmal, London: Pluto Press.

Harman, Chris 1982, *The Lost Revolution: Germany 1918 to 1923*, London: Bookmarks.

Hausenstein, Wilhelm 1920 [1909], *Der Bauern-Bruegel*, München: R. Piper & Co. Verlag.

Hausenstein, Wilhelm 1920 [1911], *Der nackte Mensch in der Kunst aller Zeiten*, München: R. Piper & Co. Verlag.

Hausenstein, Wilhelm 1920 [1913], *Bild und Gemeinschaft. Entwurf einer Soziologie der Kunst*, München: Kurt Wolff Verlag.

Hausenstein, Wilhelm 1920, *Die Kunst in diesem Augenblick*, München: Hyperionverlag.

Hausenstein, Wilhelm 1920, *Über Expressionismus in der Malerei*, Berlin: Erich Reiss Verlag.

Hausenstein, Wilhelm 1923, *Die Bildende Kunst der Gegenwart*, Berlin and Leipzig: Deutsche Verlags-Anstalt-Stuttgart.

Hausmann, Raoul 1974b [1921], 'Puffke propagiert Proletkult', in Fähnders and Rector (eds) 1974b, pp. 119–22.

Heartfield, John and George Grosz 1920, 'Der Kunstlump', *Der Gegner*, I, nos. 10–12: 48–56.

Heljenoort, Jean van 1978, *With Trotsky in Exile: From Prinkipo to Coyoacan*, Cambridge, MA; Harvard University Press.

Hermand, Jost (ed.) 1982, *Brechts Äusserungen zu den bildenden Künsten*, Frankfurt am Main: Suhrkamp Verlag.

Hermand, Jost 1996, '"Die Kunst dem Volke!" Mehrings Umgang mit dem Kulturellen Erbe', in Beutin and Hoppe (eds) 1996, pp. 17–31.

Herzfelde, Wieland 1920–21, 'Gesellschaft, Künstler und Kommunismus', *Der Gegner*, II, nos. 5, 6, 8/9, 10/11.

Herzfelde, Wieland and George Grosz 1979 [1925], 'Die Kunst ist in Gefahr. Ein Orientierungsversuch', in Schneede (ed.) 1979, pp. 126–37.

Höhle, Thomas 1956, *Franz Mehring. Sein Weg zum Marxismus 1869–1891*, Berlin: Rütten & Loening.

Horn, Ursula 1977, 'Einflüsse des Anarchismus auf die Anfänge proletarisch-revolutionärer Kunst', in *Entwicklungsprobleme der proletarisch-revolutionären Kunst von 1917 bis zu den 30er Jahren*, Arbeitskonferenz des Bereiches Kunstwissenschaft der Humboldt-Universität, Berlin, pp. 29–43.

Horn, Ursula 1978, 'Zur Ikonographie der deutschen proletarisch-revolutionären Kunst zwischen 1917 und 1933', in *Revolution und Realismus. Revolutionäre Kunst in Deutschland 1917 bis 1933*, Berlin: Staatliche Museen zu Berlin, pp. 53–69.

Hüneke, Andreas 1977, 'Die Auseinandersetzung mit den revolutionären Ereignissen von 1917 und 1918 in der deutschen Kunstkritik und theorie um 1920', in *Inter-*

nationale sozialistische Kunstprozesse seit der Oktoberrevolution, Sektion Kunstwissenschaft des Verbandes Bildender Künstler der DDR, 2. Jahrestagung, Magdeburg, pp. 79–86.

Jonas, Gisele 1988, *Schiller-Debatte 1905. Dokumente zu Literaturtheorie und Lliteraturkritik der revolutionären Sozialdemokratie*, Berlin Ost: Akademie Verlag.

Jung, Franz 1974b [1920], 'Proletarische Erzählungskunst', in Fähnders and Rector (eds) 1974b, pp. 125–8.

Kaes, Anton, Martin Jay, and Edward Dimendberg (eds) 1994, *Weimar Republic Sourcebook*, Berkeley: University of California Press.

Kambas, Chryssoula 1988, *Die Werkstatt als Utopie. Lu Märtens literarische Arbeit und Formästhetik seit 1900*, Tübingen: Max Niemeyer Verlag.

Kemeny, Alfred ('Durus') 1973 [1929], 'Zwischen "neuer" und revolutionärer Sachlichkeit', in Brauneck (ed.) 1973, pp. 365–8.

Kemeny, Alfred 1973 [1931], 'Hat die "Massnahme" Lehrwert? Diskussion über das Lehrstück von Brecht und Eisler', in Brauneck (ed.) 1973, pp. 421–3.

Kemeny, Alfred 1973 [1931], ' "Die Massnahme" im Grossen Schauspielhaus', in Brauneck (ed.) 1973, pp. 423–5.

Kemeny, Alfred 1978 [1931], 'Die über den Klassen schwebende Ästhetik', in *Revolution und Realismus. Revolutionäre Kunst in Deutschland 1917 bis 1933*, Staatliche Museun zu Berlin.

Kemeny, Alfred 1981 [1932], 'Photomontage und Buchgraphik. Zur 3. Ausstellung des Bundes revolutionärer Künstler', in März 1981, pp. 178–9.

Klein, Alfred, unter Mitarbeit von Thomas Rietzschel 1979, *Zur Tradition der deutschen sozialistischen Literatur. Eine Auswahl von Dokumenten 1926–1935*, Vol. 1, Berlin and Weimar: Aufbau-Verlag.

Koch, Hans 1959, *Franz Mehrings Beitrag zur marxistischen Literaturtheorie*, Berlin: Dietz Verlag.

Koch, Hans 1962, *Marxismus und Ästhetik. Zur ästhetischen Theorie von Karl Marx, Friedrich Engels und Wladimir Iljitsch Lenin*, Berlin: Dietz Verlag.

Korsch, Karl 1971, *Karl Korsch: Three Essays on Marxism*, London: Pluto Press.

Korsch, Karl 1973 [1922], *Kernpunkte der materialistischen Geschifchtssauffassung*, Hamburg: Association Verlag.

Korsch, Karl 2009 [1923], 'The Marxist Dialectic', www.marxists.org/archive/korsch/1923/marxist-dialectic.

Korsch, Karl 2009 [1924], 'On Materialist Dialectic', www.marxists.org/archive/korsch/1924/marxist-dialectic.

Korsch, Karl 2012, *Marxism and Philosophy*, London: Verso.

Korsch, Karl n.d. 'Dialektik des Alltags', in Korsch Archive 76/1, International Institute for Social History, Amsterdam.

Kramer, Jürgen 1977, 'Die Assoziation Revolutionärer Bildender Künstler Deutschlands', in *Wem gehört die Welt – Kunst und Gesellshaft in der Weimarer Republik*, Berlin: Neue Gesellshaft für Bildende Kunst, pp. 174–204.

Kraus, N. 1978 [1930], 'Gegen den Ökonomismus in der Literaturfrage', *Die Linkskurve*, 2, no. 3: 10–12.

Kuhirt, Ulrich 1978, 'Künstler und Klassenkampf. Zur Geschichte der Assoziation Revolutionärer Bildender Künstler Deutschlands', in *Revolution und Realismus. Revolutionäre Kunst in Deutschland 1917 bis 1933*, Berlin: Staatliche Museen zu Berlin, pp. 44–52.

Kuhirt, Ulrich 1979, 'Revolutionäre Kunst und "zweite Kultur"', in *Arbeitstagung zur proletarisch-revolutionären Kunst, Akademie der Künste der DDR, Kunst im Klassenkampf*, Berlin: Humboldt-Universität, pp. 101–20.

Kühn, Gertraude, Karl Tümmler, Walter Wimmer (eds) 1978, *Film und revolutionäre Arbeiterbewegung in Deutschland 1918–1932*, 2 vols, Berlin: Henschelverlag Kunst und Gesellschaft.

Kurella, Alfred 1979 [1931], 'Ein *Versuch mit nicht ganz tauglichen Mitteln*', *Kritik der 'Massnahme', Versuch von Brecht, Dudow und Eisler*, in Klein 1979, pp. 383–99.

Le Blanc, Paul 2017, 'The Anti-philosophical Marxism of Karl Korsch', *International Socialist Review*, 104, https://isreview.org/issue/104/anti-philosophical-marxism-karl-korsch.

Lenin, V.I. 1934 [1920], *'Left Wing' Communism: An Infantile Disorder*, London: Martin Lawrence.

Lewis, Ben 2017, 'Marxism after Marx: Karl Kautsky's Disputed Legacy', *Historical Materialism*, 25, no. 3: 141–7.

Lifshitz, Mikhail 1976, *The Philosophy of Art of Karl Marx*, London: Pluto Press.

Lih, Lars T. 2008 [2005], *Lenin Rediscovered*, Chicago: Haymarket Books.

Linkskurve, Die 1976–80 [1929–31], Vols. 1–3, Bund Proletarisch-Revolutionäre Schriftsteller Deutschlands, republished by Frankfurt am Main: Materialis Verlag.

Linkskurve, Die 1971 [1932], Vol 4, republished by Frankfurt: Druck-Verlags-Vertriebs Kooperative.

Löwy, Michael 1979, *Georg Lukács: From Romanticism to Bolshevism*, London: NLB.

Lüdecke, Willi 1973, *Der Film in Agitation und Propaganda der revolutionäre deutschen Arbeiterbewegung (1919–1933)*, Berlin: Oberbaumverlag.

Lukács, Georg 1952, 'Observations on the Problems and Tasks of Art History', *Communist Review*, October: 309–16.

Lukács, Georg 1954, *Beiträge zur Geschichte der Ästhetik*, Berlin: Aufbau-Verlag.

Lukács, Georg 1954 [1933], 'Franz Mehring 1846–1919', in Lukács 1954, pp. 318–403.

Lukács, Georg 1971 [1923], *History and Class Consciousness: Studies in Marxist Dialectics*, London: Merlin Press.

Lukács, Georg 1980, *Essays on Realism*, edited by Rodney Livingstone, trans. by David Fernbach, Cambridge, MA: The MIT Press.

Lukács, Georg 1980 [1931–32], 'The Novels of Willi Bredel', in Lukács 1980, pp. 23–32.

Lukács, Georg 1980 [1932], '"Tendency" or Partisanship?', in Lukács 1980, pp. 33–44.

Lukács, Georg 1980 [1932], 'Reportage or Portrayal?', in Lukács 1980, pp. 45–75.

Lukács, Georg 1983 [1922], *Lukács: Reviews and Articles*, trans. by Peter Palmer, London: Merlin Press.

Luxemburg, Rosa 2009, *Selected Political and Literary Writings*, Pontypool: Merlin Press.

Luxemburg, Rosa 2009 [1904–05], 'Franz Mehring, *Schiller, A Portrait of his Life for the German Worker*', trans. by Esther Leslie, in Luxemburg 2009, pp. 16–19.

Luxemburg, Rosa 2009 [1913], 'Nach 50 Jahren', trans. by Esther Leslie, in Luxemburg 2009, pp. 27–30.

Märten, Lu 1903, 'Die künstlerischen Momente der Arbeit in alter und neuer Zeit', *Die Zeit*, 51: 800–4.

Märten, Lu 1912, 'Zur ästhetisch-literarischen Enquete', *Die Neue Zeit*, 2, no. 47: 790–3.

Märten, Lu 1914, *Die Wirtschaftliche Lage der Künstler*, München: Georg Müller.

Märten, Lu 1920, *Historisch-Materialistisches über Wesen und Veränderung der Künste* (Eine pragmatische Einleitung), Stuttgart-Degerloch: Verlagdruckerei Carl Häring.

Märten, Lu 1921, 'Die revolutionäre Presse und das Feuilleton', *Der Gegner*, II, no. 6: 186–92.

Märten, Lu 1924, *Wesen und Veränderung der Formen / Künste. Resultate historisch-materialistischer Untersuchungen*, Frankfurt am Main: Der Taifun-Verlag.

Märten, Lu 1925, 'Trotzki: "Literatur und Revolution"', *Internationale Presse-Korrespondenz*, 56: 682–4.

Märten, Lu 1928, 'Die Eigengesetzlichkeit des Rundfunks', *Die Bücherwarte*, 8, Beilage 'Arbeiterbildung': 105–17.

Märten, Lu 1978 [1920], 'Geschichte, Satyre, Dada und Weiteres II', reprinted in *Revolution und Realismus. Revolutionäre Kunst in Deutschland 1917 bis 1933*, Berlin: Staatliche Museen zu Berlin, pp. 85–6.

Märten, Lu 1980 [1931], 'Zur frage einer marxistischen Ästhetik', *Die Linkskurve*, 3, no. 5: 15–19.

Märten, Lu 1982 [1903], 'Die Zentralisation der Hauswirtschaft', *Genossenschaftspionier*, 14: 14–18.

Märten, Lu 1982 [1904], 'An die Frauen des Proletariats!', in May (ed.) 1982, pp. 18–21.

Märten, Lu 1982 [1911], 'Von der Mietskaserne', in May (ed.) 1982, pp. 32–4.

Märten, Lu 1982 [1918], 'Sozialismus und Künstler', in May (ed.) 1982, pp. 34–8.

Märten, Lu 1982 [1918], 'Proletkult', in May (ed.) 1982, pp. 43–5.

Märten, Lu 1982 [1921], 'Kunst und historischer Materialismus', May (ed.) 1982, pp. 95–8.

Märten, Lu 1982 [1925], 'Kunst und Proletariat', in May (ed.) 1982, pp. 109–16.

Märten, Lu 1982 [1929], 'Historischer materialismus und neue gestaltung', in May (ed.) 1982, pp. 129–36.

Marx, Karl and Friedrich Engels 1974, *The German Ideology*, Part One, together with Marx's 'Introduction to a Critique of Political Economy', edited with Introduction by C.J. Arthur, London: Lawrence & Wishart.

Marx, Karl and Friedrich Engels 1977, *Manifesto of the Communist Party*, Moscow: Progress Publishers.

März, Roland 1981, *John Heartfield. Der Schnitt entlang der Zeit*, Dresden: Verlag der Kunst.

May, Reinhard 1979, 'Theorie der "Formen" wider Theorie der "Künste"? Lu Märtens Versuch, eine marxistische ästhetische Theorie in Deutschland, Anfang der zwanziger Jahre zu konzipieren', in *Arbeitstagung zur proletarisch-revolutionären Kunst, Akademie der Künste der DDR, Kunst im Klassenkampf*, Berlin: Humboldt-Universität, pp. 84–92.

May, Reinhard (ed.) 1982, *Lu Märten. Formen für den Alltag. Schriften, Aufsätze, Vorträge*, Dresden: VEB Verlag der Kunst.

Mehring, Franz 1891, *Kapital und Presse. Ein Nachspiel zum Falle Lindau*, Berlin: Verlag von Kurt Brachvogel.

Mehring, Franz 1903, *Meine Rechtfertigung. Ein nachträgliches Wort zum Dresdner Parteitage*, Leipzig: Verlag der Leipziger Buchdruckerei.

Mehring, Franz 1929, *Zur Literaturgeschichte. Von Calderon bis Heine*, mit Vorwort von Eduard Fuchs und Einleitung von August Thalheimer, Berlin: Soziologische Verlaganstalt.

Mehring, Franz 1931, *Zur Geschichte der Philosophie* 1931, mit Einleitung und Anhang von August Thalheimer, Berlin: Soziolologische Verlaganstalt.

Mehring, Franz 1936 [1918], *Karl Marx: The Story of his Life*, trans. by Edward Fitzgerald, London: George Allen & Unwin.

Mehring, Franz 1961, *Gesammelte Schriften. Ansätze zur deutschen Literatur von Hebbel bis Schweichel*, Vol. 11, edited by Hans Koch, Berlin: Dietz Verlag.

Mehring, Franz 1975 [1893], *Die Lessing-Legende*, edited by Hans Koch, Berlin: Dietz Verlag.

Mehring, Franz 1975, *On Historical Materialism*, London: New Park Publications.

Metscher, Thomas 1996, 'Franz Mehrings philosophische Schriften', in Beutin and Hopper (eds) 1996, pp. 63–77.

Morawski, Stefan 1965, 'Lenin as a Literary Theorist', *Science and Society*, 29, no. 1: 2–25.

Mülder, Friederich 1996, 'Schiller und Heine in den Büchern Franz Mehrings', in Beutin and Hoppe (eds) 1996, pp. 79–97.

Nisbet, Hugh B. 2012/2013, *Lessing Yearbook/Jahrbuch XL*, Göttingen: Wallstein Verlag.

Ottwalt, Ernst 1971 [1932], '"Tatsachenroman" u(nd) Formexperiment. Eine Entgegnung an Georg Lukács', *Die Linkskurve*, 4, no. 10: 21–6.

Piscator, Erwin 1963, *The Political Theatre*, translated with chapter introduction and notes by Hugh Rorrison, London: Eyre Methuen.

Plekhanov, G.V. 1982 [1908], *Fundamental Problems of Marxism*, London: Lawrence and
  Wishart.

Podro, Michael 1991, *The Critical Historians of Art*, New Haven, CT: Yale University Press.

Raphael, Max 1913, *Von Monet zu Picasso. Grundzüge einer Ästhetik und Entwicklung der
  modernen Malerei*, München: Delphin Verlag.

Raphael, Max 1975, *Arbeiter, Kunst und Künstler*, edited by Tanja Frank, Frankfurt am
  Main: S. Fischer Verlag.

Raphael, Max 1978, *Revolution und Realismus. Revolutionäre Kunst in Deutschland 1917
  bis 1933*, Berlin: Staatliche Museen zu Berlin.

Raphael, Max 1981, *Proudhon, Marx, Picasso: Three Essays in Marxist Aesthetics*, edited
  by Inge Marcuse, with introduction by John Tagg, London: Lawrence and Wishart.

Revolution und Realismus. Revolutionäre Kunst in Deutschland 1917 bis 1933 1978, Berlin:
  Staatliche Museen zu Berlin.

Richter, Hans 1965, *Dada: Art and Anti-Art*, New York: Oxford University Press.

Rohrwasser, Michael 1975, *Saubere Mädel Starke Genossen. proletarische Massenliteratur?*, Frankfurt am Main: Verlag Roter Stern.

Schleifstein, Josef 1959, *Franz Mehring. Sein marxistisches Schaffen*, Berlin: Rütten &
  Loening.

Schmitt, Hans-Jürgen and Godehard Schramm (eds) 1974, *Sozialistische Realismuskon-
  zeptionen. Dokumente zum 1. Allunionskongress der Sowjetschriftsteller*, Frankfurt-
  am-Main: Suhrkamp Verlag.

Schneede, Uwe M. (ed.) 1979, *Die zwanziger Jahre. Manifeste und Dokumente deutscher
  Künstler*, Köln: DuMont Buchverlag.

Schneider, Michael 1985, 'Der Wissenschaftler als Zeitgenosse: zur Wiederentdeckung
  Fritz Sternbergs', in *Friedrich Ebert Stiftung, Archiv für Sozialgeschichte*, pp. 678–86.

Schüller, Hermann 1920–21, 'Proletkult-Proletarisches Theater', *Der Gegner*, II, no. 4:
  109–14.

Schüller, Hermann 1974b [1920], 'Thesen über proletarische Kultur und die kulturellen
  Aufgaben revolutionärer Arbeiter vor der Diktatur', in Fähnders and Rector (eds)
  1974b, pp. 160–2.

Schütz, Erhard H. 1973, 'Zur Kontinuität des Geschichtsoptimismus in der materialistischen Literaturtheorie', *alternative*, 89: 71–81.

Schwartz, Frederic J. 1996, *The Werkbund: Design Theory and Mass Culture before the
  First World War*, New Haven, CT: Yale University Press.

Schwartz, Frederic J. 2006, 'Walter Benjamin', in *Marxism and the History of Art: From
  William Morris to the New Left*, edited by Andrew Hemingway, London: Pluto Press.

Sektion Kunstwissenschaft des Verbandes Bildender Künstler der DDR, 2. Jahrestagung,
  1977, *Internationale sozialistische Kunstprozesse seit der Oktoberrevolution*, Magdeburg.

Solomon, Maynard (ed.) 1979, *Marxism and Art: Essays Classic and Contemporary*, Sussex: Harvester Press.

Sternberg, Fritz 1963, 'Conversations with Trotsky', https://www.marxists.org/archive/trotsky/bio/sternberg.htm.

Sternberg, Fritz 2014, *Der Dichter und die Ratio. Errinerungen an Bertolt Brecht*, edited by Helga Gebing, Berlin: Suhrkamp Verlag.

Strauss, David Friedrich 1835–36, *Das Leben Jesu*, Tübingen: C.F. Osiander.

Sulzer, Dieter 1982, *Der Nachlass Wilhelm Hausenstein*, Marbach am Neckar: Deutsche Schillergesellschaft.

Taylor, Seth 1990, *Left-Wing Nietzscheans: The Politics of German Expressionism 1919–1920*, Berlin: Walter de Gruyter.

Thalheimer, August 2000, *Über die Kunst der Revolution und die Revolution der Kunst*, Giessen-Wieseck: Köhler.

Thalheimer, August 2004, *August Thalheimer and German Communism*, London: Porcupine Press.

Trotsky, Leon 1981, *Leon Trotsky on Literature and Art*, edited with an Introduction by Paul N. Siegel, New York: Pathfinder Press.

Valentin, Maxim 1981 [1930], 'Agitproptruppen', *Die Linkskurve*, 2, no. 3, in März 1981, pp. 18–19.

Valentin, Maxim 1978 [1930], 'Agitpropspiel und Kampfwert', *Die Linkskurve*, 2, no. 4: 15–17.

Weber, Hermann 1977, *Wem gehört die Welt – Kunst und Gesellschaft in der Weimarer Republik*, Berlin: Neue Gesellshaft für Bildende Kunst.

Weber, Hermann 1982, 'Ein vergessener Theoretiker: Ein undogmatischer Marxist, wieder in Erinnerung gebracht', *Die Zeit*, http://www.zeit.de(1982)06/ein-vergessener-theoretiker.

Willett, John (ed.) 1977, *The Theatre of Bertolt Brecht*, London: Eyre Methuen Ltd.

Willett, John (ed.) 1990, *Bertolt Brecht Letters 1913–1956*, edited with commentary and notes, trans. by Ralph Mannheim, New York: Routledge.

Williams, Jenny 2012, *More Lives than One: A Biography of Hans Fallida*, London: Penguin.

Williams, Raymond 1986, 'The Uses of Cultural Theory', *New Left Review*, 158.

Wittfogel, Karl A. 1922, 'Grenzen und Aufgaben der revolutionären Bühnenkunst', *Der Gegner*, III, no. 2: 39–44.

Wittfogel, Karl A. 1973 [1925], 'Über proletarischer Kultur', in Brauneck (ed.) 1973, pp. 194–206.

Wittfogel, Karl A. 1973 [1930], 'Mehring: Zur Literaturgeschichte. Der Pionier des marxistischen Literaturkritik in Deutschland', in Brauneck (ed.) 1973, pp. 391–6.

Wittfogel, Karl A. 1977 [1930–31], 'Zur Frage der marxistischen Äesthetik', *Beitraäge zur marxistischen Äesthetik*, pp. 7–40.

Wittfogel, Karl A. 1977 [1932], 'Franz Mehring als Literaturwissenschaftler', *Beitraäge zur marxistischen Äesthetik*, pp. 50–64.

Wittfogel, Karl A. 1977, *Beiträge zur marxistischen deutschen Ästhetik*, edited by Andreas W. Mytze, Berlin: Verlag europäisischen ideen.

Wittfogel, Karl A. 1980 [1931], 'Entwicklungsstufen und Wirkungskraft proletarisch-revolutionärer Kulturarbeit', *Die Linkskurve*, 3, no. 1: 17–23.

Wizisla, Erdmut 2009, *Walter Benjamin and Bertolt Brecht: The Story of a Friendship*, trans. by Christine Shuttleworth, London: Libris.

Zetkin, Clara 1955, *Über Literatur und Kunst*, edited by Emilia Zetkin-Milowidowa, Berlin: Henschelverlag,

Zetkin, Clara 1957, *Ausgewählte Reden und Schriften*, Vol. 1, Berlin: Dietz Verlag.

Žižek, Slavoj, Stathis Kouvelakis, and Sebastian Budgen (eds) 2007, *Lenin Reloaded: Toward a Politics of Truth*, Durham, NC: Duke University Press.

CPSIA information can be obtained
at www.ICGtesting.com
Printed in the USA
JSHW041123240922
30794JS00004B/4